# Under the Blade

## The Conversion of Agricultural Landscapes

EDITED BY

## Richard K. Olson
## and Thomas A. Lyson

Westview Press

A Member of the Perseus Books Group

Copyright © 1999 by Westview Press, A Member of the Perseus Books Group

Published in 1999 in the United States of America by Westview Press, 5500 Central Avenue, Boulder, Colorado 80301-2877, and in the United Kingdom by Westview Press, 12 Hid's Copse Road, Cumnor Hill, Oxford OX2 9JJ


Library of Congress Cataloging-in-Publication Data
Under the blade : the conversion of agricultural landscapes / edited
by Richard K. Olson and Thomas A. Lyson.
    p.   cm.
  Includes bibliographical references and index.
  ISBN 0-8133-3596-5 (hc). — ISBN 0-8133-3597-3 (pb)
    1. Land use, Rural—United States.   2. Farms—United States.
3. Agricultural conservation—United States.   I. Olson, Richard K.
II. Lyson, Thomas A.
HD256.U53   1998
333.76'0973—dc21                                    98-42069
                                                      CIP

10    9    8    7    6    5    4    3    2    1

# Contents

# List of Illustrations

## Boxes

## Appendices

# Foreword

"You have a hard row to hoe," someone remarked about my work to preserve family farming and farmland. *Under the Blade: The Conversion of Agricultural Landscapes* makes my task much easier.

But I am getting ahead of my story. I grew up on an Illinois farm and have a deep affection for farm people and farmland. Even though I no longer live on the farm, I am a country girl at heart. Living with my husband and daughters in the Virginia suburbs of Washington, D.C., it always seemed right to have farmland near.

But more than 10 years ago, our area's rapid growth reached a point where the changes became unwelcome. The inconveniently heavy traffic made commuting to work and doing small errands a major, time-consuming effort. The wonderful, abundant farmland near us disappeared, almost all at once it seemed. In its place were houses everywhere.

My husband and I decided it was time to move to a less crowded area. We chose rural West Virginia, an hour and a half from our former location. Our newly purchased property in a 20-year-old development did not cause farmland loss. Being next door to a farm was a real plus. We welcomed the unusual neighborliness, the simple life, the light traffic, and all the other good things of a small town.

Several years later while out driving and admiring the beautiful West Virginia countryside, I was shocked to see a For Sale sign advertising a farm property for development for 400 houses. What we had left was following us. Farm For Sale signs and new housing developments began to pop up more frequently. "Wild, Wonderful West Virginia," at least in our area, was vanishing.

I have learned, as *Under the Blade* amply demonstrates, that this is happening across the United States. Yet surprisingly few people are aware of this or seem to care. They rarely think about how much farmland is lost because of population growth, nor how hard it is for farmers to make a decent profit even though they raise the food we all need to survive. The media rarely address this subject, perhaps because good food is plentiful, and for the time being U.S. farmers help feed the world.

In the Virginia suburbs, I had bought into the conventional wisdom that farming cannot survive in developing areas. But it was different this time. There was evidence that it had elsewhere, given the right kind of help. Because family farming is a way of life that deserves to continue, I made the decision to work to save farming and farmland.

Getting information for my work was not easy. I got some good information from American Farmland Trust and their book, *Saving American Farmland: What Works*. Another valuable book was *Holding Our Ground*, by Tom Daniels and Deborah Bowers. The computer with its Internet services and e-mail networks was extremely useful.

But there were still missing pieces to the puzzle. What about food security? What did our rapidly growing U.S. population and our steadily increasing loss of farmland have to do with it? "Population growth is the prime driver of farmland conversion," according to the authors of *Under the Blade* in a look at U.S. and world population pressures. Food security and the implications of food production within a global economy are examined. Included also are current trends in the industrialization of agriculture and the hidden costs of cheap food. These hot-button issues are discussed from a balanced, non-extreme perspective.

How can *Under the Blade* help those who want to save farming and farmland? If I had placed a custom order for a book to help in my work, the finished product would definitely resemble *Under the Blade*. I find most valuable its intelligent analysis, weaving together many components that influence farmland loss. It is unique in this respect, for farmland preservation books tend to concentrate on tools. I appreciate that, rather than attempt to foresee the unforeseeable, this book presents a range of alternative future scenarios concerning food security, from optimistic to pessimistic, and lets us draw our own conclusions.

To work as a farming and farmland advocate, one must involve oneself in the community. I began with a visioning committee and realized the value of a vision. Farming and farmland preservation, according to *Under the Blade*, suffer from the lack of a national vision. *Under the Blade* presents a vision of future land use in America. This vision is based on a healthy national landscape. The vision includes both a rural vision for farming and farmland preservation and an urban vision for healthy, livable cities, as well as addressing interactions between the urban and rural. The authors make a good case that current trends do not lead to such a vision.

As I continued my work, next I became involved with the Land Trust of the Eastern Panhandle. The Land Trust has begun the valuable work of accepting donations of conservation easements, a very important tool in farmland protection. This can play an essential role in preserving rural lands. However, there is not enough money as yet for purchase of development rights, so I felt there was a need for a companion effort to make farming more profitable and thereby help some farmers hold onto their land. To work on this, I became involved with the Potomac Headwaters Resource Conservation and Development Council, one of whose objectives is to strengthen agriculture. Here was a rich opportunity to work for the economic enhancement of agriculture in our area. Again, *Under the Blade* provides information to help with this work.

Before closing, I want to recommend that readers turn to "Walking the Ghost Farm," in Chapter 2. The poignant reminiscences of Atina Diffley about the loss of a farm touch one's emotions.

*Under the Blade* is an excellent source for anyone interested in learning more about issues involved in farming and farmland preservation. It can help empower anyone who wants to make a difference. Perhaps the worst-case scenario regarding our food supply will not happen in our, our children's, or even our grandchildren's lifetime. But *if* it does, and if we have lost too much of our rural landscape, how can we reinvent farmland?

*Marian Buckner,*
Member, Board of Directors, Potomac Headwaters Resource
Conservation & Development Council, Martinsburg, West
Virginia, and Advisory Board, Land Trust of the Eastern
Pahandle, West Virginia

# Preface and Acknowledgments

When we initially titled our book in progress *Under the Blade*, we thought the meaning was perfectly clear—bulldozers clearing the land in advance of development. Then we circulated the prospectus, and the comments began to arrive: "Nice title; clearly referring to the farm plows that have shaped the agricultural landscape." "A nice play on words, referring to the sword of Damocles that hangs over many rural areas in the form of the constant threat of urbanization." "Blades of grass as in the replacement of cropland by bluegrass lawns?"

After briefly considering a switch to a less ambiguous title, we realized that the title was perfectly appropriate. The issue of land use in the United States, particularly the conversion of agricultural lands to housing, roads and other development, is not clear cut. It is extremely complex and the focus of disparate beliefs and strong disagreements. Land use decisions and the consequences of those decisions are the result of many forces including the law, economics, agriculture, landscape function, population growth, sociology, ethics, and aesthetics.

No one factor predominates, but rather they interact to varying degrees to determine the fate of any particular parcel of land. Each of these factors is quite complex in its own right. In combination, the mix is downright daunting. Therein lies the difficulty in writing a book that makes sense of this complexity without trivializing the subject or losing sight of critical interactions. How do you bring the necessary expertise to bear on each subject (for example, it takes a lawyer to fully address the law) without ending up with a disjointed set of essays?

Our approach was to provide, in the Introduction and first chapter, a unifying foundation for the book that subsequent chapters would build on. In the Introduction we describe two paradigms or ways of looking at the world that help to explain land use decisions in the United States. First, a hierarchical framework that shows the relationships between decisions at larger scales (e.g., national) and smaller scales (e.g., state, local, or individual parcels), and second, the main economic system, capitalism. In Chapter 1, we also present data on land use and farmland conversion trends in the United States, and an overview of population projections and estimates of future demand for agricultural products. Thus our foundation has four main elements.

From this common base, we let the experts address the issue of farmland loss from their particular perspectives: landscape function (Chapter 2), law (Chapter 3), economics (Chapter 4), sociology (Chapter 5), and ethics and aesthetics (Chapter 6). Although each chapter is different, they are integrated through a number of commonalities. The four foundation elements run as common themes throughout all the chapters. Cross-references among chapters are common. For example, property or inheritance taxes have significant economic effects, and both are intentionally addressed in the law and economics chapters.

The interrelationships among the different perspectives also showed in ways that we did not expect or plan. For example, Chapter 2 hammers home the point that landscape functions are the result of interactions among different pieces of the landscape. Individual parcels are not isolated from each other, and many of our environmental problems arise when individual landowners treat their land as though it had no connections to a larger area. In Chapter 3, the Supreme Court decision on Lucas v. South Carolina Coastal Commission is discussed in terms of Justice Scalia's philosophy of a "transformative economy," where parcels of land are separate and basically inert until transformed into a higher use, as opposed to an "economy of nature." In Chapter 6, a discussion of the genesis of an American land ethic highlights the writings of John Locke, a 17th century proponent of a transformative economy. Even among disciplines as different as ecology, law, and ethics, common threads emerge with regard to land use.

But what ties the book together even more, and grounds it firmly in the real world are the 22 case studies. Each describes the agriculture and the trends in the loss of farmland of a particular town, state or region. In combination, the case studies illustrate the great diversity of both problems and solutions regarding land use. They are referenced throughout the main

chapters of the book as specific examples of more general statements. Each case study, though limited to a particular geographic
area, offers lessons that are more broadly applicable. Not the
least of which is that a growing number of people share a concern
about the future of the American land.

The debate about land use and farmland preservation in the
United States is not an academic exercise. The land use decisions
that we make during the next decade will be critical in determining our future quality of life. And the evidence so far is that we
are not choosing wisely. Suburban sprawl, fragmentation of landscapes by acreages (ruburbia), and mindless commercial development are degrading landscapes and people. If the magnitude of
the problem is not evident to you, take a drive from Ft. Collins to
Colorado Springs, from Boston to Washington, D.C., from Miami
to Jacksonville or from Portland to Vancouver, B.C. Or for the quick
national overview, see the satellite image composite on page 26.

However, trend is not destiny. We can make better choices,
and in Chapter 7 we have presented some recommendations for
improved national land use policies. At the local level, the proliferation of citizens groups fighting to preserve their landscapes is
encouraging. We hope that this book will be of use to these groups
as well as to planners, politicians, teachers, and others who want
to better understand the forces behind the land use changes that
are so critically affecting their lives.

We thank all of the authors who contributed the chapters and
case studies that comprise *Under the Blade.* We also thank Steve
Fehr, Susan Holleran, and Xiaowen Huang for their contributions
to Case Study 4.

We especially appreciate the excellent work by Kristine M. Meek
of DesignLine Services, Lincoln, Nebraska in formatting and preparing the final manuscript of *Under the Blade.*

We gratefully acknowledge the financial support of the Center
for Sustainable Agricultural Systems, University of Nebraska-
Lincoln, and the W.K. Kellogg Foundation, Battle Creek, Michigan
for the preparation of this book.

The *Center for Sustainable Agricultural Systems* was formed
in 1991 within the Institute of Agriculture and Natural Resources

at the University of Nebraska-Lincoln (UNL) for the purpose of bringing together people and resources to promote an agriculture that is efficient, profitable, and environmentally and socially sustainable for the indefinite future. The Center uses a systems approach to address the complex and multidimensional challenges associated with a sustainable agriculture.

The *W.K. Kellogg Foundation* was established in 1930 "to help people help themselves through the practical application of knowledge and resources to improve their quality of life and that of future generations." Its programming activities center around the common vision of a world in which each person has a sense of worth; accepts responsibility for self, family, community, and societal well-being; and has the capacity to be productive, and to help create nurturing families, responsive institutions, and healthy communities. Areas of emphasis by the Foundation include health; food systems and rural development; youth and education, and higher education; and philanthropy and volunteerism.

*Richard K. Olson and Thomas A. Lyson*

# About the Contributors

**Richard P. Benner** is Director of the Oregon Department of Land Conservation and Development. He previously worked as a staff attorney for 1000 Friends of Oregon, and was the first Executive Director of the Columbia River Gorge Commission.

**Rasa Dale** is a graduate student and Ph.D. candidate in the Economics Department, University of California-Davis.

**Charles A. Francis** is director of the Center for Sustainable Agricultural Systems, University of Nebraska-Lincoln. He is also associated with the Agricultural University of Norway (Aas, Norway) to develop a graduate program in sustainable agriculture for the Scandinavian countries.

**Susan Jo Gehl** is a consultant working to establish a purchase of development rights program in the town of Hartford, Wisconsin. She was previously the program director of agriculture and land use issues for the Wisconsin Environmental Initiative and a policy analyst intern for the American Farmland Trust.

**Charles C. Geisler** is a professor, Department of Rural Sociology, Cornell University, and a member of the editorial boards of Rural Sociology and Journal of Rural Studies. He has worked extensively on issues affecting rural communities in both the United States and Central America.

**William Good** is a Florida farmer and a member of the Lake County Board of County Commissioners.

**Gary R. Grant** was raised on a family farm in the New Deal Community of Tillery, NC. He is the founding director of the national Land Loss Fund, and the first national president of the Black Farmers and Agriculturists Association (BFAA). His goal is to bring the issue of Black land loss to national attention, and to develop ways to reverse the trend.

**Greg Kirkpatrick** is head of the Visalia, California field office of the American Farmland Trust.

**Linda R. Klein** is an environmental consultant specializing in technical writing, communications coordination, and planning and management of ecological restoration projects. She has a MS in soil science from Washington State University, where she previously worked as a research associate in land use and soil management.

**G. Robert Lee** is the Administrator for Fauquier County, Virginia. He has served as chairman of the Shenandoah River Basin Committee, and as a member of the Virginia Commission on Population Growth and Development.

**Lawrence W. Libby** is Professor and C. William Swank Chair in Rural-Urban Policy, Department of Agricultural Economics, The Ohio State University. He formerly served as chairman of the Department of Food and Resource Economics, University of Florida.

**Tim Lindstrom** is Staff Attorney for the Piedmont Environmental Council. He served for twelve years as a member of the Board of Supervisors of Albemarle County, Virginia, and for nineteen years as adjunct professor of planning law in the University of Virginia's School of Architecture.

**Thomas A. Lyson** is a professor, Department of Rural Sociology, Cornell University. He also serves as director of the Farming Alternatives Program at Cornell, and as editor of Rural Sociology.

**Margaret Maizel** is one of the founders of the National Center for Resource Innovations (NCRI), and Executive Director, NCRI-Chesapeake, Inc., Arlington, Virginia. NCRI, a non-profit corporation, was established in 1990 through the U.S. Department of Agriculture to build integrated Geographic Information Systems for public and private decision-makers in primarily rural areas.

**Alexander Maller** is a professor, College of Architecture, University of Nebraska-Lincoln. He is one of the primary architects of Antelope Commons, an innovative urban development designed to preserve ecological functions and promote a true sense of community.

**Helle Margrete Meltzer** is a faculty member in the School of Nutrition, University of Oslo, Norway. Her research interests are in community nutrition and food security.

**Michal C. Moore** is a Regulatory Commissioner on the California Energy Commission. He teaches economic theory at California State University, San Luis Obispo and conducts research concerning the impacts of urban expansion on agricultural productivity and land prices.

**George Muehlbach** is the Geographic Information Systems coordinator at NCRI-Chesapeake, Inc., Arlington, Virginia. He has extensive experience in spatial analyses ranging from transportation corridors to wetlands data bases.

**Allen H. Olson** is a Research Assistant Professor at the University of Arkansas School of Law and a staff attorney for the National Center for Agricultural Law Research and Information. He practiced land use law in Virginia from 1977 to 1995, and now teaches land use, environmental, soil conservation and federal farm program law in the University of Arkansas agricultural law program.

**Richard K. Olson** is an agroecologist with the Center for Sustainable Agricultural Systems, University of Nebraska-Lincoln. He has written on the topics of landscape function, forest ecology, and wetland processes, and has edited six books including *Exploring the Role of Diversity in Sustainable Agriculture.*

**Ethan Parke,** a graduate of the University of Vermont College of Agriculture, owned and operated a dairy farm for 12 years. In 1992, he joined the Vermont Housing and Conservation Board as a farmland protection specialist, working with nonprofit organizations, farmers, and government officials to protect Vermont farmland through conservation easements.

**Michael Pressman** is a regional planner with 1000 Friends of Minnesota. He specializes in land conservation planning and is currently leading a private/public collaborative working to create a green corridor of permanently protected farmland, natural areas, and other open spaces using incentive-based tools.

**John P. Reganold** is a professor, Department of Crop and Soil Sciences, Washington State University, where he teaches soil science, land use, and soil conservation.

**William Riebsame** is associate professor of geography at the University of Colorado-Boulder, where he specializes in land use and resource management in the American West.

**Lauren Ross** is an environmental engineer and sole proprietor of Glenrose Engineering, Austin, Texas. She provides thoughtful and innovative consulting to industry, developers, cities, and community groups on projects and ordinances to protect water quality, soils, and habitat.

**Charles Schlough** is an Agriculture Planning Associate with Cornell Cooperative Extension of Tompkins County (NY). He wrote a comprehensive Study of Agriculture in Tompkins County, and Agriculture and Farmland Protection Plans for Tompkins and Chenango counties.

**Jeanine Sih** is a research assistant, writer, and web developer. She moved to Austin, Texas in 1992, attracted to its unique beauty, friendly people, and the commitment of the residents toward preserving Barton Springs and other priceless natural assets.

**Kate A. Smith** is vice president of AUS consultants in Moorestown, NJ. Previously she held a tenured faculty position in Agricultural Economics at the Pennsylvania State University where she was co-director of a W.K. Kellogg Foundation project on sustaining agriculture in southeastern Pennsylvania.

**W. Cecil Steward**, FAIA, is an architect and President of the Joslyn Castle Institute for Sustainable Communities, Omaha, Nebraska. Since 1973, he has held the position of dean and professor of architecture and planning in the College of Architecture, University of Nebraska-Lincoln. He currently serves as a member of the local Planning Commission for Lincoln and Lancaster County.

**Patrick A. Stewart** is an assistant professor of political science at Arkansas State University. His research interests include land use policy and decision making. He previously served as a research assistant at the Center for Agriculture in the Environment, Northern Illinois University.

**Richard Sutton** teaches landscape design in the Department of Horticulture, University of Nebraska-Lincoln, and practices landscape architecture. He is a Fellow in the Center for Great Plains Studies, and has written about the character and quality of rural landscapes.

# Under the Blade

# Introduction

*Richard K. Olson*

Cultivators of the earth are the most valuable citizens. They are the most vigorous, the most independent, the most virtuous, and they are tied to their country, and wedded to its liberty and interests, by the most lasting bonds. As long, therefore, as they can find employment in this line, I would not convert them into mariners, artisans or anything else.

— Thomas Jefferson (1785)

Our man has formed a taste for physical pleasures; he sees thousands around him enjoying them...What is he to do? To cultivate the ground promises an almost certain reward for his efforts, but a slow one...Agriculture only suits the wealthy, who already have a great superfluity, or the poor, who only want to live. His choice is made; he sells his field, moves from his house, and takes up some risky but lucrative profession...Democracy therefore...leads men to...a distaste for agriculture and directs them into trade or industry.

Almost all the farmers in the United States have combined some trade with agriculture; most of them have made agriculture itself a trade. It is unusual for an American farmer to settle forever on the land he occupies...A farm is built in the anticipation that, since the state of the country will soon be changing with the increase of population, one will be able to sell it for a good price... In such fashion the Americans carry over into agriculture the spirit of a trading venture, and their passion for industry is manifest there as elsewhere.

— Alexis de Tocqueville (1835)

Agriculture in America has never been a static undertaking. The subsistence farms of the earliest settlers were quickly transformed into exporters of excess production to eastern cities. In the Midwest, small diversified farms became larger cash grain farms whose outputs fattened Western cattle or met a demand for grain overseas. In the face of competition from regions better suited to agriculture, marginal regions such as New England saw a wholesale conversion of cropland to second-growth forest. The Spanish cattle ranches of California's Central Valley gave way to cereals, then to vegetable and fruit production, and more recently to houses, roads and malls.

All of these trends and patterns in agriculture are interrelated, but it is this last aspect of the dynamic of agriculture, the conversion of agricultural land to housing tracts, industrial parks, and other forms of development, that is the focus of *Under the Blade*. Farmland conversion is qualitatively different from other paths by which land is removed from agriculture in that it is permanent in any time frame that matters. New England farmland abandoned to second growth forest can theoretically, if erosion was not too severe, be managed as a productive forest or returned to pasture or cropland. Development forecloses any options for agriculture on a particular piece of land; if you grew up on a vegetable farm in western Long Island or a productive orchard in the Santa Clara Valley (or any of a hundred other urban fringe areas) during the 1940s or 1950s, you literally can't go home again.

Concern about farmland loss is based on four premises that will be addressed throughout this book:

1. An adequate supply of quality agricultural land embedded within functioning agricultural landscapes is absolutely essential to the economic, social, and environmental well-being of the citizens of the United States and the world. Agricultural land includes cropland, pastureland, rangeland, and managed forests. Essential functions of agricultural landscapes include not only commodity production, but air and water purification, wildlife habitat, recreation, open space, and an environment for quality rural lifestyles and cultures.

2. Conversion of farmland to development is contributing to a significant reduction in both the production and non-

production functions of U.S. landscapes, and extrapolation of current trends predicts a continuing reduction for the foreseeable future.

3. Rapid increases in both U.S. and world population are generating corresponding increases in domestic and foreign demand for U.S. agricultural production. Conversion of agricultural land to development will make it more difficult for advances in agricultural productivity to keep pace with demand.

4. The approach to development in the United States is very inefficient—a diffuse pattern that leaves impoverished urban cores behind while replacing rural landscapes with suburban sprawl that degrades many landscape functions and offers a diminished quality of life. A move toward compact, liveable cities is essential to the preservation of agricultural landscapes.

Given these premises, it is both disturbing and puzzling that U.S. agricultural and forest lands continue to be permanently converted to non-agricultural uses at an average rate of at least 1.4 million acres per year (USDA 1995). It is also puzzling that accurate, up-to-date data on the amount of agricultural land converted is difficult to obtain. The United States has better estimates of the number of cars imported each year from Japan than of the number of acres of farmland developed. Clearly, there is a discrepancy between the actual and the perceived value of this resource.

## What Controls Farmland Loss?

One of the central questions addressed in *Under the Blade* is what determines the overall rate of farmland conversion in the United States, and therefore, what changes can be made to reduce this rate? A key point is that no single factor or group predominates. Congress, the U.S. Department of Agriculture, and the National Homebuilders Association do not establish yearly quotas for farmland conversion—the ultimate rate is a function of the cumulative impact of millions of individual land use decisions. While local zoning or interactions among nearby landowners may link the fate of one farm to decisions made for another, at regional or national scales most land use decisions are independent. The many factors considered in a decision to convert a 250-acre farm in New Jersey into a mall do not include the recent conversion of a 500-acre orchard in Fresno County, California into a subdivision.

So, to answer our central question we need to examine what determines the likelihood that a particular parcel of agricultural land will be converted. The following examples illustrate five factors that play major roles in determining the future of farmland.

**Economics:** Based on commodity prices at the beginning of harvest in 1996, a dryland farmer in Lancaster County, Nebraska could afford to pay about $1,500 per acre for good farmland assuming 30% down and 8% interest. At the same time, developers were paying $11,000 per acre for parcels near the boundary of the county's main city, Lincoln, and $3,000 per acre for parcels more than 15 miles from the city's edge. The price of virtually all farmland in Lancaster County is now set by development potential rather than agricultural production potential.

**Law:** The Twin Cities region of Minnesota is the fastest growing metropolitan area in the upper Midwest (LSL 1996). A growth boundary established to restrict sprawl has had the opposite effect as developers leapfrog the boundary to obtain cheaper land with fewer restrictions. Outlying communities exacerbate the problem by zoning to encourage expensive single homes that rapidly consume land by requiring large lot sizes (DeVore 1996).

**Sociology:** In 1992, more than 40% of Iowa farmland was owned by someone more than 65 years old, while only 6.5% was owned by someone less than 35 years old (Thompson 1996). This type of age distribution is not unusual in the Midwest, and guarantees a high rate of turnover and instability in farmland ownership during the next decade.

**Landscape function:** Farmland development in areas near U.S. cities is accelerated by the paving of county roads or the extension of other urban services such as sewers or mass transit. These changes reduce the effective distance between the urban and rural areas, and therefore increase the value of land for development.

**Ethics and aesthetics:** In 1993, the Disney Company proposed to develop a Civil War theme park centered on a 200-acre parcel in northern Virginia. While the area actually occupied by the attraction would have been small, ancillary development (e.g., hotels, supporting businesses, employee housing) would have drastically changed the rural character of the surrounding landscape including many Civil War battle sites of historic interest. Much of the opposition to Disney was based not on farmland preservation *per se*, but on a broader aesthetic appeal. Court challenges and protests eventually convinced Disney to abandon the project.

These examples show the influence of five major factors in farmland conversion decisions. Although separate examples were chosen to highlight each factor, many factors interact to influence a land use decision. The advanced age of Iowa farmers is due in part to high land and equipment costs that pose a barrier to entry by young farmers, and to estate tax laws that complicate the transfer of farms to the next generation. The fight to stop Disney may have been largely motivated by a desire to preserve the aesthetics and lifestyle of this region, but economics underlay Disney's decision to attempt the project, and politics pervaded the granting to Disney of road improvements and other incentives by the state of Virginia. Any farmland conversion decision takes place in a complex context of economic, social, landscape, legal, and ethical factors.

At first glance, the number of factors affecting land use decisions and the number of people and parcels involved seem to generate an almost infinite variety of situations. It almost appears that the motivations behind land use decisions must be evaluated on a case by case basis.

This complexity presents a dilemma for any book that attempts to describe the farmland conversion problem and to prescribe policy changes to solve the problem. On one hand, the economic, legal and other aspects of the issue are each difficult enough to require the attention of an expert in the field—no single person has the necessary background and perspective to thoroughly address all the topics. On the other hand, farmland conversion is clearly a transdisciplinary process with complex interactions among multiple factors. These interactions produce outcomes that cannot be predicted or alleviated from a single perspective. How then can an integrated overview and analysis of the farmland conversion issue in the United States be produced? Fortunately, there are two frameworks that are of use.

## Two Frameworks for Evaluating Farmland Loss

### A Spatial Hierarchy

While a small piece of land—10, 100, or perhaps 500 acres—is often the focal point at which economic, social and other forces converge to cause or prevent farmland conversion, each of these factors operates within a hierarchy of spatial scales (Figure I.1). A farmer's decision to put a permanent open-space easement on her land may be based on an offer from a state-level open-space program that receives its funding from a national program established by Congress. Another farmer's bankruptcy and forced sale of land to a developer may result in part from low commodity prices established by national trade policies and crop surpluses in other countries.

Only by acknowledging these hierarchical relationships can local land use decisions be fully understood. While this may at first seem to complicate an already complex analysis, a hierarchical structure can actually simplify the task. For example, differences in tax laws affecting agriculture exist among the states, but there are commonalities imposed by federal law. Regional differences occur in prices for farm products, but for the major commodities such as corn and wheat an increasingly global economy sets the price and limits the magnitude of any variations among regions. One need not inquire at the Elm Creek, Nebraska grain elevator to find out roughly what price farmers in that town will be receiving for their corn—a call to the Chicago Board of Trade will provide a close estimate not only for central Nebraska farmers but for any American corn producer.

A hierarchical framework provides useful generalities for analyzing processes at smaller scales. Within this hierarchy, legal, economic, sociological, ethical, and ecological factors interact at every scale to directly or indirectly influence the fate of particular parcels of farmland.

This framework also helps in evaluating the consequences of farmland loss. The conversion of a parcel of farmland has economic, social, ecological, and aesthetic implications. Conversion occurs parcel by parcel, but its cumulative effects are felt at all scales.

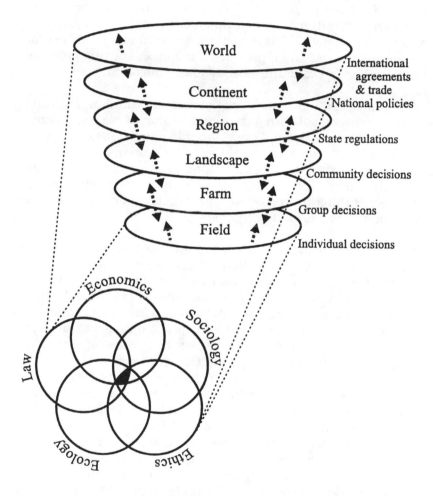

Figure I.1   Land use is influenced by decisions and conditions at different scales. Within this spatial hierarchy, the decision of how to use a particular parcel of land is influenced by economic, sociological, ethical, ecological, and legal factors. In turn, land use decisions affect each of these factors at each scale. Based on Olson and Francis (1995).

### A Socio-Economic Paradigm for Land Use Decisions

The second integrating framework consists of a common set of principles, assumptions, and conventional wisdoms held by Americans and applying to land use decisions at any level of the hierarchy. By common, I don't mean singular or unique—that is clearly not the case given the diversity of cultures and backgrounds that comprise the U.S. citizenry. I mean widespread and deeply enough entrenched to influence the majority of farmland conversion decisions. This common viewpoint is a *paradigm* for land use decisions, and it provides a common starting point for any discipline in evaluating the farmland question.

A paradigm is "the basic way of perceiving, thinking, valuing, and doing associated with a particular vision of reality. A dominant paradigm is seldom if ever stated explicitly; it exists as unquestioned, tacit understanding that is transmitted through culture and to succeeding generations through direct experience rather than being taught" (Harmon 1970). If Americans have a basic way of thinking and doing with regard to farmland use and conversion, it is based in economics.

Economics "is concerned with the way resources are allocated among alternative uses to satisfy human wants," and a resource is "a thing or service used to produce goods (or services) which can satisfy human wants" (Mansfield 1980). Agricultural land is a prominent resource whose alternative uses include production of food and fiber, production of wildlife, as a building site for homes, factories and roads, and as green space or a pleasing view. The choice to retain farmland in production or to remove it from production is an allocation of the resource among alternative uses, and as such is an economic act regardless of the rationale behind the decision. A choice is required because land is a *scarce resource*, meaning there is less of it available than is needed to meet all human wants. The choice of one particular use precludes, either temporarily or permanently, other uses and as such involves an *opportunity cost* or "the value of what these resources could have produced if they had been used in the best alternative way" (Mansfield 1980). Farmland kept in production cannot support a subdivision, while farmland developed as housing tracts cannot produce food or supply open space. Obviously, arguments about the definition of "best" use are central to land use issues and are value-based.

It is important to remember once again that beneath the broad trends and national statistics of farmland conversion are thousands of small land use decisions made as part of the process of resource allocation by individual households. Appropriately, the word "economy" is derived from the Greek *oikos*, house, and *nomos*, managing; eventually coalescing in Old French as *economie*, management of a household (Morris 1981). With approximately 99% of U.S. farmland owned by individuals, partnerships, families, or family-owned corporations (USDC 1996), most conversion decisions are a direct part of a household economy. Non-farm households indirectly influence conversion decisions as they determine how resources are allocated through their purchases of housing, food, and fiber, and their political choices on the spending of tax dollars for sewer extensions, road improvements or programs to purchase development rights. Clearly, the economic views of American families have a significant effect on trends in farmland conversion.

The dominant economic view in the United States is capitalism, "an economic-cultural system, organized economically around the institution of property and the production of commodities and based culturally in the fact that exchange relations, that of buying and selling, have permeated most of the society" (Bell 1979). Capitalism is characterized by four main principles (Mansfield 1980):

**Private ownership of capital and resources:** Factories, equipment, inventories, land, and mineral deposits are owned directly by individuals or indirectly by stockholders in corporations. Each separate piece of capital has an owner and a market value.

**Freedom of choice and enterprise:** Consumers, laborers, and investors have freedom of choice in their purchases, job selection, and investments. Businesses are free to enter markets, obtain resources, and pursue their own self-interest as best they can.

**Competition:** Businesses compete in the market place for capital, resources, and sales. Less efficient businesses, farms included, often go out of business when out-competed by more efficient enterprises.

**Reliance upon markets:** The free market is the arena within which buying, selling, and other exchanges central to capitalism occur.

These principles are more than just the textbook characteristics of a particular economic system; they represent the belief of most Americans as to the way things are and ought to be. Many individual actions are based on these principles as are peoples' judgements of the actions of others. As Americans observe what is happening around them to farmland and other resources, their conclusions as to the rightness or wrongness of these events are often based on each event's conformity to the principles of capitalism.

Of course, adherence to these principles in the United States is far from absolute. Laissez-faire capitalism does not exist because most people accept and desire some limits. At the least, government is expected to prevent theft, enforce contracts, and in some way provide a level playing field and some basic rules of economic competition. Disagreements arise about the type and extent of additional restrictions. Often the arguments are couched in political, social or even spiritual terms, but all are at their core economic as they relate to the allocation of a scarce resource. For example:

- In North and South Dakota, the U.S. Fish and Wildlife Service manages many Waterfowl Production Areas established through the purchase of easements or fee-title. Although the purchases involved willing sellers, local opposition to this use of the land may be high because the farmland no longer contributes to the tax rolls or to the local farm economy.

- Some proponents of private property rights oppose the right of owners to place permanent open-space easements on their land because it restricts the options of future owners of the property.

- Cities such as Portland, Oregon that attempt to restrict growth by setting urban growth boundaries or by other means may be accused of driving up housing prices and discriminating against lower income groups.

As a democracy, the United States provides a political process for modifying economic rules. Individuals may form groups to lobby within the political arena for laws and policies that further their common goals, with the caveat that they not infringe upon basic rights guaranteed to all individuals by the United States Constitution. The body of law regarding economics and land use continually evolves in concert with changes in the dominant political philosophy of the country.

## An American Dilemma

In relation to farmland conversion, the quotes at the beginning of this chapter illustrate a contradiction or dilemma in our socio-economic system. Jefferson's comment on the importance of land ownership and agriculture to the maintenance of democracy is quoted with increasing frequency as the proportion of Americans living in urban areas approaches 75% and the proportion actively engaged in farming falls below 2% (Dacquel and Dahmann 1993). However, Tocqueville, one of the more astute observers of American society, suggested that democracy and capitalism actually promote the abandonment of farming and the conversion of farmland to other economic uses. There is no doubt that Americans still have a "taste for physical pleasures" and that enterprises other than production agriculture can often fulfill these desires far more easily and completely. The current socio-economic paradigm with its emphasis on private property rights, freedom of enterprise, and self-achievement clearly allows and supports, and sometimes forces, the transition of many farmers to other pursuits, and the allocation of their primary resource, land, to other uses.

Our goal in *Under the Blade* is to examine this situation in detail, to demonstrate that our land use dilemma has serious implications, and to propose solutions. Chapter 1 compares the sources of information available on agricultural land conversion in the United States, and provides our best estimates of current patterns and trends in conversion. These trends are then evaluated in the context of U.S. and world agricultural land resources, current production, and projected increases in population and demand for agricultural commodities.

Chapters 2 through 6 evaluate the trends and implications of farmland conversion from the five different perspectives of land-

scape function, law, economics, sociology, and ethics and aesthetics. To complement these broader overviews, we present 21
case studies of farmland conversion in different regions of the
United States, and one case study from Europe. The case studies
illustrate the great variety of farmland conversion issues and
situations that exist within our very diverse country. They also
describe the concerns of people in every region as well as their
creativity in working to design landscapes that are both
functional and pleasing to live in. The case studies serve as a
vehicle for sharing the many real-world lessons that have been
learned. Finally, Chapter 7 includes both a summary and recommendations for a national policy toward farmland preservation.

## References

Bell, D. 1979. The Cultural Contradictions of Capitalism.
    Heinemann, London.
Dacquel, L.T., and D.C. Dahmann. 1993. Residents of Farms and
    Rural Areas: 1991, U.S. Bureau of the Census, Current
    Population Reports, P20-472, U.S. Government Printing Office,
    Washington, D.C.
DeVore, B. 1996. Holding urban sprawl accountable. The Land
    Stewardship Letter 14(1):1, 8-10.
Harmon, W. 1970. An Incomplete Guide to the Future. W.W.
    Norton, New York.
Jefferson, T. 1785. Letter to John Jay, quoted in McEwan, B.
    1991. Thomas Jefferson: Farmer. McFarland & Company,
    Jefferson, NC.
LSL. 1996. Putting the pieces together. The Land Stewardship
    Letter 14(1):11.
Mansfield, E. 1980. Principles of Macroeconomics. W.W. Norton,
    New York.
Morris, W. (ed.) 1981. The American Heritage Dictionary of the
    English Language. Houghton Mifflin, Boston.
Olson, R.K., and C.A. Francis. 1995. A hierarchical framework
    for evaluating diversity in agroecosystems. pp. 5-34. In:
    R.K. Olson, C.A. Francis and S. Kaffka (eds.) Exploring the
    Role of Diversity in Sustainable Agriculture, American Society of
    Agronomy, Madison, WI.
Thompson, N. 1996. Land ownership patterns. Center for Rural
    Affairs Newsletter, April 1996, Walthill, NE.

Tocqueville, A. de. 1835. Democracy in America. J.P. Mayer and M. Lerner (eds); Translated by G. Lawrence, 1966. Harper & Row, New York.

USDA. 1995. Summary Report: 1992 National Resources Inventory. U.S. Department of Agriculture, Natural Resources Conservation Service, Washington, D.C.

USDC. 1996. Statistical Abstract of the United States: 1996 (116th edition). U.S. Department of Commerce, Bureau of the Census, Washington, D.C.

# 1

# Farmland Loss in America

*Richard K. Olson and Allen H. Olson*

The United States is blessed with an abundance of high quality farmland, rangeland and forest land. In the first part of this chapter, we describe this cornucopia in order to provide a context for evaluating the conversion of agricultural land to other uses. But simply knowing how much land we have is not sufficient for determining whether farmland loss is a problem; an equally important question is how much land do we need? The second part of this chapter looks at current and future demand for U.S. agricultural products, and the potential for the U.S. farmland base to meet those needs. Of course, agricultural commodities are only one of many services provided by agricultural landscapes, and the effects of farmland conversion on these other functions are examined in detail throughout the remainder of the book.

## What Do We Have To Lose?

Agriculture is the dominant land use in this country, occupying more than half of the land area of the contiguous United States (Table 1.1). Cropland and pastureland, the land uses that most people associate with farms, comprise just under one-half of the total agricultural land with rangeland the remainder. Forest land is the other major rural land use category (see Box 1.1 for definitions of land uses).

Table 1.1   1992 land use statistics (federal and non-federal lands) for the contiguous United States (does not include Alaska, Hawaii, Caribbean). Water, forest land, and rangeland areas based on USDA (1981a); other land category areas from 1992 NRI (USDA 1995).

| Land Class | Acres | Percentage of Total U.S. Area |
|---|---|---|
| Inland water | 46,220,000 | 2.3 |
| Coastal water and Great Lakes | 47,642,000 | 2.4 |
| Forest land | | |
|    productive | 493,569,034 | 24.9 |
|    unproductive* | 121,231,966 | 6.1 |
| Rangeland | | |
|    productive | 535,644,613 | 27.0 |
|    unproductive* | 51,291,387 | 2.6 |
| Cropland | 381,676,000 | 19.3 |
| Pastureland | 125,126,000 | 6.3 |
| Conservation Reserve Program | 32,000,000 | 1.6 |
| Other rural | 55,884,000 | 2.8 |
| Developed | 91,776,000 | 4.6 |
| Total surface area | 1,982,060,000 | 100 |

*Forest land producing less than 20 ft$^3$ of industrial roundwood per acre per year is classified as unproductive (USDA 1981a). Desert grasslands are classified as unproductive rangeland (Sims 1988).

Box 1.1   Definitions of land use categories (USDA 1987).

**Cropland:**  Land used for the production of adapted crops for harvest, alone or in rotation with grasses and legumes. Adapted crops include row crops, small grain, hay, nursery crops, orchard and vineyard crops, and other specialty crops.

**Pastureland:**  Land used primarily for the production of adapted, introduced or native species in a pure stand, grass mixture or a grass-legume mixture. Cultural treatment in the form of fertilization, weed control, reseeding or renovation is usually a part of pasture management in addition to grazing management.

**Prime farmland:**  Land on which crops can be produced for the least cost and with the least damage to the resource base. Criteria include availability of water, favorable growing season, soil quality, and slope. Approximately two-thirds of U.S. prime farmland is used as cropland with the remainder used for pasture, range, forest, or other rural uses.

**Rangeland:**  Land on which the climax vegetation (potential natural plant community) is predominantly grasses, grasslike plants, forbs, or shrubs suitable for grazing and browsing.

**Forest land:**  Land at least 10% stocked by forest trees of any size, or formerly having had such tree cover and not currently developed for non-forest use.

**Developed land:**  Urban and built-up areas including residential, industrial, commercial, and institutional land, construction sites, public administrative sites, railroad yards, cemeteries, airports, golf courses, sanitary landfills, sewage treatment plants, water control structures, spillways, highways, railroads, other transportation facilities and small parks that are surrounded by urban areas.

Total farm marketings in the United States in 1994 equaled
$179.7 billion (USDC 1996a). The top six commodities in order of
market value were cattle, dairy products, corn, soybeans, broilers, and hogs which combined accounted for 61% of total
marketings. Given that much of the corn and soybeans is fed to
livestock, U.S. agriculture clearly emphasizes meat and dairy
production. California ranks first in value of agricultural output
at $20.2 billion, followed by Texas, Iowa, Nebraska, and Illinois
(Appendix 1.1). Together, the five states produce $59.7 billion of
agricultural commodities or 33% of the U.S. total.

There are 334 million acres of non-federal rural land (24% of
the total) classified as prime farmland—land of high quality and
minimal constraints for crop production. The largest amounts
of prime farmland are found in IA, IL, KS, MN, and TX (Appendix
1.1). Sixteen percent of U.S. cropland (62 million acres) is
irrigated, and about half the irrigated acres are found in CA,
KS, NE, TX, and AR (USDA 1995).

Prime and irrigated farmland is clearly more valuable for
production than other classes of farmland. Another high value
category is unique farmland, defined as farmland used to grow
vegetables, grapes and horticultural crops including fruits, nuts
and berries that have unique soil and climatic requirements
(Sorensen et al. 1997). For example, Hanson (1996) writes "The
only region *in all of America* with enough temperature to produce
naturally dried raisins for three weeks in late August and September is the Central Valley of California. Men of the nineteenth
century went broke, toiled for no good reason, died before they
discovered that the ground beneath them was not just excellent
grain soil, not merely the ideal home for figs and peaches, but the
*only* region in all of America for raisins. Half the world's supply is
their legacy."

The combination of soils, climate and irrigation water found in
the Sacramento and San Joaquin Valleys support more than 250
commodities in addition to raisins, and the valleys account for
15% of U.S. vegetable production and 38% of fruit production
(Sorensen et al. 1997). Fresno County, CA is the most productive
farm county in the United States. On the other side of the country, Lancaster County, PA has the most productive non-irrigated
agriculture in the United States (see Case 3). Other unique areas
include South Florida (winter vegetable production) and western

Michigan, where the lake-induced micro-climate supports or-chards that account for most of the U.S. tart cherry production.

Any farmland bordering a major urban area is unique in terms of its proximity to that city. More than half the value of U.S. farm production is generated in counties in or near urban areas (Sorensen et al. 1997). Farmland at the urban fringe is critical to the development of localized food systems (see Chapter 5). It also provides other services to the city including recreation opportunities, water supply, and aesthetic enjoyment (see Chapter 2) that are not as easily obtained from distant sources as is food. Farmland statistics at the national or state level tell only a small part of the story. Losses that are trivial at a national scale may be devastating at a local scale.

## What Are We Losing?

### Uncertainty and Early Controversy

There is not complete agreement as to the number of acres of farmland lost to development in the United States since World War II or as to the current rate of farmland conversion. Much has been written on the subject since 1981 when the National Agricultural Lands Study (NALS; USDA 1981b) found that farmland was converted to non-farm uses at the rate of three million acres a year between 1967 and 1975.

NALS, a joint effort of the United States Department of Agriculture and the President's Council on Environmental Quality, sparked considerable controversy. Criticism of the study related to both the accuracy of its farmland loss estimates and its conclusions as to the importance of the losses. Indeed, critics of NALS have focused primarily on the question of whether we need all our farmland and upon our ability to bring new farmland into production to replace that lost by conversion. They argue that technology will allow the production of more food on less acreage and that forest and rangeland could be brought into crop production if needed.

Criticism of the NALS numbers was also encouraged by the fact that NALS largely ignored the non-production functions of farmland, focusing instead on the need for farmland to meet relatively short-term world food requirements. By the time NALS was published, the food scarcity of the 1970s was giving way to the crop surpluses of the 1980s, undercutting the study's credibility. Lost in this early debate was a discussion of the environmental and aesthetic values of farmland and the need to feed future generations.

NALS was followed by many other studies, reports and articles. These include the twice per decade land resource surveys of the Census of Agriculture (Bureau of the Census 1994) and the National Resources Inventory (USDA 1995), reports by USDA's Economic Research Service (USDA 1984,1994), the Farming on the Edge reports by the American Farmland Trust (AFT 1993, 1997), and articles by Fischel (1982), Simon and Sudman (1982), Heimlich and Krupa (1994), and Pimentel and Giampietro (1994). These studies have reported farmland losses between 1982 and 1992 ranging from one to four million acres per year. This raises the question of why these estimates differ, and what is the "real" rate of conversion.

### Criteria for Evaluating Data Sources

In comparing farmland conversion numbers from different studies, many factors need to be considered:

1. Farmland includes cropland, range, and pasture. Farmland conversion can be measured either by looking at all farmland or by breaking it into separate components. Cropland and rangeland are not found in the same relative proportions in all agricultural areas, and may be converted at differing rates. Also, cropland can be, and frequently is, planted to grasses and becomes pasture. Rangeland is put to the plow to create cropland.

2. Farmland can be developed into residential, commercial, industrial or institutional uses or can be taken out of agricultural use by abandonment. Distinguishing the two types of conversion is important. Abandoned farmland is more easily returned to production than built-on farmland.

3. Forest land is generally not included in the definition of farmland. However, farmland can be converted to forests, and forests can be cut to create farmland. Similarly, wetlands can be drained to make farmland, and forests and

wetlands can be developed into urban uses. Some conversion studies include forest land located on farms, but not free standing forest land that is not closely associated with farming or ranching operations.

4. Studies may or may not look at farmland quality as well as quantity. Quality can be measured by soil types, water resources, climate, parcel size, adjoining land uses, capital infrastructure, proximity to markets and other factors. The rate of conversion of good farmland may differ from the rate of conversion of farmland as a whole, and studies frequently look at prime farmland as a separate category. Other studies have added a unique farmland category to include certain productive farmland not covered by the prime farmland definition.

5. Some studies look at changes in the number and size of farms as well as changes in the amount of farmland. The definition of a farm is important in such studies. Farms may be defined by parcel size, land use, the value of agricultural products sold or net income from agricultural activities, and the study results will depend on the definition used.

6. Studies may report farmland conversion numbers on a national or regional basis or with regard to specific metropolitan areas. Regions and metropolitan areas may be defined in various ways, and different study periods may be used. Different geographic areas and time frames will show widely varying percentages and rates of farmland conversion as will the extrapolation of different regional or metropolitan farmland conversions to estimate national trends.

### *Two Main Data Sources*

Most recent studies of farmland conversion are based on one or both of two major data sources—the Department of Commerce's Census of Agriculture and the U.S. Department of Agriculture's National Resources Inventory (NRI). The Census of Agriculture is conducted every five years, most recently in 1997. Data is obtained primarily from mail surveys for categories including land in farms, size of farms, amount of cropland and pastureland, and value of land, buildings and harvested crops. There is no category for developed land.

The NRI is also conducted every five years, and is a survey of non-federal lands based on a grid of 800,000 sample sites. Data is derived from aerial photos and other remote sensing techniques as well as on-site inspection. The NRI does not include a category for land in farms, and its operational definitions for forest-, pasture-, and croplands (see Box 1.1) differ from those of the Census of Agriculture. However, the NRI does measure developed land, a major benefit to studies of farmland conversion.

Each of these data sources is described in more detail in Appendix 1.2. The key point is that there are differences in the methodology and definitions of land categories used by these two surveys. As a result, estimates of the area of land in certain categories (e.g., cropland) differ between the two sources.

### Recent Changes in Farmland and Developed Land

The Census of Agriculture shows that between 1982 and 1992, land in farms declined from 987 million acres to 946 million acres (Table 1.2), a difference of approximately 41 million acres or an average reduction of 4.1 million acres per year. Approximately 9 million acres of this reduction may be accounted for by farms that were wholly enrolled in the Conservation Reserve Program (CRP), and therefore no longer classified as farmland (see Appendix 1.2). Because the census does not survey developed land, it is not possible to determine from the census what portion of the non-CRP land removed from the land in farms category has actually been built upon or how much of that land is being held on speculation for future development. One also cannot tell how much was converted to forest land.

Total cropland declined from 445 million acres to 435 million acres during the same period, roughly 1 million acres per year. Again, part of this decrease is attributable to the enrollment of whole farms into the CRP. Other cropland was converted to pasture, woodlands and orchards. The census does not tell how many cropland acres were developed into residential, commercial, industrial or other nonagricultural uses.

Fortunately, the NRI does measure developed land. The NRI reports show an increase of 14 million acres of developed land between 1982 and 1992, an average of 1.4 million acres per year. Of the 14 million acres of development, 2.4 million acres came from pastureland, 2 million acres from rangeland, 5.4 million acres from forest land, and 4 million acres from cropland (Table 1.3). The NRI also finds that 4 million acres of prime farmland were converted to development between 1982 and 1992. As of 1992, there remained 334 million acres of prime farmland in the United States, 65% of which was in cropland.

Table 1.2  Farms, farmland, and cropland, 1982–1992 (Bureau of the Census 1984, 1989, 1994).

| Category | 1992 | 1987 | 1982 |
|---|---|---|---|
| Farms (number) | 1,925,300 | 2,087,759 | 2,240,976 |
| Land in farms (acres) | 945,531,506 | 964,470,625 | 986,796,579 |
| Total cropland (acres) | 435,365,878 | 443,318,233 | 445,362,028 |

Table 1.3  Land converted to development in the United States (excluding Alaska) during the period 1982 to 1992 (USDA 1995). U.S. population increased during this period by 23 million.

| Land category | Acres converted | Acres converted per capita population increase |
|---|---|---|
| Cropland | 3,910,000 | .17 |
| Pastureland | 2,383,000 | .10 |
| Forest land | 5,367,000 | .23 |
| Rangeland | 2,029,000 | .09 |
| Other rural land | 269,000 | .01 |
| Water/Federal land | 21,000 | .001 |
| Total | 13,979,000 | .60 |

### NRI Underestimates Development

An important point is that the NRI clearly undercounts developed land. It fails to include within the residential category most land located within large lot subdivisions. The NRI classifies as residential only that portion of the land immediately surrounding the residence, basically the lawn and outbuildings. Where the distinction between the lawn and the remainder of the property is unclear, the residence portion is deemed to end fifty feet behind the substantial structure most distant from the road, usually the house.

The remaining land in each lot is placed in a category corresponding to its vegetative cover, i.e., pasture, hayland or woodland. This means that the overwhelming majority of land located in subdivisions with lot sizes of ten, twenty-five or fifty acres, often called farmettes or ranchettes, is reported by the NRI as agricultural or forest whether or not the land is actually used for agricultural production or commercial timbering.

The houses themselves are reported in an "other rural lands" category unless there are at least five structures, residential or commercial, located within a half-mile of each other along one side of a road or within a quarter-mile of each other if located on both sides of the road. In the latter case, the houses, lawns and outbuildings are reported as part of an urban and built-up area, that is developed land, but the remaining land in the large lots is again assigned to an agricultural or forest category.

Large lot subdivisions have proliferated in many areas of the country. They provide relatively few housing units but have the potential to take large quantities of farmland out of production. Limited agricultural activity may continue on some large lots, perhaps a few cattle or horses or a small orchard. In most areas, large lots are too small to support commercial agricultural production. In addition, they fragment agricultural regions, reducing the critical mass of farmland necessary for long term farming, and increasing land use conflicts between the large lot residents and the remaining farmers. The fragmentation also degrades other landscape functions such as wildlife habitat and scenic views. The NRI's inclusion of large lot subdivisions in agricultural land use categories has resulted in a significant under-reporting of converted farm and forest land acreage, and of the functional impacts of that conversion.

## Spatial and Temporal Patterns of Farmland Loss

### *What Regions Face the Greatest Threat?*

Spatial patterns of land conversion correspond to the patterns of population settlement. As illustrated by the nighttime satellite images in Figure 1.1, most regions of the United States are subject to considerable urbanization and development pressure. Still, rates of land conversion are not uniform throughout the country, nor are agricultural activities equally important in every region. In terms of the threat to the agricultural resource base, regions with relatively large amounts of good farmland and high rates of conversion of land to development represent the highest risk.

Using a framework of Major Land Resource Areas (relatively homogeneous areas of soil, climate, water resources, land use and types of farming), the American Farmland Trust (AFT 1997) identified the twenty most threatened regions based on the correlation of large amounts of prime and unique farmland with high rates of farmland conversion (Figure 1.2). Relative rankings among the twenty regions were determined based on each area's market value of agricultural production, development pressure, and land quality. Using these criteria, the five most threatened regions are (1) Sacramento and San Joaquin Valleys of central California, (2) the Northern Piedmont region centered in southeastern Pennsylvania, Maryland, and northeastern Virginia, (3) Southern Wisconsin and Northern Illinois Drift Plain, (4) Texas Blackland Prairie (eastern Texas), and (5) Willamette and Puget Sound Valleys of Oregon and Washington.

### *America is Sprawling*

The efficiency of land use in the United States is decreasing as we adopt a sprawling development pattern. In 1982, there was 0.34 acre of built land (e.g., housing, roads, factories) per U.S. resident (Appendix 1.3). Had development density remained constant, the population increase of 23 million experienced by the United States from 1982 to 1992 would have resulted in conversion of 7.8 million additional acres. Instead, built land increased by 14 million acres or 0.60 acres per capita population increase (Table 1.2). Individual states showed even greater decreases in land use efficiency (Appendix 1.3). Pennsylvania had 0.25 acres built land per capita in 1982, but added three acres of

Figure 1.1  Nighttime lights of the USA is a composite of satellite images from the Defense Meteorological Satellite Program that illustrates the spatial distribution of population. Available through the DMSP homepage at www.ngdc.noaa.gov/dmsp/dmsp.html.

Figure 1.2   The twenty agricultural regions most-threatened
by farmland conversion (AFT 1997). See text for analysis criteria. Regions in order of greatest threat are: 1. Sacramento and
San Joaquin Valleys, 2. Northern Piedmont, 3. Southern Wisconsin and Northern Illinois Drift Plain, 4. Texas Blackland
Prairie, 5. Willamette and Puget Sound Valleys, 6. Florida Ev-
erglades and Associated Areas, 7. Eastern Ohio Till Plain, 8.
Lower Rio Grande Plain, 9. Mid-Atlantic Coastal Plain, 10. New
England and Eastern New York Upland, Southern Part, 11.
Ontario Plain and Finger Lakes Region, 12. Nashville Basin,
13. Central Snake River Plains, 14. Southwestern Michigan
Fruit and Truck Belt, 15. Central California Coastal Valleys,
16. Columbia Basin, 17. Imperial Valley, 18. Long Island-Cape
Cod Coastal Lowland, 19. Connecticut Valley, 20. Western
Michigan Fruit and Truck Belt.

development for each new resident gained from 1982 to 1992. IL, KY, MA, MS, and OH all added built land during this decade at a rate per new resident that was more than five times the per capita level in 1982. WA, NV, and CA were the only states to decrease their per capita amount of developed land during this period.

In the 5 counties surrounding Philadelphia, a 3.5% population increase from 1970 to 1990 was accompanied by a 34% increase in developed land (see Case 3). The Chicago area population grew by 4% from 1970 to 1990 while the urbanized area increased by 46% (1000 Friends 1997). During 1982 to 1992, five states (IA, LA, ND, WV, WY) lost population, but still experienced a combined increase of 580,000 acres of developed land (Appendix 1.3). Given the rapid growth of the U.S. population, changes in the efficiency with which land is used for development will have significant effects on the overall amount of farmland conversion.

### Paving the Best Soils

Although earlier analyses (e.g., Heimlich and Krupa 1994) suggested that prime farmland is not disproportionately converted to urbanization, the NRI data suggests otherwise. Twenty-three percent of non-federal rural land is classified as prime farmland. Four million acres of prime farmland were converted to development from 1982 to 1992 (Sorensen et al. 1997), which is 29% of the 14 million acres of rural land converted during this period.

The conclusions from the NRI data are supported by more recent studies (Imhoff et al. 1997, Petersen et al. 1997) in which urbanization patterns as determined from satellite images of nighttime lights (see Figure 1.1) were superimposed on soil productivity maps. For the nation as a whole, the most productive soils are the most urbanized (Table 1.4). California is particularly wasteful in paving its best soils, while in Illinois, development has generally occurred away from the most productive land.

### Future Conversion

A drawback shared by the Census of Agriculture and the NRI is that they report at five year intervals. There is no comprehensive national data on farmland conversion after 1992. Confirmation of the actual amount of acreage lost between 1992 and the present

Table 1.4  Relative proportions of soil productivity classes under urban use (Petersen et al. 1997).

| Soil productivity level | United States | | Pennsylvania | | California | | Illinois | |
|---|---|---|---|---|---|---|---|---|
| | % of total area* | % of soil type urbanized | % of total area | % of soil type urbanized | % of total area | % of soil type urbanized | % of total area | % of soil type urbanized |
| Low | 42.3 | 1.4 | 16.8 | 4.2 | 67.5 | 1.8 | 3.6 | 52.5 |
| Moderate | 29.2 | 3.1 | 40.2 | 2.4 | 23.6 | 9.4 | 12.0 | 13.4 |
| Moderate high | 22.2 | 4.1 | 38.6 | 5.3 | 8.4 | 13.6 | 32.1 | 7.3 |
| High | 5.3 | 4.7 | 4.4 | 12.1 | 0.5 | 14.4 | 52.3 | 3.2 |

*Does not sum to 100% because of exclusion of water area.

*Under the Blade*

will have to await the results of the 1997 agricultural census and the 1997 NRI. Survey forms for the 1997 census were mailed in December of 1997. The first data will not be available until the spring of 1999. New NRI data is not expected until late 1998.

Meanwhile, the economic and population growth of the mid-nineties, local and regional studies of farmland conversion, and anecdotal evidence derived from driving around the country all suggest that the rate of farmland conversion after 1992 remains high. Population growth is the primary driver of farmland conversion. More people require more houses, roads, factories, offices, schools and other development. How much more depends on the type of housing people desire (and can afford), on their wealth and levels of consumption, on government decisions regarding road construction and other infrastructure projects, and a variety of other factors influencing land use decisions. During the period 1982–1992, 0.6 acre was developed for each additional resident (Table 1.3). Approximately one-half (0.27 acre) of the development occurred on crop- and pastureland with most of the remainder on forest- and rangeland.

While we lack comprehensive data on the conversion of rural land during 1992–1996, population estimates for each state are available. If per capita rates of development during 1992–1996 were similar to those during 1982–1992 (Table 1.3), then more than six million acres of cropland, pastureland, rangeland and forest land were converted from 1992 to 1996. The ten states with the highest estimated losses during this period are CO, FL, GA, IL, KY, MS, NC, OH, TN, and TX.

The population of the United States in July 1996 was 265 million, 2.4 million more than in July of 1995 (Bureau of the Census 1996a). If conversion continues at the 1982–92 rate, then each year's increment to the U.S. population will ultimately result in the conversion of 1.44 million acres. Based on state population projections to the year 2025 (Bureau of the Census 1997), and each state's 1982–1992 per capita rates of land conversion (Appendix 1.3), between 42 million and 48 million acres of rural land will be converted between 1996 and 2025. The ten states contributing the most to this total will be AL, CA, FL, IL, KY, NJ, NC, PA, TN, and TX.

By the year 2050, the United States could have as many as 500 million residents (Ahlburg and Vaupel 1990). Will 140 million acres of agricultural and forest land be converted to development between 1997 and 2050? Although estimates of population or per capita conversion rates are highly uncertain when projected out 50 years, the population estimate is based on conservative estimates of the two main demographic variables, total fertility rate (TFR) and immigration. TFR, the average number of children born per female, has increased from 1.7 in 1976 to 2.1 in 1996 (Bureau of the Census 1996b). Legal immigration averaged 735,000 per year during the 1980s, and rose to more than 1 million per year in the early 1990s (INS 1994). Illegal immigration in the 1990s is at least 300,000 per year (CIS 1994) and likely much higher. Because recent immigrants have a higher TFR than native born women, the U.S. TFR is likely to continue to rise with continued high rates of immigration. World population growth of 80 million annually steadily increases pressures to immigrate to the United States. Half a billion Americans in 2050 is not implausible.

Where these Americans choose to live will determine which states, counties and towns have the greatest farmland loss. The pattern in the early 1990s was for foreign immigrants to settle along the periphery of the country. From 1990 to 1995, two-thirds of foreign immigrants settled in 10 metropolitan areas including Los Angeles, New York, San Francisco, Chicago, and Miami (Frey 1996). However, these cities also had large negative net domestic migration as native residents moved, often to cities in the interior. Cities with large positive net domestic migration included Atlanta, Las Vegas, Phoenix, Portland, and Denver.

This internal migration away from the coast (Figure 1.3) is accompanied by an increase in movement to smaller towns and rural areas (Lessinger 1997). Fourteen of the counties with the highest domestic migration rates in the early 1990s were nonmetropolitan, including Elbert County, CO, Park County, CO, Stone County, MO, and Valley County, ID (Frey 1996). The development of an information economy with opportunities for telecommuting will accelerate this trend (Chinitz and Horan 1996). The low density development that accompanies this rural migration (see Case 17) is an important contributor to the overall decrease in land use efficiency occurring in the United States.

THAT'S JAKE                              By Jake Vest

Figure 1.3   Crowding and social unrest in the coastal regions of the United States are prompting many people to migrate to the interior of the country in search of open space and a higher quality of life. "That's Jake"© Tribune Media Services, Inc. All rights reserved. Reprinted with permission.

### How Much Farmland Do We Need?

The estimated annual loss of farmland in the United States is large, but so is the amount of farmland remaining. Hart (1991) wrote "Some fret, quite unnecessarily, about the loss of prime farmland to urban encroachment; at the present rate of encroachment the United States will run out of farmland somewhere around the year 2500." Actually, at current rates of loss the last prime farmland will be paved somewhat later than 2500, but we won't quibble about the exact date. It will be awhile before there is *no* farmland left.

However, this is the wrong question, a red-herring that diverts attention from the real issue, which is how much agricultural land will be required to provide in perpetuity to the citizens of the United States the goods and services that they desire? We can certainly agree that the amount is considerably more than none. Some would argue that it is more than currently exists.

Others would argue that it is not possible for a capitalist society to overexploit, either now or in the future, farmland to the point that deprivation results. According to neoclassical economic theory, as land becomes more scarce, its price should increase. This in turn will trigger the substitution of less costly resources for land in agricultural production. Because it is absurd to envision meeting human needs for food and fiber without any land, there should come a time when the price of agricultural land exceeds that of all competing uses, and conversion of farmland stops. The market will determine how much farmland is enough. The fact that we are still converting farmland to housing tracts and roads proves that there is still "excess" agricultural land.

But, the market is not perfect; its inefficiencies are well-known and accepted by even the strongest proponents of capitalism. In fact, the 1996 Nobel Prize for Economics was awarded for research on asymmetric information, a common condition where all parties in an economic transaction do not have equal knowledge, so the market is not as efficient as we might like to believe. Insufficient or incorrect information can distort price signals, and near term pressures are often given more weight in economic decisions than are future concerns. Also, price signals do not work instantaneously. Economic trends have momentum, and it is possible to overshoot an optimal response.

In the case of farmland conversion decisions, even if the parties have *equal* knowledge, none of them have *adequate* knowledge of the ecological, economic, and social implications of their act. We don't know if U.S. capitalism in a global economic system will give the correct signals—we have never faced a situation of such rapid growth in population and resource consumption. To have blind faith that an invisible hand will turn many individual actions into the global good is taking a real risk. Farmland, once paved or built on, cannot be reclaimed at reasonable cost, and a shortage of farmland would have serious impacts on all Americans. Prudence dictates that we consider the future supply and demand scenario for U.S. farmland, so that we can take action to shape the future if current trends do not seem to be leading to an optimal situation.

As we mentioned at the begining of this chapter, agricultural landscapes provide many ecological services in addition to growing crops and livestock. These non-production functions will be discussed in subsequent chapters, so for now we will consider only the future ability of U.S. agricultural lands to produce adequate food and fiber for domestic consumption and export needs.

### Our Current Land Cushion

In the late 1990s, agricultural production in the United States is more than adequate. On average, Americans spend less than 14% of their income (USDC 1996a) for a plentiful and varied diet while exporting more food than any other country. Although some Americans have inadequate diets, the problem is one of poverty (or ignorance), not food scarcity.

As a rough estimate of how much cushion or surplus land the United States has for agricultural production, we can look at the 1994 export and set-aside statistics. Total U.S. farm sales in that year were $180 billion of which exports equaled almost $46 billion. Correcting for agricultural imports of $27 billion gives net exports equal to about 10.5% of total farm sales. At the same time, 32 million acres of cropland were enrolled in the Conservation Reserve Program, and 45 million acres of cropland were not cultivated for other reasons (USDA 1995). Thus, approximately 83% of U.S. crop-, pasture-, and rangelands were devoted to production for domestic consumption, while 17% contributed to export and soil conservation or was uncultivated.

This gives us an idea of how much slack we have, on a land basis, in providing for domestic food and fiber needs under current conditions. The balance at any point in the future depends of course on (1) future demand (domestic and export), (2) the amount of agricultural land remaining in production, and (3) the productivity of that remaining land.

## Estimating Future Demand

In the United States, future demand will largely be a function of population growth. Most Americans already consume adequate (often excessive) amounts of calories from a diet heavy in animal products, so little per capita increase in consumption is expected. However, the U.S. population growth rate of 1.1% per year drives an equivalent annual increase in domestic demand for food. Based on projected population increases, domestic demand for agricultural products in the year 2020 will be 29% higher than in 1994, and will almost double by the year 2050.

As Table 1.5 shows, the high rate of U.S. population growth combined with continued conversion of agricultural land eliminates the current 17% cushion before the year 2020. Indeed, Gever et al. (1986) predict that the United States will cease to be a net food exporter within the period 2007 to 2025.

However, demand for U.S. food exports is likely to increase during this time. The 1997 world population of 5.9 billion is projected to reach about 10 billion by 2050 (United Nations 1992; medium fertility rate projection). Ninety percent of this increase will occur in the developing countries. Population growth alone will generate a 70% increase in global food requirements.

Table 1.5   Per capita land availability (acres) in the contiguous United States, 1992 and projected for 2020 and 2050 based on estimated population growth and conversion of land to development. Shown in ( ) is the percent change from 1992.

| Land Class | 1992 | 2020 | 2050 |
| --- | --- | --- | --- |
| Forest land | 2.41 | 1.77 (-27) | 1.11 (-54) |
| Rangeland | 2.30 | 1.72 (-25) | 1.13 (-51) |
| Cropland and pasture | 2.11 | 1.52 (-28) | 0.94 (-55) |
| Inland and coastal waters and Great Lakes | 0.37 | 0.28 (-24) | 0.19 (-49) |
| Other rural | 0.22 | 0.16 (-27) | 0.11 (-50) |
| Developed | 0.36 | 0.43 (+19) | 0.49 (+36) |
| Total Area | 7.76 | 5.88 (-24) | 3.96 (-49) |

But, unlike the U.S. population, large segments of the world population are currently undernourished, requiring significant increases in food production, processing and availability just to bring world diets to acceptable levels. U.S. Undersecretary of State Timothy Wirth (Anon 1997) reported that nearly 1 billion people world-wide are malnourished. Simply ensuring an adequate diet for the current world population will require 50% or greater increases in the availability of plant-derived calories in some regions. When population growth to the year 2050 is included, plant-based food availability will need to double in Latin America and Asia, triple in the Arab countries and West Asia, and increase five-to-sevenfold in parts of sub-Saharan Africa (Burdett 1996).

To achieve these increases, many countries will require increased imports as well as greater local production. Gardner (1997) estimates that by 2035 approximately half of the world's population will depend on imports for 20% or more of their staple foods. Because of the huge numbers of people involved, even a small per capita increase in imports would have a major effect on the global food trade. Brown (1995) calculates that for the Chinese government to meet their stated goal of a 3-egg per week increase in per capita consumption, China will require additional grain (to feed the laying hens) equal to Canada's total average annual grain exports. Obviously, global demand for U.S. food exports is likely to increase in the coming half-century. In a global economy, this extra demand will come in direct competition with U.S. consumers.

### Estimating Future Productivity

With much greater demand for food and a reduced land base, both in absolute and per capita terms, the key question is whether production from the remaining U.S. agricultural lands can increase sufficiently to meet demand. Certainly past performance provides a sense of optimism;   from 1950 to 1990, U.S. grain yield per acre increased 176% (Brown 1997a). This increase was achieved in part by development of higher yielding varieties and hybrids, but also by increases in agricultural inputs including fertilizer, machinery, energy, pesticides, and irrigation. Nebraska's total agricultural output tripled during the period 1936 to 1996, with one-third of the increase attributed to increased inputs (Jacob 1997). Nationwide, annual water withdrawals for irrigation increased from 71 billion gallons in 1940 to

137 billion gallons in 1990 (USDC 1996a) with a total of 49 million acres irrigated in 1992. Quantities of fertilizers and pesticides used increased more than 400% from 1950 to 1987 (Doering 1992).

However, the rate of increase in grain production declined from a high of 3.8% per year during the 1950s to 1.0% per year during the 1980s (Brown 1997a), a rate less than the current rate of population growth. Yield response per unit of additional input declined as the biophysical limits of the agroecosystems were approached, and as opportunities for expanding irrigation declined. The easy gains have been made.

Future gains will not only face this problem of diminishing returns, but one of diminishing inputs as well. The three main non-labor inputs in agriculture—land, water, and energy—all offer reason for concern. While paving land clearly takes it out of production, there are many more subtle processes that degrade soils and reduce productivity. Much of the topsoil present at the time of European settlement has been eroded. Iowa, one of our best agricultural states, has lost 50% of its topsoil (Pimentel and Giampietro 1994). In 1992, U.S. crop- and rangelands were still losing 2.1 billion tons of topsoil per year to erosion (USDA 1995). Rates of water erosion exceeded sustainable levels on 136 million acres, while wind erosion exceeded sustainable levels on 116 million acres. Salinization has reduced production on at least 48 million acres of irrigated cropland and pasture (Sorensen et al. 1997) including four million acres in California (Shafroth 1989), and soil compaction is a problem nationwide. All told, the productivity of an additional 2 million acres of U.S. cropland is seriously impaired each year due to land degradation (Pimentel and Giampietro 1994).

Twenty-one percent of irrigated land in the United States receives water from aquifers that are being depleted, and so cannot continue to be irrigated at current rates (Brown 1997a). The Ogallala aquifer that supports irrigation in much of the Great Plains is already partially depleted at its southern end. Irrigated acreage in the Texas High Plains declined 26% from 1979 to 1989, and with current depletion of the Ogallala estimated at 12 billion cubic meters per year, irrigated land continues to convert to dry-land agriculture in Texas, Oklahoma, Kansas and Colorado (Postel 1996). Groundwater overdrafts in California average 1.6 billion cubic meters per year, while aquifer drawdown has led to the abandonment of more than 300,000 formerly irrigated acres in Arizona (Abernethy 1993). In the West, most surface sources of irrigation water are fully used. In many years, no water reaches the mouths of the Colorado and Rio Grande Rivers (USDC 1996a) because of diversions for irrigation. In years of low precipitation, there is no buffer to maintain irrigation, and throughout the West conflicts are escalating among alternative users of surface water for agriculture, urban and industrial uses, and wildlife.

Just like some groundwater, oil is a nonrenewable resource, and U.S. agriculture uses a lot of it. The food system (including production, transportation, processing, and marketing) in the United States accounts for 17% of total U.S. energy consumption or the equivalent of about 425 gallons of oil per capita per year (Pimentel and Pimentel 1996). For reference, this is three times the per capita energy use for all purposes, agricultural and non-agricultural, in the developing countries.

The energy used to grow crops includes diesel fuel and gasoline to run machinery for tillage and irrigation, and also the energy consumed in manufacturing and transporting fertilizers, pesticides, and equipment. A total energy accounting for dryland field corn production in Iowa shows energy inputs totaling 67 gallons oil equivalent per acre or more than one unit of energy input for each four units of energy output in corn (Pimentel and Burgess 1980). Irrigated agriculture is particularly energy intensive because of the cost of pumping groundwater. Irrigated corn in Nebraska requires three times the energy of rain-fed corn.

Once the food is grown, the energy cost of the rest of the food system including processing and shipping is high. The energy required to grow the contents of a can of sweet corn is only 15% of the total energy required to put that corn on the dinner table (Pimentel and Pimentel 1996). Overall, the U.S. food system uses 10 calories of energy for each 1 calorie of food consumed.

This productive but highly energy intensive food system exists in a world of rapidly depleting fossil energy supplies. Crude oil production in the conterminous United States peaked in 1970 (Hatfield 1997), and average daily production is currently declining by about 300,000 barrels per year (Gutfeld 1992). In 1995, the United States imported 52% of its oil (USDC 1996a), and by 2020 will have exhausted its economically recoverable domestic reserves (Cleveland and Kaufman 1991, Kaufman 1991). U.S. natural gas reserves will not last much longer than oil, particularly if population growth and rising oil prices increase the current rate of natural gas consumption. The extremely low price of oil and natural gas in the mid- to late 1990s accelerates their depletion.

Thus, the United States will relatively soon be totally dependent on foreign sources of oil and natural gas. Unfortunately, at current rates of global oil consumption, the most optimistic estimates of global reserves provide a 60-year supply. In reality, global oil production will peak sometime about 2010, and steadily decline from that point, just as U.S. production has been declining since 1970 (Hatfield 1997). Falling production will coincide with rising demand, particularly in developing countries; from 1985–1997, energy use increased 30% in Latin America, 40% in Africa, and 50% in Asia. Based on supply and demand, prices will rise. Even the knowledge of impending shortage could cause large price increases within the next decade (Dyer 1997). U.S. agriculture will face stiff competition for this primary energy source, and rising prices for all inputs. The main alternative energy sources, coal and nuclear power, are not as versatile and easily used as oil, and present significant environmental problems. In any case, their price would be expected to increase in concert with that of oil.

### The Global Context

In a global economy, the end of cheap energy affects all countries. Higher energy costs will hinder the ability of third world countries to increase their food production at the same time that their economies, and thus their ability to pay for food imports, are disrupted. All of the processes of land degradation that are reducing the productivity of U.S. farmland and thus requiring greater inputs to compensate are going full bore in the rest of the world. Urbanization throughout the third world is consuming prime farmland. In China, the conversion of cropland to development may exceed one million acres per year (Gardner 1997). Groundwater overdrafts threaten extensive acreages in China and India, and salinization affects an additional 5 million acres of irrigated land worldwide each year (Postel 1996). Including erosion, land degradation removes 12 to 25 million acres of cropland per year from global production. Global increases in grain yield fell from an average of 2.1% per year during 1950–1990 to 0.7% per year in the first half of the 1990s (Brown 1997b), less than the 1.5% annual increase in world population. All of these trends make it unlikely that substitutes for U.S. agricultural production will be readily available.

Other global trends will add to the uncertainty surrounding the future productivity of U.S. agriculture. With ten of the warmest years in the last century having occurred since 1980, and an increase in average global temperature of 0.6° C in the past hundred years, there is increasing evidence for a change in global climate due to emissions of carbon dioxide and other greenhouse gases (Santer et al. 1996). In the United States, agriculture in the Great Plains may be particularly susceptible to rising temperatures, particularly if irrigation is curtailed (Heinz 1997). Warming trends will likely be accompanied by an increase in the frequency of extreme events such as severe storms (Flavin 1996).

Overall, rapid population growth, resource depletion, and environmental degradation are contributing to a decline in the stability of the global socioeconomic system of which U.S. agriculture is increasingly a part. Kaplan (1994) points to the growing anarchy in West Africa, the Balkans, the former Soviet Union, and the sprawling slums of Rio de Janeiro, Calcutta and dozens of other mega-cities as indications of a difficult future. Massive migrations of environmental and economic refugees, the decline of governmental authority in many countries, and an increasing ethnic balkanisation all contribute to a future in which it will be more difficult for agriculture to sustain the gains in production needed to keep pace with population growth as well as to alleviate current food shortages.

### Prudent Policies

U.S. agriculture faces a future of soaring demand, decreasing availability of the inputs that have supported past yield increases, and degradation of significant portions of the land base. Given these trends, there is a high probability that the current buffer of U.S. farmland will disappear within the next two decades. For the United States, this would mean increased domestic food prices and a greater trade deficit as agricultural exports were curtailed. Globally, the loss of the world's largest food exporter would greatly hinder efforts to counter periodic regional famines such as those in Somalia or Ethiopia, and to alleviate chronic malnutrition.

Technological advances will no doubt contribute to increases in agricultural efficiency and productivity. For example, improved photovoltaic cells will help in the transition to renewable energy, and improved irrigation techniques can greatly increase water use efficiency. But, there is no adequate substitute for land, particularly prime farmland in regions with sufficient rainfall, and good farmland located close to the cities where the products will be consumed. Loss of farmland limits our options in dealing with future crises and shortages. Given the uncertainty facing our food system, it would seem prudent to retain as much good farmland as possible. If the most optimistic technological scenarios come to pass, the land remains available for other uses. If the more pessimistic future is realized, we will praise our foresight in preserving farmland.

## References

1000 Friends. 1997. Stopping sprawl. Landmark 22(1):11-14.

Abernethy, V. 1993. Population Politics. Plenum Press, New York.

AFT. 1993. Farming on the Edge: A New Look at the Importance and Vulnerability of Agriculture Near American Cities. American Farmland Trust, Washington, D.C.

AFT. 1997. Farming on the Edge. American Farmland Trust, Washington, D.C.

Ahlburg, D.A., and J.W. Vaupel. 1990. Alternative projections of the U.S. population. Demography 27:639-652.

Anonymous. 1997. Nearly 1 billion estimated hungry. Lincoln Journal Star, April 4, 1997, col. 1, 5A.

Brown, L.R. 1995. Who Will Feed China? W.W. Norton, New York.

Brown, L.R. 1997a. Facing the prospect of food scarcity. pp. 23-41. In: L. Starke (ed.) State of the World 1997. W.W. Norton, New York.

Brown, L.R. 1997b. Can we raise grain yields fast enough? WorldWatch 10:8-17.

Burdett, H. 1996. Calculating food needs. Popline 18:1-2.

Bureau of the Census. 1984. Census of Agriculture, 1982. Vol. 1, Geographic Area Series: Pt. 51, U.S. Summary, Final Report. Government Printing Office, Washington, D.C.. Available: http://govinfo.kerr.orst.edu/cgi-bin/ag-list?01-state.usa [30 January 1998]

Bureau of the Census. 1989. Census of Agriculture, 1987. Vol. 1, Geographic Area Series: Pt. 51, U.S. Summary, Final Report. Government Printing Office, Washington, D.C.. Available:

http://govinfo.kerr.orst.edu/cgi-bin/ag-list?01-state.usa [30 January 1998]

Bureau of the Census. 1994. Census of Agriculture, 1992. Vol. 1, Geographic Area Series: Pt. 51, U.S. Summary, Final Report. Government Printing Office, Washington, D.C.. Available: http://govinfo.kerr.orst.edu/cgi-bin/ag-list?01-state.usa [30 January 1998]

Bureau of the Census. 1996a. ST-96-1, Estimates of the Population of States: Annual Time Series, July 1, 1990 to July 1, 1996. Population Estimates Program, Population Division, U.S. Bureau of the Census, Washington, D.C.

Bureau of the Census. 1996b. Resident population projections of the United States: Middle, low, and high series, 1996-2050. U.S. Department of Commerce, Washington, D.C.. Available 10/21/97 at http://www.census.gov/population/projections/nation

Bureau of the Census. 1997. Projections of the Total Population of States: 1995 to 2025. U.S. Department of Commerce, Washington, D.C.. Available 10/21/97 at http://www.census.gov/population/projections/state

Chinitz, B., and T. Horan. 1996. Communications technology and settlement patterns. Landlines 8:1, 4-5.

CIS. 1994. Immigration-related statistics – 1994. Backgrounder No. 1-94, Center for Immigration Studies, Washington, D.C.

Cleveland, C.J., and R.K. Kaufman. 1991. Forecasting ultimate oil recovery and its rate of production: Incorporating economic forces into the models of H. King Hubbert. The Energy Journal 12:17-46.

Doering, O. 1992. Federal policies as incentives or disincentives to ecologically sustainable agricultural systems. pp. 21-36. In: R.K. Olson (ed.) Integrating Sustainable Agriculture, Ecology, and Environmental Policy. The Haworth Press, Binghamton, NY.

Dyer, G. 1997. Economics, geology will send oil prices climbing by 2002. Lincoln Journal Star, May 11:7B.

Fischel, W. 1982. The urbanization of agricultural land: A review of the National Agricultural Lands Study. Land Economics 58:236-259.

Flavin, C. 1996. Facing up to the risks of climate change. pp. 21-39. In: L. Starke (ed.) State of the World 1996. W.W. Norton, New York.

Frey, W.H. 1996. Immigrant and native migrant magnets. American Demographics (November):37-40, 53.

Gardner, G. 1997. Preserving global cropland. pp. 42-59. In: L. Starke (ed.) State of the World 1997. W.W. Norton, New York.

Gever, J., R. Kaufmann, D. Skole, and C. Vorosmarty. 1986. Beyond Oil: The Threat to Food and Fuel in Coming Decades. Ballinger, Cambridge.

Gutfeld, R. 1992. U.S. crude output during 1991 was lowest since 1950. Wall Street Journal, Jan. 16:A6.

Hanson, V.D. 1996. Fields without Dreams. The Free Press, New York.

Hart, J.F. 1991. The Land that Feeds Us. W.W. Norton, New York.

Hatfield, C.B. 1997. Oil back on the global agenda. Nature 387:121.

Heimlich, R.E., and K.S. Krupa. 1994. Changes in land quality accompanying urbanization in United States fast-growth counties. Journal of Soil and Water Conservation 49:367-374.

Heinz, B. 1997. Global warming: Researchers find Plains at risk for climate change. Water Current 28:4-5.

Imhoff, M.L., W.T. Lawrence, C.D. Elvidge, T. Paul, E. Levine, M.V. Privalsky, and V. Brown. 1997. Using nighttime DMSP/ OSL images of city lights for estimating the impact of urban land use on soil resources in the United States. Remote Sensing of Environment 59:105-117.

INS. 1994. Statistical Yearbook of the Immigration and Naturalization Service, 1994. Immigration and Naturalization Service, Washington, D.C.

Jacob, S. 1997. Nebraska's ag productivity increased 80 percent in past 50 years. The Scarlet, January 31, 1997, p. 4.

Kaplan, R.D. 1994. The coming anarchy. The Atlantic Monthly (February):44-76.

Kaufmann, R.K. 1991. Oil production in the lower 48 states: Reconciling curve fitting and econometric models. Resources and Energy 13:111-127.

Lessinger, J. 1997. Boom Counties. Socioeconomics, Inc., Bow, WA.

Petersen, G.W., M.L. Imhoff, E. Nizeyimana, S.W. Waltman, and W.T. Lawrence. 1997. An assessment of soil productivity loss in the U.S. due to urbanization. Poster 325, Agronomy Abstracts, American Society of Agronomy Annual Meetings, Anaheim, CA, 26-31 October.

Pimentel, D., and M. Burgess. 1980. Energy inputs in corn production. pp. 67-84. In: D. Pimentel (ed.) Handbook of Energy Utilization in Agriculture. CRC Press, Boca Raton, FL.

Pimentel, D., and M. Giampietro. 1994. Food, Land, Population, and the U.S. Economy. Carrying Capacity Network, Washington, D.C.

Pimentel, D., and M. Pimentel (eds.) 1996. Food, Energy, and Society. University Press of Colorado, Niwot.

Postel, S. 1996. Forging a sustainable water strategy. pp. 40-59. In: L. Starke (ed.) State of the World 1996. W.W. Norton, New York.

Santer, B.D., K.E. Taylor, T.M.L. Wigley, T.C. Johns, P.D. Jones, D.J. Karoly, J.F.B. Mitchell, A.H. Oort, J.E. Penner, V. Ramaswamy, M.D. Schwarzkopf, R.J. Stouffer, and S. Tett. 1996. A search for human influences on the thermal structure of the atmosphere. Nature 382:39-46.

Shafroth, M. 1989. Changes and challenges in the Central Valley. American Farmland (summer):1-3.

Simon, J., and S. Sudman. 1982. How much farmland is being converted to urban use? International Regional Science Review 7:257-272.

Sims, P.L. 1988. Grasslands. pp. 265-286. In: M.G. Barbour and W.D. Billings (eds.) North American Terrestrial Vegetation. Cambridge University Press, Cambridge.

Sorensen, A.A., R.P. Greene, and K. Russ. 1997. Farming on the Edge. American Farmland Trust, Center for Agriculture in the Environment, Northern Illinois University, DeKalb, IL.

United Nations. 1992. Long-Range World Population Projections: Two Centuries of World Population Growth, 1950-2150. U.N. Population Division, New York.

USDA. 1981a. An Assessment of the Forest and Rangeland Situation in the United States. Forest Resource Report No. 22. U.S. Department of Agriculture Forest Service, Washington, D.C.

USDA. 1981b. National Agricultural Lands Study: Final Report. U.S. Department of Agriculture, Washington, D.C.

USDA. 1984. U.S. Cropland, Urbanization, and Landownership Patterns. U.S. Department of Agriculture, Economic Research Service, Washington, D.C.

USDA. 1987. Statistical Bulletin Number 756, Basic Statistics, 1982 National Resources Inventory. U.S. Department of Agriculture, Soil Conservation Service, Washington, D.C.

USDA. 1994. Urbanization of Rural Land In the United States. U.S. Department of Agriculture, Economic Research Service, Washington, D.C.

USDA. 1995. Summary Report: 1992 National Resources Inventory. U.S. Department of Agriculture Natural Resources Conservation Service, Washington, D.C.

USDA. 1996. America's Private Land: A Geography of Hope. U.S. Department of Agriculture, Natural Resources Conservation Service, Washington, D.C.

USDC. 1996a. Statistical Abstract of the United States: 1996 (116th edition). U.S. Department of Commerce, Bureau of the Census, Washington, D.C.

USDC. 1996b. World Population Profile: 1996. U.S. Department of Commerce, Bureau of the Census, Washington, D.C.

Appendix 1.1  Cropland and prime farmland in 1992 (USDA 1995), and total farm marketings in 1994 (USDC 1996a), by state.

| State | Cropland (1000 acres) | Prime farmland (1000 acres) | Prime farmland as percentage of total land area | Farm marketings ($ million) |
|-------|------|--------|-----|--------|
| AL | 3,147 | 7,325 | 23 | 2,904 |
| AZ | 1,198 | 975 | 1 | 1,869 |
| AR | 7,730 | 13,033 | 39 | 5,276 |
| CA | 10,052 | 5,715 | 6 | 20,238 |
| CO | 8,940 | 1,667 | 3 | 4,029 |
| CT | 229 | 305 | 10 | 473 |
| DE | 499 | 414 | 33 | 660 |
| FL | 2,997 | 1,046 | 3 | 5,978 |
| GA | 5,173 | 7,704 | 21 | 4,716 |
| HI | 274 | 251 | 6 | 498 |
| ID | 5,600 | 3,343 | 6 | 2,955 |
| IL | 24,100 | 21,043 | 59 | 8,223 |
| IN | 13,513 | 13,120 | 57 | 4,838 |
| IA | 24,988 | 18,555 | 52 | 10,084 |
| KS | 26,565 | 23,411 | 45 | 7,687 |
| KY | 5,092 | 5,739 | 23 | 3,230 |
| LA | 5,972 | 12,142 | 44 | 2,013 |
| ME | 448 | 1,060 | 5 | 483 |
| MD | 1,673 | 1,184 | 19 | 1,345 |
| MA | 272 | 313 | 6 | 459 |
| MI | 8,985 | 7,775 | 21 | 3,419 |
| MN | 21,356 | 20,561 | 40 | 6,522 |
| MS | 5,726 | 10,381 | 35 | 2,916 |
| MO | 13,347 | 14,329 | 32 | 4,524 |
| MT | 15,035 | 998 | 1 | 1,857 |
| NE | 19,239 | 12,280 | 25 | 8,561 |
| NV | 762 | 279 | <1 | 299 |
| NH | 142 | 147 | 3 | 152 |
| NJ | 650 | 720 | 15 | 768 |
| NM | 1,892 | 148 | <1 | 1,524 |
| NY | 5,616 | 4,682 | 15 | 2,858 |

*Continues*

Appendix 1.1  *Continued*

| State | Cropland (1000 acres) | Prime farmland (1000 acres) | Prime farmland as percentage of total land area | Farm marketings ($ million) |
|---|---|---|---|---|
| NC | 5,960 | 6,706 | 22 | 6,369 |
| ND | 24,743 | 11,645 | 26 | 2,935 |
| OH | 11,929 | 11,823 | 45 | 4,475 |
| OK | 10,081 | 14,420 | 33 | 3,864 |
| OR | 3,776 | 3,517 | 6 | 2,652 |
| PA | 5,596 | 4,035 | 14 | 3,755 |
| RI | 25 | 67 | 10 | 81 |
| SC | 2,983 | 3,290 | 17 | 1,362 |
| SD | 16,436 | 6,517 | 13 | 3,343 |
| TN | 4,857 | 6,161 | 23 | 2,152 |
| TX | 28,261 | 36,828 | 22 | 12,552 |
| UT | 1,815 | 843 | 2 | 819 |
| VT | 635 | 328 | 6 | 481 |
| VA | 2,901 | 4,768 | 19 | 2,159 |
| WA | 6,745 | 2,313 | 5 | 4,720 |
| WV | 915 | 545 | 4 | 403 |
| WI | 10,813 | 8,882 | 26 | 5,384 |
| WY | 2,272 | 335 | 1 | 778 |

Appendix 1.2    Primary sources of data for studies of farmland conversion.

### Census of Agriculture

The Census of Agriculture has been conducted by the Bureau of the Census since 1840, and is currently undertaken in years ending in 2 and 7 with the most recent data coming from the 1992 survey. Responsibility for the Census of Agriculture was shifted from Commerce to USDA's National Agricultural Statistics Service for the 1997 census.

The Census of Agriculture presents data for the United States as a whole and then breaks it down by state, county, and for each zip code containing five or more farms. Data includes number of farms, land in farms, size of farms, value of land and buildings, amount of cropland, amount of pasture, land use characteristics, the amount and value of harvested crops, and the number and value of livestock and poultry.

Land in farms is defined in the census as acres used for crops, pasture or grazing. This category also includes woodland, or- chards, land enrolled in the Conservation Reserve and Wetland Reserve Programs, farmstead sites and other land controlled by the farm operator. Cropland and pasture are subsets of land in farms. Cropland includes harvested acreage, idled, fallowed and failed acreage, and cropland that is used for pasture or planted to cover crops. Cropland enrolled in the Conservation Reserve Pro- gram, which requires the land be idled and planted to grasses or trees, is included in this category unless the entire farm has been put into the CRP. In this case, the CRP land is dropped from the cropland category altogether.

The census contains no data on the quality of farmland. It also does not contain a category for forest land apart from farm wood- lands nor a category for developed land. Indeed, large acreages of woodland and wasteland not held for agricultural purposes have been excluded when reported by farm operators in individual sur- vey responses.

The Bureau of the Census obtains data mainly from mail sur- veys with some follow up by telephone or personal contact. In 1992, the Bureau used a mailing list of 3.55 million names that had a high probability of being farm operators or owners. It used three different types of survey forms. Follow up forms and calls were used to ensure a high response rate, and the responses were edited for consistency and reasonableness based on comparisons with other farms in the same area and data from past censuses. Statistical estimation procedures were used to fill gaps caused by farmers who did not respond.

### The NRI

The National Resources Inventory (NRI) is a survey of non-federal lands conducted by the USDA Natural Resources Conservation Service. NRCS's predecessor, the Soil Conservation Service, conducted limited studies of soil erosion and land and water resources beginning in 1934. The first NRI was conducted in 1977 using 70,000 sample sites to collect data on soil capability, land use, conservation needs, prime farmland, potential cropland and flood-prone areas.

National Resources Inventories were performed in 1982, 1987 and 1992 using 800,000 sample sites. Sampling included aerial photographs and other remote sensing techniques as well as on-site inspections. Remote sensing and computer-based technologies were more heavily used in 1992 than in 1982 and 1987, but the 1982 and 1987 databases have been updated to make them comparable to the 1992 NRI. Statistical methodologies are applied to the databases to produce regional and national estimates for the sample variables.

The NRI contains no land-in-farms category, and the NRI definitions of cropland, pasture, and forest land differ from those used in the Census of Agriculture (see Box 1.1 for the NRI land use definitions). CRP lands are not catalogued in the NRI as cropland, but are instead included in the "other rural land" category. The NRI also surveys the quality of land with categories for prime farmland and for farmland capability class, a ranking of soils according to their suitability for agricultural production. Finally, a particularly important difference between the Census of Agriculture and the NRI is that the NRI has a category for developed land.

### Comparing the Two Surveys

The NRI figures are probably more accurate than those of the Census of Agriculture. The NRI's use of sample sites is arguably superior to the survey techniques of the Census Bureau, and its inclusion of developed land categories is a major improvement on the agricultural census. The NRI does a better job of accounting for CRP land, and its ranking of farmland by quality is extremely useful.

However, the Census of Agriculture has its own advantages. It combines land use data with crop and livestock production data, including inventories and dollar amounts of sales, to provide information unavailable from the NRI. For example, the American Farmland Trust used Census production data in combination with NRI farmland quality data in evaluating the loss of productive agricultural lands near high growth metropolitan areas (AFT 1997). The Census' mailing survey technique is exhaustive and the response rate good. The census data should be reliable for the categories that it covers.

Appendix 1.3  Per capita developed land, by state, for 1982 and for the population increase from 1982 to 1992 (USDA 1995).

| State | Developed land per capita, 1982 (acres) | Population increase, 1982-1992 | New development, 1982-1992 (acres) | Newly developed land per new resident, 1982-1992 (acres) |
|-------|------|-----------|-----------|------|
| AL | 0.44 | 205,639 | 323,600 | 1.57 |
| AZ | 0.36 | 951,264 | 365,100 | 0.38 |
| AR | 0.53 | 101,699 | 97,200 | 0.96 |
| CA | 0.17 | 6,062,976 | 800,100 | 0.13 |
| CO | 0.45 | 402,552 | 309,300 | 0.77 |
| CT | 0.23 | 137,334 | 83,700 | 0.61 |
| DE | 0.28 | 90,415 | 35,200 | 0.39 |
| FL | 0.33 | 3,041,810 | 1,192,900 | 0.39 |
| GA | 0.41 | 1,117,596 | 759,900 | 0.68 |
| HI | 0.15 | 154,023 | 23,600 | 0.15 |
| ID | 0.51 | 93,172 | 93,900 | 1.01 |
| IL | 0.25 | 172,845 | 240,200 | 1.39 |
| IN | 0.34 | 183,933 | 228,500 | 1.24 |
| IA | 0.60 | -80,004 | 49,800 | N/A |
| KS | 0.78 | 112,407 | 122,700 | 1.09 |
| KY | 0.35 | 69,113 | 367,900 | 5.32 |
| LA | 0.34 | -78,874 | 269,700 | N/A |

*Continues*

Appendix 1.3  *Continued*

| State | Developed land per capita, 1982 (acres) | Population increase, 1982-1992 | New development, 1982-1992 (acres) | Newly developed land per new resident, 1982-1992 (acres) |
|---|---|---|---|---|
| ME | 0.53 | 99,343 | 98,100 | 0.99 |
| MD | 0.22 | 626,466 | 149,000 | 0.24 |
| MA | 0.19 | 226,672 | 232,900 | 1.03 |
| MI | 0.35 | 302,958 | 462,700 | 1.53 |
| MN | 0.53 | 343,118 | 240,000 | 0.70 |
| MS | 0.47 | 55,432 | 144,400 | 2.61 |
| MO | 0.43 | 259,283 | 203,700 | 0.79 |
| MT | 1.26 | 19,301 | 82,000 | 4.25 |
| NE | 0.77 | 22,235 | 37,500 | 1.69 |
| NV | 0.35 | 452,364 | 82,500 | 0.18 |
| NH | 0.43 | 166,667 | 151,800 | 0.91 |
| NJ | 0.17 | 380,348 | 298,100 | 0.78 |
| NM | 0.52 | 219,537 | 161,600 | 0.74 |
| NY | 0.16 | 509,343 | 221,600 | 0.44 |
| NC | 0.43 | 821,403 | 941,300 | 1.15 |
| ND | 1.85 | -33,646 | 106,700 | N/A |
| OH | 0.29 | 243,222 | 471,600 | 1.94 |
| OK | 0.54 | 1,031 | 158,400 | 153.64 |
| OR | 0.36 | 312,668 | 164,000 | 0.52 |
| PA | 0.25 | 143,791 | 436,000 | 3.03 |
| RI | 0.17 | 47,711 | 25,800 | 0.54 |
| SC | 0.45 | 386,972 | 407,600 | 1.05 |
| SD | 1.55 | 19,004 | 63,600 | 3.35 |
| TN | 0.37 | 373,890 | 436,100 | 1.17 |
| TX | 0.45 | 2,366,004 | 1,401,500 | 0.59 |
| UT | 0.29 | 253,359 | 107,800 | 0.43 |
| VT | 0.50 | 52,053 | 65,400 | 1.26 |
| VA | 0.32 | 895,596 | 446,400 | 0.50 |
| WA | 0.37 | 870,862 | 287,900 | 0.33 |
| WV | 0.29 | -142,439 | 114,600 | N/A |
| WI | 0.45 | 267,082 | 249,300 | 0.93 |
| WY | 0.99 | -42,448 | 40,000 | N/A |
| US ex Alaska | 0.34 | 23,209,263 | 13,979,000 | 0.60 |

# 2

## A Landscape Perspective on Farmland Conversion

*Richard K. Olson*

### What is a Landscape?

It may seem odd for the word *farm* to be absent from the title of a book about the loss of farmland. Instead we have the term *landscape*. The purpose of this chapter is to demonstrate that this substitution is not only appropriate, but essential to an understanding of this complex problem. As described in Chapter 1, decisions and actions affecting the fate of farmland in the United States take place at a variety of scales ranging from individual fields and farms to regions and ultimately the Earth. Within this spatial hierarchy, the landscape is the scale at which the greatest number of factors coalesce, and at which the largest number of functions are influenced.

What is a landscape? Forman and Godron (1986) define landscape as "a heterogeneous land area composed of a cluster of interacting components that is repeated in a similar format throughout." Most of us know it as what we view from a moderate height, such as the top of a hill, or from the window of a moving vehicle. Our view encompasses a variety of landscape components: patches such as fields and pastures; linear elements including roads, hedgerows, and streams; and single houses or groups of homes. These components are not randomly distributed, but form identifiable patterns.

The patterns that we view depend of course on where we are. In the ridge and valley province of Pennsylvania, forested ridgetops alternate with cultivated valleys. In the Georgia Piedmont, cultivated uplands are dissected by forested watercourses. In the Couteau of North Dakota, rolling expanses of wheat and grazing land are dotted with prairie pothole wetlands and framed within a 1 mile square matrix of county roads. In the Los Angeles Basin, a dense grid of streets covers the landscape with commercial buildings along the larger roads and residential units elsewhere.

Most of the United States is now comprised of what Hiss (1990) refers to as working landscapes whose appearance is the result of the interactions of human culture with natural factors including climate, topography, vegetation, and soils. For example, Figure 2.1 shows the remaining forest cover in a Wisconsin (2.1a) and Ohio (2.1b) landscape in the early 1900s. The forest pattern in the Ohio landscape makes it clear that a series of inaccessible ridges has confined agriculture to the valley bottoms in a complex pattern. In contrast, the Wisconsin pattern suggests a more uniform terrain with cultivation possible in most places, and social factors dominate the landscape—the remnant forest patches are mainly square and linear-edged, conforming to human patterns of land survey and ownership.

### Structure and Function are Related

Why do landscape patterns matter? Because the function of a landscape is related not just to the types of components that make it up, but to their spatial relationships. For example, housing developments and farms often interact negatively— homeowners are bothered by noise, dust, and odors, and farmers experience vandalism and trespass. Two important functions of rural landscapes—living space and food production—are affected. If the homes in a landscape are clustered and separated from farms by a greenspace, these problems are minimized. If the same number of homes are dispersed throughout the countryside, interactions between homes and farms are more frequent. Understanding the relationships between structure and function is essential to successful landscape planning, and this chapter is devoted to increasing this understanding.

### Agricultural Landscapes Have Many Functions

Discussions of farmland conversion often focus on only the two functions mentioned above—living space and food production. In their excellent book *Our Ecological Footprint*, Wackernagel and Rees (1996) illustrate the full range of landscape functions with a clever thought exercise. Imagine enclosing a city such as New York under a huge plastic dome that allows light to pass but nothing else. The city is cut off from the surrounding countryside. Now imagine the effect of this enclosure on the environment of the city. The air grows stale and polluted, sewage accumulates, supplies of clean water and many raw materials are depleted, and of course so is food. Of less immediate concern to the trapped residents, their world no longer includes most other species, opportunities for recreation and aesthetic enjoyment of rural areas, and an environment conducive to rural cultures (can you imagine the Amish maintaining their culture within the dome?). Rural landscapes provide many functions other than food production (Table 2.1).

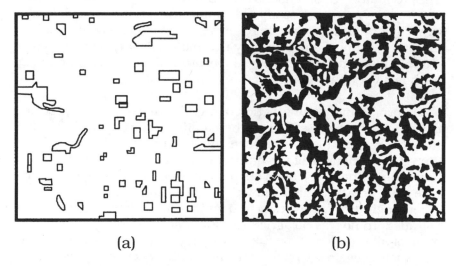

(a)                                              (b)

Figure 2.1   Shape and distribution of forest patches in two agricultural landscapes: (a) remnant forest patches, Cadiz Township, Green County, Wisconsin in 1902 (Curtis 1956), and (b) remaining forest land (black areas) in the 1930s near Washington, Ohio (Bowen and Burgess 1981). Both areas shown are approximately 10 km on a side.

Table 2.1   Functions of agricultural landscapes.

| | |
|---|---|
| • Conversion of solar energy to food and fiber | • Modification of climate |
| | • Waste assimilation |
| • Water supply and quality | • Biodiversity |
| • Air supply and quality | • Aesthetics |
| | • Culture and community |

   The next step in this exercise is to expand the dome's edge
beyond the city limits. How large an area of the surrounding landscape needs to be enclosed to allow the domed city to be sustainable? The answer depends on the population of the city, their
consumption patterns, and the characteristics of the surrounding
landscape. Denver, located in semiarid shortgrass prairie, would
require a much larger area per capita to feed its population than
would Des Moines, Iowa. In a humid climate, New York City still
depends for its water supply on watersheds totaling 1900 square
miles (Coombe 1996). Phoenix would have to expand its dome a
very long ways to enclose enough water. In fact, it does this in a
sense by importing Colorado River water. When we consider oil
and other forms of energy, many raw materials, and even much
of our food supply, the ecological footprint of an American city
extends across the globe.

   The productivity and function of a landscape depends on both
its natural characteristics and the modifications imposed by
humans. Agriculture is a massive modification that has greatly
altered the functions of the natural ecosystems that form its
foundation. Some functions such as production of food and fiber
have been greatly enhanced by these structural alterations.
Others including biodiversity and water quality have been
degraded. In no way do agricultural landscapes provide maximum
levels of all functions. The functions they do provide are, however,
the baseline against which we measure the effects of development. This chapter examines how development pressures interact
with landscape features to change the structure and function of
agricultural landscapes, and how this knowledge can be used to
reduce any negative impacts of development.

### The Urban/Rural Interface

The boundary between rural and urban areas is a transition zone of rapid change (spatially and temporally) in landscape structure. Functional changes are also rapid as a landscape managed for biological production is modified in a way that greatly reduces biological productivity. As such it is an excellent place to study the effects of farmland conversion on the structure and function of agricultural landscapes. Because such a large portion of U.S. agricultural land is now part of or influenced by the urban/rural interface (Sorensen et al. 1997), an understanding of its dynamics is of more than academic interest.

### Proximity as a Factor in Land Use

According to agricultural location theory (Tarrant 1974), within the general constraints of climate, the type of agriculture practiced in a particular area is determined not just by soil and topographic characteristics, but by the location of the area relative to markets, the demand of those markets, and transportation costs. J. von Thünen applied this theory in describing concentric circles of different types of agriculture surrounding a city (Figure 2.2), with higher value, more perishable crops grown in the inner circle (Haggett 1979). In the northeastern United States, Hart (1991) describes a ring of land closest to the city with greenhouses and nurseries, an outer ring with fruit and vegetable farms, and beyond that dairy farms. As the city expands, the rings move outward so that, "The children of dairy farmers become truck farmers, their grandchildren develop greenhouses or nurseries, and their great-grandchildren sell their land to developers and retire to areas that have milder climates." Expanding cities influence land use and agriculture far beyond the urban boundary.

Zones of land use are rarely clearly defined, however. Even Figure 2.2 indicates a distortion of the agricultural rings caused by a river, and many natural features can influence agricultural patterns (e.g., Figure 2.1b). Similarly, expansion of an urban area rarely occurs along an even, concentric front. Barriers such as steep slopes, rivers, and political boundaries, and facilitators such as roads and sewer lines affect development patterns. In Ulster County, New York, a one-hour drive from the New York City metropolitan area, the probability of conversion of rural land to urban use was negatively correlated with elevation and slope, but increased with proximity to heavy-duty, unlimited access high-ways (LaGro and DeGloria 1992).

Not surprisingly, agricultural land adjacent to urban land is more likely to urbanize than agricultural land further away (Turner 1988). In Illinois, Iverson (1988) found that urban land use was not correlated with landscape characteristics, but rather with proximity to surrounding urban areas. For any urban area, escalating land prices at the rural interface increase the availability of inputs for land conversion, and many environmental constraints to development are overcome. For example, construction of a new sewer line opens to much denser development an area whose soils have a limited capacity for waste assimilation from septic tank leachfields. The location of the sewer will have a major influence on the pattern of development.

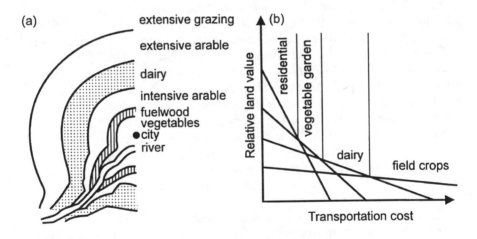

Figure 2.2  (a) Thünen's concept of concentric land use around an imaginary urban center based on the cost and frequency of transporting agricultural products. Also shown is his view of how a river providing easy transport would modify the zones. (b) Competitive land values based on transportation costs. Concentric zones result because activities with a greater need for closeness to the center are able to value land higher than those with less need. From Loomis and Connor (1992).

The effective distance of a parcel from the urban boundary is not fixed. Construction of a new highway or a decrease in gasoline prices can increase mobility, and reduce the "friction of distance" (LaGro and DeGloria 1992) that restricts development in outlying areas. Bennet, a small town 10 miles southeast of Lincoln, NE, has approved a new subdivision that will double the number of homes in the town in anticipation of the widening of Route 2 and the subsequent reduction of commuting time to Lincoln. Bennet is physically no closer to Lincoln, but functionally the distance has been narrowed. At a larger scale, Charlotte, NC is completing a 65-mile outerbelt that represents a change in landscape structure that will lead to massive changes in landscape function (Box 2.1). The location of a major new highway, especially the location of its interchanges, has a major influence on subsequent patterns of development.

### The Lessening Importance of Proximity

As described in Chapter 1, an increasing amount of development is no longer tied directly to major urban centers or to any town at all. The post-interstate highway system development boom has for the first time brought heavy development pressure on all sorts of settings simultaneously—suburbs, distant rural areas, and resort communities (Hiss 1990). Any place within two hours drive (a city's "commuter shed") is a potential bedroom community, and any place within five to six hours travel is a potential vacation residence. Based on these criteria, most rural landscapes in the United States are at risk from development (see Chapter 1, Figure 1.1).

Technological changes unrelated to transportation are also reducing physical constraints on development patterns. Prior to an administrative code revision in 1980 that allowed the installation of alternatives to sewered or leach-field development, more than 50% of Wisconsin land was considered unsuitable for unsewered development due to soil conditions (LaGro 1996).

Box 2.1   Region faces huge challenge with outerbelt's arrival.

When Mecklenburg county commissioner Tom Bush last week predicted Charlotte's outerbelt highway "is going to suck the very life out of everything inside it," he was exaggerating. We hope.

Interstate 485 is perking along—at $1.4 billion the largest public works project in N.C. history. By year's end, a fourth of it will be open. Completion date is 2008.

Most people assume it will make driving easier. And it will— for a time. But like squirrels to birdseed, developers flock to new roads. Development brings more traffic, not less.

Local political and civic leaders, with support from developers, have long touted the outerbelt as the solution to congestion, even as many other cities were experiencing the opposite. Hardly any local transportation professionals believed it was necessary, but they didn't openly oppose. "That bulldozer was way too big for anybody to get down in front of," says Bill Coxe, the county's transportation planner.

Now we have us an outerbelt. And only now are civic leaders getting worried. Beltways in such cities as Detroit and Kansas City bled businesses out of downtown. Washington's inspired miles of suburban sprawl. Atlanta saw sprawl and congestion and is considering a 211-mile, $5 billion Outer Perimeter.

### A Glimpse of the Future

Is this region ready for what the outerbelt will bring? Consider Pineville. Near I-485, development has exploded. As far as the eye can see are parking lots, shopping centers and a forest of fast-food joints, chain restaurants and gas stations. Bulldozers dot lots stripped of vegetation. Even in early afternoon, turning left from Pineville-Matthews Road onto I-485 takes three light changes. Once on the loop, you peer through the polluted haze (fed primarily by auto exhaust) and the vista is studded with communications towers. Inside the new stores, surroundings are pleasant and merchandise attractive. Outside, the scene is clogged, ugly and unpleasant.

*Continues*

Box 2.1  *Continued*

For now, I-485 ends at N.C. 49. "Whitehall. Shopping Center. Offices. Restaurants. Apartments," says a billboard looming over cleared land. Drive down Whitehall Park Drive, in Whitehall Technology Park. Across the street from a construction site and CIMTEC Automation & Control Inc., a small area is fenced. It is the Whitehall Nature Preserve, 45 acres of nationally significant upland bog, formerly home to thousands of salamanders. Yellow signs note "Salamander XING." But where will the salamanders cross to? The CIMTEC parking lot? And if they cross, will they ever return?

### What the rules allow

The outerbelt will have 30 interchanges. Unless development rules change—quickly—this scene will be replicated over and over: Apartments and homes isolated from workplaces and stores, all floating in asphalt seas. Farms and fields a distant memory, parks far away. Nightmarish traffic. Declining areas inside the belt.

Already businesses are leapfrogging farther out, following growth, abandoning the center. Experts predict this will continue. Throughout the region, governments are unprepared for the cost of outerbelt driven growth: more schools, more roads, more landfills, more police, eviscerated centers, air and water pollution problems.

Charlotte-Mecklenburg planners hope to encourage development that is more compact and less auto dependent. So far they've been successful with plans for one interchange—Prosperity Church Road. But in most localities, the rules produce sprawl.

Does the region have the skill, and the will, to counter the problems the outerbelt will bring? A few other cities have successfully used such measures as urban growth boundaries, regional government and strong public transit systems. If this region hopes to continue economically strong its leaders must begin, together, to confront the challenges and find solutions.

— Editorial, *The Charlotte (NC) Observer*, 7-20-97

Mounded drain fields and holding tanks now allow accelerated low-density rural development in much of the state. As communications technologies improve and information becomes a major commodity, the role of proximity in guiding development patterns decreases still further. Many companies can locate virtually anywhere, and their workers can live almost anywhere. California and Arizona have passed laws requiring large companies to get a certain percentage of their workers off the streets during peak commuter hours (Weimer 1996). The intent is to reduce air pollution by pushing companies to promote telecommuting. Ironically, this is likely to promote growth in outlying suburbs at a time when Phoenix, a metropolitan area larger than Delaware, is trying to slow sprawl by offering lower development fees in central areas to encourage in-filling (Egan 1996a).

Ramsey (1997) described a new type of migrant to rural areas in the West. Dubbed lone eagles, they are brokers, consultants, writers and others who are moving to outlying areas because they can do most of their business by phone or internet (see Case 17). Retirees form another mobile group that is altering rural growth patterns. As a result, rural areas in the West have gone from population decline in the 1980s to faster than average growth in the 1990s. In Washington state, only half the 27 rural counties had net in-migration in the 1980s, while all did in the first half of the 1990s. Nationally, migration accounted for 43% of the population growth that occurred in the early 1990s in non-metro counties (Johnson and Beale 1994).

Fuguitt and Brown (1990) found that 35% of U.S. adults expressed a preference for living in rural areas and small towns within 30 miles of medium-sized cities. Many are doing so as improvements in transportation infrastructure and technology have reduced the constraints of distance and physiography on spatial patterns of land use. While proximity still matters, the pace and process of growth is becoming more diffuse, less controlled, and less orderly. Geography and natural landscape features influence development less as our philosophy shifts toward dominating rather than working with landscapes, and our technology gives us the increasing ability (at least temporarily) to do so. Because of this approach, we ignore the opportunity to design with nature, and to retain and make full use of the many services that landscapes provide.

Will the trend toward more diffuse development continue or will the "friction of distance" and other constraints reassert themselves? The cheap-energy environment in which our current sprawl is taking place is coming to an end (see Chapter 1). What type of development will be supported by a resource-poor economy remains to be seen, but one conclusion ought to be obvious. Rather than continuing to construct inefficient landscapes until forced to stop, prudence dictates that we consider the types of landscapes that can function best under the coming constraints, and begin to design and build them now while we have the resources to do so.

The next four sections of this chapter consider how development affects the watershed, agricultural production, cultural, and aesthetic functions of agricultural landscapes. Descriptions of effects are followed in each case by examples of actions and policies that can help to mitigate negative effects.

## Watershed Functions

Virtually all freshwater for human use comes from watersheds, either as surface runoff or through recharge of groundwater. The quantity and quality of water leaving a watershed depends on both the types of land use within the watershed and the spatial arrangement of those uses. For example, agricultural watersheds in the Georgia Piedmont are a mosaic of cultivated uplands dissected by riparian forests (Kesner and Meentemeyer 1989). Although runoff from the fertilized croplands contains large amounts of nitrogen, the riparian forests act as filters and the quality of water in the streams is generally high. If the same proportions of land were in crops and forest, but the forests occupied the uplands while fields were cultivated to the stream edge, water quality would be much poorer. In landscape function, spatial relationships matter.

Many agricultural landscapes do not have good water quality, and agriculture is the main contributor in the United States to nonpoint source pollution (Baker 1992). Best management practices (BMPs) to improve water quality include riparian buffer strips, grassed waterways and restoration of wetlands. Obviously, the correct placement of these features in the landscape is critical to their proper functioning. Development places new components in the landscape that will also influence watershed function.

### Effects of Development

The construction phase of development can cause particularly severe effects on water quality. From 50% to 100% of the soil eroded from construction sites reaches streams compared to less than 10% of the soil eroded from most agricultural fields. In the Milwaukee River South Watershed, which includes a mixture of developed and agricultural land, 62% (16000 tons per year) of the total annual sediment load to the river comes from construction sites as opposed to 13% from cropland (Wise 1990).

In completed developments, the greatest impact is caused by the increased volume and velocity of water running off impervious surfaces. The surface area of buildings and pavement ranges from 10% to 20% for low density single family residential developments to more than 90% for commercial development (Tourbier 1994). As the proportion of the landscape covered with impervious surfaces increases, the amount of precipitation lost as runoff increases and the amount soaking into the ground decreases (Table 2.2).

The increase in total surface flow is accompanied by an increase in hydrologic variability. For example, the 2.2 square mile Whetstone Creek watershed is largely encompassed by the city of Marquette, Michigan. A one-inch rain often causes the creek to rise from 6 inches to 8 feet in depth in less than 20 minutes, and sedimentation is a major habitat and water quality problem (USEPA 1995). In the Puget Sound region of Washington, major floods used to be quarter-century events. Now significant flooding occurs virtually every winter as rains run off an increasingly large area of paved or built land that previously would have soaked up the water and released it slowly (Egan 1996a).

Storm sewers and good drainage can remove water from developed areas, but the impact is simply transferred downhill and downstream. From the experience of the Metropolitan Washington (D.C.) Council of Governments (Schueler 1991), it is almost impossible to maintain the quality of unique areas such as cold water trout streams and extensive stream, wetland, and floodplain complexes if upland imperviousness exceeds 10% to 15%.

Table 2.2  Typical water budgets (eastern U.S.) corresponding to differences in impervious surfaces due to development. Data from Tourbier (1994).

| Percent paved surfaces | Evapo-transpiration | Runoff | Shallow infiltration | Deep infiltration |
|---|---|---|---|---|
| 0 (natural ground cover) | 40% | 10% | 25% | 25% |
| 10-20 | 38% | 20% | 21% | 21% |
| 35-50 | 35% | 30% | 20% | 15% |
| 75-100 | 30% | 55% | 10% | 5% |

Development also reduces surface- and groundwater quality. The first flush of urban runoff can be as polluted as raw sewage (Tourbier 1994), containing high levels of phosphorus, nitrogen, and trace metals. Urban and suburban runoff is a major source of water pollution in the United States, so much so that stormwater discharge now requires a permit (USEPA 1990).

Barton Springs is a significant source of drinking water for the city of Austin, Texas and residents in surrounding counties. The Barton Springs Edwards Aquifer that supplies the springs is especially vulnerable to pollution because it is a limestone aquifer overlain by thin soils and containing numerous sinkholes and channels through which surface water can enter the aquifer with little natural filtration (see Case 16). Unsewered development in many rural areas of the United States poses similar threats to groundwater (e.g., LaGro 1996).

### Reducing Hydrologic Effects of Development

As the density of development increases, so does the hydrologic impact and the difficulty of instituting remedial measures (USEPA 1992a). Not only does the volume of runoff increase, but the areas available for instituting BMPs for stormwater control are reduced. Wetlands and other holding areas have a limited capacity, and often can't be made large enough to detain the runoff from even an average rainstorm if much of the landscape is paved. Advanced planning to identify the types and amounts of hydrologic BMPs required, and to set-aside the optimal locations for these BMPs is essential.

Most land use planning fails to mitigate the impact of development on water quality and hydrology because regulations and controls are adopted piece-meal in response to individual impacts. Success requires a comprehensive strategy including development of and adherence to a watershed master plan (USEPA 1992a). The first step is watershed delineation and the identification of problems. Virginia uses hydrologic unit planning as a process to identify and prioritize water quality problems on a watershed basis (USEPA 1992b). Four hundred and ninety-one watershed units have been delineated by the state, and incorporated in a geographic information system (GIS) along with information on spatial patterns of water quality, land use, and other natural resources.

The Milwaukee River South Watershed Plan, developed by Wisconsin's Department of Natural Resources-Southeast District and Ozaukee County, necessarily includes both urban and agricultural elements (Wise 1990). Urban BMPs include local controls on construction erosion, improving stormwater management, better urban housekeeping, and reduction of streambank erosion. Agricultural BMPs include field erosion controls, controlling manure, nutrient and pesticide runoff, and streambank repair and fencing. Marquette, MI established a stormwater management utility in 1993 in which all developed or undeveloped parcels are charged a fee based on their relative contribution to stormwater runoff and their potential contribution to decreased water quality (USEPA 1995). Construction by the landowner of retention basins or other means of reducing stormwater runoff and water quality degradation result in a decreased utility fee, and cost sharing and technical assistance are available for construction of these BMPs.

Often, the only way to protect watershed functions is to impose limits on total development. A citizen's initiative water quality ordinance passed in August of 1992 to protect the Edwards Aquifer outside Austin, Texas limited impervious cover in developments to 15% to 25% depending on location within the recharge zone. Post-development runoff could show no increases in average annual loads of 13 pollutants including sediment, nutrients, pathogens, heavy metals, and herbicides (Ross 1992; see Case 16). The North Thurston Urban Growth Management Area which includes the city of Olympia, Washington is attempting to reduce the amount of impervious surface in new development by offering density credits to developers, reducing vehicle-oriented pavement with narrower residential streets and less parking area, and using permeable surfaces like paving blocks for low-use areas (USEPA 1994).

## Agricultural Production

From 1990 to 1994, the Youngstown-Warren area of Ohio lost 11.5% of its farmland (Sorensen et al. 1997). Can we assume that agricultural production in this area declined 11.5%? Not necessarily. Agricultural production is a landscape-level function, so the effect of development is more complex than a simple decline in production proportional to the farmland lost. It matters which farmland was developed, and what replaced it.

A key characteristic of any landscape is heterogeneity. Different patches have different characteristics. Farmland is often described on the basis of soil quality with prime farmland having the best soils for crop production. Because level, well-drained soils are also easiest to build on, there is concern that in some cases prime farmland may be developed at a disproportionately high rate (Sorensen et al. 1997; also see Chapter 1, Table 1.4). If so, production could decline more than the percent reduction in acreage. Alternatively, if prime farmland is protected and development occurs on marginal land, the impact on production would be lessened.

It is still not that simple, however. The spatial patterns of the landscape components are critical in influencing landscape function including production. For example, many farms are not a single parcel, but are comprised of several non-contiguous parcels, some of which are rented. Because rented land is more susceptible to sale for development, a farmer may have to replace lost fields with more distant properties, assuming replacements are available at all. Increased travel time with slow moving farm equipment reduces the efficiency and increases the cost of farming—when weather conditions and weed growth offer limited windows for field operations, timeliness is critical.

As another example, farmers depend on more than their land—they require the support of an extensive service infrastructure including seed and chemical dealers, equipment dealers, and market outlets. As the agricultural activity in an area falls below a critical mass, purveyors of these services may consolidate or go out of business. Farmers have to travel further for parts and services, and the extra costs in time and money reduce profits and production. Regarding the infrastructure needed to grow cotton, Hart (1991) wrote "A farmer cannot grow cotton unless a gin is convenient, but a ginner cannot remain in business unless the local farmers are growing enough cotton to sustain his operation...The door is slammed on any prospect for future cotton production in an area when its last gin closes down."

### Landscape Views of the Urban Edge

One view of agriculture at the urban edge stresses the localization diseconomies caused by the increased population and juxtaposition of developments and farmland. Negative effects include land use conflicts; complaints or lawsuits about noise, odor, dust; and restrictions on the number of animals, aerial spraying, and other routine farming activities (Lisansky 1986, Lisansky and Clark 1987). Vandalism and trespass often increases with population (Hart 1991) as does harassment of livestock by dogs, a problem that has eliminated sheep production and even affected cattle production in rural areas near San Francisco (Forero et al. 1992).

Another view sees the urban edge as a zone of opportunity for agriculture. Urbanization economies are derived from closer proximity to markets and the potential for production of higher value crops (Katzman 1974, Winsberg 1981). Transportation costs may be lower, opportunities for u-pick or Community Supported Agriculture greater, and chances for supplemental off-farm income increased. According to Whatley (1987), a successful pick-your-own operation must be located on a hard-surfaced road within a radius of 40 miles of a population center of at least 50,000.

Andrews and Chetrick (1988) examined the relationship between population density, proximity to metropolitan areas, and agricultural production for 51 counties near the New York and Philadelphia metropolitan areas. Their analysis controlled for differences in productivity due to different levels of inputs (land, capital, fertilizer, labor, livestock) so localization diseconomies (from higher population) and urbanization economies (closer proximity to markets) could be identified. Aggregate agricultural production was estimated as market value of agricultural products sold. Their study showed that a 1% increase in population in a suburban county reduced the agricultural output of the average farm in that county by 0.1–0.2% *independent of any change in the levels of inputs used.* Given the average population density in New Jersey in 1978 of 974 persons/sq. mile versus 371 in New York and 261 in Pennsylvania, the authors conclude that "a farmer in New Jersey, employing exactly the same input combination and the same state-of-the-art technical methods as a farmer in a less densely populated neighboring state, could achieve an output that is from 7% to 20% smaller solely because of the difference in population density in the location where the farming activity is undertaken." The efficiency at which inputs are converted to agricultural goods is reduced by surrounding population growth, strong evidence that agricultural production is a landscape-level, not just a farm-level function. The study showed no clear evidence for positive urbanization economies.

In a study of agriculture at the urban fringe in Ventura County, California, Brand et al. (1996) (see also Case 21) concluded:

- Quantifiable costs increase at the urban fringe, with estimates as high as 5-6% of total operations costs per acre.

- The highest increased cost of operation at the urban fringe is the entry price for land purchase or rental.

One of the most insidious and pervasive costs experienced by growers is the most difficult to quantify: the extra time required to comply with new regulations, forestall complaints from urban neighbors, move equipment on crowded roads, and shift equipment from the field to a secure nighttime storage area.

### The Perception of Impermanence

Another insidious and difficult to quantify factor at the urban fringe is the impermanence syndrome, a set of economic behaviors that accompanies land speculation. William H. Whyte in *The Last Landscape* describes a predictable sequence of events that presages the conversion of an agricultural landscape. He defines a "greed line" that moves in advance of development, changing attitudes of owners toward their land. Investments in soil conservation and farm infrastructure stop. Even when much open space remains, its ownership is being transferred to speculators who may lease it or just leave it idle. Thibault and Zipperer (1994) examined land use changes in a 36 km² area adjacent to Syracuse, New York. In 1926, 80% of the area was in agricultural production, and 20% in forest and wetlands. By 1988, 60% of the area was urbanized, and 40% in forests, old fields and wetlands. Although much agricultural land was left, none was in production. Ewing (1994) estimates that as much as one acre of farmland is idled for every acre converted to urban uses in the Northeast.

Vegetable producer Dan Guenthner received police visits after spreading manure on several acres of rented land near Orono, Minnesota, a suburb of the Twin Cities. The city complained that the vegetable fields weren't manicured enough; trespass was a problem; and his landlords were under constant pressure to sell to a developer. Guenthner moved three times within Orono before moving to Wisconsin, a member of a significant roving population of vegetable and small fruit growers (DeVore 1996).

The potential advantages to agriculture of proximity to the urban edge are negated when the edge keeps advancing, and when the edge is fuzzy (e.g., leap-frog development) rather than clearly defined. Farmers seeking land that meets Whatley's criteria of proximity and accessibility will be in direct competition with developers, and developers can pay more.

### Maintaining Production in the Face of Development

Is there a land use strategy that can maintain a viable agriculture close to an urban area? One thing is clear—a piecemeal approach to farmland preservation will not work. Isolated, fragmented farms cannot function well. They need to be part of a functioning agricultural landscape. Preservation programs such as Purchase of Development Rights that obtain easements for individual farms must be targeted to areas where a critical mass of farmland and farm infrastructure can still be maintained.

Under current economic conditions, farming cannot compete with development for access to and use of land. Because development pressures are greatest at the urban edge, farming will always be in retreat unless a legislative line is drawn beyond which development cannot occur. Oregon requires its municipalities to delineate urban growth boundaries that separate developable land from land to be maintained in agriculture (see Case 19).

Development continues because the boundaries are placed to accommodate 20 years expected growth, but it occurs in a well-defined area where existing transportation and service infrastructures can be used. With sprawl reduced, so are the interfaces between agriculture and urban uses, and the associated conflicts. Outside the growth boundaries, the impermanence syndrome is reduced (although not eliminated; urban growth boundaries can be expanded), and farmers have the opportunity to actually benefit from proximity to markets.

Economic opportunities include direct marketing through farmer's markets, Community Supported Agriculture (CSA), and the high-value vegetable and nursery crops envisioned for Thünen's inner ring (Figure 2.2), but without Hart's final step of selling to a developer. These strategies not only provide economic diversity and a better chance of keeping protected rural land in farming, but also develop links between the farm and urban community that offer the best longterm hope of preserving agricultural landscapes.

Communities are motivated to protect their municipal watersheds from development because the service performed by the watershed is obvious as are the negative effects of conversion. In a global food market, most people see no relationship between their local landscape and their food supply. Direct links between farmers and consumers can alter this perception, and provide a strong motivation for protecting that landscape. Analogous to the watershed is the concept of the *foodshed* (Kloppenburg et al. 1996) or *marketscape* (Lyson and Green 1996)—a geographic area defined by the flow of agricultural products from producers to consumers, and by other interactions among components of the food system. As discussed in Chapter 5, relocalization of the food supply through the development, in concept and practice, of foodsheds is an important step in sustaining both agriculture and the landscapes in which this is practiced.

## Cultural Functions

### *Preserving the Past*

*...generations that we know not, heart-drawn to see where and by whom great things were suffered and done for them, shall come to this deathless field, to ponder and dream...*

— From the address of General Joshua L. Chamberlain at the dedication of the Maine Monuments, Battlefield of Gettysburg, October 3, 1889, Lakeside Press, Portland, Maine, 1898 (CWSAC 1993).

To ponder, dream, and increasingly observe the intrusion of housing developments and souvenir shops. The Civil War Sites Advisory Committee (CWSAC) was established in 1991 in response to the threat to the nation's Civil War heritage from development on and near battlefield sites. Of 384 principal battlefields, "Nineteen percent (71) of the Civil War battlefields are already lost as intact historic landscapes. Half of the 232 principal battlefields that currently are in good or fair condition are now experiencing high or moderate threats. Most of these sites will be lost or seriously fragmented within the coming 10 years, many very soon. Only one-third of the principal battlefields currently face low threats."

At a time when the need is great for common values to bind the nation together, it is essential that citizens be able to reflect upon and understand the historical events that shaped our country and its values. The defining struggles by and among Americans took place not in a vacuum, but within the context of the American landscape. Without an understanding and appreciation for the historical landscape, we can't reach an emotional understanding of the events. Reading about these events is not sufficient; just as the Declaration of Independence and the Liberty Bell serve as touchstones of our common heritage (and therefore our common present), walking the path of Pickett's charge, standing by the trenches at Vicksburg, or kneeling by the ruts of the Oregon Trail help to ground us in a common heritage. If we so change our landscapes as to obscure our past, do we not corrupt our present and deplete our future?

Preservation of just the main site of an historic event is not sufficient. To the visitor, any sense of what happened, of a connection to the past, is destroyed if the cavalry charge ends in a McDonald's parking lot or if the battalion's flank is threatened by a subdivision. All of the terrain visible from the site, the viewshed, is integral to its cultural function. For example, Waterford, Virginia, an 18th Century village of about 100 houses, is part of the Waterford National Historic Landmark. The boundaries of the Landmark go beyond the edge of the village to include most of the land visible from the village (Stokes 1989). This delineation is intended to protect both the village and its pastoral setting, and proposed developments within the viewshed are construed as threats to the integrity of the village.

Obviously, it is not possible to maintain the viewsheds of most historic sites as museums. An alternative strategy derived from the design of biological reserves (Kemf 1993) involves a core protected area surrounded by a zone of compatible land use which in most cases is agriculture. Many of the Civil War battlegrounds were in agriculture at the time. For historic sites that weren't, agricultural landscapes still retain more natural features than other land uses.

### Sustaining the Present

Working landscapes also preserve current culture in the form of communities. Berry (1987) writes that the essential elements of community include the integration of people and land with the local economy; a greater reliance on local resources and knowledge than on external inputs; and the transfer of values and knowledge between successive generations. Throughout rural America, communities are being destroyed by changes in landscape structure that preclude maintenance of these critical elements.

In *After the Fire: The Destruction of the Lancaster County Amish*, Testa (1992) describes the accelerating residential and tourist development of the Lancaster County landscape, some of the finest farmland in the United States and for three centuries the foundation of an Amish community in every sense of Berry's definition. Now, loss of farmland coupled with rising land prices forces many Amish to work off the farm. Traffic clogged roads are not conducive to buggy travel (Box 2.2), and the sheer press of tourists is disruptive. Hart's (1991) prescription that people in this situation "sell their land to developers and retire to areas that have milder climates" is not an option. A community based on a sense of place and a faith that limits contact with the outside world cannot survive in Miami. Throughout America we are giving up rural communities in trade for an expansion of megalopolis, the antithesis of community.

Of course, the Amish contribute to their own demise. They have large families, too many to stay on the farm, and many must seek work off-farm. Also, not all are good stewards of the land, and Amish communities in Pennsylvania, Ohio and other regions are not replays of the movie *Witness*. Indeed, farmers of any culture in any region rarely meet the Jeffersonian ideal of the noble agrarian, and adherence to such rural myths can impede effective policy to preserve rural communities (Browne et al. 1992). Nevertheless, farmers are different from urban dwellers, and these differences are important.

Box 2.2  Truck-buggy crash kills three. Port Trevorton, PA.

In another deadly clash between modern technology and a simpler way of life, a tractor-trailer plowed into a horse-drawn wagon carrying seven children from an Amish family, killing three of them.

The truck driver tried to stop when he spotted the black wagon Wednesday night, but his rig jackknifed when he hit the brakes. It was at least the ninth accident in recent years involving Amish buggies and motor vehicles.

"It was devastating," state Trooper Fred Dyroff said. "I've been to a lot of accidents and this one really bothered me. He hit the buggy and people went flying."

Mary Martin, 14, and her sisters Erma, 12, and Vera, 7, were killed.

Truck driver Terry Chism, 32, of New Albany, Miss., suffered only minor injuries. No charges were brought against him.

— Lincoln (NE) Journal Star, 27 Sept 1996, p. 4A

Hanson (1996) writes "The farmer is perhaps not inherently noble, law abiding, or even ethical. But he is different, vastly different, from almost all other types of citizens, whose methods of wage labor, whose house, whose values and material outlook, are now all roughly similar. He is distinct because he is shaped solely by the growth of plants, his success dependent on his degree of skill in coercing food from the earth..." As discussed in Chapter 1, the number of farmers has been declining precipitously, mostly for reasons other than farmland conversion; they lost their land although the land was not lost. However, in many areas loss of land or high prices due to competition are important in determining that there will not be another generation on the farm.

Will they be missed? In a general sense, our country needs diversity. Farmers are different, and add another perspective to viewing and solving our common problems. Specifically, we need their hard-won knowledge of farming and of the land, their agriculture, if we are to have any hope of developing a sustainable agriculture. Do we really think that the biotech gene-jockies or the shop-till-you-drop children of the urban mall can take the lead in creating healthy and productive landscapes?

Jackson (1987) writes "My concern here is the serious reduction of people on the land who can pass on to future generations the skills, the traditions, the passions, and the values they will need to farm well on the smaller energy inputs inherent in the use of "contemporary" energy. Contemporary energy is that which arrives from the sun and is harvested in a horizontal manner over the landscape, rather than from a vertical well or mine." When a landscape is converted, not only is the agricultural function lost, but so is the knowledge inherent in that place and its people, part of what Jackson refers to as an information implosion.

In the end, beyond the talk of cumulative impacts and the good of the nation, it is individuals who bear the direct effects of conversion. Hart (1991) recalls a visit in 1983 to Wear Cove, a valley in east Tennessee next to Great Smoky Mountains National Park, and a prime area for tourist and second home development. Developers were offering up to ten times the agricultural value for farmland in the valley. As Hart concluded an interview with Wear Cove's leading farmer, the man asked him for a favor. "Pray for me!" he said. "I know I can't stay here, but I don't want to leave...My family has lived here for four generations, and I don't want to see the valley go the way of Pigeon Forge. A lot of people in the valley are watching me to see what I do, and the whole valley is going to go if I sell out, but how can I possibly stay here? I can't sleep nights for worrying about what I should do. Please pray for me!"

Of course, some farmers would gladly take the money, and there is the happiness of new primary or vacation homeowners, happy to have escaped some blighted landscape as they contribute to the ruin of another one. But many suffer, and after the development have only the double-edged sword of memories for comfort and despair (Box 2.3).

Box 2.3   *Walking the Ghost Farm* by Atina Diffley.

---

Our fifth generation, 120-acre family farm has been developed into executive suburbia, with rolling sod lawns, driveways, curbs and sidewalks to protect the residents from "dirt." Now everything is clean and tidy. It's named Autumn Ridge, for the ridge they took away the ridge the new residents will never be able to stand on gazing at the valley below, the valley that will never again be filled with corn and melons.

When I walk on the farm development, I become dizzy and disoriented. I see two images as I trod where a path once was. My eyes see the homes that exist now, the street with the curve ahead, while superimposed over the present my feet feel the old paths and continue to seek them out, though they run through someone's backyard or into their garage.

My memory sees the trees, swamps, animals, plants and hills that once were. Double images appear, overlapping each other. Hills rise through people's homes and yards, trees stretch their limbs through windows, crops grow in garages. Shall I walk the ghost farm or the suburban streets?

My ears still hear the crows laughing about how they stole my first tomatoes of the season. I can close my eyes and hear the crackling sound of corn growing in the still of a hot July night.

---

*Continues*

Box 2.3 *Continued*

My hands and feet can still feel the soil, knowing by feel alone whether it's sand or clay, wet or dry, south or north slope.

I can still feel the wind at the end of a long, glorious June day, lightly blowing dust against my sun-warmed sturdy legs.

I can still smell the rich sweetness of spring soil, corn growing and melons ripening, fall leaves drying.

Through the soles of my feet, I can feel the strength and balance the land radiated and gave to me as a gift.

My heart can still feel the fullness of loving a piece of land so fully and feeling I belonged on it, sharing its beauty.

All this and more crowds through me as I try to walk where something else once was. Something that now exists only in hearts and memories. Something that can never be brought back.

Layer upon layer, superimposed, my senses become over-whelmed and it's time to move on.

Beyond the now present street lights representing suburban values of safe/white cleanliness.

Beyond a community that forgot to leave room for nature.

Beyond what feels like certain death of life itself.

How many more deaths must occur before we put an end to this madness known as progress?

— From The Land Stewardship Letter, Vol. 14, No. 1, Jan/Feb 1996, pages 2-3.

## Aesthetic And Scenic Values

### *Sowing the Seeds of Ugliness*

The bottomland along the Little Pigeon River north of Gatlinburg, Tennessee "in 1958...still grew corn. By 1983 it had erupted into the kind of place that gives tourism a bad name: a continuous roadside strip, 4.6 miles long, of motels, eating places, souvenir shops, and commercial entertainments such as water slides, rides, waxworks, "museums," horror shows (intentional and otherwise), and all manner of other grotesqueries" (Hart 1991).

The spatial configuration as well as the particular contents of any landscape provide visual information to which people respond (Schauman 1988). Landscape structure is related to aesthetics as it is for any landscape function with the important difference that the aesthetic function is mediated by the viewer's mind; in this one case perception is reality.

Still, there is more consistency in aesthetic evaluations of landscapes than we might think. We can all identify examples of just plain ugly development that has ruined the visual appeal of a landscape, and in most cases other observers would agree. What do these crummy looking areas have in common? Built cheap and not to last, they are mass produced with no consideration of regional building traditions, e.g., thick adobe walls in the Southwest, high ceilings in the South (Kunstler 1993). Buildings are placed without consideration of their relationship to the landscape; boxes on 1-acre lots in a symmetric pattern, and linear developments along a road. The technology of earth moving allows placement without respect to topography. High energy inputs for cooling, heating, and lighting allow boxy architecture without regard to form and function.

Some landscapes are more visually forgiving of poor design than others. Scenic evaluation includes the concept of fragility, defined as a range of landscape conditions from a high capacity to absorb change without diminishing the visual environment to an inability of the landscape to accept any additions (Schauman 1988). Wooded, rolling terrain with limited viewsheds can hide a multitude of sins. Other terrains don't handle it well, at least not the type of architecture we build. In the Colorado short-grass prairie, "The biggest development in Douglas County is Highlands

Ranch, an unincorporated community of more than 10,000 homes on broad streets in the wind-swept, treeless prairie just south of Denver. Some of the homes look as if they were just dropped from the sky" (Egan 1996a).

A big part of looking good is looking like you belong. Even in open terrain, appropriate architecture can complement the natural setting. In the desert Southwest, adobe houses with their muted earth tones and natural materials look like an extension of the earth, not an imposition from above. And not coincidentally, the thick walls greatly reduce heating and cooling costs. Function follows form, and we avoid the trap of the average American home which uses more energy in three years of operation than it took to build it.

But, aside from any efficiencies inherent in good design, is there a reason to preserve the aesthetic values of a landscape? What threat is a diminished view? Hiss (1990) writes "...the danger, as we are now beginning to see, is that whenever we make changes in our surroundings, we can all too easily shortchange ourselves, by cutting ourselves off from some of the sights and sounds, the shapes or textures, or other information from a place that have helped mold our understanding and are now necessary for us to thrive. Overdevelopment and urban sprawl can damage our own lives as much as they damage our cities and countryside."

### Preserving Scenic Values

At the regional scale, the first step in preserving scenic landscapes is a landscape inventory followed by an evaluation of which landscapes are distinctive and a priority for preservation. Massachusetts and Rhode Island have both conducted statewide scenic assessments to identify high quality landscapes (Hiss 1990). The six-state New England Governors Conference assembled a list of all unprotected open spaces and working landscapes that New Englanders generally consider to contribute to the distinctiveness of their region. The list is used to guide preservation and development planning.

To evaluate and compare scenic qualities of different landscapes, evaluation criteria have been developed that can be consistently applied by trained observers. Using a classification system for agricultural landscapes, Schauman (1988) rated the scenic quality of different landscape units in Whatcom County, Washington. The Whatcom County Land Trust uses these ratings to accept donations of scenic easements. Vermont uses an evaluation system to have citizens rate and designate scenic roads, while Monroe County, Pennsylvania identifies major viewsheds as part of its comprehensive planning process.

Foster (1996) states that a place is recognized by its cultural and natural history and the unique aesthetics that these produce, and that most new development looks foreign because it does not attempt to fit this identity. To plan development that fits their working landscape, a community must (1) define the key visual elements that characterize the landscape, and (2) consider the likely effects of current land use regulations on these characteristics. Photographs of identifying characteristics and key features of the landscape can be used in a community process to develop a sense of what the residents value most. Computer derived images can be used to simulate the look of different development scenarios (Foster 1996), and public choices can then be used to develop regulations that will allow and encourage the preferred alternatives. Regulations need to be crafted carefully to avoid unintended consequences. For example, minimum lot sizes intended to preserve rural qualities often accelerate land conversion and a diffuse sprawl, while prohibiting cluster development that could actually achieve the desired goal (see Case 6).

Preservation of scenic landscapes will ultimately require the general acceptance that scenic functions are public values, and that use of private property must conform to the preservation of these values. Viewsheds are often large, and there will never be enough money to buy visual easements on most lands. Inappropriate development on a very small portion of a viewshed can greatly diminish its scenic value. A contentious example in the Blue Ridge Mountains of Virginia involves the building of homes on the tops of knolls, providing choice views for a few homeowners, and greatly diminished scenic values for most residents and tourists.

In Europe, the building of these knoll-top homes would be considered "cropping public value," actions that strip part of a public value from a landscape and convert it into cash value for private gain (Hiss 1990). There is a strong public perception that some landscape functions are public benefits (see Case 22), and private actions that detract from these functions are takings that can be regulated. Similar ideas that exist in American land use law (Chapter 3) and even economic theory (Chapter 4) need to be cultivated and strengthened.

## Designing Optimal Landscapes

In addition to the functions discussed above, landscape planning needs to consider the effects of development on species habitat (Vogel 1989, Wheeler 1996), air quality (Horowitz 1982), and even local climate (Pielke and Avissar 1990). Given the many functions that landscapes provide, the conflicting priorities of people for promoting different functions, and the impossibility of maximizing all functions within a particular landscape, how do we go about designing an optimal landscape? Figure 2.3 shows an iterative process by which a community can develop and refine a comprehensive land use plan to optimize the functioning of their landscape. It requires broad involvement of residents in defining their preferred future as well as an in-depth understanding of landscape functions and the relationship of land use policy to those functions. It is an ecological design process that recognizes the importance of place and the connection of humans to that place (Van der Ryn and Cowan 1996).

The essential first step is to describe the current structure and condition of the landscape. "What is here? What will nature permit us to do here? What will nature help us to do here?" (Berry 1987). What is the topography, hydrology, biodiversity? Who are the people who live here? What do they do for a living? How do they interact with the land? What are the major problems and opportunities facing the community? And by community we mean an area of landscape scale, quite likely larger than a single town. Landscape processes rarely coincide with political boundaries, and compacts among many governments may be required to achieve landscape goals. For example, Westminster, Colorado implemented a plan including limits on development and the purchase of open space, but was then engulfed by greater Denver. "The lesson is: We can't do this alone, in isolation," said John Carpenter, the town's community development director. "There are things we have no control over, no matter how many laws we pass in Westminster" (Egan 1996b).

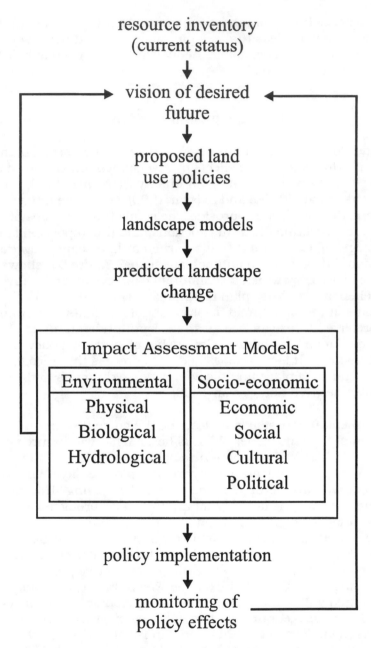

Figure 2.3  An iterative process for landscape planning. Mechanisms for monitoring the actual effects of policy decisions and comparing them with the desired effects are essential parts of the process.

McHarg (1969) in *Design with Nature* presented one of the earliest treatises on landscape design, using an approach he called physiographic determinism to design optimum patterns of development for landscapes near Baltimore, Washington, D.C. and other cities. He organized information on spatial patterns of topography, geology, surface- and groundwater, floodplains, stream courses, vegetation and existing development, and integrated them as overlays to provide a foundation for planning. His plans identified optimal locations for projected residential and commercial growth that would preserve the landscape's agricultural, hydrologic, water quality, habitat, and aesthetic functions.

Although the resource inventory is essential to the planning process, the focal point is the community's vision of their preferred future. The cliché may be tired, but if you don't know where you are going, you truly won't get there. The best way to achieve a community vision is through a formal planning process that involves all community members (Sargent et al. 1991). While consensus is unlikely in a large and diverse community, a large majority of the community needs to feel a sense of ownership of the vision if policies to achieve it are to have a chance of being implemented.

The next steps in the planning process (Figure 2.3) are to propose policies and regulations to achieve the vision, and to evaluate the likely effects of these policies before implementing them. Geographic Information Systems (GIS) are useful tools not only for organizing spatial data, but for operating spatially-based models of landscape function (Aspinall 1993) that can be used in comparing the landscape effects of alternative policies. The visual outputs of GIS are an excellent way to illustrate to citizens the potential outcomes of alternative land use policies (see Case 4). Monroe County, PA is currently undertaking a comprehensive planning process that relies heavily on a county GIS (Box 2.4). Because local agencies often lack the funds or expertise to conduct spatial analyses, McHarg (1997) proposes the development of uniform ecological planning methods to be used by all government agencies, supported by federally-financed collection and synthesis of the necessary environmental data. Lovejoy et al. (1997) suggest that the Internet provides a cost effective means for local groups to access both decision tools and data for planning purposes. Of course, not all potential effects of alternative policies need to be, or indeed can be, evaluated with computer models.

Particularly when social impacts of landscape changes are being considered, assessments may be subjective and rely on judgement.

Box 2.4   Landscape planning in Monroe County, PA.

Located in the heart of the Poconos, the character of Monroe County has been defined by its landscape. Forests, rivers, abundant wildlife, and a scenic topography that includes the spectacular Delaware Water Gap have contributed to a high quality of life for its residents and provide the foundation for a tourist industry and more than 10000 jobs. Agriculture uses about 6% of the county's area, contributing to its scenic beauty as well as to crop and livestock production.

However, paradise is threatened. Located within 100 miles of New York City and Philadelphia, the population of the county grew almost 40% in the 1980s with another 90,000 residents expected by 2020. Thirty-five percent of the county is currently developed, primarily in single-family homes on ½- to 1-acre lots. Only 1/4 of the housing units are on central sewage systems, with individual septic tanks and drain fields presenting a threat to groundwater quality. Agricultural land in 1992 had declined 23% in ten years, and roadside development has eliminated many scenic views. A Comprehensive Plan for the county developed in 1981 that leaves most planning decisions at the township level has not been effective. Half the development occurring since 1981 has been in areas not planned for growth by 2000, and total residential acreage in 1991 was three times that projected by the Plan.

A new planning effort led by the Monroe County Planning Commission relies heavily on a Geographic Information System (GIS) containing digital maps of major landscape features including elevation, slope, soil type, groundwater recharge areas, surface waters, vegetation, land use, roads, and township boundaries. Areas visible from key viewing points ("viewsheds") are mapped as is critical wildlife habitat. When overlaid, these maps provide a spatial representation of the current condition of the landscape, allowing the identification of critical areas for biological, geological and visual functions of the landscape as well as the identification of the most threatened areas. Equally important is the analysis of spatial relationships among land-

*Continues*

Box 2.4 *Continued*

scape components. For example, black bear habitat is distributed in patches that need to be linked by travel corridors for
the bears to prosper. A GIS-analysis shows that the habitat
areas are generally well protected, but the corridors are not.

With the understanding of landscape condition and function
provided by the GIS, the citizens of Monroe County have a tool
to use in planning future development and evaluating alternative development scenarios. One alternative, the Township
Plan, would promote in-filling and higher densities in existing
subdivisions, and locate new high density residential and
mixed-use development near existing town centers. Areas with
high landscape value as identified with the GIS would be conserved through purchase of conservation easements. At the
other extreme, the Build-out alternative foresees basically unregulated development resulting in a transformation of the
county into a metropolitan suburbia with the loss of most
landscape functions.

Analyses conducted with the GIS make clear that effective
planning in Monroe County must occur at the county or even
regional scale. Surface waters, groundwater, wildlife, and views
cross township lines. Decisions on road and sewer placement
have effects on development far beyond their immediate corridors. Preserving most of the landscape qualities that make
Monroe County so unique is still possible, but only at considerable expense and with some restrictions on the use of private
lands. Landscape analysis with the GIS is a critical tool for
planning and for building citizen consensus by visually illustrating alternative futures. References: Monroe County Planning Commission (1996a, b) and Steinitz et al. (1994).

After an iterative series of evaluations and refinement of policies, the only true test is to implement the policies and evaluate
the actual against the desired outcomes. Planning is an ongoing
effort; conditions change, unexpected events occur, and mid-
course corrections are needed. Successful planning requires
monitoring of outcomes and the use of evaluation criteria to determine if the preferred future of the community is actually being
achieved or if additional policy changes are needed (see Box 2.4).
The price for creating a desirable landscape, as with liberty, is
eternal vigilance.

A moratorium on development is not an option for most communities. But a community does have a choice as to the type of development that will occur, and there are alternatives that retain many of the valuable functions of agricultural landscapes (Figure 2.4; see also Case 14). With will, perseverance, and some imagination, healthy and beautiful landscapes are possible.

Figure 2.4   An illustration of contrasting development approaches, opposite page (Stokes 1989).

Top: The Jones farm as it is. Located on a country road, the Jones farm still embodies the distinct visual character of a late-nineteenth century American farm. It retains its farmhouse, outbuildings, farm pond, orchard and woodlot. Adjacent fields are still used for both cultivation and grazing. Respect for the natural environment is evident in the retention of wetlands in the foreground, vegetation along the stream, and trees on steep slopes to the right.

Middle: Short-sighted development of the Jones farm has resulted in environmental damage and destruction of much of its historic character. The original architecture of the farmhouse has been modified, and historic outbuildings and landscape elements have been removed. Development has occurred in the floodplain, and the wetland has been filled. Development along the road has reduced the farmland and gives the landscape a cluttered appearance. Construction on the steep slope not only mars the scene, but also could result in erosion.

Bottom: The same amount of development can occur without environmental degradation and loss of historic character. Traditional buildings and prime farmland can be retained, and construction on steep slopes, wetlands, and floodplains can be avoided. This development has the same number of units as the one shown in (middle), but the design is more sensitive. Ten of the units have been clustered in the former orchard. More trees have been retained in the woodlot. Although there is development on the hillside, the houses are not on as steep a slope, fewer trees have been cut, and the buildings are less obtrusive.

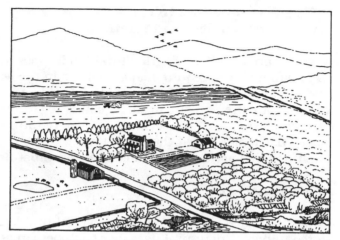

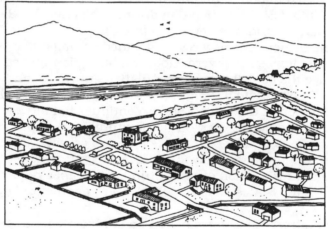

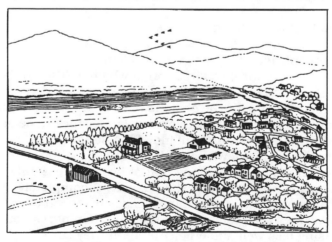

## Five Prerequisites to the Preservation of Landscape Functions

The successful preservation of agricultural landscapes at any scale, local to national, will require major changes in the ways we perceive and manipulate our lands. These changes in laws, ethics, and attitudes are prerequisite to saving lands regardless of the region in which they are located, the type of agriculture they support, or the particular threat they face. If we want to preserve healthy and functional agricultural landscapes, we must have:

### 1. A stable population:

As people are added to the population, agricultural land is converted to non-agricultural uses. For each person added to the United States population during the period 1982–1992, 0.6 acre of land was developed (see Chapter 1, Table 1.3). While the loss per new resident varied among different locales, it was never zero. Good land use planning can reduce the contribution of population growth to land loss, but not eliminate it, at least for any significant period. If the population of the United States continues to increase by 2.4 million people per year, our agricultural landscapes will continue to rapidly degrade. Population growth at reduced rates will ultimately have the same effect; it will just take longer. Preservation of agricultural landscapes requires that the United States adopt a policy of zero population growth.

### 2. Regulation of land use based on landscape management:

Buildings are erected from a single blueprint. Imagine a construction project in which the plumbers, electricians and other contractors worked independently of a master plan, or even more absurdly a situation in which a different builder designed and erected each separate room. We don't attempt such endeavors for the obvious reason that the building would not stand. Yet we allow our landscapes to be shaped piecemeal by thousands of individual landowners, most of whom have no knowledge of landscape function, and are constrained by regulations that at best address only a few landscape functions and then usually incompletely. Not surprisingly, the result in most cases has been degraded landscapes that perform even the function of residential housing less well and efficiently than they could.

Development must be regulated within comprehensive plans that consider all landscape functions, the degree of each function that should be maintained, and the spatial arrangement of landscape components needed to maintain those functions. Planning boards need to have the authority and knowledge to evaluate development proposals from a landscape perspective and block actions that would have unacceptable impacts. Because local control can be synonymous with no control, some local governments will require an incentive to adhere to a landscape planning process. In 1970, Sen. Henry Jackson introduced legislation to require states to adopt federally-approved statewide plans to preserve agricultural land or lose significant federal funding (Peterson 1983). A similar approach, strengthened to include all landscape functions, should be implemented.

### 3. A citizenry that understands landscape functions:

Ian McHarg (1997) writes "The phenomenal increase in urban concentrations, combined with exponential population growth and the reduction of the agricultural component in society and economy, have produced asphalt people who know little of nature and care less. To such people, knowledge of nature is apparently irrelevant to their success or future." I would add that almost no one understands ecosystems or rural communities or any of the other complex systems that combined form an agricultural landscape. And we certainly have the power to change these landscapes, and are doing so with increasing frequency.

Without an educated populace, we lack a pool of people from which to draw for planning boards or as elected officials to establish policies. And unless a majority of citizens understand the implications of farmland loss and uncontrolled development, officials who support preservation will not be elected and policies to preserve agricultural landscapes will not be implemented. Many Americans don't go to college, so pre-college education needs to teach landscape functions. Groups interested in farmland preservation can support this by developing curricula for elementary through high school. To reach adults, farmland preservation groups need to include a landscape perspective in their public education efforts, which may require educating themselves on this subject first.

**4. Research to support policy decisions and land use management:**

We know a lot about landscape functions. Still, there is much that we don't know. Landscape management has clearly lagged behind most applied sciences in terms of research effort. Theories of landscape management need further development and testing in specific situations. Models of landscape function must be rigorously validated to withstand legal challenges, yet simple enough to be easily used in community planning.

**5. A commonly held land ethic:**

Morals, values, and ethics provide the constraining envelope within which individual and community decisions are made. When this envelop becomes tattered, our unrestrained free choices often cause negative effects. A return to values is frequently espoused as a cure for many of America's ills, although which values and how to achieve them are subjects of much debate. Bill Bennett addressed the problem by writing *The Book of Virtues: A Treasury of Great Moral Stories*. Perhaps what we need is a Book of Landscape Virtues in which fables illustrate the damning consequences of urban sprawl and the redeeming virtues of enlightened landscape design. Until such a book appears, the writings of Leopold, Berry, Jackson, and McHarg provide a fine start. We should be reading these to our children.

*We abuse land because we regard it as a commodity belonging to us. When we see land as a community to which we belong, we may begin to use it with love and respect.*
— Aldo Leopold

## References

Andrews, M.S., and J. Chetrick. 1988. Agricultural productivity in densely populated areas. Landscape and Urban Planning 16:311-318.

Aspinall, R. 1993. Use of geographic information systems for interpreting land use policy and modelling effects of land-use change. pp. 223-236. In: R. Haines-Young, D.R. Green, and S.

Cousins (eds.) Landscape Ecology and Geographic Information Systems. Taylor & Francis, London.

Baker, L.A. 1992. Introduction to nonpoint source pollution in the United States and prospects for wetland use. Ecological Engineering 1:1-26.

Berry, W. 1987. Does community have a value? pp. 179-192. In: W. Berry, Home Economics. North Point Press, San Francisco.

Bowen, G.W., and R.L. Burgess. 1981. A Quantitative Analysis of Forest Island Pattern in Selected Ohio Landscapes. Publication ORNL-TM-7759, Environmental Sciences Division, Oak Ridge National Laboratory, Oak Ridge, TN.

Brand, P.S., J. McCluskey, G. Goldman, E.S. McNiel, M. Moore, E.K. Young, A.D. Sokolow, and D. Strong. 1996. The Value of Agriculture to Ventura County: An Economic Analysis. Ventura County Agricultural Land Trust and Conservancy, Ventura, CA.

Browne, W.P., J.R. Skees, L.E. Swanson, P.B. Thompson, L.J. Unnevehr. 1992. Sacred Cows and Hot Potatoes: Agrarian Myths in Agricultural Policy. Westview Press, Boulder.

Coombe, R.I. 1996. Watershed protection: A better way. pp. 25-34. In: W. Lockeretz (ed.) Environmental Enhancement Through Agriculture. Center for Agriculture, Food and Environment, Tufts University, Medford, MA.

Curtis, J.T. 1956. The modification of mid-latitude grasslands and forests by man. pp. 721-736. In: W.L. Thomas (ed.) Man's Role in Changing the Face of the Earth. The University of Chicago Press, Chicago.

CWSAC. 1993. Civil War Sites Advisory Commission Report on the Nation's Civil War Battlefields. Prepared by the staff of the CWSAC, National Park Service, Washington, D.C.

DeVore, B. 1996. Holding urban sprawl accountable. The Land Stewardship Letter 14:1, 8-10.

Egan, T. 1996a. Urban sprawl strains western states. New York Times, 29 December.

Egan, T. 1996b. Portland's hard line on managing growth. New York Times, 30 December.

Ewing, R.H. 1994. Characteristics, causes, and effects of sprawl: A literature review. Environmental and Urban Issues (Winter):1-15.

Forero, L., L. Huntsinger, and W.J. Clawson. 1992. Land use change in three San Francisco Bay Area counties: Implications for ranching at the urban fringe. Journal of Soil and Water Conservation 47:475-480.

Forman, R.T.T., and M. Godron. 1986. Landscape Ecology. John Wiley & Sons, New York.

Foster, K. 1996. Citizens use photo-realistic visualization process to specify qualities needed to sustain a rural environment. The Rural Landscape 8:4-8.

Fuguitt, G.V., and D.L. Brown. 1990. Residential preferences and population redistribution: 1972–1988. Demography 27:589-600.

Haggett, P. 1979. Geography: A Modern Synthesis. Harper & Row, New York.

Hanson, V.D. 1996. Fields without Dreams: Defending the Agrarian Idea. The Free Press, New York.

Hart, J.F. 1991. The Land that Feeds Us. W.W. Norton, New York.

Hiss, T. 1990. The Experience of Place. Knopf, New York.

Horowitz, J. 1982. Air Quality Analysis for Urban Transportation Planning. MIT Press, Cambridge, MA.

Iverson, L.R. 1988. Land-use changes in Illinois, USA: The influence of landscape attributes on current and historic land use. Landscape Ecology 2(1):45-61.

Jackson, W. 1987. The information implosion. pp. 11-16. In: W. Jackson, Alters of Unhewn Stone. North Point Press, Berkeley, CA.

Johnson, K.M., and C.L. Beale. 1994. The recent revival of widespread population growth in nonmetropolitan areas of the United States. Rural Sociology 59:655-667.

Katzman, M. 1974. The Von Thuenen paradigm, the industrial urban hypothesis, and the spatial structure of agriculture. American Journal of Agricultural Economics 56:683-696.

Kemf, E. (ed.) 1993. The Law of the Mother: Protecting Indigenous People in Protected Areas. Sierra Club Books, San Francisco.

Kesner, B.T., and V. Meentemeyer. 1989. A regional analysis of total nitrogen in an agricultural landscape. Landscape Ecology 2:151-163.

Kloppenburg, J., Jr., J. Hendrickson, and G.W. Stevenson. 1996. Coming in to the foodshed. Agriculture and Human Values 13:33-42.

Kunstler, J.H. 1993. The Geography of Nowhere. Simon & Schuster, New York.

LaGro, J.A., Jr. 1996. Designing without nature: Unsewered residential development in rural Wisconsin. Landscape and Urban Planning 35:1-9.

LaGro, J.A., Jr., and S.D. DeGloria. 1992. Land use dynamics within an urbanizing non-metropolitan county in New York State (USA). Landscape Ecology 7:275-289.

Lisansky, J. 1986. Farming in an urbanizing environment: Agricultural land-use conflicts and right-to-farm. Human Organization 45:363-371.

Lisansky, J., and G. Clark. 1987. Farmer-nonfarmer conflicts in the urban fringe: Will right-to-farm help? pp. 219-229. In: W. Lockeretz (ed.) Sustaining Agriculture Near Cities. Soil and Water Conservation Society, Ankeny, IA.

Loomis, R.S., and D.J. Connor. 1992. Crop Ecology: Productivity and Management in Agricultural Systems. Cambridge University Press, Cambridge.

Lovejoy, S.B., J.G. Lee, T.O. Randhir, and B.A. Engel. 1997. Research needs for water quality management in the 21st century: A spatial decision support system. Journal of Soil and Water Conservation 52:18-22.

Lyson, T.A., and J. Green. 1996. The Agricultural Marketplace: Implications of Alternative Food Systems for Communities and Landscapes in the Northeast. Farming Alternatives Program, Department of Rural Sociology, Cornell University, Ithaca, NY.

McHarg, I.L. 1969. Design with Nature. Natural History Press, Garden City, NY.

McHarg, I.L. 1997. Natural factors in planning. Journal of Soil and Water Conservation 52:13-17.

Monroe County Planning Commission. 1996a. Fiscal Alert. MCPC, Stroudsburg, PA.

Monroe County Planning Commission. 1996b. Environmental Alert. MCPC, Stroudsburg, PA.

Peterson, G. 1983. Methods for retaining agricultural land in the urban fringe in the U.S.A. Landscape Planning 9:271-278.

Pielke, R.A., and R. Avissar. 1990. Influence of landscape structure on local and regional climate. Landscape Ecology 4:133-155.

Ramsey, B. 1997. 'Lone eagles' are helping shape latest incarnation of American West. Lincoln Journal Star, 26 January, Section E, pp. 1E, 4E.

Ross, L. 1992. Austin voters win one for Barton Springs. Nonpoint Source News-Notes, #25. U.S. Environmental Protection Agency, Washington, D.C., pp. 4-5.

Sargent, F.O., P. Lusk, J.A. Rivera, and M. Varela. 1991. Rural environmental planning for sustainable communities. Island Press, Washington, D.C.

Schauman, S. 1988. Countryside scenic assessment: Tools and an application. Landscape and Urban Planning 15:227-239.

Schueler, T.R. 1991. Mitigating the Adverse Impacts of Urbanization on Streams. In: Watershed Restoration Sourcebook, Metropolitan Washington Council of Governments, Washington, D.C.

Sorensen, A.A., R.P. Greene, and K. Russ. 1997. Farming on the Edge. American Farmland Trust, Center for Agriculture in the Environment, Northern Illinois University, DeKalb, IL.

Steinitz, C., D. Olson, A. Shearer, I. Fairley, and S. McNally. 1994. Alternative Futures for Monroe County, Pennsylvania. Harvard University Graduate School of Design, Cambridge, MA.

Stokes, S.N. 1989. Saving America's Countryside: A Guide to Rural Conservation. The Johns Hopkins University Press, Baltimore.

Tarrant, J.R. 1974. Agricultural Geography. John Wiley & Sons, New York.

Testa, R. 1992. After the Fire: The Destruction of the Lancaster County Amish. University Press of New England, Hanover, NH.

Thibault, P.A., and W.C. Zipperer. 1994. Temporal changes of wetlands within an urbanizing agricultural landscape. Landscape and Urban Planning 28:245-251.

Tourbier, J.T. 1994. Open space through stormwater management: Helping to structure growth on the urban fringe. Journal of Soil and Water Conservation (Jan/Feb):14-21.

Turner, M.G. 1988. A spatial simulation model of land use changes in a piedmont county in Georgia. Applied Mathematics and Computation 27:39-51.

USEPA. 1990. National Pollutant Discharge Elimination System Permit Application Regulations for Storm Water Discharges: Final Rule. U.S. Environmental Protection Agency, Washington, D.C.

USEPA 1992a. The Anacostia: An urban watershed begins restoration. EPA News-Notes #21, May 1992. pp. 13-14.

USEPA 1992b. Virginia develops watershed targeting process. News-Notes #22.

USEPA 1994. Olympia, Washington, studies reduction of impervious surfaces. Nonpoint Source News-Notes #37, pp. 16-17.

USEPA. 1995. Stormwater utility in Marquette, MI. Nonpoint Source News-Notes. Issue #40, pp. 16-17.

Van der Ryn, S., and S. Cowan. 1996. Ecological Design. Island Press, Washington, D.C.

Vogel, W.O. 1989. Response of deer to density and distribution of housing in Montana. Wildlife Society Bulletin 17:406-413.

Wackernagel, M., and W. Rees. 1996. Our Ecological Footprint. New Society Publishers, Philadelphia.

Weimer, D. 1996. Program helps telecommuters feel part of the FPL team. The Palm Beach Post, December 26, p. 9B.

Whatley, B.T. 1987. How to Make $100,000 Farming 25 Acres. Regenerative Agriculture Association, Emmaus, PA.

Wheeler, D.P. 1996. Ecosystem management: An organizing principle for land use. pp. 155-172. In: H.L. Diamond and P.F. Noonan (eds.) Land Use in America. Island Press, Washington, D.C.

Winsberg, M. 1981. Intensity of agricultural production and distance from the city: The case of the southeastern United States. Southeastern Geographer 21:54-62.

Wise, H. 1990. Milwaukee River South declared a priority watershed in Wisconsin. Nonpoint Source News-Notes, #9. U.S. Environmental Protection Agency, Washington, D.C., pp. 14-15.

# 3

# The Law of the Land

*Allen H. Olson*

Europeans imposed law on the American landscape from the moment they stepped from their ships and planted the flags of their sovereigns. The colonizers imported the law of the mother country, declared it to be superior to the laws and customs of the indigenous people and began to apply the law to those who fell under their dominion. They used law to decide who would hold title to the land that they had discovered, conquered or settled, who could occupy or use the land and for what purposes. Law was the mechanism by which the European powers created their own property rights in the lands of the New World, rights that did not exist before their arrival, rights that supplanted a much different view of the nature of property held by the native peoples.

This chapter examines the legal framework that evolved from these imported laws, and under which farmland conversion decisions are now made. It begins with a discussion of the evolution of property law in the United States and then describes five types of laws that influence land use. The chapter gives federal, state and local examples of each of these types of laws and analyzes the effectiveness of different farmland preservation programs. It concludes with an analysis of the "takings issue" and makes recommendations for more effective land use controls of farmland.

## Creation of Property Rights in the United States

The laws of Great Britain, and to a lesser extent, France and Spain, became the foundation of the law of property in the fledgling United States. The United States Supreme Court recognized European discovery as the basis of land title in its 1823 decision in Johnson v. McIntosh.[1] Chief Justice Marshall wrote for the Court that discovery conferred upon the European sovereign exclusive title in the discovered lands good against all other European nations. The United States succeeded to the title acquired by the British. The Indians retained a right of occupancy in the discovered lands but lost their right to convey the lands to others. The government of the United States could convey title in discovered lands to individuals subject to the Indian right of occupancy. Furthermore, the United States could extinguish the right of occupancy either by purchase from the Indians or by conquest. The Court would add many years later that the Fifth Amendment to the United States Constitution did not require compensation be paid to Indians whose land was taken by conquest.[2]

Prior to independence, individuals or companies could acquire title to land only by a grant from the crown. Upon independence, the new government recognized the private property rights created under British rule. However, much of the land area of the United States, particularly that located in the western territory, remained in the public domain. The Articles of Confederation had given to the central government the right to "disposal of the soil." State governments ceded their claims to lands west of Pennsylvania to the national government in the years between 1784 and 1786. Upon adoption of the Constitution in 1789, title to the public domain vested in the new federal government. Later, the Louisiana Purchase, the Mexican War and other western land acquisitions would vastly expand the public domain (Opie 1994).

Disposal of the public domain became a crucial, long term issue for the new country. Between 1785 and 1929, 1.25 billion acres were transferred out of the public domain. Land was sold and sometimes given to settlers for homes and farms. Other land went to speculators, railroads, ranchers, mining interests, state governments and schools. Laws enacted by Congress like the Survey Ordinance of 1785, the Homestead Act of 1864 and the Kincaid Act were the authority for these transfers, and these statutes created private property rights in the land for the new owners (Opie 1994).

The homestead laws were intended to provide land for farmers who would live on their farms (Browne et al. 1992). In 1850, 239 million acres were being used for farming and grazing. By 1930, the amount of land in farms had increased to 987 million acres, most of it privately owned. The frontier was formally closed in 1936 with the passage of the Taylor Grazing Act, and no more public land was available for homesteading or sale. With the exception of certain grazing land in the far West, agriculture had become an activity conducted primarily on private lands (Lehman 1995).

Title, however, is only one aspect of land ownership. Ownership also includes other rights, such as the right to use property, the right to sell property and the right to pass on property at one's death. Property rights are frequently compared to a "bundle of sticks". Each stick represents a particular right, and the sticks may be separated. For example, an owner holds the title "stick", but his tenant temporarily holds the occupancy and use "sticks." Law is not only the mechanism that creates property rights; law also defines the nature of the rights. Once created, property rights are not absolute—changes in law may produce changes in property rights.

## History of Land Use Regulation

As the country approached the twentieth century, the attention of lawmakers shifted from the transfer of the public domain to private ownership to questions of how private land was being used. Conflicts arose between laws intended to regulate private land use and property rights claimed by land owners. Other conflicts occurred between laws that encouraged or subsidized certain uses of land and laws that attempted to regulate the adverse effects of such uses. These conflicts produced lively, and often bitter, debates that continue today. Property rights and land use have been major topics of public discourse throughout this century. Few subjects produce such impassioned argument as does government regulation of private land use. Similarly, government subsidies of private land use have been both loudly championed and roundly condemned.

Agricultural land has been at the forefront of much of this debate. The dustbowl of the 1930's focused public and legislative attention on farmland soil erosion. Farm subsidy programs were also enacted during this period to secure national food supplies, alleviate rural poverty and keep farmers on their land. As cities sprawled following World War II, farmland was often converted to meet suburban needs, and conflicts between agricultural and residential land uses became major issues by the late 1960's and early 1970's (Lehman 1995).

The 1970's became the decade of federal environmental regulation with Congress enacting major legislation addressing air and water pollution, pesticides and herbicides, solid waste, toxic waste and endangered species. Much of this legislation targeted industrial and municipal sources of pollution, but agriculture was not completely spared. State and local governments also enacted environmental laws and began to strengthen their land use laws. New legislation intended to slow farmland conversion reached its peak in the early 1980's following publication of the National Agricultural Lands Study (USDA 1981a,b,c).

Since the 1930's, agriculture has been highly subsidized by farm programs that support commodity prices and farm income, provide subsidized credit, and offer extensive technical assistance. During the 1930's and again in the 1985, 1990 and 1996 farm legislation, eligibility for subsidies was tied to the adoption of farming practices that conserved soil, protected water quality or preserved wetlands (Kelley and Lodoen 1995).

The federal income tax and federal estate tax are also creations of the twentieth century, and the focus of even more debate than property rights. Both types of taxes have also been imposed by the majority of states. Real property taxes assessed by local governments to finance schools, streets, police protection and other local services have increased steadily nationwide and in dramatic spurts in urbanizing areas. All three types of taxes play a significant role in farmland conversion and preservation.

As the scope and intensity of land use and environmental regulation has increased, so has opposition to such regulation. The late 1980's and 1990's have spawned numerous property rights and "wise use" movements that seek to limit the regulation of the use of private property. Legal challenges to land use and environmental regulations usually focus on the takings clause of the Fifth Amendment to the Constitution, which provides that private property shall not be taken for public use without just compensation.[3] Until 1922, the takings clause had been ruled to apply only to the direct, physical appropriation of real property. The Supreme Court held in that year that it also applied to regulations that went "too far."[4] Courts have struggled ever since to determine when a regulation of land goes too far, and the issue has yet to be completely decided.

## Types of Laws Influencing Land Use

There are at least five types of laws that influence land use and farmland conversion:

1. Laws that directly regulate the use of land; for example, zoning (Box 3.1), subdivision control, site plan approval, and environmental regulations such as effluent and emission limitations.

2. Laws that give an individual landowner the right to seek redress for damage done to his property by the use of a neighboring property; for example, nuisance laws (Box 3.2).

3. Laws that tax the use of land, either directly or indirectly. Taxes may be levied on income derived from the use of the land, on capital gains from the sale of the property, or on the value of the land as part of an inheritance. Local governments impose real property taxes on land, the amount sometimes depending on how the property is used.

4. Laws that subsidize a particular use of land. Federal programs that support commodity prices or farm income may promote agricultural land use while federal and state highway and sewer projects favor residential and commercial uses of property.

5. Laws that allow or encourage, but neither mandate nor subsidize, certain land uses; for example, state statutes that authorize the voluntary donation of conservation easements or government funded educational programs on methods to control farmland erosion.

Box 3.1  Zoning.

Zoning is the primary form of land use control in the United
States. New York City adopted the first comprehensive
zoning ordinance in 1916, and other cities followed suit.
Rural zoning did not become prevalent until the late 1960's
and early 1970's, and many rural areas still have no form of
zoning. The basic premise of zoning is the separation of land
uses—each type of land use is given its own zone in which
other land uses are prohibited. Conflicts between incompatible uses are thus avoided. Differing compatible uses may be
permitted together in mixed zones. The principle legal basis
for zoning is the *police power*—the authority of government
to enact laws promoting the health, safety, morals and
general welfare of its citizens. The police power is conferred
on the states by the *Tenth Amendment* to the United States
Constitution[5], and the states in turn delegate the police
power to local governments. The United States Supreme
Court first upheld the constitutionality of zoning in 1926 in
*Village of Euclid, Ohio vs. Ambler Realty Co.*[6]

Box 3.2  Nuisance.

A nuisance is generally defined as an unreasonable interfer-
ence with the use or enjoyment of land. Determining what is
unreasonable will involve a balancing of the nature of the
offending use with the use and location of neighboring
properties. A rendering plant operating in a residential area
is an extreme example. Certain agricultural operations, such
as feedlots and hog barns, may also be considered nuisances
when located near homes or other types of businesses. *Right-
to-Farm* statutes have been enacted in every state in an
attempt to limit farmers' nuisance liability. Some of these
statutes protect farmers whose operations predate the
neighboring non-farm use. Other statutes only limit the
liability of farmers who follow agricultural best management
practices, and some statutes combine both concepts (AFT
1997). The effectiveness of right-to-farm laws is questionable
given the many court decisions holding agricultural operations to be nuisances despite the statutes (Hamilton 1992).

Laws may fall into more than one category. For example, a law that taxes income obtained from a specific use of land on a more favorable basis than income derived from other uses of the same land in effect provides a subsidy for the favored use. Similarly, zoning ordinances that allow high-profit uses such as residential development on some parcels, while limiting other parcels to lower profit activities such as agriculture, may provide extra value to the residential parcels by limiting the supply of developable land. This windfall to the owners of the residentially-zoned land is arguably a subsidy. The different types of laws do not function in a vacuum but interact in often complex ways.

Laws addressing farmland conversion come from several sources including:

- Statutes enacted by Congress and by state legislatures.

- Ordinances enacted by counties, cities, towns and other local governments

- Regulations issued by federal, state and local administrative agencies

Federal and state courts refine statutory law by their interpretations made in the course of applying the statutory law in individual cases. Some law, such as the concept of nuisance, is derived from the English common law as modified by state court decisions through the years. Common law is, for the most part, judge-made law and not the product of legislation.

Superimposed over statutory, administrative and common law are the provisions of the United States Constitution. States also have constitutions that may contain provisions identical or similar to those found in the Constitution. State courts, however, may give such provisions interpretations that differ significantly from those given the corresponding provisions of the federal Constitution.

Laws are the means by which a democracy implements public policy. Public policies are meaningless without effective laws, while contradictory public policies will often result in laws that appear at cross purposes. The success of any policy, including those intended to preserve farmland, will depend on the type of laws chosen to implement the policy, the resources allocated to enforce those laws, the level of public support for the laws, and the presence or absence of conflicting laws.

## Federal Law

The federal government has rarely attempted to regulate land use directly—state and local governments have had almost exclusive jurisdiction in this area. However, the New Deal era saw much discussion about the federal role in reducing soil erosion on American farmland. Federally supported Soil Conservation Districts were encouraged to adopt land use programs. Many districts formed land use committees, but little mandatory land use regulation was enacted. World War II production needs generally put an end to this experiment (Lehman 1995).

The concept of federal land use regulation did not die, however. In 1973, Congress debated the Land Use Policy and Planning Assistance Act that would have required the states to adopt comprehensive statewide land use plans, but would not have mandated the content of such plans. Supporters of the bill cited the loss of agricultural land to sprawl as a major argument for enactment. The bill passed the Senate but was narrowly defeated in the House of Representatives, and Congress has not seriously addressed any form of national land use planning since (Lehman 1995). Nevertheless, Federal law continues to have a major influence on the location and rate of farmland conversion.

### Federally Funded Projects

Federally funded public works projects such as roads and sewers have encouraged sprawl. Dams have inundated farmland, and federal facilities such as military bases have converted other acreage. Development spawned by federal projects has frequently consumed more farmland than is taken by the projects. The public works funding authorized by federal statutes has been both in the form of direct federal expenditures for construction and as grants to states and localities. These laws have in effect subsidized the economic activities that resulted in farmland conversion (Council on Environmental Quality 1974).

Other types of federal public works projects have subsidized agricultural production. Irrigation projects funded by the Bureau of Reclamation, for example, have permitted the cultivation of millions of acres of arid land that otherwise could not have been farmed. This water has provided a continuing subsidy to agriculture, though one that may expire as other uses compete for the water and the irrigation reduces the soil's productivity. Ironically, the water from the federal projects may ultimately allow the conversion of this farmland to urban uses.

### National Environmental Policy Act

Other federal statutes have been enacted to mitigate the environmental and land use effects of federal and federally funded projects. These can be generally referred to as environmental review statutes (Olson and Rosenberg 1978). However, many of these laws contain only procedural requirements, and once the required reviews are completed, the projects may proceed regardless of their effects.

The best known of these laws is the National Environmental Policy Act of 1970[7], which gave rise to the environmental impact statement or EIS. An EIS is required of all major federal actions significantly affecting the quality of the human environment. A major federal action can include federal construction projects, federal grants and the issuance of federal permits for private activities. In the EIS, the federal agency must analyze the environmental impacts of the proposed action and alternatives to the proposed action. Short-term gains must be weighed against permanent losses of productivity and resource availability.

Regulations[8] implementing the act specify that environmental impacts include both direct and indirect effects. Indirect effects include those caused by private development facilitated by the project such as the housing subdivisions that follow a federally funded sewer line. Federal agencies have been specifically required to address in their EIS the effects of proposed projects on prime and unique agricultural lands.[9]

The National Environmental Policy Act does not require, however, that the federal agency abandon or modify an action shown to have an adverse effect on the environment including agricultural land. All that an agency is required to do is study the project or other federal action and make public its findings. Political pressure may then be brought to bear on the project or the project may be challenged in court on other grounds, but NEPA itself will provide no legal basis to stop it once the procedural requirements of the Act have been satisfied.

### Farmland Protection Policy Act

In 1981, Congress passed the Farmland Protection Policy Act.[10] The act begins with a statement of seven Congressional findings. These findings include that the nation's farmland is a unique natural resource, that each year a large amount of the nation's farmland is irrevocably converted to nonagricultural use, that continued farmland conversion may threaten the ability of the United States to produce sufficient food and fiber to meet its domestic and export needs, and that federal actions in many cases result in farmland conversion. The act then states its purposes to minimize the extent to which federal programs contribute to the unnecessary and irreversible conversion of farmland to nonagricultural uses and to ensure that to the extent practicable federal programs are compatible with state, local and private programs to protect farmland.

The act applies to federal and federally financed construction projects and to the management of federal lands but not to federal construction related to national defense, to private construction requiring a federal permit or license or to construction on lands already zoned for or otherwise committed to development. USDA provides evaluation criteria for use by federal agencies,[11] and technical assistance to states, local governments and nonprofit organizations that wish to develop farmland preservation programs.

However, procedural compliance is all that is required of an agency. A federal agency that has reviewed a program or a project and determined that it will cause significant farmland conversion may nevertheless proceed with the program or project without modification. Furthermore, with one exception (court action by a state governor—which no governor has yet done), there is no private right of action to enforce even the act's procedural requirements (Daniels and Bowers 1997). Section 4209 of the act states that the statute:

"...shall not be deemed to provide a basis for any action, either legal or equitable, by any person or class of persons challenging a Federal project, program, or other activity that may affect farmland..."

### Farms for the Future Act

Congress enacted the Farms for the Future Act in 1990.[12] The act authorized the federal government to guarantee loans to state trust funds made by private lenders. The loans in turn were to be used by the trust funds to purchase threatened farmland or to purchase development rights or conservation easements (Box 3.3) on such land. Only Vermont's farmland preservation program (see Case 1) used the act, purchasing easements on 44,000 acres of farmland (AFT 1997). The Farms for the Future Act is now inactive.

Box 3.3   Conservation Easements.

A conservation easement is a voluntary, legally recorded agreement that places restrictions on the use of land. The holder of the easement, usually a governmental agency or a private, nonprofit organization, has the right to enforce the restrictions. A conservation easement can be thought of as relinquishing some of the "sticks" from the proverbial "bundle of sticks" that make up property rights. The land-owner retains all rights not specifically deeded to the holder of the easement. An easement may either be for a term of years or in perpetuity. Conservation easements on agricultural land prohibit or severely limit the subdivision of the land and its development for nonagricultural uses. Easements generally do not grant the public any right of access. The owner may farm and reside on the property and may sell the land or will or give it to his or her children. The property remains subject to the easement, however, following the sale, inheritance or gifting. Conservation easements can be either donated or sold, and donors of permanent conservation easements may receive substantial tax benefits. Private organizations that hold and enforce conservation easements are often referred to as "land trusts."

## FAIRA Farmland Protection Program

Additional funding for farmland preservation was authorized in the 1996 farm legislation, the Federal Agricultural Improvement and Reform Act (FAIRA).[13] Section 388 of FAIRA, known as the Farmland Protection Program, authorizes the Secretary of Agriculture to purchase conservation easements or other interests on not less than 170,000 nor more than 340,000 acres of farmland with prime, unique, or other productive soil. Eligible land must be the subject of a pending offer to purchase a conservation easement by a state or local government. The easement must be for the purpose of protecting topsoil by limiting non-agricultural uses of the land. The act authorizes the Secretary to use not more than $35 million of Commodity Credit Corporation funds to make such purchases.

USDA, acting through its Natural Resources Conservation Service (NRCS), made an initial round of easement purchases in fiscal year 1996. The agency entered into cooperative agreements with 37 state and local governments in 17 states. The agreements obligated USDA to pay $14.3 million toward the purchase of conservation easements on approximately 76,000 acres on 200 farms. The state and local government recipients were required to match the federal grants on a 50-50 basis. Each easement is required to contain a clause authorizing the NRCS to enforce the easement if the state or local government fails to do so.

NRCS agreed to pay only $1.92 million to purchase easements in fiscal 1997. Grants were made to six state and five local programs. However, the balance of the $35 million authorization is expected to be available in 1998.

The current cost of agricultural conservation easements ranges from $500 to $10,000 per acre (AFT 1997). With more than one million acres of farmland being developed each year, it is obvious that the Farmland Protection Program's $35 million authorization is woefully inadequate to save but a tiny percentage of threatened acreage.

## Farm Loan Programs

Under the 1985 Farm Bill,[14] farmers unable to repay certain loans from the Farm Services Agency (FSA), previously the Farmers Home Administration, are permitted to discharge part of the loan balance by selling FSA a fifty-year conservation easement on wetland, upland or highly erodible land that secures the loan. However, few farmers have expressed interest in the easement program (Daniels and Bowers 1997). The 1985 farm legislation also authorizes FSA to place conservation easements on farmland that comes into federal ownership through foreclosure on its loans.[15] The Secretary of Agriculture is also required to place easements on certain foreclosed wetlands properties.[16] These provisions have had limited use as well.

### FAIRA Farm Programs

Federal farm legislation has supported commodity prices and farm income since the 1930's, and these subsidies may have prevented or delayed some farmland conversion by keeping farmers in business. However, the Federal Agricultural Improvement and Reform Act of 1996 has replaced price and income supports with a series of fixed, declining payments to farmers that will terminate in the year 2002. Thereafter, farm prices will be determined by the market and, absent new legislation, the historic safety net for farm income will disappear (USDA 1996).

Federal programs that may continue to subsidize agriculture in the next century include crop revenue insurance that protects farmers from major declines in crop prices. Soil and water conservation payments under federal programs like the Conservation Reserve Program and the Environmental Quality Improvement Program may also subsidize farmers by paying them to idle highly erodible land and by funding other projects necessary to control soil erosion and other agricultural pollution (USDA 1996).

It is questionable how much farmland will be preserved by farm programs that subsidize production or conservation but do not require permanent restrictions on conversion. Some FAIRA programs use conservation easements, but most do not. The Wetlands Reserve Program employs both permanent and thirty-year term easements to protect wetlands that might otherwise be farmed. The Conservation Reserve Program, on the other hand, uses ten- to fifteen-year contracts to take highly erodible farmland out of production. Once these contracts expire, there are no restrictions on either returning the land to production or converting it to other uses. In these two examples, permanent protection from conversion to residential, commercial or industrial uses is afforded only a portion of wetland areas and none of the agricultural land.

Subsidy programs may defer but ultimately will not prevent farmland conversion. The subsidies are unlikely to compete with rapidly escalating real estate prices particularly as their amounts decline under FAIRA. Linking mandatory, permanent restrictions on farmland conversion to eligibility for those subsidies that remain would be a more effective approach to preserving farmland.

### Federal Estate Taxes

The estate tax is a percentage of the value of a person's estate, generally payable within nine months of death. Each individual has a personal exemption from estate and gift taxes, known as the unified credit, which shelters combined lifetime and testamentary (conveyed in a will) gifts up to a certain maximum amount. While the maximum has been $600,000, the Taxpayer Relief Act,[17] enacted by Congress in 1997, gradually increases the amount of the exemption to $1,000,000 in the year 2006. The exemption amount in 1998 is $625,000. An individual may also give or will an unlimited amount of property to a spouse free of estate and gift taxes through the marital exemption.

The Taxpayer Relief Act also provides for the exclusion of up to $1,300,000 of qualified family-owned business interests from a decedent's taxable estate. However, this amount includes the unified credit amount, so the maximum exclusion is $1,300,000, not $1,300,000 plus the unified credit. Some family farmers may be able to take advantage of this exclusion.

In areas facing urbanization, farming operations that are land rich but cash poor must often be sold, in whole or in part, to pay federal estate taxes notwithstanding the unified credit and the marital exemption (Daniels and Bowers 1997). In some states, state estate and inheritance taxes must be paid as well. Estate tax thresholds may be exceeded by the farms' land values alone. It is not uncommon for farmland in high growth areas to sell for $5,000 to $10,000 per acre or more. A five hundred acre farm valued at $6,000 per acre might be appraised for estate tax purposes at $3,000,000 excluding the value of the improvements. Obviously, farm structures, the farmhouse, equipment, livestock and other property can substantially increase the estate tax value of what is generally regarded as a medium-sized farming operation.

Even when properly used, the marital exemption, the unified credits of both farm spouses and the family-owned business interests exclusion will not be sufficient to avoid all estate taxes in this example. Substantial sums will be due. Estate tax rates begin at 37% and quickly move to the top rate of 55%.

With advance planning, some additional relief may be afforded by the valuation provisions of Section 2032A of the Internal Revenue Code.[18] 2032A allows farmland to be valued for estate tax purposes at its farmland value rather than its value for development. If the unified credits and other exclusions have already been used, there will still be tax owed on the 2032A land, but the amount will be less. The benefits of 2032A are capped at $750,000, that is the provision can only be used to reduce the estate tax value of farmland by a maximum of $750,000. Under the Taxpayer Relief Act, this amount will be increased by a cost of living adjustment for the estates of people dying after 1998.

The assumption in our example of the proper use of two unified credits and other exemptions is often incorrect. The estate planning and document drafting necessary to take advantage of the unified credit and other provisions of the tax code are complex and expensive. Farmers are often reluctant to pay lawyers and accountants when there are more immediate needs for their limited cash. Also, many farmers have incomplete information about estate and inheritance taxes. The unified credit of the first spouse to die is frequently lost. Many farmers begin estate planning only after the death of their spouse who has left everything to him or her.

In general, it is larger, wealthier farmers who take advantage of the tax breaks afforded by good estate planning. These are the same farmers who may be best able to pay some tax. In areas with high priced farmland due to development pressure, estate taxes do not help redistribute land to new and beginning farmers or level the playing field between new entries and the children of farmers. Instead, estate taxes push farmland away from farmers into the hands of developers and handicap the farmers who manage to pay the taxes on their parents' estates, either by depleting limited cash resources or by forcing the sale of a part of the farm.

The combination of estate taxes and rising farmland prices also makes it difficult for farmers to address the interests of their non-

farming heirs. The children who leave the farm may be less likely
to let their shares of the farm ride with their farming siblings if
the value of those shares has grown large through inflated real
estate prices. It is harder for the farmer to come up with other
resources, such as cash or insurance proceeds, sufficient to fund
an equal inheritance for the non-farming children. The pressure
grows to sell the farm, and developers, not farmers, do the bidding.

### Tax Breaks for Farmland Preservation

Section 170(h)[19] of the Internal Revenue Code permits a charitable deduction to be taken against income taxes for the value of
conservation easements. The value of an easement is determined
by subtracting the fair market value of the property subject to the
easement from the fair market value of the property before the
easement is donated. In areas where the development value of
farmland is higher than its agricultural value, this deduction can
be significant, ranging from 10% to 50% of the property's original
value depending on the restrictiveness of the easement. Landowners who sell conservation easements for less than their full value
may be able to take a deduction for the difference. Unfortunately,
many farmers do not have enough ordinary income to take advantage of the full tax deduction even though it may be taken over six
tax years.

Beginning in 1998, the gift of a conservation easement may
also reduce a farmer's estate tax burden by excluding a portion of
the value of easement encumbered land from the farmer's gross
estate. Section 508 of the Taxpayer Relief Act[20] permits the exclusion from a decedent's taxable estate of up to 40% of the value of
land subject to a conservation easement. The maximum exclusion
is $100,000 in 1998. The exclusion maximum increases incre-
mentally to $500,000 in 2002 and later years. The exclusion is in
addition to the maximum exclusion allowed for family-owned
business interests. However, this exclusion is limited to easement
lands located within 25 miles of a metropolitan area, national
park or national wilderness area, or within 10 miles of a national
urban forest. The act imposes other limitations.

Section 508 is a watered down version of legislation promoted
by the Piedmont Environmental Council of Virginia for many
years. The original proposal would have excluded 100% of the
value of easement encumbered land located within 50 miles of a

metropolitan area or national park. The effectiveness of the new legislation in preserving farmland remains to be seen.

In some states, easement encumbered farmland is automatically valued for real estate tax purposes at its agricultural use value rather than its value for development purposes. In states where this is not the law, the easement may nevertheless help to reduce the tax assessment on the land.

Despite the tax breaks, there are limits to the amount of farmland that will be preserved through the donation of easements. Easements are voluntary. Some farmers, or their heirs, desire to cash in on the farm's development value. They often view that value as their retirement policy. If only a few farmers in a given area donate easements, the patchwork of farms left when the others sell out may not provide the critical mass needed to support a viable agriculture. Also, easements may not be given on the best farmland in a region, leaving farmers on the least productive land and developers on the good farmland.

Table 3.1   Farmland preserved by major land trusts (Daniels and Bowers 1997).

| Land Trust | Farmland Acres Preserved |
|---|---|
| Montana Land Reliance | 76,347 |
| American Farmland Trust | 40,266 |
| Vermont Land Trust[1] | 36,580 |
| Marin (CA) Agricultural Land Trust | 25,600 |
| Columbia (NY) Land Trust | 6,647 |
| Napa County (CA) Land Trust | 6,050 |
| Lancaster (PA) Farmland Trust | 4,300 |

[1]With the Vermont Housing and Conservation Board.

## State and Local Law

### *Zoning*

The most common type of farmland preservation program at the state and local level is direct regulation through zoning. Except in large cities, most zoning ordinances contain agricultural zones. The uses permitted in such zones vary widely from jurisdiction to jurisdiction. In many jurisdictions, agricultural zones are simply holding areas for land slated for future development. In the meantime, farming and low density residential activities are permitted by right. Eventually rezonings will be granted permitting higher density residential or commercial uses. This type of zoning ordinance does little to preserve farmland even in the short term. It may even encourage premature farmland conversion by allowing developers to leapfrog over more expensive land closer to the city to create new communities on the urban fringe.

Other agricultural zoning ordinances are enacted with the objective of long-term farmland preservation. These true agricultural zoning ordinances can take several forms. In each case, however, agricultural activities are the preferred land use, and uses that would conflict with agricultural activities are limited, prohibited or regulated. Agricultural zones include:

- Large lot zones where only one dwelling unit is permitted on each parcel with minimum parcel sizes mandated from 10 acres to 200 acres or more (Table 3.2).

- Area based allocation zones where the number of permitted dwellings is based on the size of the overall parcel, but where the lots are required to be small (1-3 acres) and clustered so as to preserve the maximum amount of farmland.

- Exclusive agricultural zones where only farming activities and associated residential and commercial uses are permitted.

- Conditional use zones where only farming activities are permitted by right, but other activities may be permitted as special uses upon an affirmative showing that they will not conflict with the agricultural uses.

Table 3.2   Examples of county agricultural zones using minimum lot sizes (Daniels and Bowers 1997).

| County | Minimum Lot Size in Acres on Which to Build a Dwelling | Main Type of Farming |
|---|---|---|
| Woodford, Kentucky | 30 | horses |
| DeKalb, Illinois | 40 | cattle, grains |
| Fresno, California | 40 | fruits, vegetables |
| Baltimore, Maryland | 50 | horses, grains |
| Marin, California | 60 | dairy, cattle, sheep |
| Rock, Minnesota | 80 | cattle, grains, hogs |
| Waseca, Minnesota | 160 | grains, hogs |
| Deschutes, Oregon | 320 | cattle |
| Madera, California | 640 | cattle |

In jurisdictions with **large lot** agricultural zoning, subdivided parcels must contain the minimum acreage specified by the ordinance. With limited exceptions, such as mother-in-law apartments and houses for farm laborers, only one dwelling may be constructed on each parcel. However, that dwelling is not required to be occupied by a farmer or otherwise used for farm purposes. Non-residential improvements are usually limited to barns, garages and other farm type structures. Industrial and commercial land uses not associated with farming are prohibited.

Using a 320-acre (half-section) farm as an example, a large lot zoning ordinance with a forty-acre minimum lot size would permit the farm to be divided into eight parcels of equal size. The minimum lot size must be chosen carefully if large lot zoning is to preserve agricultural land and promote actual agricultural use of that land. If the lot size is too small, farms may be sold as hobby farmettes, estate properties or recreational lands. If the lot size is too large, it may make it difficult for beginning farmers to acquire land, and agriculture in the area will stagnate.

There are two types of **area based allocation** ordinances used by counties and townships. The first is a fixed area based ordinance such as "quarter/quarter" zoning where one non-farm dwelling lot is permitted for each quarter of a quarter section of farmland (40 acres). To preserve farmland, however, the lot size is restricted, often to a maximum of one to three acres.

In our example, under quarter/quarter zoning, eight residential lots could be subdivided from the 320-acre farm (eight quarter quarters). But, if each lot is limited to two acres in size, a total of only 16 acres of the farm is used for residential purposes (not counting the original farmhouse). The balance of 304 acres is preserved for agricultural use as a single farm.

The other type of area based ordinance is variable area based zoning in which lots are allocated according to a sliding scale with the permitted residential density decreasing as the size of the farm increases. As with fixed area based ordinances, the maximum lot size is kept small. Under a variable area based ordinance, a 160-acre farm might be permitted four lots. The 320-acre farm would only be allowed six lots, and a 640-acre farm would be permitted ten lots. In our example, the variable area based ordinance preserves more farmland than the fixed area based ordinance.

Both fixed and variable area zoning frequently include the requirement that the residential lots be clustered together on one part of the farm. This maximizes the size of the remaining farm fields, minimizes the interface between the residential lots and the agricultural land to reduce land use conflicts, lowers infrastructure costs and keeps lots off of the better agricultural soils on the farm.

**Exclusive agricultural zoning** ordinances prohibit all non-farm structures and land uses within agricultural zones. Such ordinances may require site specific review of all new farm dwellings. **Conditional use zoning** allows non-farm dwellings or other non-agricultural uses in otherwise exclusive agricultural zones upon an individualized determination that such dwellings are compatible with the surrounding agricultural uses. Special use permits and special exceptions are often used to approve or deny a proposed conditional use.

An exclusive agricultural zoning ordinance would prohibit altogether the subdivision of our 320-acre farm. It would allow the construction of one or more dwellings on the farm only if the dwellings were to house the farm owner or persons employed on the farm. The ordinance might also allow the construction of additional houses for family members of the farm owner even if they did not work on the farm.

Most agricultural zoning ordinances are enacted by counties and townships. State enabling legislation authorizes such ordinances but rarely mandates their adoption. Oregon is an exception (see Case 19). The state's 1973 Land Conservation and Development Act required its counties to inventory farmland and to adopt exclusive agricultural zoning for their best farmland.[21] All Oregon counties have complied. More than 16 million acres of agricultural land have been protected from development (AFT 1997). Washington State, Vermont, New Jersey, Hawaii and Maryland also have enacted statewide legislation addressing both growth management and farmland preservation. Although important, to date none of these have been as effective as Oregon's law.

Whether zoning ordinances can successfully preserve farmland depends on a number of factors. The first is the political will of the electorate and their officials. Zoning preserves farmland when the community is committed to that objective. Zoning can be easily changed, however. New voters and new officials can quickly undo even the best agricultural zoning programs.

The administrative competence of government officials is another factor. A loosely administered ordinance or one not based on sound planning or good science is susceptible to legal challenge or the erosion of public support. Officials who grant too many variances weaken the ordinance; so do officials who apply the ordinance so inflexibly as to produce absurd results. Underfunding of planning offices is one reason for poor administration. Conflicts of interest on the part of officials who are also landowners is another. A third is pressure exerted by family and friends, particularly in rural communities.

The economic health of the farming community is a major factor. Farmers who are making money and intend to stay in agriculture are more likely to support strict agricultural zoning. They see such zoning as a way to help maintain the critical mass of farmland and to isolate farmland from conflicts with other land uses. Farmers who are in financial distress are less likely to support such zoning. They wish to preserve all of their options including the sale of their land for development.

The amount of growth pressure from surrounding areas is also important. Farmland close to metropolitan areas with high growth rates is at risk even when restrictively zoned. The more competing uses there are for farmland that provide higher returns than farming, the harder it becomes to maintain the zoning. The political and economic pressures placed on local government by development interests are difficult to withstand.

Although it is the most common agricultural preservation program, agricultural zoning is hardly universal. The National Agricultural Lands Study (USDA 1981a,b,c) reported that 270 counties in the United States had agricultural zoning in 1981. A recent survey by the American Farmland Trust found that 700 counties and townships had some form of agricultural zoning. These jurisdictions were located in 24 states. However, 62% of these jurisdictions were in Wisconsin and 13% were in Pennsylvania. The survey authors believe that, given the limited response rate to the survey, they may have underestimated the actual number of counties with agricultural zoning (AFT 1997). On the other hand, Daniels and Bowers (1997) found just more than 500 jurisdictions nationwide using agricultural zoning.

There are 3,043 counties in the United States. Obviously the vast majority do not regulate agricultural land use. The same can probably be said for most townships.

Subject to the constitutional and statutory limitations discussed later, preservation of agricultural land by zoning does not require landowners to be compensated. Land use regulation has the effect of "wiping out" that portion of the farmland's value attributable to otherwise possible nonagricultural uses such as housing developments and shopping centers. Zoning may enhance, however, the farmland's value as agricultural land by protecting it from conflicting uses. Agricultural zoning may also increase the value of nearby land zoned for residential or commercial development by limiting the amount of land available for those uses, in effect giving the latter landowners a "windfall." The value of homesites close to an agricultural zone may also be increased because of the desire of many people to live near protected open space.

Box 3.4   Agricultural Districts.

Agricultural district programs should not be confused with agricultural zoning. Agricultural districts are voluntary associations of farms in a particular geographic area formed to keep land in agriculture. Sixteen states have laws authorizing the creation of agricultural districts. Farmland owners join agricultural districts for fixed, renewable terms. The benefits of district membership vary widely from state to state. They may include eligibility for property tax relief, limits on annexation and eminent domain, limits on local government regulation of agricultural activities, protection against nuisance suits, and eligibility for purchase of development rights programs. A few programs prohibit the development of land in the district for the duration of its term and place restrictions on withdrawing from the district before the term expires. Agricultural districts do not preserve farmland permanently.

### *Purchase of Development Rights*

Other types of programs attempt to preserve farmland by compensating farmers for part or all of the development value of their property. Fourteen states have programs to purchase farmland development rights. These programs are usually referred to either as PDR (purchase of development rights) or PACE (purchase of agricultural conservation easements). The state programs have protected more than 450,000 acres (Table 3.3), and there are also local PDR programs that have protected additional acres (Table 3.4).

In PDR programs, farmers whose land is located in areas planned for long-term agricultural use are paid the difference between the value of their land for development purposes and its value for farming. Conservation easements are then placed on the farmland restricting its use to farming and related purposes, usually in perpetuity. The farmers retain ownership of their land subject to the restrictions and continue to farm. The land can be sold or willed to an heir, but the easement restrictions run with the land and are binding upon all future owners.

PDR programs have an element of permanence missing in regulatory schemes and enjoy great acceptance among farmers

Table 3.3   Purchase of agricultural conservation easements by
state PACE programs to March 1998 (AFT 1998a).

| State | Year of inception | Acres (parcels) preserved | Funds ($ million) spent |
|---|---|---|---|
| Connecticut | 1978 | 25,658 (170) | 75.6 |
| Delaware | 1991 | 16,107 (66) | 17.9 |
| Maine | 1987 | 540 (3) | 0.5 |
| Maryland | 1977 | 139,828 (968) | 127.2 |
| Massachusetts | 1977 | 40,040 (441) | 96.2 |
| New Hampshire | 1979 | 5,500 (35) | 5.1 |
| New Jersey | 1983 | 43,294 (278) | 129.0 |
| Pennsylvania | 1988 | 107,626 (845) | 172.2 |
| Rhode Island | 1981 | 2,429 (31) | 13.2 |
| Vermont | 1987 | 69,693 (202) | 34.8 |
| U.S. total* | | 459,864 | 684.0 |

*Colorado, Kentucky, California, Michigan and New York also
have PACE programs.


Table 3.4   Status of selected local PACE programs, March 1998
(AFT 1998b).

| Jurisdiction | Year of inception | Acres protected | Farms protected | Funds spent to 1997 | Funding source |
|---|---|---|---|---|---|
| San Juan Co., WA | 1991 | 972 | 10 | $1,822,401 | real estate transfer tax |
| Sonoma Co., CA | 1990 | 25,146 | 62 | $38,830,056 | .25% sales tax, state bonds |
| City of Boulder, CO | 1984 | 1,092 | 6 | $6,833,732 | sales tax |
| Forsyth Co., NC | 1984 | 1,236 | 20 | $1,869,965 | county budget reserve, FPP[1] |
| U.S. total | | 143,389 | | $255,000,000 | |

[1]Farmland Protection Program of the 1996 Federal Agricultural
Improvement and Reform Act.

because they provide compensation and are voluntary. But, current PDR programs have several major problems, the first being chronic underfunding. Legislatures and local governing bodies have not appropriated enough money to permit the purchase of all development rights needed to protect farmland within their jurisdictions. The federal Farm Protection Program's commitment of $35 million to assist state and local governments in purchasing easements is helpful to select jurisdictions but clearly inadequate to address the larger problem.

Second, the voluntary nature of most programs means that government may be outbid by developers for key parcels, particularly when funds are limited. This can result in a checkerboard pattern of protected and unprotected land. Land use conflicts increase, and the critical mass of farmland necessary to sustain agriculture in the area may not be preserved.

Third, there is an overriding question whether society should have to pay for the preservation of valuable farmland resources, particularly when those resources are economically productive to the owners as farmland. If some compensation is justified, the question becomes how much. Should the farmer be paid for the entire development value of his or her land including the portion of the land value attributable to public improvements such as roads, sewers and schools paid for by the taxpayers? Or should the farmer be paid some lesser amount?

The most successful PDR programs will likely be those that purchase development rights in areas already subject to a good comprehensive plan and restrictive agricultural zoning. The planning will have reduced the rise of land values by keeping public infrastructure out of the agricultural area. The zoning will have regulated away part of the farmland's development value leaving less to be compensated by the PDR program.

A final question is who should pay for PDR programs. There are several options including local or state taxpayers, federal taxpayers, real estate developers and owners of land in areas planned for residential, commercial or industrial development. Zoning land for high density uses confers value on that land. That value may be even greater when large amounts of other land in the jurisdiction are zoned for agricultural use. Building roads and other public improvements near land also increases its value. Land planned and regulated for development receives benefits far in excess of taxes paid on the land. A portion of this windfall might be the appropriate source for funding PDR programs. Taxation would be one way to tap the windfall. Governments could use ad valorem taxes, transfer taxes, capital gains taxes or a combination thereof for this purpose.

### Transfer of Development Rights

A few jurisdictions have adopted a different type of "windfalls for wipeouts" program known as transfer of development rights (TDR). Under this system, development is severely limited in agricultural zones, but parcels in such zones are assigned a certain number of development rights. These rights cannot be used on the agricultural parcels but may be sold to landowners in receiving zones that are planned for development.

The landowners who purchase the development rights are then permitted to develop their receiving zone properties to higher residential or commercial densities than would otherwise be allowed. When properly implemented, the program will create a market in the development rights. The bidding of buyers and sellers of those rights will determine their price at any given time. The price received by landowners in the agricultural zone for their development rights compensates them for the development restrictions imposed on their property. The receiving zone owners in turn are made to pay for the extra value given their land by being zoned for development.

TDR programs are tricky. First there must be political acceptance. Then the right amount and type of land must be placed in the agricultural and receiving zones. There must be demand for higher densities in the receiving zones and enough development rights in the agricultural zones to satisfy that demand, but not so many as to depress their price to the point that farm owners are not adequately compensated. The administrative costs of such programs are high, and governing bodies and their staffs must be fairly sophisticated to make them work. However, unlike PDR programs, there are no capital outlays.

Montgomery County, Maryland is probably the best example of a jurisdiction that has successfully implemented a TDR program. Nationwide, relatively few farmland acres have been protected by TDR programs, but these programs may hold more promise in the future.

Table 3.5   Examples of local governments with TDR programs for farmland, 1997 (AFT 1997).

| Jurisdiction | Date ordinance enacted | Total acres protected | Notes |
|---|---|---|---|
| Charles Co., MD | 1991 | 315 | Sale of one right results in easement on balance of property |
| Montgomery Co., MD | 1980 | 38,251 | Mandatory program |
| Lumberton Township, NJ | 1985 | 0 | |
| Windsor, CT | 1993 | 0 | Open space preservation program |
| Shrewsbury Township, PA | 1991 | 15 | Rights may be transferred to low-quality farmland only |
| Island Co., WA | 1984 | 88 | |

Box 3.5   Differential Assessment.

Differential assessment is a form of farmland tax relief found in 49 states that allows eligible farmland to be assessed for property tax purposes at its value for agricultural use rather than at its fair market value (which reflects its value for development). There are three different forms of differential assessment—preferential assessment, deferred taxation and restrictive agreements. Each type can result in substantial tax savings for farmers, which may allow a farmer to stay in business and avoid selling out to developers. However, the relief is often temporary. Other factors, such as the farmer's retirement or conflicts with residential neighbors, may eventually lead to the conversion of the farm. Differential assessment programs have frequently been abused by land speculators who buy farmland, lease the property to a neighboring farmer, and pocket the tax savings while waiting for the best time to sell or develop the property. Some programs recapture a portion of the unpaid tax if the property is developed, others do not.

## The Takings Issue

Agricultural zoning, purchase of development rights and transfer of development rights represent three different approaches to restricting non-agricultural uses of farmland. All three recognize that farmland has a "development value" for urban uses in addition to its agricultural use value. Agricultural zoning regulates away, without compensation to the owner, all or part of farmland development value. PDR programs use government funds to compensate owners for part or all of their land's development value. TDR programs make the owners of land planned for development compensate those whose land is to be preserved for agricultural use.

The decision on whether to compensate farmland owners for lost development value is first and foremost a political decision. No farmland preservation program will be implemented without public support. A decision to regulate rather than compensate will be subject to additional scrutiny under the takings clause of the Fifth Amendment to the United States Constitution, under the takings provisions of some state constitutions and, in a few states, under the standards set by state takings legislation.

"...nor shall private property be taken for public use without just compensation."

— Fifth Amendment, United States Constitution

The concept of a takings has evolved dramatically since the adoption of the Bill of Rights, and it will continue to evolve as the nation faces new land use challenges. How the takings concept is interpreted and applied in the future will be the single most important legal factor in determining where and how the country uses its land. This in turn will be decided by politics. The relative weights assigned by the community to preserving the public goods associated with farmland on the one hand and maximizing private property rights on the other will determine which property rights may be regulated without compensation and which may be restricted only through the exercise of eminent domain.

## The Evolution of the Takings Clause

There were few precedents for the takings clause during the colonial period and those were limited to the physical expropriation of property. The Massachusetts Body of Liberties, adopted in 1641, contained a provision requiring compensation for the government seizure of personal property. The 1699 Fundamental Constitutions of Carolina, drafted by John Locke, required compensation for real property taken for the construction of highways. These provisions, however, were the exceptions, and compensation for the physical taking of property was generally left to the discretion of the colonial legislatures (Treanor 1995).

The takings clause of the Fifth Amendment was not one of the provisions of the Bill of Rights that the states demanded as a limitation on the powers of the federal government. This restriction apparently originated with the drafters of the Amendments and was not debated at the state ratifying conventions. The statements of James Madison and others indicate that the intent of the provision was to require compensation only when the government physically took property. The takings clause may have been included primarily as a response to the rather arbitrary confiscation of private property by armies during the Revolutionary War.

Prior to 1870, there were relatively few decisions of the United States Supreme Court interpreting the Fifth Amendment takings clause. Later that century and in the first part of the next, the Supreme Court addressed the takings clause in the context of statutes enacted to abate nuisances. These cases began to set the boundaries and limits of the police power and made a clear distinction between the exercise of the police power and the exercise of the power of eminent domain. The latter required the payment of compensation under the Fifth Amendment. The former did not.

The 1892 case of Mugler v. Kansas[22] was the principal decision in this series. In Mugler, the Supreme Court upheld a Kansas statute declaring that establishments manufacturing alcoholic beverages were nuisances and directing that they be closed. The statute rendered Mr. Mugler's brewery virtually worthless. Justice Harlan wrote for the Court:

The power which the States have of prohibiting such use by individuals of their property as will be prejudicial to the health, the morals, or the safety of the public, is not,—and, consistently with the existence and safety of organized society, cannot be—burdened with the condition that the State must compensate such individual owners for pecuniary losses they may sustain, by reason of their not being permitted, by a noxious use of their property, to inflict injury upon the community.

The Court made fundamental changes to Fifth Amendment takings jurisprudence in 1922. Ignoring the precedent set by *Mugler* and other earlier cases, Justice Oliver Wendell Holmes stated for the majority in the case of Pennsylvania Coal v. Mahon[23] that:

[t]he general rule at least is that while property may be regulated to a certain extent, if regulation goes too far it will be recognized as a taking.

The concept of a regulatory taking was thus born.

*Pennsylvania Coal* involved a challenge to a Pennsylvania statute which prohibited companies from mining coal when its removal would cause subsidence. In this case the coal company owned the mineral rights but not the surface rights of the property at issue. The Court found that this statute did indeed go "too far" by making it commercially impractical to mine coal with nearly the same effect as if the coal had been appropriated by the state.

In reaching this decision, the Court employed a balancing test in which the regulatory interests of the state were compared to the "extent of diminution" of the value of the property. Holmes wrote:

[w]hen it reaches a certain magnitude, in most if not in all cases there must be an exercise of eminent domain and compensation to sustain the act. So the question depends on the particular facts.

The *Pennsylvania Coal* decision provided, however, little specific guidance as to how much "diminution of value" is excessive and when a regulation has gone "too far." Also unaddressed was the question of compensation for a regulatory taking during the period of time between the statute's enforcement and the date it is declared unconstitutional.

For many years after, the Supreme Court made little attempt to define the limits of the regulatory taking concept established in *Pennsylvania Coal.* Then between 1978 and 1994, the Court issued a series of opinions that taken together constitute current federal takings law. These decisions have not addressed all the unanswered questions in *Pennsylvania Coal,* and they contain some contradictory statements. Much is left for future decisions, including the application of the takings clause to specific agricultural zoning ordinances.

The holdings of the principal Supreme Court takings cases concerning land use regulation are summarized in Box 3.6. In these decisions, the Court expanded upon the concept of a regulatory taking discovered by Holmes in Pennsylvania Coal. The Court first created a balancing test for takings of less than all of a property's value, then established a categorical rule for regulatory takings depriving property of all economic value. It recognized a remedy in damages for temporary regulatory takings. In certain situations the Court shifted the burden of proof from the offended landowner to the government imposing the regulation. The Court addressed, but did not fully resolve, the question of how you define property for the purpose of imposing takings analysis. Lastly, the Court created new rules for determining when the government may require that a portion of regulated property be dedicated to public use without having to pay for it.

What do these Supreme Court decisions mean to jurisdictions that wish to regulate the use of agricultural land rather than compensate owners for lost development value? They certainly mean that local and state governments will have to be careful in how they draft land use regulations and particularly in how they develop individualized, factual records supporting their decisions. The "legitimate state interest" behind the regulation must be defined with precision. The application of the regulation to specific land must be backed up with good general and site specific planning. A failure to do so may give property owners a basis to challenge the regulation with severe financial and land use consequences for the losing jurisdiction.

Box 3.6   U.S. Supreme Court Takings Decisions—1978–1994.

**Penn Central Transportation Company v. City of New York (1978):**[24] No taking; upheld an historic landmarks preservation law that prohibited the construction of an office tower atop Grand Central Station; applied a balancing test weighing the nature of the government action, the economic impact on the property owner, and the extent to which the regulation interfered with distinct investment-backed expectations.

**Agins v. Tiburon (1980):**[25] No taking as to zoning ordinance as a whole; no decision as to whether ordinance as applied to this specific property was a taking because owner had not applied for a permit; Court held that the application of a general zoning ordinance to a particular property will effect a taking only if the ordinance does not advance legitimate state interests or if it denies an owner economically viable use of the land; the question requires a weighing of private and public interests.

**First English Evangelical Lutheran Church v. County of Los Angeles (1987):**[26] Court did not rule on whether interim ordinance preventing any construction in a flood ravaged area caused a taking, but held that damages would be an available remedy for an ordinance causing a temporary regulatory taking during the period of time the unconstitutional ordinance was in effect.

**Nollan v. California Coastal Commission (1987):**[27] Taking; California Coastal Commission conditioned permit to rebuild beach house on dedication by owners of easement providing public access to beach; Court held there was not an essential nexus between the easement exaction and the state interest in providing beach access.

**Lucas v. South Carolina Coastal Council (1992):**[28] Taking; Coastal Council imposed regulation prohibiting all construction on two beachfront lots; Court announced new rule that a *per se* taking occurs when a regulation deprives a landowner of all economically beneficial or productive use of his land; the Penn Central balancing test does not apply in such

*Continues*

Box 3.6 *Continued*

> cases; exception to the new rule when the prohibited use not part of owner's title such as restrictions based on the state's nuisance laws.
>
> **Dolan v. City of Tigard (1994):**[29] Taking; permit to expand store conditioned on dedication of a greenway and a bike path to the city; Court held that degree of the exactions demanded by the city were not roughly proportional to the projected impact of the land owner's project.

On the other hand, none of the decisions described in Box 3.6 should be used to support the belief that agricultural zoning is dead. The Supreme Court has not gone nearly as far in restricting land use regulation through the Fifth Amendment as the popular press and certain property rights groups would suggest. Zoning is still a constitutionally permissible means of land use regulation. The Supreme Court cases all begin by stating that zoning or other forms of land use regulation are a legitimate exercise of the police power. The issue to be decided is whether the application of an ordinance to a particular parcel causes a taking. Regulations may still reduce the value of property without effecting a taking. The question remains, by how much.

None of the Supreme Court takings decisions has involved situations where government has imposed restrictions severely limiting the use of large parcels of land. The agricultural zoning options described earlier have survived challenges in state and lower federal courts but have not been tested under the Fifth Amendment in the highest Court. The properties before the Court have generally been of only a few acres in size or smaller, and have been residential or commercial in nature, not agricultural.

However, under its current takings rules, the Supreme Court should uphold most properly administered agricultural zoning ordinances that are based on sound planning. There is a legitimate state interest in preserving farmland and in protecting the agricultural economy of a particular area. Few agricultural zoning ordinances will deprive a farmland owner of all economically beneficial use of such property unless his or her property is too small, too arid or has very poor soils. In addition to farming uses, most agricultural zoning ordinances permit limited residential or commercial development.

## The Future of the Takings Issue

### Economy vs. Ecology

The more important question, as our population and the demand to convert farmland to other uses increases, is in what direction will takings law evolve? The Supreme Court's future approach to an agricultural zoning takings case may depend on whether the Court views farming as merely a holding activity to be pursued only until the property owner can realize the property's "highest and best" use through some type of development or whether the Court sees intrinsic, long term value in farming itself. This in turn may depend on whether the Court takes a traditional economic view or an ecological view of the nature of real property ownership.

Professor Joseph Sax believes that the *Lucas* decision (see Box 3.6) reflects Justice Scalia's philosophy of a "transformative economy" where parcels of land are separate, boundary lines are crucial, landowners have no obligations and land is inert waiting for its owner to exercise his dominion to transform the land into something better than its original condition. Economic development has a preference over other values in this scheme (Sax 1993).

Conversely, *Lucas* shows Scalia's distrust of the "economy of nature" where connections dominate, single ownership of an ecological unit is rare, land is governed by ecological needs, landowners have certain obligations to their property and land has a dual purpose, both transformative and ecological.

Agricultural zoning programs will fare best if the Court appreciates the interrelationships between land and farming and between farming and the long term interests of society, and understands how those connections depend on the ecological relationships among different parcels of land (see Chapter 2). Agricultural zoning will suffer if the Court views farming as an economically inferior use of land to be conducted on isolated parcels until better uses come along.

## Takings vs. Givings

Another issue likely to be addressed in future takings cases is the "givings issue" (Thompson 1994). Should, in cases where compensation for lost development value is required, a government have to pay for that portion of a property's development value attributable to public infrastructure financed by taxpayers rather than the landowner? A new road, sewer or school built near farmland almost always increases the development value of that land. If the government must compensate the farmland owner for that increased value when it purchases development rights on the farm, government is not paying the land owner for value created by the owner or by the normal action of the market. It is paying for value created by public funds expended on public works. If government is not required to pay for this part of farmland value, PDR dollars will buy development rights on much more farmland. In cases where government is regulating away development value, courts should find fewer compensable takings.

The U.S. Supreme Court may not always have the last word on what regulations cause takings. The constitutions of most states contain takings provisions. In some state constitutions, the takings language is identical to that of the Fifth Amendment. In other cases, the language is quite different. State courts may interpret the state takings clause in accordance with federal takings jurisprudence, or they may give the state takings prohibition a different, usually broader, interpretation. A state or local regulation found not to cause a taking under the Fifth Amendment may nevertheless be held unconstitutional under the state constitution.

Twenty states have enacted takings legislation. The majority of these laws simply require that new state or local regulations be reviewed prior to enactment to determine whether they will have adverse effects on property values. They do not necessarily stop the regulation from being implemented and do not require that compensation be paid to the affected land owners.

Four states, however, have passed laws that require compensation be paid if a law or regulation reduces the value of land subject to the regulation. Texas requires compensation be paid if the reduction in value exceeds 25%. In Louisiana, the percentage is 40%, and in Mississippi, 25%. The Florida statute requires compensation but does not specify a percentage. These takings statutes apply only to state and local laws and regulations, not to federal laws (AFT 1997).

### The Future of Farmland Preservation Law

Many perceive a trend towards a more expansive interpretation of the Fifth Amendment and similar state constitutional provisions and in favor of the enactment of additional state takings legislation. The continuation of such a trend would certainly limit existing farmland preservation programs and discourage new ones. However, no natural or absolute law commands that such a trend be followed.

Until 1922, there was no such thing as a regulatory taking. Nine judges invented that concept. It is not found in the Constitution. Nine judges could certainly overrule the holding of *Pennsylvannia Coal* and later cases. Although a complete reversal is unlikely, future regulatory takings cases could just as well limit the scope of a taking as expand it. The same would apply to state courts.

State takings legislation can be repealed. This has already occurred in Arizona. Takings legislation has even less claim to permanence than the court-made regulatory takings concept. The definition of a taking is fundamentally a political issue. Society must decide whether it can afford to allow the continued conversion of massive amounts of farmland and, if not, whether it can afford, or should be required, to pay farmland owners not to develop that land. It is a question of resource allocation, both between competing land uses and between the present and future generations. In making these decisions, society is again creating and defining property rights as it did during the founding of the country. The objectives may be different now, but the process is much the same.

If the answer is to preserve land and to either pay no compensation or to limit it to extreme situations, the takings issue will gradually go away. Legislators, Presidents, governors, and judges, whether appointed or elected, will read the political will of the electorate and interpret the takings clause accordingly. If instead, society's response is ambivalent or favors unlimited property rights, the takings clause and related legislation will be the legal mechanism used to preserve property rights, and rapid farmland conversion will continue.

Even without the limitations imposed by the takings clause, farmland preservation laws are not likely to solve the problem if implemented just at the local level or even at the state level. Farmland conversion is a national problem, and only national policies and programs can assure that all farmland requiring protection is saved.

National programs could help avoid the parochial nature of local decision making and keep local jurisdictions from sacrificing farmland as they bid against each other for economic development. National programs could use a combination of regulations and incentives to assure that farmland was preserved at the local level. They could help ease the burden on certain agricultural areas where farmland preservation would foreclose other economic opportunities.

National programs would not necessarily replace local and state efforts. State and local programs could be used as the mechanism to implement national policy. Strong national policies would also reduce the conflict between federal laws that encourage development and those that promote farmland preservation.

## Recommendations for Changes to the Law

In addition to the general need to restrict the application of the takings clause and to develop strong national farmland preservation policies, there are specific changes or applications of the law that would favor the preservation of farmland. These include:

- Use conservation easements in farmland preservation programs whenever possible to assure that farmland is preserved permanently and not subject to the whims of elected local government officials.

- Where land use regulation is ineffective, increase funding for Purchase of Development Rights programs. Funding should be obtained by taxing real estate speculation profits and the windfall portion of development value attributable to owning land zoned for development. Funding could also be obtained by taxing the benefits accruing to neighboring property owners from the preservation of farmland in their area.

- Condition eligibility for federal farm program benefits on farmland preservation. Require farmland owners to encumber their land with permanent conservation easements before receiving payments.

- Condition state and local eligibility for federal monies on the state adopting and enforcing effective farmland preservation laws.

- Deny federal, state and local subsidies to infrastructure investments that stimulate farmland conversion.

- Exempt from federal and state estate taxes the full value of farmland that is encumbered by a permanent conservation easement.

Law is not immutable. Our founding fathers created a new legal order on the continent, and those laws evolved as the country grew. Law must continue to evolve if we are to have any success in preserving adequate farmland resources for future generations.

## Endnotes

1. 21 U.S. (8 Wheat.) 543 (1823).
2. Tee-Hit-Ton Indians v. United States, 348 U.S. 272 (1955).
3. U.S. Const. amend. V.
4. Pennsylvania Coal Co. v. Mahon, 260 U.S. 393 (1922).
5. U.S. Const. amend. X.
6. 272 U.S. 365 (1926).
7. 42 U.S.C. §§ 4331 et seq.
8. 40 C.F.R. § 1502.16.
9. Executive Office of the President, Council on Environmental Quality: Memorandum for Head of Agencies on Analysis of Impacts on Prime or Unique Agricultural Lands in Implementing the National Environmental Policy Act (August 11, 1980).
10. 7 U.S.C. §§ 4201 et seq.
11. 7 C.F.R. §§ 658 et seq.
12. 1990 Act, §§ 1465 et seq.; 7 C.F.R. pt. 1980, subpt. J.
13. 7 U.S.C. §§ 4201 et seq.
14. 7 U.S.C. § 1997; 7 C.F.R. § 1951.909 & Exh. H.
15. 7 U.S.C. § 1985(c)(3)(B).

16. 7 U.S.C. § 1985 (g).
17. I.R.C. §§ 2010, 2033A.
18. I.R.C. § 2032A.
19. I.R.C. § 170(h).
20. I.R.C. § 2031(c).
21. ORS §§ 215.203 et seq.
22. 123 U.S. 623 (1887).
23. 260 U.S. 393 (1922).
24. 438 U.S. 104 (1978).
25. 447 U.S. 255 (1980).
26. 482 U.S. 304 (1987).
27. 483 U.S. 825 (1987).
28. 505 U.S. 1003 (1992).
29. 512 U.S. 374 (1994).

# References

AFT. 1997. Saving America's Farmland. American Farmland Trust, Washington, D.C.

AFT. 1998a. American Farmland Trust summary available 7 July 98 at http://farm.fic.niu.edu/fic-ta/tafs-pacestate2.pdf

AFT. 1998b. American Farmland Trust summary available 7 July 98 at http://farm.fic.niu.edu/fic-ta/tafs-paceloc2.pdf

Browne, W.P., J.R. Skees, L.W. Swanson, P.B. Thompson, L.J. Unnevehr. 1992. Sacred Cows and Hot Potatoes: Agrarian Myths in Agricultural Policy. Westview Press, Boulder, CO.

Council on Environmental Quality. 1974. Cost of Sprawl. U.S. Government Printing Office, Washington, D.C.

Daniels, T., and D. Bowers. 1997. Holding Our Ground: Protecting America's Farmland. Island Press, Washington, D.C.

Hamilton, N.D. 1992. Right-to-farm laws revisited: Judicial consideration of agricultural nuisance protections. Journal of Agricultural Taxation and Law 14:195-228.

Kelley, C.L. and J.A. Lodoen. 1995. Federal Farm Program conservation initiatives: Past, present, and future. Natural Resources & Environment (winter): 9:3:17.

Lehman, T. 1995. Public Values, Private Lands: Farmland Preservation Policy, 1933-1985. University of North Carolina Press, Chapel Hill.

Olson, A.H. and R. Rosenberg. 1978. Federal environmental review requirements other than NEPA: The emerging challenge. Cleveland State Law Review 27:195-229.

Opie, J. 1994. The Law of the Land: Two Hundred Years of American Farmland Policy. University of Nebraska Press, Lincoln.

Sax, J.L. 1993. Property rights and the economy of nature: Understanding Lucas v. South Carolina Coastal Council. Stanford Law Review 45:1433-1455.

Thompson, E. 1994. The government giveth. The Environmental Forum (Mar/Apr.):22-26.

Treanor, W.M. 1995. The original understanding of the Takings Clause and the political process. Columbia Law Review 95:782-887.

USDA. 1981a. National Agricultural Lands Study: Final Report. U.S. Department of Agriculture, Washington, D.C.

USDA. 1981b. National Agricultural Lands Study: The Protection of Farmland: A Reference Guidebook for State and Local Governments. U.S. Department of Agriculture, Washington, D.C.

USDA. 1981c. National Agricultural Lands Study: Case Studies on State and Local Programs to Protect Farmland. U.S. Department of Agriculture, Washington, D.C.

USDA. 1996. Provisions of the Federal Agriculture Improvement and Reform Act of 1996, AIBN 729, U.S. Department of Agriculture, Economic Research Service, Washington, D.C.

# 4

## The Economics of Farmland Conversion

*Lawrence W. Libby and Patrick A. Stewart*

### Introduction

This chapter presents an economic perspective on the causes and consequences of farmland conversion. It also considers the alternatives for policy intervention in the pattern and pace of land use change, and potential impacts of those alternatives. Land, the productive factory of agriculture, goes out of farming and into other uses and from other uses into farming as the result of thousands of individual decisions—by farmers, developers, communities, public officials, consumers, taxpayers—based on the available use options and information about their likely impact. While land use conversion may appear haphazard, even chaotic, there is a certain logic or at least a predictability to those changes. Economics helps one understand the process of land use change and predict the particular use pattern that emerges.

### Economics and Choice

Economics is about the process of human choice. It is about how people in the real world decide how best to use their time, energy and other resources to achieve what they want. Personal values and attitudes shape what a person thinks is important, while cultural and social mores establish acceptable bounds on personal action. A person lives and decides things within a complex structure of rules that governs his or her interactions with others. The rules of the game of land use include laws that establish rights of ownership and the rights of non-owners to define the limits of private action (see Chapter 3). The rules also direct the process of exchange within a market; they define what is being bought and sold and enforce transactions.

As a social science discipline, economics is a set of abstractions that may be used to understand a complex market that entails many individual transactions. These abstractions enable the practitioner to identify the causes and effects of changes in resource use. The "tendency to economize" is an observation about human behavior fundamental to the discipline and its role in analyzing resource use. People tend to seek as much "good" as possible from a given budget of time, dollars and other resources. They will likely accept anything valuable if it is free and are not inclined to pay for something if they can get it free (the "free rider" problem). They respond in predictable ways when the price of a given product or service increases or decreases relative to other prices. They know that at some point consuming another unit of a certain product produces less utility than did the previous unit, and eventually entails more additional cost than benefit.

The economizing tendency, then, is a prediction about human choice that is robust in understanding patterns of land use at the urban fringe, a farmer's decision to sell land and seek another line of work, or a community's inclination to seek development. These basic behavioral observations may be formally expressed in mathematics and are the conceptual underpinning for such statistical tools as econometrics or linear programming. But at root, they are quite simple, even intuitive, observations about how people seem to act. People preferring a given pattern of land use express those preferences in a market, or they organize and press their demands for an institutional change that reinforces their interests. While we *know* that real people are motivated by more than self interest and economizing, that they care about their neighbors and future generations and act with notions of right and wrong (see Chapter 6), they seem to act "as if" they were economizers; at least assuming so can be extremely useful in predicting land use patterns. Within the general process of economizing, choices regarding time and scarcity are particularly important.

## Treatment of Time

The old saying that "time is money" must have been authored by an economist! Time is a scarce resource to be allocated among different activities that are valued by an individual. Except for the most clever, people cannot do many things at once, so a real cost of engaging in a particular activity is the value of what else you might have done at that time. This is what economists refer to as *opportunity costs.*

Time is particularly important in farmland issues because the choices we make today in the use of productive land will clearly affect the options available to future decision makers. Future returns to any resource use are by nature uncertain, as are the economic and social conditions that will shape choices made by future land users. A current resource owner will choose among relevant land use options based on expected returns to those uses through a reasonable planning horizon. Anticipated returns are worth less than present returns because the owner is uncertain about the future benefits and must sacrifice today to receive future benefits. On the other hand, those who do not own the land under consideration will likely have different values for present and future land uses. Because the opportunity costs of foregoing present gains for future returns are less for non-owners than for owners and the potential costs of the loss of future land use options are higher, conflict between owners and non-owners is predictable. In other words, *the social rate of time preference differs from the private rate.*

The rate of resource use through time is particularly important for non-renewable exhaustible natural resources, including farm-land (Heal 1986). Future consumers will have fewer non-renewable resources, but may have higher levels of technology and capital to complement those natural resources. However, the limited supply of physical resources necessary for plant growth is still a concern for many people. There is no precise "optimal" rate of depletion or conversion of farmland with time because future users are unable to state their needs.

Thus, economics can help interpret the allocation of the productive capacity of good farmland through time, but the techniques of standard economic analysis can prescribe no single best distribution for future farmland use. Rather, it is a matter of competing judgements about the tradeoff between present and future land use (Ferejohn and Page 1978).

### Economics and Scarcity

Thomas Robert Malthus foresaw in 1798 an inevitable imbalance between human reproductive success and the capacity to produce food. He observed that population tends to increase geometrically, while food production only increases arithmetically. This inevitably leads to scarcity, widespread hunger and eventual social destruction.

World population has, however, continued to increase at a rapid pace, particularly in the developing countries where population tripled between 1930 and 1990, from 1.3 billion to 4.1 billion. The rate of natural increase in developing countries is nearly three times that of developed countries. Recent United Nations statistics show a world population of nearly 6 billion worldwide and predict an increase to 9.4 billion by 2050 (United Nations 1996).

Malthus has yet to be proven wrong, of course. Population continues to rise at about 1.5% per year (PRB 1997), but predictions of impending doom have been largely ignored as more is learned about potential substitutions for scarce resources and more efficient use of current resources (Stiglitz 1979). Ultimately, however, there must be some widely accepted means for reducing the rate of global population increase or Malthus may well be right.

The United States is richly endowed with natural resources critical to the nation's industrial growth, food supply, and general economic progress. Impending scarcity of any nonrenewable natural resource (including farmland)[1] is signaled by an increase in relative cost of those production inputs. When that happens, people adjust. They have the incentive to find new resources, or man-made substitutes in production processes. Thus physical resource scarcity is mitigated by human innovation, reducing reliance on the primary natural resource (Barnett and Morse 1963).

In the farmland case, there is no indication that the land component of food production inputs has yet become economically scarce. The relative cost of land in food production, and in fact the real price of food, have both declined since the early 1900's (Schultz 1977). The increase in the *economic* supply of farmland in the twentieth century has come largely through the substitution of capital and management for land and labor. These substitutions have come not because of real scarcity, but the realization that economic improvement in the United States and elsewhere requires freeing people and land from the day-to-day rigors of producing food. This was primarily the result of deliberate public policy rather than market adjustment. Once output per acre increased, people left for the cities and total land in farming declined. So in a real sense, we are living off the surplus from past investments. The economics of food scarcity *could* cause the re-cultivation of farmland by clearing of buildings and parking lots, though the pain of waiting for hunger to trigger such an adjustment process would be substantial.

The economics of scarcity is really about the process of human adjustment through time. Resource markets adjust as individuals respond to the changing economic results of a declining supply of exhaustible natural resources. But markets cannot handle all of the adjustments people may desire. Some natural resource services cannot be distributed through markets because the cost of excluding non-paying users is high. Public policies explicitly dealing with those natural resource services are required.

Markets are nested in an institutional context that establishes rights of market participants and the terms for their participation. Changes in the rules for resource access, including private property rights, are brought about through the policy process. Such policy changes adjust the terms and conditions for market exchange to reflect value placed on the non-owner services of the land. For example, active farmland may also produce wildlife habitat, a land service considered scarce by some participants in the policy process. Options for the farmer may be adjusted accordingly to increase the supply of habitat. When the concept of natural resource scarcity is expanded to include such non-priced land services, one may be more cautious about future availability of farmland. Further, some of the technological substitutions forming the basis for optimism about future supply of resources may have negative side effects on the non-priced services. Energy intensive fertilizers and pesticides raise concerns about long term energy consumption and may affect water quality (Daly 1979).

Decisions affecting certain non-market natural resource services may be irreversible, or reversible only at considerable cost
(Krutilla and Fisher 1975). The decision to convert highly productive farmland to a shopping center is for all practical purposes
irreversible because of the cost of re-conversion and the likelihood
of permanent destruction of ecological function. Thus, resources
are not fully mobile among competing uses. No parcel of farmland
is unique in services generated. But each small, seemingly incon-
sequential land use decision may have results that are very
expensive to reverse and may contribute to a situation with significant "dead end" problems for society. "Marginalism can lead
us into a perverse process in which society becomes progressively
worse off" (Kelso 1977).

### Economics and Real Human Behavior

While conventional economic theory is built on the assumption
of self-interested, profit maximizing behavior, we know that real
individuals are more complex than that. They will sacrifice to help
others even when reciprocity is not expected. Some departures
from self-interested economizing behavior may be from confusion
regarding the rules of the system rather than altruism[2] (Andreoni
1995). Other research suggests the importance of emotions such
as guilt, fear of risk, and sense of duty in modifying purely economic decisions (e.g., Frank 1991, Scholz and Pinney 1995).
Farmland protection policies that appeal to citizens' and land
owners' sense of duty may be more successful than those that
rely solely on enforcement of laws and regulations.

However, Milton Friedman, arguably the "pope" of neoclassical
economics, contends that alternative assumptions of human behavior are irrelevant to the inherent beauty of the economic model
built on the self-interest assumption. Whether or not the self-
interest assumption is an accurate description of human
motivation, it is useful in predicting results. Accuracy of prediction is the true test of a theory, he says, not the realism of its
assumptions, and on that basis the neo-classical model earns
high marks (Friedman 1953). The pattern of land use that evolves
with space and time at the mostly rural periphery of a city indicates the tendency of landowners to maximize economic returns.

As we attempt to determine how people behave, it is apparent that the institutional structure that defines rights of the

transacting parties is critical to any system of exchange or trade including the sale of land. People with different perceptions of risk and value come to agreement on the exchange of services and products of remarkable diversity, with no one really running the system. There seems to be an innate orderliness to it all, based on how humans behave when in search of improvement. "Somehow it (a pricing system) is a product of culture; yet in important ways, the pricing system is what makes culture possible. Smash it in the command economy and it rises as a Phoenix with a thousand heads ...." (Smith 1982). Economic theory is really a shorthand, a series of abstractions that describe patterns of human action, but in the process it must sacrifice information on the detailed actions of real people. People tend to go with "what worked last time," or rely on experience to avoid past mistakes. Uncertainty is rampant; its presence creates predictability of behavior in decision-making. The neo-classical assumption of perfect knowledge in selecting preferred options is really a special case; *un*certainty is the reality (Heiner 1983).

We contend that land policies of the future must be built on a more complete understanding of human motivation and action; that economic models based solely on an assumption of self-interest are not sufficient. Neoclassical economics helps us understand the direction of land use change; what is needed is an understanding of the magnitude and causes of these changes. Only then can truly effective land use policies be implemented.

## Land as an Economic Commodity

The assertion is often made that the primary reason we do not do better at protecting the quality of our landscape is that we treat land as a commodity rather than a resource. This distinction makes a good punch line, but has little real substance. Land has value to people for the services it generates. Some of those are captured in market price, though many are not. All of the benefits, the important attributes of land, have relevance *only* because people say so and are willing to act on that belief. In conventional economics, a buyer will pay for land based on what he expects to get from it in the foreseeable future. Expected future returns must be adjusted to reflect uncertain future economic conditions and opportunities missed by investing in land instead of an alternative.

In farming, land is the factory for food production, the combination of water, minerals and organic matter that supports plant growth when management, capital and labor are brought to the task. There are important *substitution effects*[3] as capital or management may generate more returns per unit of land. Further, land may itself be consumed when sand, gravel or minerals are extracted or when soil erosion rates exceed replacement rates.

Land is also location, a place to put income generating services relative to other activities. Its value comes from where it is, rather than its physical productivity. Land is unique in that its location is fixed. Certain factors like terrain, elevation, proximity to highways, cities, lakes, or mountains will influence location value.

Land also has value as a consumer good. Some people will buy land just to own it, for the intrinsic value of having exclusive physical access to a resource of unique character and location. Other on-site services may include habitat for wildlife, scenic beauty and isolation. A buyer's willingness to pay for given parcels of land will combine these various sources of utility in a unique way.

Non-owners of land also enjoy its services. Land provides scenic countryside, groundwater recharge, wildlife habitat, conversion of organic waste to useable nutrients, and its inherent importance as an ecological system (Brewer 1981). The balance between exclusive rights of the land owner captured in land price and non-exclusive rights of others to benefit from various land services are established in the institutions and rules that govern our society.

The overall pattern of land use evolves in a predictable fashion as people bid for land services within the structure of rules that influence how land may be used and the relative value of those uses. Those rules may include a local zoning ordinance, environmental restrictions, impact fees and taxes that affect the relative attractiveness of different land parcels, or that protect certain non-owner services. Farming is relatively land intensive, meaning that it takes more land per unit of output than is the case for some other land uses. Such land uses as housing or shopping centers are very capital intensive; others place a very high locational or consumer value on small land parcels. A new residence, for example, requires little land but benefits to the owner are substantial. As a result, if the rules permit, land will be bid away from farming to competing uses (Box 4.1). While there may be inertia of current use—that is, a crop farmer may find it difficult to convert to specialty horticulture, even for higher economic returns per unit of land, and he may resist the offers of non-farmers to convert his land to house lots—the tendency for change is clear and inexorable.

Box 4.1   Competition for land.

Studies at the urban edge uniformly show a large difference between the price that conventional farmers can afford to pay for land for agricultural use, and the price that a developer can afford to offer. Following are three examples drawn from the case studies presented later in this book:

(1) Case 13:  A dryland corn/soybean farmer in Lancaster County, NE might realistically pay $1,500 to $2,000 per acre for good farmland, while developers are paying $10,000 to $25,000 per acre for land near the boundary of the city of Lincoln.

(2) Case 17:  Rocky Mountain ranchland, valued at $1,500 to $2,000 per animal unit,* sells for two to ten times that amount for ranchette development.

(3) Case 21:  In southern Ventura County, CA, land acquisition costs must be below $10,000 per acre for a citrus operation to produce a profit. Actual acquisition prices near urban expansion areas are $25,000 to $35,000 per acre.

In some regions, intensive production of specialty vegetables or other niche crops can gross $10,000 or more per acre (e.g., Gettings 1990) and potentially outbid developers for small amounts of land. But given the low prices received for most agricultural products, it is impossible for most types of conventional agriculture to compete for land with residential or commercial development in the absence of citizen actions to remove the economic differential. For example, agricultural zoning or the purchase of development rights help to maintain agriculture in areas facing development pressure by removing development as a legal option, and proper estate planning (see Chapter 3) can enable the intra-generational transfer of farmland, denying developers the opportunity to bid.

* "Animal unit" refers to the amount of rangeland required to support a cow-calf pair.

Thus, in a real sense, access to land is a commodity that may be bought, sold or otherwise transferred within a structure of rights and obligations that define a land market. Competition for land has no meaning outside of that institutional infrastructure. And those rules and incentives change with time reflecting prevailing preferences and attitudes of the population.

## The "Why" of Farmland Protection—An Economic Perspective

We know that land use patterns result from many individual buyer and seller decisions made *within* an institutional context that defines the land market. Each transaction is based on expected returns to both parties. Economic theory says that an owner will keep a resource in a particular enterprise until the value of an alternative use exceeds returns to the current use. As discussed above, the expected returns for a buyer making a *bid* or a seller holding a *reservation price*, would reflect the utility derived from the many services that land produces. Some of those benefits may be measured in dollars, others not, but if they are exclusive to the owner or buyer, their value will be recorded in the price.

Some services or impacts of alternative land uses are experienced by parties beyond the buyers and sellers. Market prices do not capture *all* costs and benefits of land use options. In fact, virtually any transaction between two parties has consequences for others, costs which they cannot avoid or benefits for which they cannot be held accountable.[4] When external costs or benefits become significant enough to encourage those affected to organize and petition for protection, we have an *externality* that is policy relevant. If the pressure is great enough, the policy process may yield a change in market rules to force the people generating that negative externality to absorb it as part of the cost of production, or stop the activity altogether. On the benefit side, the producer of the positive externality may be rewarded for providing it, to encourage continuation, or even denied the right to stop. An example of the latter is the requirement that farmers continue providing endangered species habitat as a positive by-product of farming. These rule changes are the substance of land use policy.

Land markets may also fail to reflect that in some cases the transition from one use to another is irreversible. As discussed, no land use change is reversible without cost. For some uses the cost of reversing a decision to use resources in a particular way is very high, and for some the cost is infinite. A series of "rational" land use choices may produce a pattern of change preferred by no one, and irreversible when the ecological attributes necessary for food production and other services are destroyed. Some land use attributes are true *public goods* in the sense that enjoyment or consumption by one person does not limit their availability for others. Examples of this extreme case of positive externality are the vicarious enjoyment one may get from knowing that a particular species or fragile ecosystem is protected or the sense of security that future generations will have enough food (Krutilla and Fisher 1975, Libby 1997).

Reasons given for changes in policy to encourage retention of good farmland basically involve these positive externalities of actively farmed land that are not reflected in the returns to the farmland owner. These additional benefits suggest a social utility for farmland greater than private utility and therefore a socially optimal quantity of farmland that is greater than results from market transactions (Lopez et al. 1994). Further, failure to include the unpriced services of agriculture may result in lower investment in agricultural research and development than is socially optimal or desirable (Ervin and Schmitz 1996). The most important of these unpriced services are discussed below.

### Long Term Food Security—A Continuing Controversy

The question of adequacy of U.S. farmland to meet domestic and global food demand arrived on the national policy agenda with release in 1981 of the National Agricultural Lands Study (NALS; USDA 1981). The study reported that farmland was being converted to non-farm uses at the rate of three million acres a year. Of that total, one million acres a year were being permanently lost from farming.

The specter of rising food prices, declining exports and food shortage was picked up by the national media. "Typical headlines ran *The Peril of Vanishing Farmland* (New York Times), and *Farmland Losses Could End U.S. Food Exports* (Chicago Tribune)" (Easterbrook 1986). Shortly thereafter, questions were raised about the validity of the data and particularly the inferences drawn. Writing in *Science*, economist Julian Simon observed cynically that "false bad news" sells books and attracts grant dollars (Simon 1980). Brewer and Boxley (1981), both of whom had provided analyses as part of NALS, were likewise concerned that special interests, including public agencies, misconstrued objective data to suit their own needs. They questioned whether such large questions with obvious political significance were really amenable to objective analysis, or could be insulated from misrepresentation in the media.

Much of the debate about the relevance of NALS revolved around differences among academic disciplines. Land as a physical resource may be limited by the absolute confines of the globe's surface, but as an economic resource land supply expands in response to land-freeing technology and land prices that may bring additional supply to that use. Reassessments on that basis led many analysts to conclude, "U.S. cropland is certainly adequate to meet future domestic demand. Whether it is adequate to meet high export demand is less certain, but there is no need to panic" (Barrows and Chicoine 1984), and "the U.S. is in no danger of running out of food because of disappearing farmland" (Castle 1981). Robert Solow (1974) went so far as to assert that with productivity of natural resources increasing exponentially with time, perhaps the world can get along *without* natural resources. The second USDA appraisal of the condition and adequacy of the U.S. soil, water and related natural resources (USDA 1982) concluded in 1981:

> Under all of the scenarios projected for this appraisal, assumed demands for food and fiber in the year 2030 could be met on the cropland projected to be available. Under the intermediate scenario, which generally is continued current trends, production to meet demand in 2030 is projected to require slightly more than 218 million of the 347 million acres of cropland available. Under the "high stress" scenario, which combines higher export demand and smaller increases in yield, all of the 347 million acres available would be needed to meet demand. For every crop except grain sorghum, the model projects that under intermediate conditions fewer acres would be needed in 2030 than were harvested in 1982.

More recently, Ausubel (1996) and Waggoner et al. (1996) have expressed continued optimism regarding the ability of technological advances and human ingenuity to increase agricultural production. However, even if we know *how* to sustain productivity in the long run, that knowledge must be used by the millions of farmers who work the land, and by the billions of consumers who make demands on the land. Understanding and predicting behavior of people is the province of the social sciences, including economics, yet too few economists appreciate the ecological imperatives.

Pimentel and Giampietro (1994) have a pessimistic view of future food adequacy. They predict that rapid population growth in the United States combined with continuing degradation of arable land by erosion, salinization, depletion of irrigation water, and paving will result in the population exceeding the capacity of the land to support current levels of food and fiber consumption. The same processes, occurring at even faster rates, are seen globally.

Food scarcity and environmental degradation have been described as the *most* compelling challenges facing future global communities, creating the context and incentives for conflict on a massive scale (Kaplan 1994). Hungry people have little stake in a political system that has tolerated or even ignored scarcity. Any political change is an improvement, producing a volatile situation. And hungry people have little interest in soil conservation or protection of wildlife habitat—their priorities are more immediate. The issue of food security is not *just* related to famine. The lack of proper nutrition has been shown to have a marked negative and potentially permanent impact on both the physical and mental development of children (McKay et al. 1987). A recent report by the Johns Hopkins University School of Public Health (Hinrichsen 1997) estimates that almost 2 billion people worldwide are malnourished, and that 18 million people, mostly children, die yearly from malnutrition and related causes.

Food production scientists face difficulties in maintaining past rates of return to conventional technology. Additional returns to fertilizer application and varietal research are declining. Much current research effort is spent on just maintaining results of past productivity research, keeping up with new plant and animal pests, physical changes like salinization or desertification, and various economic shifts. World fertilizer use accounting for much of the productivity increase of the first seventy years of this century is declining in the 1990's as farmers throughout the world see the cost of additional applications falling below economic returns (Brown 1996). Even China, apparently still on the increasing returns portion of the production function for wheat and rice during the 1980s and early 1990s has seen a recent decline in fertilizer use.

In sum, the food adequacy rationale for farmland protection is really about risk management through time. It is about comparing the risks of basing future food production on a reduced land base with the consequences of protecting land for future food production and thereby foregoing other possibilities. In statistical jargon, this issue is about comparing the consequences of Type I and Type II errors on the hypothesis that there will be adequate farmland to meet future needs for food and fiber. The consequences of the Type I error, rejecting the true hypothesis and retaining more farmland than needed, would appear to be less socially disruptive than accepting a false hypothesis and preserving less land than needed for long term food security, the Type II error (Figure 4.1).

|  |  | Outcome if current farmland loss trends continue: | |
|  |  | Adequate farmland for future needs | Inadequate farmland for future needs |
| Policy decision | Continuation of current policies | No problem | Major disruption (Type II error) |
| | Policies to reduce rates of farmland conversion | Excess farmland (Type I error) | Manageable problems |

Figure 4.1   Payoff matrix illustrating the four possible outcomes of two different farmland preservation policies. Implementing more effective policies to preserve farmland is a conservative strategy, which if wrong results in the allocation to farming of more land than necessary. If continuation of current policies proves to be the wrong choice, the ramifications are much more severe. Prudence dictates that farmland be preserved. See text for discussion.

Your position on the matter depends on your confidence about continued technological substitution, attitudes about the future and judgement about what could have been done with the land unnecessarily kept in farming. Writing in opposition to local farmland protection programs, Brewer (1981) stated, "Such programs could be difficult, costly and disruptive to local and regional economies. The argument also ignores the costs that would be incurred if U.S. agriculture finds itself faced, without warning, with super-abundance and the need to suddenly reduce the amount of cropland in production."

We happen to be risk averse on this matter. We would concur with the general advice of Kenneth Arrow and other scientists writing for the 1994 Stockholm convention on economic and environmental policy "...given the fundamental uncertainties about the nature of ecosystem dynamics and the dramatic consequences should we guess wrong, it is necessary that we proceed in a precautionary way" (Arrow et al. 1995). As a society, we simply *must* take the long view.

### Natural Resource Services

Farmland contributes to many non-production ecosystem services including water supply and quality, air quality, and biodiversity (see Chapter 2). Dollar values have rarely been assigned to these services, but recent analyses suggest that they are of major economic importance (Costanza et al. 1997; Box 4.2). Awareness of the value of these services is important to policy design.

*Biodiversity*. A public good attribute of farmland is linked to protection of wildlife habitat, endangered species and biodiversity. Popular demand for retention of lands that support endangered species of plants and animals is reflected in the Endangered Species Protection Act of 1973. It applies to some farmland already, but we argue that the sense of well-being available to citizens from simply knowing that wildlife and threatened species are protected is part of the public good aspects of farmland use. This knowledge is "non-rival in consumption and non-exclusive" in that one person's receipt does not limit its availability to others. Such knowledge is part of the general public domain.

Box 4.2   Ecosystems provide valuable "services" worth
$33 trillion.

The "services" of the earth's ecosystems "represent part of
the total economic value of the planet," and are valued at
$33 trillion per year, according to an article by 13 ecologists,
economists, and geographers in Nature (May 15, 1997).
"Because ecosystem services are not fully 'captured' in
commercial markets or adequately quantified in terms
comparable with economic services and manufactured
capital, they are often given too little weight in policy decisions," the authors wrote. "This neglect may ultimately
compromise the sustainability of humans in the biosphere.
The economies of the Earth would grind to a halt without the
services of ecological life-support systems, so in one sense
their total value to the economy is infinite."

Among the 17 services provided by ecosystems are nutrient
cycling, including "nitrogen fixation, N, P, and other elemen-
tal or nutrient cycles" (valued at $17 trillion); erosion control
and sediment retention, including "prevention of loss of soil
by wind, runoff, or other removal processes, and storage of
silt in lakes and wetlands;" soil formation, including "weath-
ering of rock and the accumulation of organic material;"
pollination, including "provisioning of pollinators for the
reproduction of plant populations;" biological control, including "keystone predator control of prey species;" and genetic
resources, including "medicine; products for materials
science; genes for resistance to plant pathogens and crop
pests; pets; ornamental species; and horticultural varieties
of plants."

According to an article about the study in The New York
Times (May 20, 1997), "nature performs a long list of other
economic services as well. Flood control, soil formation,
pollination, food and timber production, provision of the raw
material for new medicines, recreational opportunities, and
the maintenance of a favorable climate are among them."

One way to put a value on such services, according to
Newsweek (May 20, 1997), "is to figure out what it would
cost to substitute technological fixes for what nature does.
Substituting chemical fertilizer for natural nitrogen fixation,

Continues

Box 4.2 *Continued*

> for instance, would cost at least $33 billion a year. Growing
> crops without soil by substituting the hydroponic systems
> beloved of urban gardeners would cost $2 million per acre in
> the United States."
>
> Source: Reprinted from *Alternative Agriculture News*, June
> 1997, published by Wallace Institute for Alternative Agricul-
> ture.

Reasons often cited for protecting biodiversity include potential
commercial value,[5] the value people ascribe to the existence of
specific endangered species, support for an ecological balance
that requires diverse species, and the ethical proposition that
protecting wildlife habitat is simply a proper human concern
and a reasonable policy objective (Wilson 1986, Metrick and
Weitzman 1996). Several studies have measured a public willingness to pay for the preservation of ecosystems or open space even
if the respondents did not expect to personally use the land (e.g.,
Silberman et al. 1992). Failure to include such non-user benefits
in the analysis of proposed resource protection efforts would
vastly understate the returns to such efforts.

Poorer quality farmland, because it is less intensively farmed,
may provide for a larger variety of species than more intensively
farmed cropland. Actively farmed land is not ideal for endangered
species or biodiversity, but it does infinitely more for those qualities than does a shopping center or other development. This is a
further argument to protect and farm the best land, leaving the
rest to nature (Huston 1993).

*Waste assimilation.* The United States produces 130 million
tons of sewage sludge annually, spreading 54% on farmland,
forests and other land, composting 9% and landfilling or inciner-
ating the remainder. U.S. citizens also produce about 200 million
tons of municipal solid waste each year, of which 24% is recycled
or composted, and the remainder buried in landfills or inciner-
ated (Miller 1998). Costs related to disposal in landfills or by
incineration exceed $40 billion per year.

Composting of the organic fraction of municipal solid waste and application of wastewater and sewage sludge to agricultural land reduces the load to natural systems, and turns an environmental liability into an economic asset. New England farmers have been able to capture some of the community benefits of the composting capacity of their farms by accepting organic wastes for a fee and then selling the composted material for fertilizer (Halstead et al. 1996). Similarly, many Midwestern farmers have contracted with nearby municipalities to receive sewage sludge or wastewater. There are inevitable logistical problems because wastewater must be applied even when it is raining and soils are nearly saturated. Also, metals and other toxics in some sludge may present problems. Still, land application is often a low cost disposal alternative for many communities, a valuable farmland service (Williams et al. 1977).

*Hydrologic functions.* Farmland may serve to mitigate, even prevent, flooding. Increased development results in more land area impervious to water, leading to a greater possibility of flooding, with greater runoff depth and volume, and lower levels of groundwater recharge. In a study of development in Akron, Ohio from 1960 to 1984, Harbor (1994) found that commercial development, with its extensive impervious surfaces, led to a 1820% increase in average runoff compared to undeveloped conditions, and high-density residential development led to a 1000% increase. As a result, Akron suffered a potential loss of 57,000 to 469,000 gallons per square mile per day in groundwater recharge. While such commercial and high-density residential development has obvious negative hydrological implications for the communities where it is happening, downstream communities will also be affected.

The importance of such natural resource services has led the European Union to undertake specific policies to subsidize farmer provision of various ecological services. At a top rate of about $380 per acre per year, farmers alter their production practices to protect water quality and wildlife habitat. They can participate at a level suitable to their own needs from the farm (Hackl and Pruckner 1996). Thus, there is a measurable value of natural resource services acknowledged and paid by the general taxpayer to the service provider. Whitby and Saunders (1996) estimate a supply function based on the additional cost a farmer must bear to provide such services, measured as the value of the farm productivity sacrificed to provide the services. When subsidies are offered to farmers and they accept, we can assume that the value of the services provided to the public is at least as great as the cost to the farmer for providing them. This approach to value estimation is in lieu of estimating demand for the services.

### Aesthetics and Rural Character

Farming is key to the history, character and general identity of many U.S. communities. It is an aspect of the countryside that people will vote and sacrifice to retain. Some amenity value of farmland may be captured in the price an individual will pay for proximity to farmland. Studies in Oregon (Nelson 1985) and Boulder, Colorado (Correll et al. 1978, Smith 1991) have shown a correlation between proximity to agricultural open space and higher home and lot prices. In the mid-1850's, Frederick Ohlmsted carefully documented the increase in property tax collections associated with proximity to a large open area in New York City, to justify the expense of what later became Central Park (Fox 1990). An alternative explanation for higher land value in areas where open space has been protected and development limited is the supply effect of fewer developable lots (Pollakowski and Wachter 1990).

Other amenity values are non-exclusive and non-consumptive, in that the amenity cannot be appropriated and withheld from others. These benefits are estimated through survey, asking people in various ways what they *would* pay to have the aesthetic quality, or avoid losing it. Bergstrom et al. (1985) used a mailed survey to estimate what residents of Greenville County, South Carolina would pay to prevent development of 72,000 acres of prime farmland. The amount they would pay for an acre tripled when the amount of remaining farmland was reduced by 75%. Beasley et al. (1986) used a bidding game to estimate what Alaskans would pay for the amenity attributes of farmland in a situation of rapid, large-scale development. Halstead (1984) used a similar bidding procedure to estimate what residents of three Massachusetts communities would pay to avoid development of nearby farmland. In all of these cases, willingness to pay is clearly related to the many positive attributes of nearby open farmland and the negatives of development, not just the aesthetic quality of the countryside.

Willingness to pay for the aesthetic value of farmland obviously varies markedly from place to place, among different age, education and income groups, and among alternative land use scenarios. As with any good, the lower the quantity of farmland to provide the aesthetic service, the higher the price a person would pay per unit. Although a rough idea of the actual price people would pay would help policy makers see more clearly the cost of failing to protect certain farmland acres, the precise amount of value is less important than the fact that it exists, can be demonstrated, and does affect policy positions taken relative to farmland protection. In fact, these non-owner open-space amenities are consistently more important to support for farmland protection efforts than are the direct farm services of locally grown produce or contribution to the local economy (Kline and Wichelns 1996).

While economists try to measure the aesthetic and psychological values of open space in dollars, environmental psychologists suggest that open land, including farmland, also has a beneficial effect on the emotional state of individuals. Experimental studies using slides with varying levels of natural and man-made features have shown a marked preference for natural environments over urban/built environments (Kaplan et al. 1972, Kaplan and Kaplan 1989). Cross-cultural studies in the United States and Sweden using physiological measures of stress and psychological measures of emotion suggest that nature scenes in either slide (Ulrich 1981) or film (Ulrich et al. 1991) format have properties that lower levels of stress, fear, anger/aggression, and sadness while increasing positive emotions. On the other hand, urban scenes such as buildings, traffic, or suburban strip malls tend to amplify these negative emotions (for further discussion of aesthetics and farmland, see Chapter 6).

### Cost of Sprawl

Another reason cited for supporting farmland protection is to reduce the public cost of servicing linear or scattered development. Protecting farmland as open space may be an important complement to the effort to curb costly urban sprawl. Residences tend to cost more to serve than they generate in tax revenue (Box 4.3), especially when scattered around the service center. Analysts in California's Central Valley estimated that low density development could claim nearly one million acres of farmland while a more compact pattern to accommodate the same number of people would take half as much land (AFT 1995; see Case 20). Additional studies by Burchell and associates indicate that planned, guided development consumes 20% to 45% less land than does linear or unplanned growth, costs for roads and streets are 15% to 25% less, and water and sewer costs are 7% to 15% less (Burchell and Listoken 1994).

The fiscal consequences of alternative development mixes have been a topic of study by communities for several decades (Burchell and Listoken 1993). The American Farmland Trust has produced a general "cookbook" approach to estimating the cost of community services for various development assumptions (AFT 1994). Commercial and industrial land uses tend to generate far more public revenue than they cost in services, while middle in-come single family housing, even in coterminous development patterns, is a revenue drain. That conclusion has led local offi-cials to seek commercial growth and discourage residential growth. However, this single-minded response to expected fiscal impacts can produce economic imbalance—new commercial firms need trained employees, and real advantages may not be realized. In DuPage County, Illinois, for example, analysts discovered that additional non-residential growth was associated with generally rising tax levies for all residents as people demanded more ser-vices to cope with greater urban pressure (DuPage County Regional Planning Commission 1991).

Thus, local economy is a widely acknowledged and telling argu-ment for encouraging growth patterns that leave large areas of active farmland. It is not a matter of choosing between agriculture and growth, but of encouraging higher density residential devel-opment consistent with available public services while retaining a viable agriculture.

Box 4.3   The cost of growth.

Supporters of development often argue that an increase in the tax base is a way to stabilize or even reduce property taxes. However, a growing body of evidence suggests that residential development often costs more in municipal services than it produces in tax revenue. For example:

Estimated annual net revenue (taxes minus services) for residential (per housing unit) and business (per 1,000 square feet) development, Monroe County, PA (MCPC 1996).

| Type of land use | Net municipal revenue | Net school district revenue | Net county revenue | Local government total |
|---|---|---|---|---|
| Single-family detached | - $121 | - $1,439 | + $110 | - $1,450 |
| Attached or multifamily | - $167 | - $244 | + $27 | - $384 |
| Office | + $35 | + $991 | + $65 | + $1,091 |
| Factory | + $38 | + $411 | + $3 | + $452 |

Ratios of revenues to service costs for different land uses in four Midwestern communities (AFT 1993, 1994).

| City | Residential | Commercial and industrial | Farmland |
|---|---|---|---|
| Farmington, MN | 1 : 1.02 | 1 : 0.79 | 1 : 0.77 |
| Lake Elmo, MN | 1 : 1.07 | 1 : 0.20 | 1 : 0.27 |
| Independence, MN | 1 : 1.03 | 1 : 0.19 | 1 : 0.47 |
| Madison Township, OH | 1 : 1.54 | 1 : 0.23 | 1 : 0.34 |

Conversion of farmland to development increases the need for roads, police, waste disposal, and other municipal services. Particularly due to the cost of education, residential development often pays less in taxes than it requires in services.

*Continues*

Box 4.3  *Continued*

---

Commercial and industrial development more than pays for its required services. Farmland, which requires very few services, also provides a surplus of tax revenue to local government. In three Massachusetts towns (AFT 1992), residential development generated on average only $1.00 of revenues for each $1.12 of services required – a net loss to the community budget. Alternatively, industrial/commercial development ($1.00 revenue/$0.41 services) and farmland ($1.00 revenue/$0.33 services) generated surplus revenue for government.

The total cost to a municipality of farmland development depends in part on the final mix of land uses. Also, more expensive homes generate more revenue. A study in Palm Beach County, Florida estimates that a new rural home worth $750,000 will pay enough taxes to cover its services, while less expensive homes add to the county tax burden (Engelhardt 1997). Construction of 25,800 homes in the county's Agricultural Reserve would cause an estimated $1.36 billion drain on taxpayers during 50 years, even with developers paying for some of the roads and other infrastructure.

---

### Recreation

Farmlands can be a source of direct recreation enjoyment, an important reason for protecting those open lands. Some services (e.g., hunting) are associated with specific parcels, and a price may be charged for their enjoyment. Services such as scenic views are associated with landscapes, and so their value is more widely dispersed. Summer visitors to Steamboat Springs, Colorado report that the scenic vistas of ranches adjacent to the mountains add measurably to their enjoyment of the area, more than recreation investments such as trails, campgrounds, and golf courses. Analysts estimated that individuals would be willing to pay an average of from $10 to $25 per person per day (Walsh et al. 1994) for the added enjoyment derived from having open ranch land as a backdrop to the area's general attraction.

A 1988 survey of twenty-one eastern states revealed a remarkable range of fees charged by farmers for rights to hunt on their land. To hunt waterfowl on Maryland's eastern shore, for example, hunters were paying up to $8,000 per acre per year for duck blinds. On Mississippi Delta farmland, farmers typically get

$10 per acre per year from an individual to hunt doves, $30 an acre to hunt ducks, and $150 a half-day for quail (Bromley 1990). Similar fees are charged for deer, elk and other game, though a connection to active farmland is more tenuous. Because deer and elk prefer feeding in open fields near woods that provide cover, extensive crop damage may result. Some farmers would probably pay hunters to reduce the herd.

Even the day to day operations of a farm can provide an exciting (or at least interesting) visit and experience. The Mechlings have provided such an opportunity on their 206-acre grain, hay and cattle operation forty miles from Columbus, Ohio. They advertise the historic character of the farm house and the area in which the farm is located. Paying guests are interested in how a farm operates and seek the relative quiet of the country setting (Mechling 1990).

## The Economics of U.S. Farmland Protection Policy

All states and many localities have implemented at least one policy or program to require or at least encourage farmland owners to make the land use choices that keep land available for farming. We distinguish here between farmland and open space. There are non-owner amenities available from all open land and *to that extent* farmland is a category of open space. But farming is more than land, and the farmland appearing to be just open land may in fact be intensively managed. Farming is the mobilization of human capital (management and labor) to employ land (soil, water and air) in producing a desired commodity. Farming is a business, in which land is the production engine, augmented with fertilizers, pest management and other man-made interventions.

The goal of *farmland* policy is to retain conditions favorable to continued farming for the various benefits that farmland generates. Open space policy, on the other hand, deals only with the amenities from land free of structures, the relatively untrammeled natural systems that people enjoy. Not all farmland is very attractive or makes a real contribution to wildlife habitat, and some farming produces negative by-products that impose cost on other people. Farmland policy may address only the preservation of farmland as an agricultural production resource. A more comprehensive farm policy would address the beneficial non-production functions of farmland as well as the adverse environmental effects of agriculture.

Farmland policy seeks to influence the land market by adjusting the economic signals to various buyers and sellers. It responds to demands by non-owners for the full menu of services, including the "sense of security" that future consumers will have enough food. It also responds to demands by farmers that their land remain part of a critical mass of farmland necessary to support a viable agricultural industry in the region and that they be insulated from conflicts with residential land uses. *While farmland policy may seek to make farming a positive and rewarding experience for the farmer, it is safe to say that without the services to non-owners there would be little state or local farmland protection policy.* It is important, however, that policies designed to save farmland acknowledge the role of farmers. It is farmers who make farmland out of open space. Programs that consider farmland as just the absence of buildings will have little success.

Techniques employed to implement state or local farmland programs cover the full spectrum of government authority—from regulations enacted under the police power to various manipulations of the tax code to make farming attractive, to buying the private land rights necessary to keep land available for farming. Choices among these instruments or approaches are based on what is politically possible, what is legally acceptable and what seems to work elsewhere. A detailed discussion of the legal aspects of different farmland preservation programs is found in Chapter 3.

Economic performance information is important to policy design, or at least it should be. The key questions to be asked of each type of farmland preservation program are 1) whether the program actually preserves the owner and non-owner benefits of active farmland, 2) for what time period, 3) at what cost, and 4) out of whose pocket. Each farmland preservation technique implies a certain distribution of cost. "Who pays" often becomes the central policy question.

The non-owner benefits of farmland preservation are shared by many people dispersed across broad geographic areas. It is difficult to allocate the costs of preserving farmland to these non-owners and even harder to collect each individual's share.

This is because many of the non-owner benefits of farmland are indeed "public goods" in the classic economic sense. Farmland policy and programs are necessary because the market fails to assign a value to the public goods associated with farmland.

Land use planning and control to date have been implemented primarily at the state and local level. Senator Henry Jackson from Washington State proposed a national system of support for local comprehensive land use programs in 1970. The bill passed the Senate but died in the House, and no similar legislation has been given serious consideration since.

However, Congress has enacted many other statutes that indirectly affect farmland conversion and retention. These include the Endangered Species Act of 1973, the Clean Water Act of 1970, including its provisions for control of wetland conversions (section 404) and grant assistance to the states for the development of non-point source control programs (section 208), and the Coastal Zone Management Act of 1972 requiring state regulation of coastal lands.

The 1985 farm bill introduced requirements that farmers protect soil and water quality to be eligible for price and income supports. The 1996 Federal Agricultural Improvement and Reform Act includes authorization of funds for purchase of farmland development rights. Of course, the biggest kids on the block are the Federal Highway Assistance Program and the 1956 Interstate Highway Act, which have provided most of the funding for U.S. highways that have allowed people to live in the country while working in distant cities and suburbs (Nelson 1995). Other examples of federal laws affecting farmland conversion are found in Chapter 3.

*Agricultural Zoning.* Zoning is an application of regulatory authority designed to implement community land use preferences. Its purpose is to separate conflicting land uses. Zoning is sometimes based on a comprehensive plan, and deals with spatial aspects of land use, establishing geographic districts within which certain uses are permitted and others prohibited. Experience with zoning goes back to before the Declaration of Independence, when communities in the old Commonwealth of Massachusetts were granted authority to separate gunpowder mills and other dangerous activities from population centers. Initially, zoning was primarily an urban program.

Wisconsin was the first state to adapt zoning to the needs of rural areas with its rural zoning enabling act of 1889 (Solberg 1967). Agricultural zoning may designate areas for agriculture and related uses only, sometimes called exclusive agricultural zoning, or may permit a variety of low density agricultural and non-agricultural uses within the same zoning district. This second type of agricultural zoning provides minimal long-term farmland protection and may be little more than a temporary holding zone for land intended for future high density development.

What of the performance of agricultural zoning? There is evidence that exclusive agricultural zoning districts do in fact retain blocks of land for farming if the provisions are enforced and variances denied (Daniels and Nelson 1986). The economic result is complex, and effects are often off-setting. By restricting the amount of land that can be developed, such ordinances will push up the price of land that may be developed, increasing the cost of development to the buyer. To the extent that such ordinances help limit linear, sprawling development, however, cost of public services will be reduced, which will be reflected in land price. Proximity to protected open lands will often add an amenity increment to land value (Nelson 1985) as people enjoy the scenery of nearby farmlands.

Because exclusive agricultural zoning limits the right of the owner to sell for development, it presumably reduces the market value of protected farmland. Gleeson (1979) determined that the presence of growth management rules in an area near Minneapolis, Minnesota explained more than two-thirds of the difference in farmland values between development and non-development zones. A similar analysis in the province of Quebec, Canada revealed a 15% to 30% reduction in farmland value attributable to zoning (Vaillencourt and Monty 1985). Nelson's analysis of the "urban growth boundary" surrounding the city of Portland in Oregon's Washington County showed an $1,800 or 25% differential between parcels in the area designated as greenbelt and those just across the boundary where exurban development was permitted (Nelson 1988). Thus, *exclusive agricultural zoning essentially shifts the increment of land value linked to expected sale for higher value use from the farmland owner to owners of land where development is permitted.* It is easy to understand why farmers are not enthusiastic about zoning as a land use policy approach. Further, the rising price of developable land in one community may reduce the demand for land there in favor of cheaper land in a nearby community that does not have zoning.

While effective rural zoning seems to cost the farmer, there can be benefits as well. Solberg (1967) made the case as follows: "Farmers need first to realize that absence of zoning offers no protection...it permits their neighborhoods to become dumping grounds for commercial and industrial activities that are prohibited elsewhere...Sooner or later, unguided urban encroachment into productive farming areas means that farmers pay higher taxes for services demanded by others...As more non-farm people move in, other urban-agricultural conflicts arise." Henneberry and Barrows (1990) measured a *positive* impact of rural zoning on farmland values near Janesville and Beloit, Wisconsin. Farmers were willing to pay more for zoned than unzoned land, partly because they expected fewer conflicts with non-farm neighbors, but also because under Wisconsin's circuit breaker tax program farmers received state income tax credits to offset property taxes on farmland zoned for exclusive agricultural use but not on unzoned farmland.

Land prices are a product of expectations. If prospective land buyers see little likelihood that zoning or another growth management tool will substantially alter the pattern of development, because of variances or lax enforcement, regulations will have little effect on land value. Gradual implementation of open land zoning in southern New Jersey resulted in a huge increase (228%) in land value as the date for imposition of the ordinance approached, followed by a precipitous drop in value after full implementation. Owners who sold *prior* to implementation reaped major windfalls. After implementation, the fall of land prices was tempered by a waiver provision of the law. Owners able to demonstrate real hardship were permitted a waiver from development restrictions (Beaton 1991). Again, willingness to pay for a specific parcel of land depends on expected returns to that land as influenced by land use rules—not as written but as actually implemented.

Certain types of non-exclusive agricultural zoning have a perverse effect on the effort to protect farmland, and their effect on land values is inconsistent. A 10-, 35-, or even 50-acre minimum lot size may encourage scattered development, raising the development expectations of all land owners. Such is the case in Waukesha County, Wisconsin, which has a 40-acre minimum lot size in the agricultural zone (Gehl and Libby 1997; see Case 11). Lacking assurance of being protected from development, farmers were soon more interested in the possibility of "the big sale" than remaining competitive. Such expectations led to reduced priority on farming throughout the area. In this area the land value effect of zoning depended on the demand for "farmettes" or rural estates, availability of central water and sewer, and other services.

*Tax Incentives.* Taxes have always been a significant cost of doing business in any sector, but are particularly so in farming. Keene et al. (1975) estimated that land taxes consumed up to 30% of net farm income, even more at the urban fringe. Farmers pay a larger portion of their income in property taxes than do non-farmers because land is the productive factor of farm operations. In the period from 1932 to 1975, farm property taxes amounted to 8% of all property taxes while farm income was 4% of national income (Stam and Sibold 1977).

All states have enacted special property tax provisions for farmers to reduce their real property tax burden. Real property taxes are *ad valorem* taxes. They are based on the notion that the market value of land is an indicator of the owner's ability to pay. The value of farmland is a composite of its productive quality and its location relative to other economic activities. When location dominates as the value-producing variable, the serious farmer is at a significant disadvantage because he cannot convert location to income without sacrificing the productivity variable on which farming depends.

As of February 1998, 49 states employ differential assessment procedures to tax farmland on its value for producing farm income rather than on market value. Thirty-seven of those states require that a farmer pay back a portion of the benefits received under the tax program if his or her farmland is developed. Michigan relies on a "circuit breaker" system granting the eligible farmer a state income tax credit for any property taxes paid above a threshold of 7% of household income. Wisconsin, the only other state with a property tax circuit breaker (it also has use value assessment), has a sliding scale threshold with a higher proportion of household income employed for higher income farms. Eligibility for the Wisconsin tax credits is conditioned upon counties adopting farmland preservation plans and exclusive agricultural zoning.

Connecticut and Vermont also have special capital gains or conveyance tax provisions that recapture a portion of the capital gain when eligible farmland is developed (Grillo and Seid 1987). The capital gains approach is far more popular in Europe and Canada. They recognize the "unearned increment" in land value attributable to public infrastructure investments, and recapture a portion of that gain for the public (Smith 1976).

Land tax incentives are just that; they seek a socially desirable land use pattern by *encouraging* the owner to make private choices that have social utility. Unlike the case with regulation, land use behavior is not compulsory. Tax programs "work" as farmland policy only if the incentive is sufficient, when combined with farm income and any other monetary or non-monetary returns to farming, to offset the financial gain from conversion. There is no evidence that such programs *on their own* will actually preserve farmland for the long haul. They will buy some time, perhaps alter the development pattern temporarily, but are not really designed to keep land in farming for long periods. They do reduce the cost of holding land, permitting farming to continue longer than it would in the absence of such programs, but cannot withstand real development pressure. The potential for sale is always there, thus even active farmers may begin to feel "impermanent," lose the competitive edge, and begin to speculate on the possibility of future sale. The rollback or capital gains penalty involved becomes just another cost of development.

Conklin and Lesher (1977) concluded that use value assessment of farmland in rural areas outside of New York City may not protect farmland under pressure, but it does help make farming profitable further out from the urban boundary. At least these programs keep taxes from pushing land out of farming. Nelson (1990) has argued to the contrary that "[p]referential assessment does not slow the conversion of farmland to urban uses. It may even facilitate conversion." He contends that farmers become the biggest speculators of all, with their costs reduced by special tax treatment. Developers and non-farmer speculators also find an advantage in leasing land to farmers to keep eligibility for preferential tax treatment, thus keeping their own cost down while looking for a development prospect. Admittedly in such cases the public is subsidizing land speculation by owners who eventually sell for development, but perhaps that is a price taxpayers are willing to pay for the temporary open space advantages of private land.

The tax incentives do make a difference in the farmer's tax bill. Analysis of the Michigan circuit breaker program revealed that, in combination with the general homestead tax credit, the program reduced the real property taxes of a typical participant by 80% to 90%. In this program, there is less than a full recapture of the tax benefits when the farmland is converted. The tax benefit is thus capitalized into the land value. The net benefit for the owner is substantial (Anderson and Bunch 1989).

Analysis of the Wisconsin circuit breaker program revealed that mid-sized and large dairy farms received higher tax credits. Small dairy farms tend to have larger off-farm income sources and pay lower property tax, thus passing the eligibility threshold less frequently. If the program worked on net *farm* income only, smaller farms would indeed get most of the state tax credit. But progressivity with respect to all income sources means that larger farms receive more rebate of state income tax (Barrows and Bonderud 1988).

Experience shows that many rural assessors have long given *ad hoc* use value treatment to farmland. They recognize the inherent differences between farming and other land uses. Thus, a new preferential assessment law merely formalizes what has been a common practice, with little immediate impact on farmland taxes (Chicoine and Hendricks 1985). Because farmers are paying lower land taxes and the cost of public services is likely not declining, other property owners must shoulder the added burden. The gap between revenues and service demands in any locality may be picked up by the state through school aid formulae or by more fundamental changes in tax structure.

Therefore the question of "who pays" for the public benefits of farmland retention under a tax incentive approach depends on the tax source used to replace the property tax formerly paid by the farmer. Michigan, for example, has revised its tax structure to shift the funding of education from local property tax to state sales and income taxes. While that action has reduced local property taxes, it has at the same time reduced the tax incentive to farmers under their circuit breaker program. This is important if it keeps farmers from signing up for the program. To qualify for tax credits, a farmer must enter into a contract agreeing not to develop his or her land for at least ten years.

Realistically, use value, circuit breaker and capital gains incentives can be effective land use policy only if employed in conjunction with other techniques. These techniques must go beyond incentives to individual owners to support of active farming in larger areas or regions through controls on land use or more substantial and fundamental incentives.

*Acquisition.* The way to *assure* that farmland stays in farming or in a use that generates the non-owner services valued by society is to buy the right to develop that land. Thus, the owner's land use options no longer include selling for development or other non-farm use. The buyer of those rights, generally a public agency, essentially retires those rights. They cannot be exercised by the public, so development will not occur on those acres. The farmer is paid a one time price, and the acquired development rights are then separated from the bundle of rights that goes with fee simple ownership. This is done through use of a permanent conservation easement. The price paid is the estimated difference between the land's value for agricultural use and its open market value as a location for potential development. Some level of oversight is necessary to assure that development rights transferred in this manner are not in fact exercised by the owner at a later time.

The public agency may seek right of first refusal in case the owner decides to sell the land with the development restrictions in place. This is sometimes done to assure that the land remains in active farming as opposed to being sold for use as an estate. The public agency will then turn around and sell the land to a farmer. Regardless of to whom the property is sold, the conservation easement remains in place.

Outright purchase of farmland, as opposed to the purchase of development rights, is less likely than for other open space. Few public agencies want to get into the active farming business. The Southwest Florida Water Management District has purchased more than 6000 acres of grazing land and then leased grazing rights back to the original owner. They have also considered outright purchase followed by sale to a farmer willing to operate with the development restrictions in place (Frahm 1995).

Statewide programs for purchase of development rights (PDR) are in effect in about fourteen states, many in the Northeast where farmland is in relatively short supply and demand for non-owner services is well articulated. Several individual counties, townships and communities around the country where farmland is particularly important to the scenic character of the place have their own programs. Examples are Peninsula Township, Michigan, mixing an active fruit industry with tourism that includes the farming countryside as part of the attraction (AFT 1996), and King County, Washington, a scenic and productive part of that state (see Case 18). The St. Johns Water Management District in central Florida purchased development rights to a 12,000 acre ranch with funds from the farmland preservation provisions of the Federal Agricultural Improvement and Reform Act of 1996 (See Chapter 3, Tables 3.3 and 3.4).

Effectiveness of PDR as a farmland protection technique depends on the money available and how many farmers are interested. Programs are generally "arms length transactions" in which the public seeks to bid away from an owner. who is under no compulsion to sell, the development rights to his farmland. Only the farmer can assure that the land is still farmed, but with development rights gone it will not be developed. Speculation in future development value is halted and the farmer can focus on farming.

Funding for PDR is always the limiting variable and depends on voter support for targeted municipal bonds, special transfer taxes and other sources. The approach can be effective when used to retain farmland in a relatively small targeted area, but public cost of purchasing rights to vast farming areas will be prohibitive.

There are various strategies that may be employed in setting purchase priorities. Some states seek farmlands that are already under urban pressure and are therefore the most "threatened" for conversion. Price of the development rights under these circumstances is clearly higher, thus fewer acres can be protected. Other programs place a premium on large contiguous areas with relatively little pressure, where continuation of viable farming is more assured for the long run (Buist et al. 1995). The PDR program in

Massachusetts, for example, emphasizes relative "social value" of alternative development rights purchases; Connecticut, on the other hand, gives negative weight to urban pressure in their priority scheme.

Distribution of the cost of farmland development rights acquisition clearly depends on the source of funds. The farmland owner bears little of the direct cost of attaining farmland protection goals because he is compensated for the estimated value of foregone development. Cost of a special millage or local bond issue would be levied on all property tax payers, while the transfer tax is paid only by those in the real estate market. In Michigan, funds for development rights purchase come from paybacks received from farmers deciding to leave the state's farmland preservation program. Funds available at the federal level distribute the burden for farmland protection among all income tax payers.

While less common for farmland than for other open land, conservation easements may also be used to donate development rights to a land trust. The land trust enforces the terms of the easement thus preventing the land from being developed. Of the nearly 900 land trusts in operation across the country in 1990, more than half listed farmland protection as one of their purposes. The major financial incentive for the farmer to donate development rights is that the value of those rights becomes a charitable income tax deduction. Up to 30% of adjusted gross income may be deducted, and the deduction may be spread over six tax years. The donated easement may reduce the farmer's real property taxes and also reduce the estate tax value of the property when the farmer dies (Buist et al. 1995). Easements must be perpetual to qualify for a tax deduction. Private non-profit land trusts may also broker development rights transfers to public agencies.

The effectiveness of PDR programs is dependent on active enforcement by the easement holder, usually a unit of government. Public pressure may build to terminate or alter the terms of an easement as development surrounds easement protected land. Legal challenges to the easement may follow. The success of such litigation will depend on the wording of the easement and whether the easement holder makes a vigorous defense. Well drafted and actively administered easements should generally withstand attack.

## Conclusions

The central theme of this chapter is the role of economics as a conceptual language for analyzing and better understanding the human forces affecting conversion of farmland to non-farm use. People have various expectations of farmland—obviously as a source of food for themselves and others, but also for the various natural resource services it generates. Those expectations change with time. As the U.S. economy matures, with productive sectors becoming more specialized and a post-industrial service component becoming more prominent, people will expect different things from the world around them. People will learn more about how farmland and other open lands can enrich their lives and will make personal choices that reflect that knowledge. They will in turn petition their elected officials to implement land use policies consistent with those choices.

Economics can help us see the consequence of various changes in the land use rules. People do seem to respond to incentives, and do so in fairly predictable ways. Any attempt to adjust land use rules will hurt some and help others. Balance among those who gain and those who lose from policy encompasses the political conversation surrounding farmland and open space policy. There is always concern for equity or fairness of a policy as well as its effectiveness in achieving its intended purpose. While economics cannot define fairness, economic analyses can generate information that helps the interested parties know whether they favor or oppose a proposed action.

In our view, successful farmland policy will require the following elements:

First, a visible and pro-active state-level commitment to encouraging farmland retention is essential. There must be a statement of land use strategy, and it must be actively communicated to the citizens. People have to know that state leaders support local efforts, and there must be general consistency among local efforts. It helps to have the governor of a state initiate a state-wide examination of farmland issues with policy recommendations. That effort should include a review of existing conditions, the current state and local policy mix influencing use of farmland and the non-market benefits of actively farmed land to state citizens.

Second, there should be local implementation of farmland policies within the overall state structure. There are differences in
land use patterns within any state. A county is a unit of government large enough to encompass agriculture and municipalities
while being relatively close to people affected by policy change.
County and local programs should be consistent with state guidelines.

Third, farmland policies are most successful when farmers
themselves initiate action. Farmland protection is not easily
forced on farmers, because it is their actions that make farming
work. Farmland preservation that drives out the farmers makes
little sense. We are not of the "preserve it and they will come"
school that assumes that if the farmland is out there, someone
will come along and farm it. Agricultural districts in several states
rely on farmer initiative, and this is a good approach.

Fourth, farmland protection policy can only succeed when
there is strong and consistent growth management policy. The
two are distinct, but inseparable sets of policies, and neither on
its own is sufficient. Growth management channels development
away from areas planned for agriculture. Farmers will continue
investing in agriculture and providing the various natural resource services of farmland only if their future seems to be in
farming. Weak or poorly implemented growth management policy
creates the illusion of riches for all farmers and can undercut the
best of farmland retention policy. Given compelling evidence that
old development and central cities subsidize the cost of services at
the fringe, encouraging sprawl and urban decline, a growth management package must ensure that annexations, impact fees,
zoning and other exercises of local discretion are in general harmony across local boundaries.

## Endnotes

1. We consider productive farmland as a nonrenewable resource in the sense that it is fixed in physical supply and may be
destroyed by paving, removing topsoil or in other ways permanently altering its ecological character. That is not strictly true, as
in the case of oil.
2. The extensive literature on altruism suggests that this behavior evolved to further the self-interest of the altruist as there

would be greater payoffs to individuals reciprocating in long-term interactions (Trivers 1971, Axelrod 1984).

3. The substitution effect refers to the tendency to substitute less costly alternatives in a production process or in consumption to maintain a given level of output for the producer or utility for the consumer.

4. These external benefits are characterized by Schmid (1987) as high exclusion cost products or services. That is, because the benefit cannot be withheld from anyone, no one can be forced to pay in order to enjoy it, and the producer receives no compensation for providing it.

5. A large U.S. pharmaceuticals firm has a continuing contract with the government of Costa Rica to "prospect" the biologically rich rain forests of that nation for materials that may have future commercial value for medicines or drugs. Potential net value of such materials to a private firm has been estimated at $4 billion (Mendelsohn and Balick 1995).

## References

AFT. 1992. Does Farmland Protection Pay?—The Cost of Community Services in Three Massachusetts Towns. American Farmland Trust, Washington, D.C.

AFT. 1993. The Cost of Community Services in Madison Village and Township, Lake County, Ohio. American Farmland Trust, Washington, D.C.

AFT. 1994. Farmland and the Tax Bill: The Cost of Community Services in Three Minnesota Cities. American Farmland Trust, Washington, D.C.

AFT. 1995. Alternatives for Future Urban Growth in California's Central Valley: The Bottom Line for Agriculture and Taxpayers. American Farmland Trust, Washington, D.C.

AFT. 1996. Forging New Directions: Purchasing Development Rights to Save Farmland. American Farmland Trust, Washington, D.C.

Anderson, J., and H. Bunch. 1989. Agricultural property tax relief: Tax credits, tax rates and land values. Land Economics 65(1):13-21.

Andreoni, J. 1995. Cooperation in public goods experiments: Kindness or confusion? The American Economic Review 85(4):891-904.

Arrow, K., B. Bolin, R. Costanza, P. Dasgupta, C. Folke, C.
    Holling, B-O. Jansson, S. Levin, K-G. Maler, C. Perrings, and
    D. Pimentel. 1995. Economic growth, carrying capacity, and
    the environment. Science 268:520-521.
Ausubel, J.H. 1996. Can technology spare the Earth? American
    Scientist 84:166-178.
Axelrod, R. 1984. The Evolution of Cooperation. Basic Books, New
    York.
Barnett, H., and C. Morse. 1963. Scarcity and Growth: The
    Economics of Natural Resource Availability. Johns Hopkins
    Press, Baltimore.
Barrows, R., and K. Bonderud. 1988. The distribution of tax relief
    under farm circuit-breakers: Some empirical evidence. Land
    Economics 64:15-27.
Barrows, R., and D. Chicoine. 1984. Land for agriculture. pp. 12-
    21. In: D. Henderson and R. Barrows (eds.) Resources, Food
    and the Future. NCR Educational Materials Project, Iowa State
    University, Ames, Iowa.
Beasley, S., W. Workman, and N. Williams. 1986. Estimating
    amenity values of urban fringe farmland: A contingent
    valuation approach. Growth and Change 17:70-78.
Beaton, W. 1991. The impact of regional land use controls on
    property values: The case of the New Jersey Pinelands. Land
    Economics 67:172-194.
Bergstrom, J., B. Dillman, and J. Stoll. 1985. Public
    environmental amenity benefits of private land. Southern
    Journal of Agricultural Economics (July):139-149.
Brewer, M. 1981. The Changing U.S. Farmland Scene. Population
    Reference Bureau, Inc. 36:5, Washington, D.C.
Brewer, M., and R. Boxley. 1981. Agricultural land: Adequacy of
    acres, concepts and information. American Journal of
    Agricultural Economics 63:879-887.
Bromley, P. 1990. Wildlife opportunities: Species having
    management and income potential for landowners in the East.
    pp. 105-112. In: W. Grafton and A. Ferrise (eds.) Income
    Opportunities for the Private Landowner Through Management
    of Natural Resources and Recreational Access. West Virginia
    Cooperative Extension Service, Morgantown, WV.
Brown, L. 1996. Tough Choices: Facing the Challenge of Food
    Scarcity. W.W. Norton, New York.

Buist, H., C. Fischer, J. Michos, and A. Tegene. 1995. Purchase of Development Rights and the Economics of Easements, Agricultural Economic Report 718. Economics Research Service, Washington, D.C.

Burchell, R., and D. Listokin. 1993. The Development Impact Handbook and Model. Urban Land Institute, Cambridge, MA.

Burchell, R., and D. Listokin. 1994. The Economic Effects of Trend Versus Vision Growth in the Lexington Metropolitan Area. Report to Bluegrass Tomorrow, Lexington, KY.

Castle, E. 1981. Is there a farmland crisis? Christian Science Monitor, p. 23, August 31.

Chicoine, D., and D. Hendricks. 1985. Evidence on farm use value assessments, tax shifts and school aid. American Journal of Agricultural Economics 67(2):266-270.

Conklin, H., and W. Lesher. 1977. Farm value assessment as a means for reducing premature and excessive agricultural disinvestment in urban fringes. American Journal of Agricultural Economics 59:755-759.

Correll, M., J. Lillydahl, and L. Singell. 1978. The effects of greenbelts on residential property values: Some findings on the political economy of open space. Land Economics 54(2):207-217.

Costanza, R., R. d'Arge, R. deGroot, S. Farber, M. Grasso, B. Hannon, K. Linsburg, S. Noeem, R. O'Neill, J. Paruelo, R. Raskin, P. Sutton, and M. vandenBeit. 1997. The value of the world's ecosystem services and natural capital. Nature 387(15):253-260.

Daly, H. 1979. Entropy, growth and the political economy of scarcity. pp. 67-94. In: V.K. Smith (ed.) Scarcity and Growth Reconsidered. Johns Hopkins Press, Baltimore, MD.

Daniels, T., and A. Nelson. 1986. Is Oregon's farmland preservation program working? Journal of the American Planning Association 52:22-32.

DuPage County Regional Planning Commission. 1991. Impacts of Development on DuPage County Property Taxes. Unpublished Memo, April 4, 1991. DuPage County, Illinois.

Easterbrook, G. 1986. Vanishing land reappears. Atlantic Monthly, July, pp. 17-20.

Engelhardt, J. 1997. Palm Beach County relied on faulty figures for cost of growth, experts say. The Palm Beach Post, November 19, p. 10A.

Ervin, D., and A. Schmitz. 1996. A new era of environmental management in agriculture. American Journal of Agricultural Economics 78:1198-1206.

Ferejohn, J., and T. Page. 1978. On the foundations of intertemporal choice. American Journal of Agricultural Economics 6:269-275.

Fox, T. 1990. Urban Open Space: An Investment that Pays. The Neighborhood Open Space Coalition, New York.

Frahm, R. 1995. Alternative Methods of Land Acquisition. Southwest Florida Water Management District, Tampa, FL.

Frank, R. 1991. Economics. pp. 91-110. In: Mary Maxwell (ed.) The Socio-biological Imagination. SUNY Press, Albany, NY.

Friedman, M. 1953. Essays in Positive Economics. The University of Chicago Press, Chicago, IL.

Gehl, S., and L. Libby. 1997. Understanding the Rules, Practices and Attitudes Regarding Land Use in Waukesha County, Wisconsin. CAE/WP 97-5. Center for Agriculture in the Environment, Dekalb, IL.

Gettings, T.L. 1990. The new gold rush! The New Farm 12:32-37.

Gleeson, M. 1979. Effects of an urban growth management system on land values. Land Economics 55:350-365.

Grillo, K., and D. Seid. 1987. State Laws Relating to Preferential Assessment of Farmland. U.S. Department of Agriculture, Economic Research Service, Washington, D.C.

Hackl, F., and G. Pruckner. 1996. The provision of countryside amenities: External benefits of agricultural production in mountainous regions. pp. 287-288. In: W. Lockeretz (ed.) Environmental Enhancement Through Agriculture. Tufts University School of Nutrition Science and Policy, Medford, MA.

Halstead, J. 1984. Measuring the non-market value of Massachusetts agricultural land. Journal of the Northeast Agricultural Economic Council 13:12-19.

Halstead, J., T. Cook, and G. Estes. 1996. On farm composting of food and farm wastes: Economic and environmental considerations. pp. 183-191. In: W. Lockeretz (ed.) Environmental Enhancement Through Agriculture. Tufts University School of Nutrition Science and Policy, Medford, MA.

Harbor, J. 1994. A practical method for estimating impact of land use change on surface run-off, groundwater recharge and wetland hydrology. APA Journal 60:95-108.

Heal, G. 1986. The inter-temporal problem. pp. 1-20. In: D. Bromley (ed.) Natural Resource Economics: Policy Problems and Contemporary Analysis. Klewer-Nijhoff Publishing, Boston, MA.

Heiner, R. 1983. The origin of predictable behavior. American Economic Review 73:560-595.

Henneberry, D., and R. Barrows. 1990. Capitalization of exclusive agricultural zoning into farmland prices. Land Economics 66:249-258.

Hinrichsen, D. 1997. Winning the Food Race. Johns Hopkins University School of Public Health, Baltimore, MD.

Huston, M. 1993. Biological diversity, soils and economics. Science 202:1076-80.

Kaplan, R. 1994. The coming anarchy. Atlantic Monthly 273:44-75.

Kaplan, R., and S. Kaplan. 1989. The Experience of Nature. Cambridge University Press, New York.

Kaplan, S., R. Kaplan, and J. Wendt. 1972. Rated preference and complexity for natural and urban visual material. Perception and Psychophysics 12:354-356.

Keene, J., D. Berry, R. Coughlin, J. Ferncem, E. Kelly, T. Plant, and A. Strong. 1975. Untaxing Open Space. Council on Environmental Quality, Washington, D.C.

Kelso, M. 1977. The political economy of national resources policy. pp. 141-148. In: USDA (ed.) Lectures in Agricultural Economics. U.S. Department of Agriculture, Washington, D.C.

Kline, J., and D. Wichelns. 1996. Public preferences regarding the goals of farmland preservation programs. Land Economics 72:538-549.

Krutilla, J., and A. Fisher. 1975. The Economics of Natural Environments. Johns Hopkins Press, Baltimore, MD.

Libby, L. 1997. In Pursuit of the Commons: Toward a Farmland Protection Strategy for the Midwest. CAE/WP 97-2. Center for Agriculture in the Environment, Dekalb, IL.

Lopez, R., F. Shah, and M. Altobello. 1994. Amenity benefits and the optimal allocation of land. Land Economics 70:53-62.

McKay, H., L. Sinisterra, A. McKay, H. Gomez, and P. Lloreda. 1987. Improving cognitive ability in chronically deprived children. Science 200:270-278.

MCPC. 1996. Fiscal Alert. Monroe County Planning Commission, Stroudsburg, PA.

Mechling, P. 1990. Bed and breakfast. pp. 328-330. In: W. Grafton and A. Ferrise (eds.) Income Opportunities for the Private Landowner Through Management of Natural Resources and Recreational Access. West Virginia Cooperative Extension Service, Morgantown, WV.

Mendelsohn, R., and M. Balick. 1995. The value of undiscovered pharmaceuticals in tropical forests. Economic Botany 49:223-28.

Metrick, A., and M. Weitzman. 1996. Patterns of behavior in endangered species preservation. Land Economics 72:1-16.

Miller, G.T., Jr. 1998. Living in the Environment, 10th ed. Wadsworth Publishing Co., Belmont, CA.

Nelson, A. 1985. A unifying view of greenbelt influences on regional land values and implications for regional planning policy. Growth and Change (April):119-142.

Nelson, A. 1988. An empirical note on how regional urban containment policy influences an interaction between greenbelt and exurban land markets. APA Journal (Spring):178-184.

Nelson, A. 1990. Economic critique of U.S. prime farmland preservation policies. Journal of Rural Studies 6:119-142.

Nelson, R. 1995. Federal zoning: The new era in environmental policy. pp. 295-317. In: B. Yandle (ed.) Land Rights: The 1990's Property Rights Rebellion. Rowman and Littlefield, Lanham, MD.

Growth and Change (April):119-142. Federal zoning: The new era in environmental policy. pp. 295-317. In: B. Yandle (ed.) Land Rights: The 1990's Property Rights Rebellion. Rowman and Littlefield, Lanham, MD.

Pimentel, D., and M. Giampietro. 1994. Food, Land, Population and the U.S. Economy. Carrying Capacity Network, Washington, D.C.

Pollakowski, H., and S. Wachter. 1990. The effects of land use constraints on housing prices. Land Economics 66:315-324.

PRB. 1997. World Population Data Sheet – 1997. Population Reference Bureau, Washington, D.C.

Schmid, A.A. 1987. Property, Power and Public Choice. Praeger, New York.

Scholz, J. and N. Pinney. 1995. Duty, fear and tax compliance. American Journal of Political Science 39:490-512.

Schultz, T. 1977. The Economic Value of Human Time Over Time. Lectures in Agricultural Economics. U.S. Department of Agriculture, Washington, D.C.

Silberman, J., D. Gerlowski, and N. Williams. 1992. Estimating existence value for users and nonusers of New Jersey beaches. Land Economics 68:225-236.

Simon, J. 1980. Resources, population, environment: An oversupply of false bad news. Science 208:1431-1437.

Smith, L. 1976. The Ontario land speculation tax: An analysis of an unearned increment land tax. Land Economics 52:1-12.

Smith, V. 1982. Microeconomic systems as an experimental science. American Economic Review 72:923-954.

Smith, V. 1991. Protecting rivers, trails and greenways reap economic returns. Exchange (Summer):20-21.

Solberg, E. 1967. The How and Why of Rural Zoning. Agriculture Information Bulletin 196. U.S. Department of Agriculture, Economic Research Service, Washington, D.C.

Solow, R. 1974. The economics of resources or the resources of economics. American Economic Review (May):1-14.

Stam, J., and A. Sibold. 1977. Agriculture and the Property Tax. AE Report 392. U.S. Department of Agriculture, Economic Research Service, Washington, D.C.

Stiglitz, J. 1979. A neoclassical analysis of resource economics. pp. 36-66. In: V.K. Smith (ed.) Scarcity and Growth Reconsidered. Johns Hopkins Press, Baltimore, MD.

Trivers, R. 1971. The evolution of reciprocal altruism. Quaterly Review of Biology 46:35-47.

Ulrich, R. 1981. Natural versus urban scenes: Some psychophysiological effects. Environment and Behavior 13:523-556.

Ulrich, R., R. Simons, B. Losito, E. Fiorito, M. Miles, and M. Zelson. 1991. Stress recovery during exposure to natural and urban. Journal of Environmental Psychology 11:201-230.

United Nations. 1996. World Population Growing More Slowly, But Could Still Reach 9.4 Billion by 2050. Population Division, Department for Economic and Social Information and Policy Analysis, New York.

USDA. 1981. National Agricultural Lands Study: Final Report. U.S. Department of Agriculture, Washington, D.C.

USDA. 1982. The Second RCA Appraisal: Soil, Water, and Related Resources on Non-federal Land in the United States. Miscellaneous Publication 1482, U.S. Department of Agriculture, Washington, D.C.

Vallaincourt, F., and L. Monty. 1985. The effect of agricultural zoning on land prices, Quebec 1975-81. Land Economics 61:36-42.

Waggoner, P.E., J.H. Ausubel, and I.K. Wernick. 1996. Lightening the tread of population on the land: American examples. Population and Development Review 22:531-545.

Walsh, R., J. McKean, R. Rosenberger, and C. Mucklow. 1994. Recreation Value of Open Space. Unpublished Report to Routt County Board of Commissioners, Department of Agricultural and Resource Economics, Ft. Collins, CO.

Whitby, M., and C. Saunders. 1996. Estimating conservation goods in Britain. Land Economics 72:313-325.

Williams, J., L. Libby, and L. Connor. 1977. Case Studies and
    Comparative Cost Analyses of Local and Conventional
    Treatment of Wastewater by Small Municipalities in Michigan.
    AE Report 329. Department of Agricultural Economics,
    Michigan State University, East Lansing, MI.
Wilson, E.O. (ed.) 1986. Biodiversity. National Academy Press,
    Washington, D.C.

# 5

# Preserving Community Agriculture in a Global Economy

*T.A. Lyson, C.C. Geisler, and C. Schlough*

Agriculture is far more than just farmland. It is a complex socio-economic system in which the input and marketing sectors have become as or more important than the production sector. People are a critical component of agriculture, and the pattern of their social and legal relationships constitutes the structure of agriculture (Hamilton 1994). Structure is measured by factors such as size and type of farms, distribution of land ownership, and control of decision-making. Hamilton writes that "Another way of looking at the structure of agriculture is to consider who will control agriculture—who will own the land, perform the labor, market the food, and profit from agriculture?"

The structure of agriculture in the United States has changed significantly in the past half-century, part of a process of industrialization and globalization that is altering the agricultural landscape. These structural changes have important implications for how land is treated, including the likelihood of its conversion to non-agricultural uses. These structural trends also present a major challenge to the food security of American communities. We believe that a shift of these trends toward a relocalization of agriculture is required to ensure food security, and that the preservation of farmland by each community is essential to successful relocalization.

# Structural Trends

## Farm Numbers and Size

Agriculture since 1950 has been characterized by large decreases in the number of farms and farmers, and a corresponding increase in average farm size (Table 5.1). Smaller, family-labor farms have declined substantially in number as larger, increasingly industrial-like operations have become the primary source of food and other agricultural products. The proportion of Americans involved in farming has fallen below 2%. Technologically sophisticated and highly standardized production techniques have penetrated most segments of farming, and advances in plant and animal sciences have resulted in substantial increases in production.

The trend in farm numbers and size has been associated with a concentration of land and production in relatively few hands, and a highly skewed distribution of land between large and small farms (Table 5.2). In terms of gross sales, approximately 90% of U.S. agricultural output is produced by only 522,000 farms.

Table 5.1     Structural changes in U.S. agriculture since 1950 (Albrecht and Murdoch 1990, Bureau of the Census 1983, 1984, 1992, 1994).

| Characteristic | 1950 | 1982 | 1992 |
|---|---|---|---|
| Number of farms | 5,388,000 | 2,240,976 | 1,925,300 |
| Average farm size (acres) | 216 | 440 | 491 |
| Farm population | 23,048,000 | 5,620,000 | 4,632,000* |
| Farm population as percent of U.S. total | 15.3 | 2.4 | 1.9 |

*Farm population data from 1991.

Table 5.2  Percent distribution of farms—number and acreage, by size of farm, 1992 (Bureau of the Census 1994).

| Size of farm | Percent distribution | | |
|---|---|---|---|
| | Number of farms | All land in farms | Cropland harvested |
| Less than 10 acres | 8.6 | 0.1 | 0.1 |
| 10 to 259 acres | 59.3 | 11.5 | 14.0 |
| 260 to 999 acres | 23.0 | 23.4 | 37.9 |
| 1,000 to 1,999 acres | 5.3 | 14.7 | 23.4 |
| 2000 acres or more | 3.7 | 50.4 | 24.5 |

### Land Tenure and Operation

Farms are not usually single parcels of land on which the owner/operator resides. A farm often consists of many different parcels, owned by different people and widely separated. In 1988, 41% of all farmers operated at least some leased land (Rogers 1993) and 45% of U.S. farmland was rented, a figure that declined slightly to 43% in 1992 (Figure 5.1). Thus, the distribution of land among farms does not necessarily reflect the distribution of land ownership.

The Agricultural Economics and Land Ownership Survey conducted in 1988 (Wunderlich 1993) estimated that there are approximately 3 million private owners of agricultural land. Of these owners, the 4% with the largest holdings own 47% of the agricultural land, which represents 25% of the value of land and buildings. The 30% with the least land hold only 2% of the agricultural land, which is worth 11% of the value of land and buildings. Of the total land owners, 44% are not operating farms. Non-family held corporations are minor players, owning less than 1% of agricultural land.

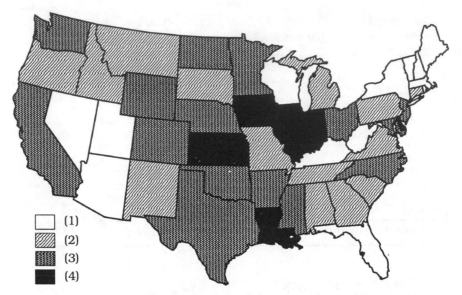

Figure 5.1   Percent of U.S. farmland, by state, rented in 1992.
(1) <30%;    (2) 30% to 40%;    (3)  40% to 50%;    (4) >50%.


### Farmland Fluidity

According to the Census of Agriculture (see Chapter 1, Table
1.2), between 1982 and 1992 there was a slight decrease in acres
of farmland (-4.2%) and cropland (-2.2%). Underlying what
appears to be a gradual loss of farmland is a more complex set of
structural dynamics, which can be expressed as the "fluidity" of
farmland. By fluidity we mean the amount of farmland and cropland, measured at the county level, that moves into and out of
production through time. Ideally, we would like to chart the
yearly/seasonal change in land at the farm level, but because the
Census of Agriculture (Bureau of the Census 1984, 1989, 1994) is
taken every five years and because the smallest unit for which
data are reported is the county, we are restricted to measuring
the cumulative changes from 1982 to 1987 and from 1987 to
1992.

Between 1982 and 1987, 1,256 counties added to their cropland base, while 1,781 counties experienced a decrease. More
than 13 million acres of cropland went out of production, but
11 million (different) acres were brought into production during
this period. Between 1987 and 1992, 1,159 counties added

cropland and 1,876 counties saw a decrease in cropland. More than 15 million acres of cropland were taken out of production, while 7.4 million acres were brought into production. Farmland (cropland plus all other lands controlled by a farmer) showed similar fluidity.

Among the states showing the largest fluxes of cropland were Montana, Nebraska, Kansas, Texas, and Mississippi. For the United States, the common perception of farmland and cropland as relatively static entities that, at best, are slowly declining across the country may not be accurate. Land is brought into and taken out of production in response to market changes and policy changes (e.g., the Conservation Reserve Program).

What has developed then is a structure in which the ownership of farmland is concentrated in a few hands, many of the owners are not involved directly in the farming of their land (absentee landlords), and the movement of land into and out of production has acquired a fluidity enhanced in part by the rental situation. How did we arrive at this position? Largely through the industrialization of agriculture, a process assisted by public policy and research priorities.

## The Industrialization Of Agriculture

### *The Conventional Model of Agricultural Production*

Conventional agriculture is the system of production that has been developed and promoted by university researchers and government personnel during the past 120 years. It represents the accumulated knowledge and wisdom about the most widely accepted procedures and techniques to grow crops and raise livestock (Heady 1976).

Conventional agriculture is grounded on the belief that the primary objective of farming should be to produce as much food and fiber as possible for the least cost. It is driven by the twin goals of productivity and efficiency. More particularly, the theoretical (and philosophical) underpinnings of conventional agriculture rest within both experimental biology and neoclassical economics (Lyson and Welsh 1993). The logic of experimental biology dictates that increasing output is the primary goal of scientific

agriculture. Neoclassical economics, on the other hand, posits
that optimal efficiency and presumably maximum profitability
in production agriculture can be achieved by balancing the
four factors of production: 1) land; 2) labor; 3) capital; and
4) management or entrepreneurship (Kay 1986).

 The prime movers behind the conventional model of production
in the United States have been the land grant universities, the
USDA, and more recently large agribusiness firms. The land grant
system brought the methods of scientific research to agriculture.
At America's land grant universities, the emphasis in the class-
room and research laboratory was on "production." The different
agriculturally related disciplines that formed during the past 120
years such as agronomy, plant pathology, plant breeding, and
entomology broke apart "farming" bit by bit into disciplinary
niches. In the process of reducing agriculture to its component
parts, land grant research in the 20th century has at its most
extreme reduced farmland to simply a medium in which crops are
produced.

    Adherents to the conventional agriculture paradigm point to
high yielding plant varieties, standardized and uniform products,
year-around availability of fresh fruits and vegetables, and "cheap
food" as evidence that the neoclassical model is working. From a
strictly economic standpoint, it is a fact that Americans spend
less of their disposable income on food than any other society
(Urban 1991). However, cheap food has hidden costs.

### Industrialization

    In many ways, conventional agriculture in the United States
reflects the adoption of a 'mass production,' 'corporate,' or 'industrial' model of food production (Friedland 1994). Agricultural industrialization involves the concentration, increased technical
advancement and ongoing integration with input and marketing
sectors of larger-sized agricultural interests (Hamilton 1993).
Capital in the form of machinery and chemicals is substituted for
land and labor in the production process. Labor tasks are routin-
ized whenever possible, and management is increasingly standardized. Professional farm managers operate their businesses
according to strict guidelines for preparing the soil, planting,
fertilizing, pest control, cultivation and harvesting (Lyson and
Geisler 1992).

While it is difficult to pinpoint a starting date for the industrialization process in the United States, it is safe to say that the mechanization of farming in the early part of the 20th century was a first giant step that led to increasing intensification, concentration, and specialization of production (Bowler 1992, Welsh 1996). From that time, farms became larger and fewer, while land was used more intensively and yields per acre increased dramatically. At the same time, farms were woven into ever tighter marketing channels.

Between 1920 and 1970, large food processors such as Green Giant, Birds Eye, Del Monte, Dole and others helped to industrialize America's food system. Early in the 20th century, most farm products, especially fruits and vegetables, were consumed in and around the region where they were produced. Production and consumption of food was fixed to a locality. The development of the canning and packaging industry, however, allowed certain foods to travel great distances without spoiling. Frozen food technology further contributed to the uncoupling of production from consumption. While non-family held corporations didn't get heavily into land ownership, they moved to dominate the input and marketing sectors, gaining in that way considerable control of the land without actual ownership.

### Between a Rock and a Hard Place

"Farming is the only business where you buy retail, sell wholesale, and pay the transportation both ways" (Carusi 1998). Farmers in 1910 received about $0.41 of the consumers' food dollar; in 1992 they received only $0.09. During the same period, the share of the input sector rose from $0.15 to $0.24, and the marketing sector from $0.44 to $0.67 (Lehman and Krebs 1996). The money in agriculture is made in the input and marketing sectors, and it is in these sectors that large corporations completely dominate, and strive to increase even further their share of the food dollar.

In 1985, four companies supplied 64% of the corn seed in the United States, and Pioneer alone supplied 38% (Raeburn 1995). The top 10 agrochemical companies accounted for 82% of global agrochemical sales in 1996, while the top 10 seed companies control about 40% of the global seed market, and consolidation is continuing (PANUPS 1998). Farm machinery is another key input,

and in 1989 four companies controlled 80% of the U.S. market
(Krebs 1992).

Mass-production food processors and distributors along with
mass market retailers have also become dominant fixtures in the
American food economy, providing abundant quantities of relatively inexpensive, standardized goods. The degree of
concentration has reached the point where in 1994 three packers
controlled the slaughter of more than 80% of the beef in the
United States (Lehman and Krebs 1996), and two companies,
Cargill and Continental, controlled 50% of U.S. grain exports.
Market share of the top four firms exceeds 45% in pork packing
and broiler production, 30% in egg and turkey production, and
70% in flour milling (Heffernan et al. 1996).

Six multinational corporations account for more than 46% of
the retail purchases of food in the United States. According to
Standard and Poors (1994), total sales of food and beverage products in the U.S. in 1992 exceeded $221 billion. The six largest
U.S. corporations and their 1992 sales (in $billion) were Phillip
Morris ($33.0), Conagra ($21.2), Pepsico ($13.7), Coca Cola
($13.0), IBP Inc. ($11.1), and Anheuser Busch ($10.7). Several
international corporations with annual sales in the billions of
dollars, such as Grand Metropolitan (UK), Nestle (Switzerland),
Unilever N.V. (Netherlands and UK), and Eridania Gruppo
Ferruzzi (Italy), also control a substantial portion of the U.S. food
dollar through their subsidiaries.

Concentration within different sectors does not tell the full
story; vertical integration gives some companies control from seed
to table. Integrated ownership is particularly important in the
production of poultry, eggs, and produce (Table 5.3). For example,
Tyson Foods owns the chickens, feed, trucks, and processing
plant; the farmer provides housing and labor (see Case 15). In the
global merger frenzy, chemical and pharmaceutical companies
are frequent purchasers of seed and food technology companies
(Box 5.1). Much of this buying is driven by the profit potential of
biotechnology, and the ultimate goal of a synthetic food industry
producing substitutes for milk, meat, and other commodities from
soybeans or simple carbohydrate feedstuffs.

Table 5.3  Value, by commodity, produced under production and marketing contracts, and under integrated ownership, 1990 (Welsh 1996).

| Commodity | Production and marketing contracts (%) | Integrated ownership (%) | Integrated control, total (%) |
|---|---|---|---|
| Broilers | 92 | 8 | 100 |
| Turkeys | 65 | 28 | 93 |
| Hatching eggs | 70 | 30 | 100 |
| Market eggs | 43 | 50 | 93 |
| Mfg. grade milk | 25 | 1 | 26 |
| Fluid grade milk | 95 | 0 | 95 |
| Hogs | 18 | 3 | 21 |
| Fed cattle | 12 | 4 | 16 |
| Sheep/lamb | 7 | 33 | 40 |
| Processed vegetables | 83 | 15 | 98 |
| Fresh vegetables | 25 | 40 | 65 |
| Potatoes | 55 | 40 | 95 |
| Citrus | 65 | 35 | 100 |
| Other fruit | 40 | 25 | 65 |

Today, the sheer size of the multinational food giants has important consequences for farmers and their farms. "Size brings economic power and this is particularly significant when set against the structure of the farming industry with its large number of relatively small producers. Some of the most dramatic recent changes in agricultural marketing reflect the power of these new markets to extract their requirements from the farming industry" (Hart 1992). Large processors and retailers centralize their purchases of farm products. Because they seek large quantities of standardized and uniform products, they have considerable power in dictating how and where agricultural production takes place, and what price the farmers will receive. One of their mechanisms for controlling what happens on the farm is the use of contracts.

Box 5.1   Mr. Green Genes?

A front page article in The Wall Street Journal, January 29 (Kilman 1998) asked "Will consumers gobble up genetically engineered food created by the same company that makes Lycra, Teflon and Stainmaster carpets? Officials at Dupont Co. believe so. And they are putting their money where their mouths are, tossing $3 billion around the breadbasket in recent months in hopes of creating the ingredients for a bioengineered menu that will yield huge profits."

"The nation's largest chemical concern predicts that within a few decades, revenue from its new crop-biotechnology venture will equal DuPont's total 1997 sales of $45.1 billion. 'The next Silicon Valley is plant biotechnology,' says William F. Kirk, a senior vice president of DuPont, noting that the deals he has made recently represent only 20% of the items on his shopping list. 'We're going to be the major player.'"

DuPont has already developed a genetically-altered soybean that contains four times the normal level of oleic acid, and hopes within ten years to have 10 million acres under contract to grow the bean. The company recently purchased 20% of the Pioneer Hi-Bred seed company as a means of developing other genetically manipulated crops. Other investments include food technology firms that transform soybeans into meat, cheese and milk replacements.

Other companies moving aggressively into crop biotechnology and food technology include Monsanto, Dow Chemical, Novartis AG, a Swiss pharmaceutical and chemical concern. Grain processors Cargill and Archer-Daniels-Midland are interested in dedicating some of their processing plants to refining genetically engineered grain, and are negotiating deals with the chemical companies.

## The Growth of Contract Farming

To ensure large quantities of standardized and uniform products, food processors enter into formal contracts with individual farmers (Box 5.2). In 1980, 23% of total farm output was contract production (Krebs 1992). Today, about 83% of processed vegetables are grown under contract and 15% are produced on large corporate farms (Table 5.3). Sugar beets, milk, seed crops, horticultural crops, and poultry are largely produced under contract. More than 20% of swine are produced under contract, an increase from only 2% in 1980 (Hamilton 1994). Even food- and feed-grain production under contract has increased to 7% from 2% in 1970, with further increases predicted as production of identity-preserved grains increases.

Box 5.2    Contracts in U.S. Agriculture.

U.S. agricultural contracts tend to be of two types: marketing and production (Welsh 1997). A marketing contract requires a farmer to sell his or her product to a particular processor or intermediary firm (contractor) but allows the farmer to make all managerial and production decisions. Most of the milk contracts in the United States, for example, as well as many grain contracts, are marketing contracts (Martin 1993). Production contracts tend to go beyond marketing contracts by specifying that farmers adhere to certain production practices decided by the contractor (Martin 1993, Martinez and Reed 1996). If a production contract specifies that farmers adhere to certain production practices, but the contractor does not provide any tangible goods (inputs) to use in production, the contract is called a production management contract. If a contract requires the contractor to provide an input, it is called a resource providing contract (Martinez and Reed, 1996).

Marketing contracts transfer minimal control from the farmer to the contractor. Production management contracts, however, give contractors more control over the production process, and resource-providing contracts give contractors the most control over the production process that is possible without buying the production operation outright—vertically integrating.

Contract farming allows food processors to exert significant control on farmers. Many contracts specify quantity, quality, price, delivery date, and in some instances, the processor is completely involved in the management of the farm, including input provision. Contract farming also supports increased farm size. Economies of scale dictate that processors are more inclined to work with large farmers whenever possible. A processor's ability to award or refuse a contract may have contributed to differences in profitability between large and small producers, and accelerated the process of farm concentration (Hart 1992).

Contract farming results in a reconfiguration of production at the local level, because it is the processor and not the farmer who determines what commodity is produced and where. In the processing industry, especially for fruits and vegetables, quality concerns dictate that crops be grown near processing plants. This requirement imposes a distance limit on producers and leads to narrowly defined supply areas revolving around the location of the processing plants.

## Globalization of the Food System

### Who's Farming in the Green Giant's Valley?

During the 1970's and 1980's a rather dramatic transformation began to take place in the food industry. A wave of mergers and acquisitions transformed what was at the time a system of large, nationally-oriented food companies into a global system of multinational food giants. In the process of this transformation, the ties between farmers and processors were restructured.

The story of Green Giant is revealing. In 1979, Pillsbury acquired the Green Giant company in what appeared to be a friendly takeover (Bengston 1991). Although at the time of the takeover Green Giant had expanded its operations beyond canning and packaging vegetables to include restaurants, meat products, and fruits, after the takeover Pillsbury divested itself of everything except the vegetable business.

In 1989, Pillsbury, which was an emerging food conglomerate in and of itself, was acquired by Grand Metropolitan, a British-based multinational food giant. Grand Metropolitan's plans for Green Giant were to make it "...the number one vegetable company in the *world* by the year 2000" (Bengston 1991).

To accomplish this daunting feat, Grand Met divested Green Giant of all of its production and processing facilities. These divestitures were made to "increase competitiveness and customer service." According to Ian Martin, the CEO of Grand Metropolitan, the goal was to make Green Giant "...a true international brand with its cartoon figure [that is] in line with all of the green values of ecology" (Wentz 1992).

In the 1990's, then, Green Giant became the first 'virtual' food corporation. Today it owns no production or processing facilities. Green Giant procures the vegetables it needs by entering into contracts with farmers around the world. It then outsources the canning and packaging of these commodities to companies like Seneca Foods, which proudly proclaims, "Give us your recipe and your specifications and we'll provide a finished product that you'll be proud to put your label on."[1] (http://www.senecafoods.com/mainpage.html) [December 1997]

### Global Trade Figures

Agricultural trade figures for the United States indicate the extent to which global food companies seek their raw materials globally. In 1995, U.S. farms produced $186 billion worth of crops and livestock, of which $55.8 billion was exported. In the same year, the United States imported almost $30 billion of agricultural products (Table 5.4). Only 28% of the imports were classified as noncompetitive, i.e., crops such as bananas that cannot be grown in the continental United States.

The real money of course is in processed foods. The largest U.S. food corporations do as much as 25% to 50% of their business in other countries. Foreign corporations such as Nestle S.A. (Switzerland) are also global, with much of their sales in the United States.

Table 5.4  Agricultural imports to the United States—value
($ million), by selected commodity, and by leading countries of
origin, 1995 (USDC 1997).

| Commodity | Value | Leading countries of origin |
|---|---|---|
| Total | 29,993 | Canada, Mexico, Indonesia |
| Competitive products | 21,586 | Canada, Mexico, Italy |
| Cattle, live | 1,413 | Canada, Mexico, Japan |
| Beef and veal | 1,447 | Australia, New Zealand, Canada |
| Pork | 686 | Canada, Denmark, Poland |
| Dairy products | 1,089 | New Zealand, Ireland, Italy |
| Fruits and preparations | 2,261 | Mexico, Chile, Thailand |
| Vegetables and preparations | 3,103 | Mexico, Canada, Spain |
| Wine | 1,153 | France, Italy, Spain |
| Malt beverages | 1,166 | Netherlands, Mexico, Canada |
| Grains and feeds | 2,362 | Canada, Italy, Thailand |
| Sugar and related products | 1,255 | Canada, Brazil, Dominican Republic |
| Oilseeds and products | 1,815 | Canada, Philippines, Italy |
| Noncompetitive products | 8,406 | Indonesia, Mexico, Columbia |
| Coffee and products | 3,263 | Mexico, Columbia, Brazil |
| Rubber, crude natural | 1,629 | Indonesia, Thailand, Malaysia |
| Cocoa and products | 1,134 | Canada, Cote d'Ivoire, Indonesia |
| Bananas and plantains | 1,140 | Costa Rica, Ecuador, Columbia |

## GATT, NAFTA, and the WTO

The globalization of the economy and the increase in the power of multinational corporations has been accelerated by the adoption of world and regional trade agreements that limit the power of national, state or local governments to impose restrictions on commercial activities. As stated in *The Wall Street Journal*, GATT (General Agreement on Tariffs and Trade) "represents another stake in the heart of the idea that governments can direct economies. The main purpose of GATT is to get governments out of the way so that companies can cross jurisdictions (i.e., national boundaries) with relative ease" (Nader and Wallach 1996).

As a condition of joining the World Trade Organization, the United States has agreed to binding arbitration of a wide range of trade disputes by a WTO tribunal in Geneva. Thus, an unelected international body has the right to overturn U.S. laws or regulations that inhibit free trade under WTO rules. Unacceptable laws could include subsidies to promote energy conservation, banning of pesticides allowed elsewhere in the world, restrictions on the export of raw logs to protect value-added timber industries, and tariffs to protect certain types of farmers from cheaper imports. Even a "support local farmers" campaign by a New England state drew European complaints as unfair government intrusion in food trade.

## Implications of Industrialization and Globalization

### Land and Labor

An industrial system of agricultural production operates at its highest economic efficiency when the factors of production can be freely substituted for one another depending on their relative cost. This has manifested itself in the United States during the last century as the substitution of chemicals and machinery for labor and land. In a global economy, the options for substitution are increased—cheaper foreign land and labor for more expensive domestic land and labor. Land, which once anchored labor, capital, and management to a particular place and formed the foundation of a family-based system of farming, is increasingly being put into a 'reserve pool' from which it can be brought into or taken out of production as global market forces dictate. If land can be easily brought into and taken out of production, then it acquires the same degree of fluidity as capital, labor and management. The net result is a system of food and agricultural production that is becoming uncoupled from place and presumably from local control.

Contract farming allows large corporations more flexibility in dealing with land than ownership does—vertical control without vertical integration. As Hamilton (1994) asks, "Why own the farm if you can own the farmer (and the crop)?" It is much simpler to add or drop contracts than to buy and sell land, and contracts leave responsibility for compliance with labor and environmental laws on the farmer, not the corporation. In several Midwestern states with laws against corporate ownership of land, contracts allow a company to become directly involved in crop or livestock production. Even without contracts, the near monopolies held by multinational corporations in providing inputs and buying the crops give them immense influence on farm operations. Lehman and Krebs (1996) state that corporate agribusiness "has sought to relegate the farm community to a small and select group of economically and politically impotent raw material producers serving a nationwide food manufacturing system. Such a system can be controlled from afar by a select number of giant corporations and economically powerful individuals."

### Impact on Communities

The effects of major structural changes in agriculture go beyond farmers to the entire rural community. We know, from a study conducted in the 1940s, that large scale, industrial agriculture can have a dampening effect on community welfare. In 1946, Walter Goldschmidt published a landmark study in which he compared the quality of life and standard of living of residents in two California farm communities, Arvin and Dinuba (Box 5.3). Arvin and Dinuba were similar in size and type of agriculture, but Arvin was dominated by a single large agribusiness firm (DiGiorgio), while Dinuba was organized around small, family farms. On every measure of social well being Goldschmidt examined, the residents of the small farm community enjoyed a more beneficial standard of living and a higher quality of life. Several replications of Goldschmidt (see Lobao 1990) have reaffirmed his basic findings, although the debate continues, most recently regarding the effects of large hog confinement operations (Box 5.4).

Box 5.3   Goldschmidt and farmland.

Farmland plays a central role in Walter Goldschmidt's (1946) classic study of three California farm communities, "As You Sow." The first sentence in the Introduction sets the tone for the entire book: "Controversy over control of the land is as old as America." His comparison of two of the farm communities, Arvin and Dinuba, rests on the relationship between farm size and tenure arrangements and the quality of life and living conditions in the communities.

The average farm size in Arvin was 497 acres when Goldschmidt conducted his study in the 1940s. In Dinuba the average farm size was 57 acres. Almost 90% of the farms in Dinuba were less than 80 acres, while more than half of the farms in Arvin were greater than 80 acres. More than three-fourths of Dinuba farmers owned all of the land they operated. Only 35% of the farmers in Arvin were full owners. Tenancy in Arvin was concentrated more among the largest farmers than in Dinuba where tenancy was more evenly distributed across all size classes. Not surprisingly, less than one-third of the land owners in Arvin lived in the community compared to 70% of the Dinuba land owners. When he examined the community well being in each of the communities, Goldschmidt observed the following:

1. Arvin had more wage laborers than Dinuba, while Dinuba had more entrepreneurs;
2. Arvin had lower living conditions;
3. Arvin had a more unstable population;
4. Arvin had a poorer physical appearance;
5. Arvin had poorer schools, parks and social services;
6. Dinuba had more religious institutions;
7. There was a higher degree of community loyalty in Dinuba;
8. In Arvin, fewer community decisions were made by community residents;
9. Arvin displayed greater social segregation;
10. Dinuba had more retail trade.

Based on his observations, Goldschmidt concluded: "The study of Arvin and Dinuba shows, therefore, that quality of social conditions is associated with scale of operations; that farm size is in fact an important causal factor in the creation of such differences and that it is reasonable to believe that farm size is the most important cause of these differences."

Box 5.4    Report: Small hog farms aid economy.

Small hog farms are better for rural economies, producing more jobs and local tax revenue than larger operations, according to an analysis of a new Iowa State University study by a Nebraska rural advocacy group. The analysis by the Center for Rural Affairs in Walthill, Neb., indicates that 23 farms of 150 sows each would create 21 more jobs and produce almost $35,000 more in revenues to local governments than one farm with 3,400 sows, if all produced at the same rate. "If a state's goal is job formation and economic growth, this study says they should do it with small hog operations instead of large ones," said Nancy Thompson, a consultant for the center who did the analysis.

But Tim Cumberland, chief financial officer for Sand Livestock Systems in Columbus, Nebraska, said the fallacy of studies indicating that more small farms are better is that they don't come true. Until last fall, the hog industry had some of the highest market prices in its history during the last 2½ years. "But we continued to see the small hog farmer exit the industry," he said. The average age of rural hog producers is the late 50s, and there aren't a lot of young farmers coming in behind them, he said. "It sounds nice that, yeah, you could have this many more jobs, but there's nobody around to do them," Cumberland said.

Daniel Otto, the Iowa State economics professor who prepared the study, said small farms tend to employ more people, while larger operations have a greater labor efficiency, often using equipment such as automated feeding systems that require fewer people. Those extra people on small farms pay taxes and buy houses and other goods, which adds to local economies, he said. "There would be more jobs and economic impacts if the hogs were produced in smaller systems," Otto said. "But the economic forces are favoring the larger systems."

Since 1980, the number of Iowa farms with hogs has declined dramatically, although the number of hogs in the state has remained fairly constant, he wrote in the study, which was prepared as part of a recent teleconference. The shift from more smaller farms to fewer large farms in Iowa is

*Continues*

Box 5.4 *Continued*

part of a national pattern, as change in the industry and global competition caused many smaller operations to drop out of the hog business. "It's better for rural communities to have more small hog farms," Otto said. "The challenge is finding ways for that to happen." One way to keep smaller operations may be through cooperatives or networks, he said. But he said he was "dubious" about placing policy restrictions on large operations and instead favored incentives for smaller operations.

Bob Ruggles, executive director of the Nebraska Pork Producers Association, said size was not the main issue to him or to most of the organizations members. "Learning how to be cost-competitive is," he said. But Thompson said Otto's study is the kind of information Iowa, Nebraska and South Dakota should look at as their leaders debate what kind of a pork industry they want. In addition to creating more jobs and local tax revenue, the smaller operations create 20 percent more net revenue for the state and pay 7 percent more property taxes than one large operation of equal output, she said. "States need to be doing more to create the pork production opportunities that will bring greater economic benefits to a community," she said.

— Anderson, J. 1998. Report: Small hog farms aid economy. Omaha World-Herald, 17 January, pp. 23, 30.

Continuing agricultural industrialization promises more negative changes for rural communities. Technological advances such as ROMPER, a robotic melon picker with sensors to detect ripe melons, will displace more farm workers (Rifkin 1996). Monopolies by processors such as beef packers drive down wages (Krebs 1992) as does the importation by these processors of cheap, often illegal, foreign labor. Huge confinement facilities for hogs and other livestock threaten water and air quality. There is growing evidence that NAFTA's implementation regulations are accelerating the loss of small and medium-size farms, and promoting the increase of corporate agriculture (Luna 1994). In an ironic effect of the agreement, the removal of barriers to the export of cheap U.S. corn to Mexico will drive millions of Mexican farmers from the land, who will then migrate with their families to the cities, many of them to the United States (Abernethy 1994).

While the structure of agriculture has obvious ramifications for rural communities, it is no less important for urban communities, particularly in terms of food security—the ability of a country or region to feed itself (Joseph 1996). By this definition, most regions of the United States are not food secure. They cannot feed themselves, but are dependent on a global food system and the transport and processing of much of their food at long distances. Even production and processing that occurs locally is generally not under local control. It is instead controlled by a handful of multinational corporations that have no allegiance to any particular country or people.

Some of the drawbacks of a lack of local control of the food system are already apparent in the inner cities of the United States. The large food retailers have abandoned these areas, leaving the residents with the choice of traveling long distances to buy food (exacerbated by a lack of mass transit) or paying inflated prices at convenience stores for a poor selection. Fresh foods are particularly limited.

Even the more affluent urban areas suffer an economic drain as most food dollars leave the community. Dependence on long distance food shipments make residents vulnerable to disruptions, as evidenced by the panic buying in food stores in advance of hurricanes or other weather problems. A highly centralized and integrated economic system is also vulnerable to global crises such as oil embargoes or a Wall Street meltdown. As consolidation reduces the number of food companies even further, lack of competition makes price increases likely (Krebs 1992). The immense power of the multinational food corporations and their influence on political decisions makes a mockery of the democratic process.

Underlying all of these issues is the degradation of land and resources caused by a system that perceives farmland as just another substitutable industrial input. This degradation poses a major threat to the sustainability of the food system (see Chapter 1). The most severe treatment of agricultural land is, of course, its conversion to development. What is the potential influence of the ongoing changes in the structure of agriculture on the rate of farmland conversion?

Box 5.5   The Community Food Projects Program.

The 1996 Farm Bill authorized a new program of federal grants to support the development of community food projects designed to meet the food needs of low income people; increase the self-reliance of communities in providing for their own food needs; and promote comprehensive responses to local food, farm, and nutrition issues. It is administered by the Cooperative State Research Extension and Education Services (CSREES) of USDA.

1997 awardees include the Field to Family Project, Practical Farmers of Iowa, Boone, Iowa. Local churches, social service organizations, community supported agriculture (CSA) groups, sustainable agriculture organizations, academia, and businesses are coming together to rebuild community ties between diverse sectors of the food system. The goals of the project are to 1) make fresh, locally grown produce available to low-income households along with the opportunity to design and develop the local food system, 2) link low-income CSA members and other Field to Family participants with churches and agencies now organizing to help families leave welfare successfully, 3) increase use of locally grown food and foster the start-up and growth of small to medium sized producers, and 4) promote the role local agriculture can play in supporting communities.

— From Community Food Security Coalition. Available 3 Aug 98 at: http://www.foodsecurity.org.

## Likelihood of Farmland Conversion

A global industrial food system has no need to protect a specific piece of farmland from development. As long as the supply of land for producing the commodities needed by large agribusiness firms is plentiful around the world, there is little incentive to support local measures to preserve farmland. In a study of urban influences on farmland use in New York, Hirschl and Bills (1994) note: "Despite much debate and exposure in both the popular press and the scientific community...a national consensus on the need for agricultural land protection has not emerged." Their analysis showed that "...maintenance of land in farm use largely depends upon economic forces that are national and regional in scope, and almost exclusively outside the purview of state and local farmland protection programs."

Given the many interacting factors that determine land use (see Introduction), it is difficult to quantify the effect that the industrialization and globalization of agriculture has had on the rate of farmland conversion. However, the structural changes that have occurred in agriculture during the past century would seem to increase the likelihood of conversion because:

- The shrinking of the portion of the food dollar that goes to farmers makes farming less profitable and the conversion of farmland to other uses more likely.

- Rented land is more susceptible to development as absentee landlords have no direct interest in continued agricultural use of the land.

- Contracts are a shaky prop for farmers—if the corporate processor shifts production elsewhere for whatever reason, the farmer may be forced out (analogous to the shifting of manufacturing overseas and the loss of local jobs).

- The decoupling of a population from local land as their food source reduces their incentive to protect their farmland from development.

- The reduction in labor use on industrial farms, the decline in local value-added food processors, and the export of most agricultural profits out of the community means that fewer local people have an economic stake in land other than for development.

There is nothing in the global industrial food system that promotes the long-term preservation of agricultural land. In the emerging global economy, farmland loss will continue, and with it the disappearance of the means for communities to regain local control and food security. What are our alternatives?

## Land and Community

### Small is Beautiful

Although structural changes in agriculture are taking their toll on community food security, it is possible with proper forethought and planning to relocalize parts of the food system, especially in the periurban areas around large metropolitan centers. However, communities can buffer and shelter themselves from the global food system only if they preserve an adequate farmland base. Successful relocalization can help to stabilize the farmland base

In this section we examine ways in which farmland can be decoupled from the global food system and re-integrated with a local food system. We have identified seven characteristics associated with the relocalization of agriculture.

1. Production is oriented toward local markets and meeting the needs of local consumers rather than national or international mass markets (Wilkins 1995).

2. Agriculture is viewed as an integral part of rural communities, not merely as production of commodities (Center for Rural Affairs 1988).

3. Producers are concerned more with high-quality and value-added products and less with quantity (yield) and least cost production practices (Waters 1990).

4. Production at the farm-level is often more labor and land intensive, and less capital intensive. Farm enterprises tend to be considerably smaller in scale than industrial producers (Bird et al. 1995).

5. Producers rely more on indigenous, site-specific knowledge and less on a uniform set of "best management practices" (Kloppenburg 1991, Kneen 1993).

6. Producers forge direct market links to consumers rather than indirect links through middlemen (wholesalers, brokers, processors) (Johnston and Bryant 1987, Lyson et al. 1995).

7. Agriculture takes up social, economic and geographic spaces not filled (or passed over) by industrial agriculture. Landscapes are reconfigured.

The relocalizing of agricultural production manifests itself in many ways (Center for Rural Affairs 1988, Farming Alternatives Program 1994, 1997). *Farmers markets* provide immediate, low-cost, direct contact between local farmers and consumers, and are an effective first step for communities seeking to develop stronger local food systems. *Organic farmers* have in many cases pioneered the development of local marketing systems, and have also eschewed conventional, chemically-intensive farming practices for those that are more environmentally benign. *Community Supported Agriculture* (CSA) projects are forging direct links between groups of member-consumers (often urban) and their CSA farms. New *grower-controlled marketing cooperatives* are emerging to more effectively tap regional markets. *Agricultural districts* organized around particular commodities (such as wine; Box 5.6) have served to stabilize farms and farmland in many areas of the country. *Specialty producers* and *on-farm processors* of products for which there are not well developed mass markets (e.g., deer, goat/sheep cheese, free range chickens, organic dairy products) and *small scale, off-farm, local processors* add value in local communities and provide markets for 'new agriculture' farmers (Box 5.7).

Box 5.6   Farm winery legislation and the growth of premium wineries in New York State. Amy Guptill, Cornell University.

In the early to mid-1970s, New York's wine and grape industry was facing a crisis. The previous two decades had seen the growth of a state industry based on production of native grape varieties for juice, jellies, and wine. The New York Crop Reporting Service estimates that New York had 42,653 acres in grape production in 1975. New York was (and still is) the second largest producer of wine in the United States (Cooper 1982). The wine sector of the grape industry was anchored by the Taylor Wine Company, which purchased its grapes largely from independent New York growers on the shores of Lake Erie and in the Finger Lakes Region. Rapidly expanding production in California and a shift in consumer preferences toward table wines made from French vinifera or French-American hybrids led to a depression in grape prices in the state (White 1982). In addition, the sale of the Taylor Wine Company to Coca Cola threatened to disrupt the traditional economic relationship between the wine giant and New York's grape growers.

*Continues*

Box 5.6 *Continued*

The New York State legislature responded in 1976 with the passage of the New York Farm Winery Bill, which attempted to assist grape growers in establishing estate wineries to realize a higher return on their grapes. In addition, the government hoped to support the high quality wine sector in the state industry and enhance its already positive reputation (Cooper 1982). The legislation substantially lowered licencing fees for farm wineries using New York state grapes and other fruits, and producing less than 50,000 gallons of wine per year. Subsequent legislation bolstered the effort by allowing vintners to more freely sell their product on site and through other retail channels.

Between 1980 and 1995, the number of wineries in New York increased from 46 to more than 100. Most of this increase involved smaller wineries (see Table 5.5). In a 1982 survey, small wine producers reported that the lower licencing fees were a significant benefit to their business. In addition, several vintners pointed out that the several pieces of legislation themselves served to attract a lot of attention to the wine industry and especially the farm winery sector. Currently, the wine industry makes a substantial contribution to New York's economy. In 1992 the New York Wine and Grape Foundation calculated that the direct and indirect benefits of the industry included over 45,000 jobs paying over one million dollars in wages, over three million dollars in sales, and $200,000 in state taxes.

The 1992 Census of Agriculture reported 34,250 acres planted in grapes, about an 8,000 acre decrease from 1975. However, measures for both years do not distinguish between acreage for varietals for wine making and native varieties (like Concord) for juices and jellies. Despite the net decline in grape acreage, it is plausible to conclude that the historical and agricultural significance of wine and grape production in New York State means that the successful development of the premium wine sector included as a benefit the preservation of a highly specialized farmland resource under conditions conducive to sustainable stewardship. Overall, then, premium wine production has played an important role in maintaining and enhancing the ecological, economic, and cultural integrity of New York's vineyard landscapes.

There is evidence that a relocalization of agricultural and food systems is taking place in regions that have been hit hard by global competition. It is not surprising that Massachusetts, New York and other states in the Northeast are in the vanguard of the relocalization efforts, though even in these states farmland is still disappearing at an alarming rate. For example, New York state has experienced a rather dramatic growth in recent years of some of these new forms of 'local' agricultural and food production (Table 5.5). Community supported agriculture did not exist in New York 10 years ago, but by 1996 there were 64 CSA farms. The numbers of farmers markets, small wineries, and community gardens have all increased. Likewise, small-scale processing, which frequently articulates with local farms increased from 380 firms in 1987 to 461 firms in 1992. U-pick operations and community kitchens also show dramatic growth in recent years. These efforts share the potential to nurture local economic development, maintain diversity and quality in products, and provide forums where producers and consumers can come together to solidify bonds of community.

One way to preserve farmland in the United States then is to increase the amount of food and agricultural products that are produced and marketed locally. Land that might otherwise be taken out of farming because it cannot profitably produce for the global marketplace can be kept in production because it serves the needs and tastes of local consumers. In the process of relocalizing at least part of the food system, farmland is transformed from simply a 'substitutable' factor of production in a global food economy to an integral part of the local community. It is at this point that economy shades into community, and decisions about the future of local farmland are made by farmers and consumers in the community and not by global market forces.

Box 5.7 Resurgence of the small.

Although large multinational corporations dominate the U.S. food system and pose major barriers to local control of food and to community food security, there are indications that economic trends may be shifting from bigger is better to small is beautiful.

Writing in *The Wall Street Journal*, Thomas Petzinger, Jr. (1998) reports that "Megamergers and consolidations are all sideshows compared with the restructuring of the economy into ever-smaller pieces. Like dandelions gone to seed, major companies have released millions of experienced workers to the wind, and they're thriving in small niches."

"In manufacturing, new economies of locality are beginning to conquer old economies of scale. Micropub Systems of Rochester, N.Y., installs entire breweries in 96 square feet; keg for keg, the premium local brews cost less than anything a giant factory can deliver. In Dillon, Mont., Great Harvest Baking is testing a complete scratch-bread retail bakery in 258 square feet. Big firms sell processed food overseas, but Ibberson Inc. of Minneapolis helps countries make their own. It builds grain-processing plants in modules the size of shipping containers—then bolts the pieces together in Asia."

"Size no longer assures stability. Microsoft and AT&T have already seen the peaks of their commercial influence."

Decentralization of food processing technology will facilitate the relocalization of the U.S. food system, but food systems also include suppliers of agricultural inputs, wholesale and retail marketers of food, and of course the farms them-selves—all areas that have seen major consolidations of control. Will the "new economies of locality" be able to gain the upper hand in the areas of seed and fertilizer production, land ownership, and the battle for the shopper's dollar? It remains to be seen if Pioneer, Con-Agra and ADM have seen the peak of their influence.

Table 5.5   Growth of local agriculture initiatives in New York State.

| Local Agriculture Initiative | No.   (Year) | No.   (Year) |
|---|---|---|
| Farmers' Markets | 6   (1964) | 180   (1995) |
| Organic Farmers | 26   (1988) | 107   (1995) |
| Small Wineries | 35   (1981) | 70   (1995) |
| Community Kitchens | 0   (1994) | 7   (1996) |
| Community Gardens | 550   (1978) | 1,500   (1996) |
| Small-scale Food Processors | 380   (1987) | 461   (1992) |
| Community Supported Agriculture (CSAs) | 53   (1993) | 64   (1996) |

Source: Farming Alternatives Program, Cornell University, Ithaca, NY.

### New Residents, New Problems

The merging of economy and community is not easily accomplished. The population pressures that lead a community to consider ways to preserve farmland complicate the social dynamics of reaching a consensus for action. In the 1990s, nonmetropolitan areas experienced a net migration gain from metropolitan places for the first time since the 1970s (Fulton et al. 1997). As Salamon and Tornatore (1994) note, the in-migration typically takes place in areas that are within easy commuting distance to metropolitan centers. The in-migrants often expand the geographic boundaries of the existing community by moving into new neighborhoods on land that was previously devoted to agriculture. They also disturb the social boundaries of the community. "Old political alliances and status hierarchies are inevitably upset...Community solidarity may be threatened by conflicts over goals, rate of development, and allocation of community resources" (Schwarzweller 1989).

Newcomers usually demand more services and infrastructure than existing residents, and the affluent in-migrants are willing

to raise taxes to pay for these services. This puts pressure on existing farm businesses and in some instances makes it too
expensive to farm. Schwarzweller provides an example of the
squeeze farmers feel from urban sprawl. In the late 1970s the
New York City metropolitan area was expanding into Suffolk
County on Long Island. Suffolk County was one of the leading
agricultural counties in the state through the 1950s and into the
1960s, producing fresh fruits and vegetables for the New York
City market and potatoes for much of the country. In 1978, farmland in the eastern part of the county (farthest from the City) was
valued at $1,500 per acre, while in the western part of the county
the development value had jumped to $7,500 per acre. Since 1980
the situation has continued to deteriorate, the number of farms in
the county has fallen from almost 800 (1982) to less than 600
(1992) and farm acreage has dropped from 50,000 acres to
35,000 acres.

The social dynamics in a rapidly growing community are complex. Often it is the newer residents who are the most vocal
proponents of farmland preservation, while long-time residents
may lead the fight for individual property rights and the ability to
cash in on land development. Perhaps the main lesson from cases
like Suffolk County is that communities wishing to preserve their
agriculture need to act now to build consensus, and institute land
use laws and agricultural development policies. By the time the
new houses are coming over the horizon, it is often too late.

### Into the Future

Complete local or regional self-sufficiency is neither practical
nor desirable. Undoubtedly there is some level of equitable international and inter-regional trade that is beneficial to both
exporting and importing communities. However, the balance between local self-sufficiency and global dependence needs to come
back towards the local, rather than continuing on its present tra-
jectory towards the global. Only in this way can we stem the
continued erosion of our farmland base.

There are many changes in government policy that could facilitate relocalization (Box 5.8). However, communities already have
many tools that can be used to effect change and move the food
system towards greater localization. Some of these tools include:

- Local economic development efforts to support food process-ing activities.

- Land use policies that protect active farm areas from random residential development.

- Zoning codes that allocate land into areas of non-farm development, areas of natural preservation, and areas for agricultural production.

- Institutional food acquisition practices that integrate local food production directly into the community.

- Local purchase of development rights programs that allow the citizens of a community to buy control of the land that supports their food system.

Kloppenburg et al. (1996) suggest that "the centrality of food to human life [makes it] a powerful template around which to build non- or extra-market relationships between persons, social groups, and institutions which have been distanced from each other." Indeed a growing number of practitioners and academics across the United States are recognizing that creative new forms of community development, built around the regeneration of local food systems, may eventually generate sufficient economic and political power to mute the more socially and environmentally destructive manifestations of the global marketplace.

Box 5.8   Structural and policy changes to support small-scale farmers.

Relocalization of community food systems involves close relationships among producers and consumers, production tailored to local demand, local processing and adding value, responsiveness to small-scale niche and ethnic markets, and the capture and cycling of profits within the community. Small-scale farms are essential to this type of economy, yet current economic and regulatory trends often work against the success of small farms.

*Continues*

Box 5.8 *Continued*

At a 15 September 1997 public hearing of the National Commission on Small Farms (Warnert 1997), farmers and other witnesses recommended changes in government policies to improve the environment for small-scale farming including:

- Increase funding in support of specialty crop production.

- Increase extension efforts for non-English speaking farmers.

- Investigate brokers to ensure that they are dealing with farmers honestly.

- Develop a marketing infrastructure for small-scale farmers.

- Encourage the formation of farmer cooperatives, which help farmers achieve more bargaining power and economies of scale.

- Coordinate nutrition programs with small scale farming, and link farmers with local low-income residents.

- Allow Community Supported Agriculture programs to accept food stamps.

- Provide a mechanism to make small loans available to small-scale farmers.

- Prohibit the import of products grown in other countries using pesticides not available to U.S. farmers.

- Shift Cooperative Extension training from an emphasis on production to an emphasis on salesmanship, labeling, adding value to products, and other marketing tactics.

## Endnote

1. This quote is taken from the home page of Seneca Foods.

## References

Abernethy, V. 1994. Editorial: A minority view on the globalization of trade. Population and Environment 15:343-345.

Albrecht, D.E., and S.H. Murdock. 1990. The Sociology of U.S. Agriculture. Iowa State University Press, Ames.

Bengston, R.E. 1991. A History of the Green Giant Company, 1903-1979. Unpublished dissertation, University of Minnesota.

Bird, E.A.R., G.L. Bultena, and J.C. Gardner (eds.). 1995. Planting the Future. Iowa State University Press, Ames.

Bowler, I.R. (ed.). 1992. The Geography of Agriculture in Developed Market Economies. John Wiley and Sons, New York.

Bureau of the Census. 1983. Farm Population of the United States: 1982. Current Population Reports, Series P-27, No. 56. U.S. Department of Commerce, Washington, D.C.

Bureau of the Census. 1984. Census of Agriculture, 1982. Vol. 1, Geographic Area Series: Pt. 51, U.S. Summary, Final Report. Government Printing Office, Washington, D.C. Available: http://govinfo.kerr.orst.edu/cgi-bin/ag-list?01-state.usa [30 January 1998]

Bureau of the Census. 1989. Census of Agriculture, 1987. Vol. 1, Geographic Area Series: Pt. 51, U.S. Summary, Final Report. Government Printing Office, Washington, D.C. Available: http://govinfo.kerr.orst.edu/cgi-bin/ag-list?01-state.usa [30 January 1998]

Bureau of the Census. 1992. Residents of farms and rural areas, 1991. Current Population Reports, Population Characteristics, P20-472, U.S. Department of Commerce, Washington, D.C.

Bureau of the Census. 1994. Census of Agriculture, 1992. Vol. 1, Geographic Area Series: Pt. 51, U.S. Summary, Final Report. Government Printing Office, Washington, D.C. Available: http://govinfo.kerr.orst.edu/cgi-bin/ag-list?01-state.usa [30 January 1998]

Carusi, C. 1998. Build a business on your farm. Nebraska Sustainable Agriculture Society Newsletter No. 61:1-2, 12.

Center for Rural Affairs. 1988. Agriculture: A foundation for rural economic development. Center for Rural Affairs Newsletter (November):5-8.

Cooper, R.C. 1982. Some Economic Aspects of Small Winery Operations in New York. Masters Thesis, Cornell University.

Farming Alternatives Program. 1994. Community Agriculture Development Profile of 32 Initiatives in New York State. Community Agriculture Development Series, Farming Alternatives Program, Cornell University. Ithaca, NY.

Farming Alternatives Program. 1997. Farming for the Future: A Guide to Sustaining Agriculture in Your Community. Community Agriculture Development Series, Farming Alternatives Program, Cornell University, Ithaca, NY.

Friedland, W.H. 1994. The global fresh fruit and vegetable system: An industrial organization analysis. pp. 173-189. In: P. McMichael (ed.) The Global Restructuring of Agro-Food Systems. Cornell University Press, Ithaca, NY.

Fulton, J.A., G.V. Fuguitt, and R.M. Gibson. 1997. Recent changes in metropolitan-nonmetropolitan migration streams. Rural Sociology 62:363-384.

Goldschmidt, W. 1946. Small Business and the Community: A Study in the Central Valley of California on the Effects of Scale of Farm Operation. Report of the Special Committee to Study Problems of American Small Business. U.S. Senate, 79th Congress, 2nd session, Committee Print 13. U.S. Government Printing Office, Washington, D.C.

Hamilton, N.D. 1993. Who owns dinner: Evolving legal mechanisms for ownership of plant genetic resources. Tulsa Law Journal 28:587-643.

Hamilton, N.D. 1994. Agriculture without farmers? Is industrialization restructuring American food production and threatening the future of sustainable agriculture? Northern Illinois University Law Review 14:613-657.

Hart, P. 1992. Marketing agricultural produce. pp. 162-206. In: I.R. Bowler (ed.) The Geography of Agriculture in Developed Market Economies. John Wiley and Sons, New York.

Heady, E. 1976. The agriculture of the U.S. Scientific American 235:107-127.

Heffernan, W., D. Constance, R. Gronski, and M. Hendrickson. 1996. Concentration of agricultural markets. pp. 61-64. In: H. Carter and C. Francis (eds.) Proceedings of Planning and Review Meeting, North Central Sustainable Agriculture Training Program, Kansas City, MO, 17-18 November 1996. Center for Sustainable Agricultural Systems, University of Nebraska, Lincoln.

Hirschl, T.A., and N.L. Bills. 1994. Urban influences on farmland use in New York State. Population Research and Policy Review 13:179-194.

Johnston, T., and C. Bryant. 1987. Agricultural adaptation: The prospects for sustaining agriculture near cities. pp. 9-21. In: W. Lockeretz (ed.) Sustaining Agriculture Near Cities. Soil and Water Conservation Society, Ankeny, IA.

Joseph, H.M. 1996. Community food security, agriculture, and the environment: A Massachusetts perspective. pp. 245-253. In: W. Lockeretz (ed.) Environmental Enhancement through Agriculture. School of Nutrition Science and Policy, Tufts University, Medford, MA.

Kay, R.D. 1986. Marginal analysis and economic principles. pp. 23-42. In: Farm Management: Planning, Control and Implementation. McGraw-Hill, New York.

Kilman, S. 1998. Green Genes. The Wall Street Journal, pp. A1,10, 29 January.

Kloppenburg, J., Jr. 1991. Social theory and the de/reconstruction of agricultural science: Local knowledge for an alternative agriculture. Rural Sociology 56:519-548.

Kloppenburg, J., Jr., J. Hendrickson, and G.W. Stevenson. 1996. Coming in to the foodshed. Agriculture and Human Values 13:33-42.

Kneen, B. 1993. From Land to Mouth. NC Press Limited, Toronto.

Krebs, A.V. 1992. The Corporate Reapers: The Book of Agribusiness. Essential Books, Washington, D.C.

Lehman, K., and A. Krebs. 1996. Control of the World's food supply. pp. 122-130. In: J. Mander and E. Goldsmith (eds.) The Case Against the Global Economy: And For a Turn Toward the Local. Sierra Club Books, San Francisco.

Lobao, L.M. 1990. Locality and Inequality. SUNY Press, Albany, NY.

Luna, G.T. 1994. Agriculture, rural workers and free trade. Northern Illinois University Law Review 14:789-798.

Lyson, T.A., and C.C. Geisler. 1992. Toward a Second Agricultural Divide: The Restructuring of American Agriculture. Sociologia Ruralis 32:248-263.

Lyson, T.A., and R. Welsh. 1993. Crop diversity, the production function and the debate between conventional and sustainable agriculture. Rural Sociology 58:424-439.

Lyson, T.A., G. Gillespie, and D. Hilchey. 1995. Farmer's markets and the local community: Bridging the formal and informal economy. American Journal of Alternative Agriculture 10:108-113.

Martin, L. 1993. Pork...the other white meat? Agricultural Economics Workshop, Department of Agricultural and Resource Economics, North Carolina State University.

Martinez, S.W., and A. Reed. 1996. From farmers to consumers: Vertical coordination in the food industry. U.S. Department of Agriculture/ERS Agriculture Information Bulletin No. 720.

Nader, R., and L. Wallach. 1996. GATT, NAFTA, and the subversion of the democratic process. pp. 92-107. In: J. Mander and E. Goldsmith (eds.) The Case Against the Global Economy: And For a Turn Toward the Local. Sierra Club Books, San Francisco.

PANUPS. 1998. Global enterprises dominate commercial agriculture. Pesticide Action Network North America Updates Service. Available: http://www.panna.org/panna/ [9 Feb 98]

Petzinger, T., Jr. 1998. The front lines. The Wall Street Journal, p. B1, 9 January.

Raeburn, P. 1995. The Last Harvest. University of Nebraska Press, Lincoln, NE.

Rifkin, J. 1996. New technology and the end of jobs. pp. 108-121. In: J. Mander and E. Goldsmith (eds.) The Case Against the Global Economy: And For a Turn Toward the Local. Sierra Club Books, San Francisco.

Rogers, D. 1993. Leasing farmland. pp. 17-25. In: G. Wunderlich (ed.) Land Ownership & Taxation in American Agriculture. Westview Press, Boulder, CO.

Salamon, S., and J.B. Tornatore. 1994. Territory contested through property in a Midwestern post-agricultural community. Rural Sociology 59:636-654.

Schwarzweller, H.K. 1979. Migration and the changing rural scene. Rural Sociology 44:7-23.

Standard and Poors. 1994. Standard and Poors Industry Surveys. Standard and Poors Corporation, New York.

Urban, T.N. 1991. "Agricultural industrialization: It's inevitable." Choices 6(4):4-6.

USDC. 1997. Statistical Abstract of the United States: 1997, 117th edition. U.S. Department of Commerce, Washington, D.C.

Warnert, J. 1997. Farmers testify at public hearings. Small Farm News (October/November):1,4.

Waters, A. 1990. The farm – restaurant connection. pp. 113-124. In: R. Clark (ed.) Our Sustainable Table. North Point Press, San Francisco.

Welsh, R. 1996. The Industrial Reorganization of U.S. Agriculture. Policy Studies Report No. 6. Henry A. Wallace Institute for Alternative Agriculture, Greenbelt, Maryland.

Welsh, R. 1997. Reorganizing U.S. Agriculture. Policy Studies Report No. 7. Henry A. Wallace Institute for Alternative Agriculture, Greenbelt, Maryland.

Wentz, L. 1992. How Martin sees Grand Met's global role." Advertising Age 63(17):11,14.

White, G.B. 1982. Economics of small farm wineries. Vinifera Wine Growers Journal (Fall):160-164.

Wilkins, J.L. 1995. Seasonal and local diets: Consumers' role in achieving a sustainable food system. pp. 149-166. In: H.K. Schwarzweller and T.A. Lyson (eds.) Research in Rural Sociology and Development: Sustainable Agriculture and Rural Communities, Vol. 6. JAI Press, Greenwich, CT.

Wunderlich, G. 1993. Agricultural landownership and the real property tax. pp. 3-16. In: G. Wunderlich (ed.) Land Ownership & Taxation in American Agriculture. Westview Press, Boulder, CO.

# 6

## Ethics and Aesthetics in the Loss of Farmland

*Richard K. Sutton*

The more the city expands and absorbs us, the firmer the belief in a rural paradise becomes.

— J. B. Jackson, *Changing Rural Landscapes*

Quit thinking about decent land-use as solely an economic problem. Examine each question in terms of what is ethically and esthetically right as well as what is economically expedient. A thing is right when it tends to preserve the integrity, stability and beauty of the biotic community. It is wrong when it tends otherwise.

— Aldo Leopold, *A Sand County Almanac*

By *aesthetic* I mean being responsive to *the pattern which connects.*

— Gregory Bateson, *Mind and Nature: A Necessary Unity*

## Introduction

Lorna Jacobs Doolittle inherited a half-section farm. Once Iowa prairie, it has been long since converted to cropland. That is all except a 40-acre parcel of potholes, prairie grasses, and wild-flowers. The Doolittle Prairie is now a tiny patch in a quilt of corn, soybeans, and pastures. She left it prairie and forewent a sizable yearly income because this place of tillable soils was also a container of fond childhood memories. Her decision was irrational to some, yet to Lorna the land had value other than money. She is now a memory too, but the tiny prairie lives on as a relict that provides a place of memories for hundreds of Story County school children who visit it yearly.

Half a continent away, New York City expanded across the west end of Long Island, replacing farms with housing, roads, and retail developments. All but one two-acre parcel, the Klein farm, which in 1990 was the only land in New York City still zoned for agricultural use, and the last working family farm within the city limits (Hiss 1990). Here, too, school children visit for a glimpse of the past. When asked why Mr. Klein had never accepted the lucrative offers of developers, his daughter replied, "Well, it still feels like country, and he didn't want to part with it."

These examples, exceptions to the normal course of events, hint at both the ethical and aesthetic aspects of land use decisions:

- Ethics are formal systems of human values that allow and require certain attitudes and actions. Van Rensselaer Potter (1977) defines ethics as "a set of culturally accepted beliefs and guidelines for decisions affecting the course of human activity, with idealistic goals in mind usually involving the adjustment of competing claims without resorting to the use of coercion, unless mutually agreed upon by members of the culture."

- Aesthetics, according to Arnold Berleant (1997), "concerns itself with the special values found in making and appreciating art and in the enjoyment of natural beauty," and it also concerns itself with "human well-being and the intrinsic satisfactions that are the living heart of experience."

Ethics and aesthetics are both useful in analyzing the relationships between humans and the land. In the context of this chapter, ethics applies to the right and wrong of permanently committing farmland to urbanization, and aesthetics applies to the resulting good or bad experiences inhabitants have before, during and after changing farmland into cities.

*Under the Blade* examines the loss of farmland from many different perspectives. My task in this chapter is to identify and explain the impact of human values on the land in general and farmland in particular. It identifies what I believe to be the driving human values that lead to wasteful land use and urban sprawl and in doing so, it aims to see the loss of farmland in ethical and aesthetic terms.

Because the loss of farmland is related to the dominant values of U.S. residents, the first objective of this chapter is to trace how these values have come about, and to consider some less popular ethical systems that might be more supportive of the preservation of rural landscapes. A second objective is to explain the relevance and importance of agricultural land to the quality of our individual and shared aesthetic experience. Finally, in attaining the first two objectives, I wish to show how ethics and aesthetics are inextricably linked.

## Land Ethics

### Historical Roots of American Land Ethics

Although the North American continent was already densely settled prior to European colonization, the rapid subjugation and in some cases extermination of the Native Americans by the Europeans ensured that the ethical systems of the Native Americans had little influence on U.S. land use. Instead, it was European ethical systems, expressed in a new environment of abundant resources and increased personal freedoms, that formed the foundation of our current land use policies and laws.

Resettlement of Europeans to North America in a period roughly from 1500 to 1800 was affected by the radical and portentous changes in the religion, economy, moral ideals and science of northwestern Europe. The renewed religious beliefs of the Reformationists, the economic morality of Locke and Smith, and the rational science of Descartes all influenced the idea of land in America as simply an exploitable commodity.

### Religiosity in Value Decisions

Where people and cultures subscribe to religious teachings, they project its tenets into their ethical relationships with the land. Western Christianity has had an important influence on the development of a European and subsequently an American land ethic (White 1967). The replacement of pantheism in Europe by Christianity was a major step toward eliminating the view of nature as sacred (Jackson 1987). The gods or spirits that inhabited specific groves, lakes or mountains were banished, and their former residences were much more likely to be viewed solely as sources of lumber, irrigation water and metal ores.

This is not to imply that Christianity preaches only an exploitative view of land. The biblical evidence is mixed, and one can find admonishment to "dress the garden and keep it" as well as to "subdue the earth." Gottfried (1995) traces back to the Old Testament the ancient Jewish relationship with the natural world that is reflected, for example, in biblical teachings that the Sabbath be applied to land which was to be fallowed every seventh year. The Dominican priest Matthew Fox (1991) points out that creation spirituality, which stresses a spiritual relationship between people and the land, is endemic to the Old Testament and carries through into the New Testament.

Although creation spirituality advanced in the 13th century beginning with the writings of St. Francis of Assisi (see Box 6.1) and Saint Thomas Aquinas, the Church soon after officially renounced this mysticism. Reformationist thinking and theology in 16th century Europe largely overlooked the importance placed by the Bible on care of God's creation. The subduing of the earth was emphasized, particularly in the attitudes of Calvinists, Lutherans and Puritans. To the Puritans settling in New England, the place was in reality a "howling wilderness"— a place in which the true nature of human morality and superiority was tested (Nash 1973, Thayer 1994).

Box 6.1   Canticle of Brother Sun, Sister Moon.

Most high, omnipotent, good Lord,
Thine are all praise, glory, honor and all benedictions.
To thee alone, Most High, do they belong
And no man is worthy to name Thee.

Praise be to Thee, My Lord, with all Thy creatures,
Especially Brother Sun,
Who is our day and lightens us therewith.
Beautiful is he and radiant with great splendor;
Of Thee, Most High, he bears expression.

Praise be to Thee, my Lord, for Sister
Moon, and for the stars
In the heavens which Thou has formed
bright, precious and fair.

Praise be to Thee, my Lord, for  Brother Wind,
And for the air and the cloud of fair and all weather
Through which Thou givest
sustenance to Thy creatures.

Praise be, my Lord, for Sister Water.
Who is most useful, humble, precious and chaste.
Praise be, my Lord, for Brother Fire,
By whom Thou lightest up the night:
He is beautiful, merry, robust, and strong.

Praise be, my Lord, for our sister, Mother Earth,
Who sustains and governs us
And brings forth diverse fruits with
many-hued flowers and grass.

— St. Francis of Assisi

### Rise of Utilitarian Thinking

Concomitant with the final de-mystification of the Church was
the rise of modern science and a reductionist world view. René
Descartes, the French philosopher of the early 1600s, advocated
the solution of problems through their disassembly into smaller,

manageable pieces. However, the method was soon perceived as synonymous with the actual structure of the world; things really are no more than the sum of their parts (Jackson 1987). We now know that the whole is often greater than, or at least different from, the sum of its parts (see Chapter 2), but Descartes provided support for the approach of making land use decisions on a parcel by parcel basis.

Furthering this concept, John Locke published in 1690 his seminal essay, "Of Property," an interweaving of religion, morals and economics (Wood 1984). To Locke, land only had value if it was used and improved by the labor of an individual. In the same period that American colonists began to push back the wilderness and improve it with their labor by cutting trees and draining swamps, the common lands of England, referred to by Locke as wastes and compared with the tractless American wilderness, were being enclosed and improved. This philosophical position was the underlying moral basis used by English colonists to justify dispossessing the Native Americans of commonly held tribal lands and appropriating them as farms.

Locke influenced English Utilitarians Jeremy Bentham (1748–1832) and John Stuart Mill (1806–1873) in asserting that land is only useful if it is improved by man's labor and produces something of utility. Much of the neoclassical economic theory espoused by Adam Smith and later 19th century industrialists is built on utilitarian principles; so much so that it could be called economic utilitarianism. In his classic *The Wealth of Nations* (1776), Smith firmly adopts for economics the Descartsian reductionist viewpoint by stressing that the annual output or revenue of a society is precisely equal to the sum of the revenues of its individual entrepreneurs. So, by each businessman seeking to maximize his own profits, the benefit to society as a whole is maximized. This is the famous *invisible hand* that turns the pursuit of individual gain into the promotion of the common good (see Box 6.2).

Thus, when Europeans arrived in America, the Church had ensured that the land would not be perceived as sacred, and Descartes had ensured that it would be treated as no more than the sum of its parts or parcels. Locke made it clear that the land had no value until "improved" by the settlers, and Adam Smith assured them that their ignorance regarding how to treat the land would not detract from the common good if each person simply acted in their own self-interest. These are the primary values that European immigrants brought to America, and the interaction of these values with the American landscape has shaped land use decisions from colonial times until today.

Box 6.2   Adam Smith on the "invisible hand."

It is only for the sake of profit that any man employs [his] capital in the support of industry, and he will always, therefore, endeavor to employ it in the support of that industry of which the produce is likely to be of greatest value, or to exchange for the greatest quantity either of money or of other goods. But the annual revenue of every society is always precisely equal to the exchangeable value of the whole annual produce of its industry, or rather is precisely the same thing with that exchangeable value. As every individual, therefore, endeavors as much as he can both to employ his capital in the support of domestic industry, and so to direct that industry that its produce may be of the greatest value, every individual necessarily labors to render the annual revenue of the society as great as he can. He generally, indeed, neither intends to promote the public interest, nor knows how much he is promoting it...He intends only his own security; and by directing that industry in such a manner as its produce may be of the greatest value, he intends only his own gain, and he is in this, as in many other cases, led by an invisible hand to promote an end which was no part of his intention. Nor is it always the worse for the society that it was no part of it. By pursuing his own interest he frequently promotes that of the society more effectually than when he really intends to promote it. I have never known much good done by those who affected to trade for the public good.

— Adam Smith, The Wealth of Nations, George Rutledge, London, 1900. Originally published in 1776.

## Coming to America

Jackson (1987) writes that "how we look at the world is how it becomes," and so values are translated into changes on the land. Yet, the exchange is not uni-directional. There is an interplay between people and the landscape in which they live; each is changed due to the presence of the other. The values developed in Europe were transplanted to another continent, where the immigrants were faced with both an abundance of land and the opportunity to own land—two characteristics absent in their homelands.

Freed from the physical constraints of Europe, the value systems held by the settlers were inadequate to prevent a destructive use of the land. The pioneers followed a pattern of development, exploitation and abandonment. Left in their wake were vast areas of degraded lands, such as the cut-over lands in Michigan, Wisconsin and Minnesota, eroded Appalachian Uplands, and later, the Dust Bowl in the southern Great Plains. In the 1790s, a new settler described Albemarle County, Virginia, home of Thomas Jefferson, as "a scene of desolation that baffles description—farm after farm worn out, washed and gullied, so that scarcely an acre could be found in a place fit for cultivating" (McEwan 1991). Jefferson stayed and made an effort to improve his farms, but many others simply moved south or west.

The dominant tendency in American history, according to Wendell Berry (1977), has been to conquer and move on, while the tendency to stay and prosper in one place has been much weaker and less successful. This attitude toward the land necessarily reflects an attitude toward certain groups of people—those who occupy the land that the exploiters wish to "improve." "If there is any law that has been consistently operative in American history, it is that the members of any *established* people or group or community sooner or later become "redskins"—that is, they become the designated victims of an utterly ruthless, officially sanctioned and subsidized exploitation" (Berry 1977).

In the earliest application of this ethic, Native Americans were dispossessed for the establishment of farms. Now, the same thing occurs in areas of urban expansion. Farmers and other rural residents are displaced by a wave of suburbanites. The developer does not stay in the place he built and continue to "develop" it as a community; he moves on to the next piece of exploitable ground.

As cities expand in concentric rings, the inner rings tend to decay as the well-to-do and the businesses that serve them move to the new developments (Box 6.3). When revitalization of the inner city is undertaken, the poor are pushed aside by gentrification, another form of conquest and exploitation.

Here we see the impact of Locke and the Utilitarians leading to an important part of America's land ethic. It describes our view of land as only a form of capital or monetary wealth. Farmland is viewed in the same way in which Locke viewed the unimproved English commons—it has low relative utility and monetary value and thus, simply awaits the entrepreneurial labor to convert it to a "higher" urban use. As a corollary to this ethic, land speculation has been a traditional and honored method to gain personal wealth. The speculator buys at the fringe and simply waits, often with agricultural production filling the time and paying the taxes until the land is converted to a more lucrative economic purpose. Ironically, speculation rarely fits Locke's vision of profits accrued from one's labor because "Its [land's] value is largely created by things unrelated to the actions of the owner..." (Lincoln 1996). Increases in land value often result from public expenditures for roads and other infrastructure, and Lincoln suggests that windfall profits "should accrue to the community as a whole, not to individuals..."

Box 6.3   The Church in the City.

> The Church in the Diocese of Cleveland has recognized the detrimental impact of suburban sprawl on the well-being of its parishioners, and is moving to address this issue as illustrated by these excerpts from The Church in the City Vision Statement:
>
> There will be some who object to the Church inserting itself into a discussion which seems beyond its proper realm. In response to these objections, we recall the words of the 1971 Synod of Bishops: "Action on behalf of justice and participation in the transformation of the world fully appear to us as a constitutive dimension of the preaching of the Gospel, or in other words, of the Church's mission for the redemption of the human race and it's liberation from every oppressive situation."

*Continues*

Box 6.3 *Continued*

As population has shifted, so too has the tax base of cities.
As people of greater means have moved from central cities to
suburbs, our cities and our city parishes remain home to
growing concentrations of people of reduced income, fewer
educational opportunities, and with little or no access to
employment in the suburbs where jobs have moved as well.

In hindsight it is clear: over the past 40 years there was little
balance between building new suburbs and rebuilding our
cities—particularly city housing. More balance would have
given people more choice between city and suburb. The lack
of choice and the consequent dominance of outmigration
helped to create stark separations of people: city vs. suburb
and even suburb vs. suburb. The poor and minorities have
been isolated in concentrations that severely limit opportunities for a decent and secure life.

What has become clear in these decades of change is that
government, federal, state and local, has played a major part
in shaping the imbalance. Government facilitates and encourages development of new, ever-more-distant suburbs,
and outmigration, by building highways and streets, by
widening roads, by building water and sewer extensions. The
effect of those installations is extremely powerful: where they
are located is where homes are built. By constantly locating
almost all new housing in outer-edge suburbs, overwhelming
outmigration is inevitable. Without question there has been,
and is, strong public demand to live in outer suburbs, and
government's support of that demand is not itself the issue.
Urban problems have been greatly exacerbated because
balanced support for the maintenance and redevelopment of
cities (and now inner suburbs) has been absent.

But it is not only government that has been instrumental in
these events. Builders, real estate brokers, developers, banks
and others share responsibility for what has happened.
Many have taken the easiest route to the greatest profit (in
suburbs) and have ignored the need for reinvestment in
maintenance and redevelopment in the city—thereby denying opportunity to those who would prefer to live in the city.
If the imbalance of investments continues as it is, we can

*Continues*

Box 6.3 *Continued*

expect urban decline, and all of its negative aspects, to spread on an even broader scale. Neighborhoods that had been stable will erode, then suburbs, beginning with those closest to the city.

The Church has been sent by Christ to reveal and communicate the love of God to all people. In fulfilling its mission, the Church must take into account various social conditions which impact upon this mission. Hopefully it is clear from what has been described above that we are challenged on two fronts: we must recognize and respond to the needs of those, the urban poor, who have been terribly hurt by the outmigration of the non-poor and employers; and we must become engaged in changing the practices of our governments that have contributed to the disastrous situation before us.

— The full text of the Vision Statement is available at http://www.citc.org

## Toward a Viable American Land Ethic

Lincoln is far from alone in offering suggestions for alternative ethical views. The tendency to develop, destroy and move on was decried as early as the mid 1800s by George Perkins Marsh. Other 19th century figures, such as John Muir, Frederick Law Olmsted and Gifford Pinchot, argued for the preservation of the public's common interest in the resources of the West. Matthew Fox (1991) refers to the writings of Walt Whitman, Emily Dickenson, Robert Frost, Wendell Berry, John Muir, Rachel Carson and Annie Dillard as evidence that a creation-centered spirituality retains some hold in North America.

Many examples of individual actions (for example, the Doolittle Prairie and the Klein Farm) and societal actions provide further evidence that economic utilitarianism is not the only principle guiding American land use decisions. Many of our shared public goods in the form of land such as national parks, state school lands, county conservation areas, and municipal watersheds came about and continue to be preserved not simply because of the quantifiable recreation user-days, rent, wildlife harvested, or acre-feet of water that these public areas supply. These lands endure because they also provide intangible goods and shared meaningful memories.

Elizabeth Anderson (1993) describes public spaces, such as parks or open space, as shared goods which cannot be accurately valued only as private goods in a free market. "In a democratic society we are free to participate in collective decisions that affect everyone. This is the freedom to be included rather than exclude others. When exit is impossible, when decisions concern shared goods, or where freedom can be effectively exercised by all only in public spaces of free and equal association, democratic freedom supersedes market freedom." This is the political and ethical basis for local elective bodies debating and approving or denying land use changes. Economist Daniel Bromley (1991) states that "The fundamental policy problem in any economy is to determine the location of the boundary that divides the proper domain for collective choice from the proper domain of atomistic choice (the market)." So how might we determine this boundary as we consider the loss of farmland?

### Ethical Systems Beyond Economic Utilitarianism

Theologian John Cobb (1993) looks beyond the economic utilitarian viewpoint and posits that ethical systems should contain answers to two basic questions: (1) What is good or desirable? and knowing that, (2) What are the principles of "right action" that must follow? With regard to land use decisions, these questions are generally answered from one of four perspectives:

1. For yourself in the present

2. For yourself for the rest of your life

3. For all [hu]man[s] for the indefinite future

4. In general

Perspectives one and two dominate classical economics, and indeed the theories of Adam Smith suggest that these are the proper approaches for maximizing the public good. The third perspective sets up an artificial dichotomy between humans and the "environment," missing the essential place of humans in the environment. The fourth is the only approach that Cobb thinks is "stable and acceptable" through time and space. A thing is right when it maximizes value in general.

"In general" refers to all landscape functions including habitat for other species, water supply, waste assimilation, aesthetics and of course agricultural production. As Chapter 2 clearly shows, land use decisions that do not consider relationships among different parcels of land lead to degradation of landscape functions. Aldo Leopold (1949) addressed the "in general" in *A Sand County Almanac* where he encourages humans to take a biocentric view of ethical relationships. Leopold's land ethic is a radical holistic approach to human interaction with the environment, and a recognition that humans are an integral part of the biotic community. According to him, "Ecologically, an ethic is the limitation on freedom in the human quest for survival. It is the setting aside of instinct and competition in favor of cooperation." Leopold goes on to say, "Philosophically, an ethic is the distinction between social and anti-social conduct." Ethics and ecology are related through their common emphasis on the *relationships* among members of the biotic community.

Relationships between people and the land are the foundation of farming and the preservation of farmland, but it is essential to realize that these relationships include both farmers and non-farmers. Farming is an ecological endeavor, but it is also a cultural undertaking that involves all people. "If you eat, you're involved in agriculture" reads a popular bumper sticker. Wendell Berry (1990), when asked what city people can do to reverse the decline of American farming and rural life, replied "Eat responsibly."

This may sound at first like a flippant answer, but of course it is not. Eating responsibly acknowledges the unbreakable bond between all people and the land. Consuming the bodies of other creatures is one of the most profound indications of our membership in the biotic community, and a clear reminder of the need to consider the effects of our actions "in general." Responsibility requires knowledge of the implications of one's actions and demands modification of those actions to produce a right outcome.

Unfortunately, many Americans lack the knowledge that is required of responsibility. Berry (1990) writes "Most urban shoppers would tell you that food is produced on farms. But most of them do not know on what farms, or what kinds of farms, or where the farms are, or what knowledge or skills are involved in farming. They apparently have little doubt that farms will continue to produce, but they do not know how or over what obstacles." One of those obstacles of course is the paving of those farms, subsidized by taxpayer funding of roads and sewers. Another is consumer preferences for highly processed foods that help to put 93 cents of every food dollar in a pocket other than the farmer's. Yet another is the acquiescence of taxpayers in the funding of agricultural research that supports the food industry rather than farmers. However, most Americans eat their Big Macs™ in blissful ignorance of their contribution to these problems.

Such profound ignorance of a relationship that is absolutely essential to our existence and well-being is truly irresponsible and unethical. A viable land ethic would recognize the interrelationships of all people, all land, and all life; would demand personal understanding and accountability for the effect of one's actions on these relationships; and would emphasize the preservation of the integrity, stability, and beauty of these relationships.

The rationale for this land ethic derives not just from concern for our own well-being, but from what Burkhardt (1989) argues is "a general obligation we have to respect and secure the rights of future generations." Some would argue that future generations do not exist and therefore do not have rights. This logic is antithetical to the continuity of biology and human culture. One can simply look backward and ask: Is the quality of our lives affected by previous generations? And because it obviously is we can ask: Have they diminished our options and our rights to a clean, productive and healthy environment through their decisions regarding land and resource use? As we look backwards, the answer is yes. Looking forward, how will our descendants judge us?

## Land Aesthetics

"No matter how important such resources as prime agricultural soil, clean water, and wildlife habitat may be, they rarely have the emotional appeal of a beautiful countryside setting. A love for scenic beauty often provides the common bond among people who work for the protection of wetlands, historic houses, and farmland. A community leader may strive to protect the economic

well-being of local farmers, realizing that this is the key to farmland retention, but may be motivated—consciously or not—by the
pleasure of observing scenic farmland and farming activity"
(Stokes 1989).

Much of our discussion of the ethics of farmland preservation
has related to the future availability of resources to meet the basic needs of our descendants. Yet we live our lives in the present,
and assuming our basic needs are met, much of the quality of our
lives depends on the quality of the landscape of which we are a
part. As Jean Giorno illustrated in his classic fable *The Man Who
Planted Trees*, ugly, degraded, dysfunctional landscapes result in
ugly, degraded, dysfunctional people. But landscapes can be restored or better yet, humans can plan their interactions with
landscapes to avoid degradation and to enhance the structures
and functions that make life more meaningful.

### Connecting Ethics and Aesthetics

All of us have seen at some time a particular building, machine
or implement that was so perfectly designed for its purpose that it
just looked right, and in this rightness was beauty. Indeed, ma-
chines and tools, not usually thought of as art, have been
exhibited in art museums as a demonstration that the aesthetic
emerges from the proper relationship between form and function.

Landscapes are no different; we can tell when a working landscape is properly designed. People show significant agreement in
their evaluations of what makes a landscape look good, and often
these are the same characteristics that promote necessary landscape functions. Our ethics and values, through their influence
on our actions, determine the quality of the landscape, and the
aesthetic is a guide to right form and function. Ethics and aesthetics are inextricably linked, and aesthetics are far more than
just a trivial consideration of artistic taste. Yi Fu Tuan (1993)
links ethical and aesthetic issues in the agricultural landscape
when he says, "Agricultural land is good, hence also desirable and
pleasing. Americans share this view. However, when Americans
appraise a landscape, they use the word good in an explicitly
moral sense." In a larger sense Tuan (1979) says, "Yearning for an
ideal and humane habitat is perhaps universal. Such a habitat
must be able to support a livelihood and yet cater to our moral
and aesthetic nature."

Following are some examples to support the contention that
landscape development that has a form that supports good function will be more aesthetically pleasing than development that
detracts from good function:

- Water is essential to life, and humans have an innate attraction to it. In studies of visual preferences, views incorporating water are universally popular (Smardon et al. 1986).
  However, most housing developments deal with the accelerated run-off from impervious surfaces by channeling the
  water quickly off-site, often in underground stormwater
  systems. This strategy contributes to downstream flooding
  and reduced water quality. Developments that deal with
  water by preserving or constructing ponds, wetlands, and
  natural floodplains mitigate many of the hydrologic problems
  and provide functional open spaces that the residents enjoy.

- In mountainous and hilly regions of the United States,
  homes are frequently built on ridgetops in order to provide
  the owner with excellent views, but in the process degrading
  the views of all other residents, a result referred to in Europe
  as "cropping public value." These exposed houses also have
  higher heating and cooling costs, and the steeper, longer
  access roads accelerate erosion and fragment habitat.
  Municipalities that zone against ridge-top homes improve
  landscape function and retain a landscape that people enjoy.

- New developments often have no large trees and present a
  sterile, uninviting look. Vegetation moderates local climate,
  and a single tree can provide the same cooling effect as ten
  room-size air-conditioners working 20 hours per day (Lyle
  1994). A residential landscape with trees is not only more
  aesthetically pleasing, it is more energetically efficient.

Knowledgeable landscape design can substitute ecological and
aesthetic intelligence for energy, materials, and dollars, an approach that I will revisit later in the chapter. For now, I will
address three particular aesthetic problems caused by the loss of
farmland, each stemming from the ways in which we alter the
structure of rural landscapes: (1) loss of or reduced contact with
nature, (2) loss of a sense of place and shared community, and (3)
additional noise and cluttered spaces.

## Loss of Contact with Nature

Environmental psychologist Rachel Kaplan (Kaplan and Kaplan 1989) has explored the importance of nearby nature to human well-being. Her research showed that city apartment dwellers were more satisfied with their lives if they could see or visit nearby nature on a daily basis, if only a shade tree, patch of shrubs or a tiny flower garden. E.O. Wilson (Kellert 1993) suggests that humans have an innate need, which he calls *biophilia*, for contact with a variety of species. This need is derived from an evolutionary history as a member of a diverse global ecosystem where such contact was both constant and essential. Lewis (1996) concludes, "*Homo sapiens* learned to survive by listening to [seeing] and learning from nature. Acknowledging its reverberations within us beyond the symbols of our apparent success as a twenty-first-century civilization to the basic truth that we are still creatures dependent on earth; whatever we inflict on the planet we inflict on ourselves."

When we replace farmland with urban sprawl, we are eliminating our most prevalent remaining connection to nature. Rene Dubos (1980) declares, "Over much of the world, farmland has become the most distinctive feature of the scenery. It constitutes the "Nature" that has replaced wilderness in the minds of both rural and urban people." Joan Nassauer (1997) in her article entitled "Agricultural Landscapes in Harmony with Nature" describes an ideal scene: "Where elevated viewpoints create opportunities for panoramic views over rolling hills, new landscape patterns that create more small fields, more crop variety, more hedgerows, and more wooded patches will help the public see nature in the countryside."

What they see helps people not only to meet an innate need for contact, but to refine their understanding of and appreciation for the non-urban world. This could be as simple, but critical, as understanding that food comes from farms, not supermarkets. At a deeper level, it involves the development of what Aldo Leopold referred to as a land aesthetic (Callicott 1983). Leopold suggested that the land aesthetic, like the formal aesthetics of art objects, must be developed both from study and *first hand experience*. Green (1981) claims that the aesthetic importance of open land and the preservation of productive farmland is demonstrated by the large numbers of recreationists who use it for such diverse activities as hunting or nature and bird study.

### Loss of Place and Shared Community

Driving on Route 1 along the east coast of Florida, you pass through Juno Beach, North Palm Beach, Lake Park, and other towns. But unless you catch the "Welcome to..." signs, the continuous band of strip sprawl provides no clues that you have left one place and entered another. Berleant (1997) observes that "Where cities once had protective boundaries, there is now neither boundary nor any protection." As cities merge into amorphous, monotonous blurs of suburban development, the inhabitants lose their ability to discern social units such as neighborhoods and towns or ecological units such as watersheds. Loss of identity exacerbates ignorance and indifference to shared social and environmental problems.

The erasure of natural phenomena and landmarks all happens in the guise of short-term economic self-interest. Berleant points out, "Cities that succumb to the exclusiveness of economic values are like opportunists, people who put a price on their integrity and lose their identity in the process."

### Noise and Cluttered Space

William Irwin Thompson (1991), a cultural historian, has described noise as the solvent of modern civilization. It pervasively enters our minds and our relationships, slowly dissolving and changing their quality and meaning and ultimately their outcomes. Greenbelts appeal to the urbanite's need for respite from the dreary, cluttered, and noisy city—an all-encompassing assault on our perceptions of our immediate, daily environment (Whyte 1968). Radio ads extoll the peace and quiet of rural subdivisions, playing on our experiences of the city as noisy. Yet implicit in these ads is that we are, presumably, far enough away from one's rural neighbor not to hear his riding mower putting acres of lawn under the blade. In rural areas one is also presumably buffered by space from feedlots, hog factory farms, freeways, landfills, sewerage lagoons, rail corridors and airport approach patterns.

But it is not only what we hear and smell that affects our sensitivities. Sullivan (1994) examined residents' preferences for scenes of the urbanizing fringe of rural Washentaw County, Michigan, near Ann Arbor, in order to understand the aesthetic and non-economic values that residents found there. He states,

"Preference is viewed as an expression of bias toward adaptively suitable environments, environments that include support elements, and spaces that are useful and supportive to human functioning." His survey of preferences for a range of landscape scenes found that regardless of the type of resident (farmer, county official, homeowner or multi-family occupant), *views of trees or farmland with defined edges of trees were highly rated.* Other scene groupings which contained more built elements and fewer trees were rated lower. His explanation for the impact of trees is that their spatial definition creates a pleasant feeling of mystery in the observer.

## Stemming the Loss of Farmland at the City's Edge

The movement of people into our rural landscapes is a push-pull phenomenon operating within a trend of an overall increase in U.S. population (see Chapter 1). The push of urban problems, like threats of violence and lack of shared public spaces, repels while the pull of quiet, serene, nature in exurbia attracts. However, only the economically advantaged can participate in this exodus, leaving an even more impoverished group within the city and reinforcing the incentives for flight by those who are able. Suburban and exurban immigrants find that the quiet, the serene, and the natural soon disappears under the relentless march of urbanization, and another wave of people pushes further into the countryside.

To stem the tide, cities must get denser, but land must be used in a way that maximizes productive human relationships and supports shared community values. Cities must become more civil and livable. At the same time, the inherent productivity, pattern, character, and process of the countryside must be preserved and indeed strengthened. Recognizing the duality of the push-pull phenomenon, LaGro (1996) suggests that "A prudent strategy, therefore, would be to couple rural growth management programs with efforts to improve the quality of life in existing urban communities, thereby reducing the push factors that stimulate migration from urban to rural areas." However, if the strategy is to be successful, it requires a third component, a significant change in the ethics of the American people.

### *Improving the City*

The decreases in crime that occurred in some U.S. cities in the mid-1990s were attributed to community policies based on the broken-window theory. This theory holds that a single broken window in a block of buildings sets a tone that encourages more vandalism, so a broken window though trivial in itself should be fixed immediately. This has been used as an analogy for various zero-tolerance policing strategies, but it is also another demonstration of the link between aesthetics and the proper functioning of communities. Three methods of improving the aesthetics and overall health of U.S. cities are:

### 1. Preserve and restore nearby nature.

Unless experienced on a regular basis, our perceptions of natural seasons, sights and sounds atrophy. A city's green infrastructure, its gardens, parks, school yards, cemeteries, golf courses, drainageways and undeveloped open spaces, bring natural aesthetic values close to the daily lives of its inhabitants. Cities must do more to preserve, link and expand their systems of public open spaces. This does not mean narrowing these spaces' use to heavily programmed and single-purpose, active recreation, such as lighted ball-fields with bleachers, domed tennis courts, and parking lots—these simply encourage users to drive in from a distance. Nor does it mean that all of these open spaces should be publicly owned and maintained.

It does mean that expanded space and enhanced care will both be needed. Within the most urban of areas are many opportunities for establishing bits of nature. Hiss (1990) describes how a local group created "Brooklyn Bridge Meadow by planting native wildflowers—many of them collected from vacant lots in Brooklyn—on a small triangle of once dusty land between City Hall and the entrance ramps to the Brooklyn Bridge." Just as important, new buildings need to be regulated not to block views of natural features, and public access to natural areas needs to be promoted. The Brooklyn/Queens Greenway, a forty-mile bicycle and pedestrian path, is not only an open space itself, but links many city parks and botanical gardens. In doing so, it increases the effective natural area for millions of residents.

Conversion of vacant lots into community gardens provides both green space and green goods. The National Gardening Association estimated in 1989 that $18 billion worth of food is produced each year in the United States by household and community gardens (Joseph 1996)—an amount greater than the wholesale value of all vegetables produced by U.S. commercial farms (USDC 1996). Gardens improve the health and nutrition of the community, and strengthen the bonds among the residents and between the residents and the land (Box 6.4, 6.5).

As an added incentive, a community that is permeated by open space not only gains an improvement in quality of life, but in real estate values. Public investment in green spaces, by increasing the property values of adjacent lots, may result in overall economic benefits to the community including increased property tax revenues.

Box 6.4   From "Rooted in Community: Community Gardens in New York City."

---

During 1997, twenty gardens were bulldozed and an unknown number of still operating gardens have lost their leases to operate on city-owned land. Approximately 738 community gardens still in existence remain vulnerable to the City's policy to sell them to developers for housing or commercial development.

Community gardens...have unique physical features and reflect the individuality of their members. The wealth of activities and events taking place in gardens is enormously significant to engendering a sense of community among neighborhood residents. Far more people than regular garden members enjoy and use community garden spaces. Community gardens bring together people of all ages and ethnicities, as well as people residing in other neighborhoods. Moreover, community gardens are visual amenities in the neighborhood, as well as special places which host community-based activities.

Their destruction will destroy more than some plants, trees , and benches. It will rip the heart out of the community.

— A Report to the New York State Senate written by Carole Nemore of the Senate Minority Office (Available 3 Aug 98 at http:\\www.cityfarmer.org)

Box 6.5   Urban gardens in Havana.

Born of necessity resulting from the collapse of the Soviet
Union and the imposition of the U.S. trade embargo, Cuba
has become a leader in research and development of low-
input, sustainable agriculture (Nation 1997). This effort
includes the promotion of urban gardening, a program recently documented by Moskow (1997).

Havana has approximately 26,000 self-provision gardens sup-
plying some food to an estimated one in ten city residents.
Households with gardens reported average reductions in food
expenditures equal to 40% of average income. Sales and donations of food from gardens also enhanced the local food supply.

In addition to fresh, affordable food, Havana's urban gardens
have delivered many other benefits to the city. Moskow writes
that "In Havana, the replacement of unsightly landscapes
with gardens is one of the many unintended benefits of a
program which was designed to deal with the country's food
crisis. Because of the incredibly large scope of the program
the city form itself is being changed alongside some of the
city's functions."

"Replacing vacant lots with gardens has improved neighborhood safety. A number of the gardeners said the transformed
lots had been unsafe areas where people had previously been
afraid to walk. Two participants in the study mentioned that
the area they gardened had once been referred to as the 'Hill
of Fear.' It had been restored to a lovely series of gardens."

"These gardens create a prominent pattern throughout much
of Havana, making food production very transparent. While
the peripheral areas contain more gardens than the city
center, many parts of Havana support food gardens. The
gardens bring the multiple aesthetic and environmental
benefits of increased vegetation to the city as well as decreased food transportation and storage requirements."

Many inner-city Americans could benefit from local food
production. And while the food itself may be less of an immediate incentive for most urban Americans than for Cubans,
the aesthetic and environmental benefits of urban gardens
should tip the scales toward their inclusion in urban design
and redesign in the United States.

## 2. Density control and site planning for amenity.

Population density in cities and towns must increase. Suburban patterns spawned by the post-war love affair with the automobile must be abandoned, while blighted inner city areas and abandoned industrial complexes must be redeveloped. Large-scale urban renewal has largely been a failure, but small scale, lot by lot, or block by block rebuilding can replace a portion of the development occurring at the urban fringe. Cities have the advantage of existing utilities and services that can reduce development costs. Should a community decide that its growth should happen through infill, reuse and rebuilding, it will need political will, leadership and vision (see Case 20). It will also need to ensure that poorer residents will not be displaced as property values increase.

In his book, *Finding Lost Space*, Roger Trancik (1986) points out that our existing cities have a variety of spaces that are under-utilized and can be used more efficiently. But doing so will require that out-moded ordinances and practices regarding street sizes, setbacks and minimal lot size be revamped. More careful land subdivision and design (see Case 14), prescribed building footprints, zero-lot lines, and careful placement of indoor and outdoor functions are needed. Most of our subdivisions have carelessly-placed homes in which split-level designs are foisted on flat sites or oriented with thoughtless placement of windows. This precludes privacy or stymies a potential view of nearby open space. Every window, room, doorway, curbcut, tree and fence must be conceptualized as part of an overall planning process and not left to whim or happenstance. Developers, engineers and surveyors alone are simply not up to this task, they must be required to team with architects, landscape architects, and interior designers. But most importantly, the future residents must be full partners in the design process. If so, denser living patterns can correspond with an improved quality of life (Box 6.6).

At best, opportunities exist for the intentional use of good design to teach people about natural systems and functions. Van der Ryn and Cowan (1996) describe "a new kind of aesthetic for the built environment, one that explicitly teaches people about the potentially symbiotic relationship between culture, nature, and design. It is a powerful approach, since new ideas are learned most rapidly when they can be expressed visually and experienced directly." This approach has been termed *visual ecology* (Thayer 1976) and promotes designed environments that can:

- Help us see and become more aware of the abstractions we superimpose on the land

- Make complex natural processes visible and understandable

- Unmask systems and processes that remain hidden from view

- Emphasize our unrecognized connections to nature

Box 6.6   Effective clustering.

An excellent example of well-planned clustered housing is St. Francis Square in San Francisco, where three hundred dwellings are arranged in three-story buildings around three courtyards. The reason that this scheme works so well is partially that it is a co-op, which is very important, but also because its site planning enhances the social and community life of the residents. The site plan is such that when you're walking down an adjacent street, you're not likely to misinterpret the communal courtyards as public parks. People at St. Francis Square come out and use these spaces, because they're on the natural routes from home to car or laundry or garbage area, and because of the attractive planting, benches, and pathways. People meet each other and look out for each other. This scheme is in a moderately high-crime district. It's right next to an eight-lane highway, and yet, inside, it's a very beautiful, well-maintained green oasis in the city. There is literally a 200 - 300 person waiting list to move in. So, there are many, many people who still want to live downtown if we can create green and pleasant and quiet places for them.

Because it's a co-op, the residents have been able, over the years, to change the physical design of the outdoor spaces. They've rebuilt every play area, they've changed the position of pathways, they've taken out trees and put in trees. They've

*Continues*

Box 6.6 *Continued*

> voted to put in solar panels, and additional lighting, and
> fencing. I'm convinced that a very necessary part of a satis-
> factory living situation is having control: having power over
> changes in the environment as needs change through time.
>
> — Clare Cooper-Marcus, from Design as if People Mattered,
>           pp. 121-129 in Van der Ryn and Calthorpe (1991).

### 3. Open space subdivisions.

A major feature in many exurban residential developments and
high property value urban neighborhoods is the golf course. In
the next decade, millions of acres are projected to be converted
to golf courses with adjacent homes. This is in spite of the fact
that about half of those purchasing homes near a course have
no intention of playing golf. They are interested in the protected
open space. Though in the process of changing their image and
management practices, golf courses have traditionally been
sources of excessive chemical and water usage, far more on a
per acre basis than the farmland they supplanted.

Randall Arendt (1996) in his book, *Conservation Design for
Subdivisions*, proposes that the golf course be replaced by
community-controlled open space. This is accomplished by
putting nearly the same number of dwellings per subdivision
but on smaller lots. At the same time natural or sensitive
features are protected. If a large enough area is left undeveloped, it could be maintained as productive farmland. This
could be anything from a community pasture or hayfield to
truck farming, orchards, or nursery production. Perhaps this
common space could be a focus for community-supported
agriculture, where the bulk of produce grown goes to the
residents.

### *Strengthening the Rural Community and Landscape*

Improving the city will help to preserve the countryside, but by
itself will not be sufficient to prevent its exploitation. To achieve
that will require first a vision of the type of rural community,
economy, and landscape we want, and then a set of actions

crafted specifically to achieve that vision. It is a tired cliché, but if you don't know where you want to go, you probably won't get there. Each community needs to undertake a planning process to develop a vision for its countryside (see Chapter 2, Figure 2.3). Once a common vision is developed, then the necessary laws and policies can be determined. Laws frequently turn out to be insufficient or even counter-productive to meeting desired goals, so a thorough evaluation of the likely effect of proposed laws or policies is essential as are opportunities for mid-course corrections after new rules have been implemented. Although goals and strategies will vary in different locales, the successful approach will likely be a coordinated mix of public and private actions including:

**1. Agricultural zoning.**

If a city's vision includes a boundary with a large area of predominantly agricultural land, the only way to achieve that goal is through zoning of the land for exclusive agricultural use. Given the effect of urban proximity on land prices for development, agriculture can never compete economically at the urban edge. No municipality can afford to purchase the development rights to more than a small fraction of the land needed to maintain a critical mass for a viable agricultural economy and infrastructure. A majority of the citizenry will have to be willing to deny certain developers and landowners the right to maximize short-term profits in order to promote the long-term public good.

**2. Land trusts.**

In an era of stretched fiscal resources and mistrust of government, it is unrealistic to think that local governments can purchase or control all the lands that need protection. The land trust represents a way to privately preserve substantial areas from urban development (Daniels and Bowers 1997). It simply requires private owners who come together under a common goal (or threat) to pledge their lands for a larger, more common good. These landholders may or may not be farmers, but in the best sense of Leopold's land ethic, they are putting a limitation on their economic freedom in exchange for preservation of the landscape. They are setting aside an instinct for self interest and competing land development in favor of cooperation and preservation.

## 3. Community Supported Agriculture.

Rural landscapes are not, nor should they be, museums. They are living, changing communities and even if some restrictions are placed on the economic uses of the land, the landowners need to be able to earn a living from their holdings. Rather than simply dictate land use policies, urban residents can be non-exploitive partners in the rural economy by direct purchase of produce from farmers rather than heavily-processed "value-added" food from the supermarket (see Chapter 5 on relocalizing agriculture). Arrangements vary from roadside produce stands selling produce to farmer's markets to subscriptions or Community Supported Agriculture (Lapping and Pfeffer 1997).

In this last arrangement, city dwellers subscribe to the produce or animals raised on smaller, more intensively managed farms. These small specialized farms are quite unlike the traditional industrial farm with its large inputs, extensive fields, large machinery and anonymous distant markets. The subscriber may be required to contribute some labor to the farm and may also be involved with the year-to-year planning. The farmer owns the land and is the day-to-day supervisor and marketer. Instead of visiting the bank for a production loan, the farmer may ask for an advance payment on what is to be produced the next season. In all of these various arrangements the consumers are more involved in the production of their food and begin to have a personal connection and a stake in the use and future of a piece of productive land.

## Changing Values

It is fine and good to describe policies and actions that would slow our exploitation and destruction of farmland, but there are some major changes required before we are likely to embrace these actions. Earlier I stated that values precede actions, and somewhere during our long history as a people we have acquired some values that lead to misuse of the land. How can we make the changes within ourselves that will lead to a more just treatment of the land? At the beginning of this chapter, I discussed the role of Christianity in the evolution of our ethics. To conclude the chapter, I need to close the circle and return to those teachings.

Fox (1991) says that "Letting go is at the heart of spiritual growth and of economic and ecological justice...In the Gospel of Matthew, letting go—repentance—precedes justice." We have acquired some poor values, and if we are to survive, we need to let go of them so they can be replaced by ethics that will promote our survival and well-being. We need to exchange:

- The ethic of unending growth for an ethic of limits.

- The ethic of consumption for an ethic of sufficiency.

- The ethic of conquest for an ethic of nurturing.

Annie Dillard (1974) wrote that letting go is one way to see, and "When I see this way I sway transfixed and emptied." Once emptied, perhaps we can see and follow a path to a future that degrades neither land nor people.

## References

Anderson, E. 1993. Value in Ethic and Economics. Harvard Press, Cambridge.

Arendt, R. 1996. Conservation Design for Subdivisions. Island Press, Washington, D.C..

Bateson, G. 1976. Mind and Nature: A Necessary Unity. Bantam, New York.

Berleant, A. 1997. Living in the Landscape: Toward an Aesthetics of Environment. University Press of Kansas, Lawrence.

Berry, W. 1977. Culture and Agriculture: The Unsettling of America. Avon, New York.

Berry, W. 1990. The pleasures of eating. pp. 125-131. In: R. Clark (ed.) Our Sustainable Table. North Point Press, San Francisco.

Bromley, D.W. 1991. Environment and Economy: Property Rights and Public Policy. Blackwell, Cambridge.

Burkhardt, J. 1989. The morality behind sustainability. Journal of Agricultural Ethics 2:113-128.

Callicott, J. B. 1983. Leopold's land aesthetic. Journal of Soil and Water Conservation 38:329-332.

Cobb, J. 1993. Ecology, ethics and theology. In: H. Daly and K. Townsend (eds.) Valuing the Earth. MIT, Cambridge.

Daniels, T. and D. Bowers. 1997. Holding Our Ground: Protecting America's Farmland. Island Press, Washington, D.C..

Dillard, A. 1974. A Pilgrim at Tinker Creek. Harpers Magazine Press, New York.

Dubos, R. 1980. The Wooing of Earth. Scribner, New York.

Fox, M. 1991. Creation Spirituality: Liberating Gifts for the Peoples of the Earth. HarperCollins, New York.

Gottfried, R. 1995. Economics, Ecology and the Roots of Western Faith. Rowman-Littlefield, New York.

Green, B. 1981. Why should the countryside be conserved? pp. 8-25. In: B. Green (ed.) Countryside Conservation. Allen & Unwin, London.

Hiss, T. 1990. The Experience of Place. Knopf, New York.

Jackson, W. 1987. Alters of Unhewn Stone. North Point Press, San Francisco.

Joseph, H.M. 1996. Community food security, agriculture, and the environment: A Massachusetts perspective. pp. 245-253. In: W. Lockeretz (ed.) Environmental Enhancement through Agriculture. Center for Agriculture, Food and Environment, Tufts University, Medford, MA.

Kaplan, R., and S. Kaplan. 1989. The Experience of Nature: A Psychological Perspective. Cambridge Press, New York.

Kellert, S.R. 1993. The biological basis for human values of nature. pp. 42-72. In: S.R. Kellert and E.O. Wilson (eds.) The Biophilia Hypothesis. Island Press, Washington, D.C.

LaGro, J., Jr. 1996. Designing without Nature: Unsewered residential development in rural Wisconsin. Landscape and Urban Planning 35:1-9.

Lapping, M., and M. Pfeffer. 1997. City and country: Forging new connections through agriculture. pp. 91-104. In: W. Lockeretz (ed.) Visions of American Agriculture. Iowa State University Press, Ames.

Leopold, A. 1949. A Sand County Almanac. Oxford Press, New York.

Lewis, C. 1996. Green Nature, Human Nature. University of Illinois Press, Urbana.

Lincoln, D.C. 1996. Ethics, business, and land. Land Lines 8, No. 6.

Lyle, J.T. 1994. Regenerative Design for Sustainable Development. John Wiley & Sons, New York.

McEwan, B. 1991. Thomas Jefferson, Farmer. McFarland Publishing, Jefferson, NC.

Moskow, A. 1997. Havana's self-provision gardens. Urban Ecologist, No. 2. Available: http://www.best.com/schmitty/ue97n2b.htm [13 January 1998]

Nash, R. 1973. Wilderness and the American Mind. Yale
    University Press, New Haven.
Nassauer, J. 1997. Agricultural landscapes in harmony with
    nature. pp. 59-76. In: W. Lockeretz (ed.) Visions of American
    Agriculture. Iowa State University Press, Ames.
Nation, A. 1997. Cuba shifts to no-input grass farming. The
    Stockman Grass Farmer 54:1-7.
Potter, V.R. 1977. Evolving ethical concepts. Bioscience 27:251-
    253.
Smardon, R.C., J.F. Palmer, and J.P. Felleman (eds.). 1986.
    Foundations for Visual Project Analysis. John Wiley & Sons,
    New York.
Stokes, S.N. 1989. Saving America's Countryside: A Guide to
    Rural Conservation. Johns Hopkins University Press,
    Baltimore.
Sullivan, W.C., III. 1994. Perceptions of the rural-urban fringe:
    Citizens' preferences for natural and developed setting.
    Landscape and Urban Planning 29:85-101.
Thayer, R.L., Jr. 1976. Visual ecology: Revitalizing the aesthetics
    of landscape architecture. Landscape 20(2):37-43.
Thayer, R. 1994. Gray World, Green Heart: Technology, Nature,
    and the Sustainable Landscape. Wiley, New York.
Thompson, W. 1991. The American Replacement of Nature. Dell,
    New York.
Trancik, R. 1986. Finding Lost Space: Theories of Urban Design.
    Van Nostrand Reinhold, New York.
Tuan, Yi Fu. 1979. Thought and landscape. pp. 89-102. In: D.W.
    Mienig (ed.) Interpretation of Ordinary Landscapes. Oxford
    Press, New York.
Tuan, Yi Fu, 1993. Passing, Strange and Wonderful: Aesthetics,
    Nature and Culture. Island Press, Washington, D.C..
USDC. 1996. Statistical Abstract of the United States: 1996
    (116th ed.). U.S. Bureau of the Census, Washington, D.C.
Van der Ryn, S., and P. Calthorpe. 1991. Sustainable
    Communities: A New Design Synthesis for Cities, Suburbs and
    Towns. Sierra Club Books, San Francisco.
Van der Ryn, S., and S. Cowan. 1996. Ecological Design. Island
    Press, Washington, D.C.
White, L. 1967. The historical roots of our ecological crisis.
    Science 155:1203-1207.
Whyte, W. 1968. The Last Landscape. Anchor Books, New York.
Wood, N. 1984. John Locke and Agrarian Capitalism. University
    of California Press, Berkeley.

# 7

## A National Policy for Farmland Preservation

*R.K. Olson, A.H. Olson, and T.A. Lyson*

### Introduction

Farmland preservation is by definition a future-oriented activity. For the near future, the goals are usually quite specific and clear—to preserve the current look of a rural landscape that brings us pleasure, to allow a particular family to continue farming, to maintain a local CSA. Actions taken in contemplation of the more distant future are about preserving options—biological, economic, social—for ourselves and for future generations. The longer the time frame being considered, the greater the uncertainty surrounding the decision process.

In any case, farmland preservation is about actions designed to ensure a particular future. Which actions should be taken depend on which future is desired. The cliché is no less true for being well-worn: if you don't know where you want to go, you probably won't get there. It is equally true that without a plan to reach your goal, you probably won't get there.

Many farmland preservation efforts suffer from lack of a clearly articulated vision of what the people want to accomplish, of what they want their future landscape and community to be. Emphasis is placed on tools (e.g., purchase of development rights, minimum lot-size zoning) rather than on the desired outcome. If a vision or goals are developed, they are often too vague to serve as a framework for developing concrete plans or for measuring progress.

In contrast, an architect starts with a client's vision of a home, and translates the vision into the goal of a specific house on a particular site, and a plan to achieve that goal in the form of blueprints and time lines. Progress toward the goal is easily measured. The most appropriate tools to accomplish the project are selected as part of the planning process.

In this chapter, we describe our vision of an optimal future urban and rural landscape for the United States. We then define this vision in terms of measurable goals, and outline a national policy for achieving these goals. In recognition of political reality, we also outline some more modest changes at the federal level to improve the climate for farmland preservation at the state and local levels.

Our focus in this chapter is national. The twenty-two case studies following this chapter offer a variety of state and local perspectives, and throughout the preceding chapters, many examples of approaches and tools suitable to local action have been given. Also, several excellent books including Saving American Farmland: What Works (AFT 1997), Holding Our Ground: Protecting America's Farmland (Daniels and Bowers 1997), and Saving America's Countryside: A Guide to Rural Conservation (Stokes et al. 1997) describe in detail the laws and techniques that communities can use to protect their farmland. They provide a much better how-to manual than we can present in a single chapter.

Instead, we examine the changes that are necessary at the national level if local efforts are to have a chance to succeed. In the Introduction (Figure I.1), we described the hierarchy of spatial levels from field to world at which decisions are made that influence land use. Not only can the right policies at the federal level support local farmland preservation, but the wrong policies can, and are, contributing to the failure of many local efforts.

## A Vision of Future Land Use in America

Our vision of a future America has no particular time frame. There are certain characteristics that we would like to see at any time, whether next year or in 500 years. Although the vision could be stated in different ways, the characteristics we promote are mostly just common sense in terms of what supports a good quality of life for the citizens of any country. We envision a United States that has:

- An amount of farm-, range-, and forest land adequate to provide all current and future U.S. citizens with a varied and affordable diet; a plentiful supply of lumber, fiber, and non-food agricultural products; and an excess of production for export and as insurance against bad weather, disruption of inputs, or other unforeseeable problems.

- An equitable distribution of farmland with respect to population that gives every American the opportunity to be part of a local or regional food system that promotes food security, sustainable agriculture, economic opportunities from value-added processing of locally grown foods, and greater citizen control of the sources of their food. A hard, fixed edge between development and agricultural land provides a secure interface that enhances the locational advantages of farming on the edge, and allows the formation of longterm relationships between farmers and consumers.

- Adequate amount and types of rural lands (e.g., farm, forest, range, and non-agricultural) to maintain high levels of non-production functions including water supply, air quality, wildlife habitat, aesthetics, and rural cultures.

- Affordable, quality housing for all Americans; clean, crime-free cities and towns pervaded by a strong sense of community and abundant human interactions, and designed to be energy efficient, aesthetically pleasing, environmentally sound, and accessible to nature.

Although others might state their vision of American land use somewhat differently, we feel that few would argue against our goals. Plentiful and affordable food is a basic human right, and prudence suggests that a cushion of land be maintained in expectation of the inevitable setbacks to production (e.g., the drought of the 1930s, the corn blight of 1970). Agriculture is an inherently uncertain undertaking; technological advances are likely but not guaranteed. Some may argue that we have no responsibility toward future generations, but most people have concern for the well-being of their grandchildren and the future of their country.

Our reliance on rural lands for many non-production functions was clearly described in Chapter 2. Some of these functions (e.g., aesthetics, air quality) require open lands in close proximity to population centers—they cannot be imported. Others such as water supply can be imported from some distance, but at great cost to both the importing and exporting region.

Food security is enhanced by participation of the residents in a local food system which in turn requires adequate farmland in proximity to each city and town. To a resident of New York City, an acre of farmland at the city's edge contributes more to the food security and economy of the city than an acre of land in California or Mexico. A local economy is strengthened by adding value to locally grown food rather than importing processed meals. Food security depends on the relocalization of agriculture (see Chapter 5), and this requires local land.

Ultimately, the fate of farmland is inextricably tied to the fate of the cities. Our typical sprawling pattern of development not only consumes farmland at high rates, but results in cities that are ugly, inefficient, and the antithesis of community. Given that 80% of Americans live in urban areas, cities that don't work create a major push of people into the countryside.

## Current Trends Do Not Lead Toward the Vision

### Local Trends

The case studies provide a more detailed look at conversion trends and effects in 21 different locations throughout the United States. Many of the major U.S. agricultural regions are included, and reading the case studies illustrates a rich diversity of agriculture, conversion pressures, and approaches to farmland protection. No two regions are exactly alike.

However, a general theme emerging from a reading of the studies is that most regions face tremendous threats to farmland and rural landscapes, and current preservation efforts are often inadequate. Quotes taken from the case studies illustrate the problems and negative trends:

*Barriers to maintaining the SE Pennsylvania food and farm system currently outweigh the opportunities. Changes in policies, programs, attitudes, and behavior are required for agriculture to survive.*

*Significant negative changes have occurred in western Washington's agricultural resource base, despite the many farmland protection strategies in place in the 14 counties... Western Washington's farmland protection programs have been ineffective.*

*Planning, zoning and special tax laws have failed to protect prime agricultural land in Waukesha County [WI]. In late 1996, virtually the entire County is zoned for development, and it appears as if the majority of agricultural lands remaining will soon be lost forever.*

*The future of, and the ability for, agricultural production in Lake County [Florida] have been forever changed. The necessary infrastructure for agricultural production is disappearing as labor converts to the construction industry and a slightly higher average wage than those employed in agriculture. The opportunity for local agriculture still exists, but many of the larger agriculture parcels have been sold off, and fragmentation is reducing many of the parcels to a size that challenges the economy of scale for many of the agricultural operations attempting to use them...*

Even Oregon (Case 19), whose land use and farmland protection program is the strongest in the country, has fallen short of its goals during the past 20 years as graded by the citizen group 1000 Friends of Oregon (Table 7.1). The overall grade is only fair, and the group's conclusion is that Oregon's "land use laws are not strong enough or working well enough to protect our quality of life" (Liberty 1997).

All is not doom and gloom though. The case studies are full of hard won lessons that can serve as the foundation for effective actions in the future. Oregon's program may have deficiencies, but it still stands out as an amazing attempt by its citizens to take control of their future. Oregon's citizens have noted the weaknesses in the program, and have developed an Agenda for Livability (1000 Friends 1996) with specific recommendations to correct them. Case 19 describes mid-course corrections already made to Oregon's program that have improved the future outlook.

DeKalb County, IL (Case 10) has had some success—*Not only has the comprehensive land use plan had the desired impact on farmland prices, it has also withstood recent legal challenges.*

The Vermont Housing and Conservation Board (Case 1) has created a successful public/private partnership—*While real estate prices have remained constant or have risen slightly, VHCB's average cost of conserving farms has decreased due to the extraordinary fundraising efforts of the program's nonprofit partners.*

The case study for Albemarle County, Virginia (Case 6) offers five recommendations, not yet implemented but eminently feasible, to improve the county's land use trends. Most of the case studies offer such recommendations. We draw on these elsewhere in this chapter, but for now we reiterate that this body of local knowledge is critical to success at the national scale.

Most of the case studies do not convey the sense of surrender and inevitability shown by Waukesha County (Case 11). But they do suggest an uncertain future. They also indicate that the near future will be critical in shaping America's landscapes.

*The farmers in Fauquier County are truly farming in the shadow of suburbia and the policies and programs that are adopted in the next few years will likely determine the fate of the community's rural areas (Case 5).*

*Are efforts like this (land trusts and PDR programs), in places like Jackson, Wyoming or Montana's Gallatin Valley just delaying tactics, or might they be the roots of a new approach to sustainable pastoral land uses in at least some areas of the Rockies? This is not an easy question to answer (Case 17).*

Table 7.1   An evaluation of the success of Oregon's land use program (Liberty 1997). A: outstanding, B: Good, C: Fair, D: Poor,
F: Failing.

| Land use protection category | Oregon's performance measured against its objectives | Oregon's performance measured against other states |
|---|---|---|
| Farm and forest land protection | B- | B+ |
| Natural and scenic resources | D | none |
| Stopping sprawl | C | B |
| Transportation reform | B | A- |
| Affordable housing | B | A- |
| Citizen involvement | D | none |
| Governance | C | none |

### A National Overview

On a national scale, the information presented in Chapters 1
through 6 describes a country that is moving away from our
vision of a quality future. Population growth and farmland loss
are resulting in a rapid decline in the per capita availability of
agricultural land (see Chapter 1; Table 1.5). All of the excess
production currently available for export could be needed for
domestic consumption by 2020. Technological advances that
increase yields per acre are counteracted by resource depletion
and land degradation.

Most food in America is consumed far from where it is grown;
17% of what we eat is imported from other countries (USDC
1996). Many states import more than 80% of their food, and the
food in an average U.S. meal travels 2000 miles before it is eaten
(Lehman and Krebs 1996). This energy-extravagant food system is
the result of an ongoing globalization of agriculture (see Chapter
5) that places the average American ever further, both physically
and mentally, from the source of their food. Six multinational
corporations control half of the U.S. food market.

This global economy is cited by some as evidence that farmland loss is not a local or regional concern because food can be imported from elsewhere. Others (e.g., Brecher and Costello 1994, Olson and Francis 1995, Mander and Goldsmith 1996) show that globalization decreases food security for many populations including the urban populations of the United States.

Urban sprawl and diffuse rural development are degrading the non-production functions of many U.S. landscapes (see Chapter 2). Ecosystem services worth billions of dollars are lost (see Chapter 4). Even the intended function of developed landscapes— a place for people to live and work—is ill-served by current patterns of development. Sprawl is ugly, energy intensive, and not conducive to the development of community (see Chapter 6). In a vicious cycle, roads built to accommodate increasing traffic support the construction of sprawling suburbs requiring cars to get around and creating more traffic. Modern developments isolate people from each other and from the countryside.

It is clear that current trends in U.S. land use are not leading toward a desirable future. Fortunately, trend is not destiny, and there is still time to change our direction. Following are some suggestions on how to do so.

## A National Land Use Policy

### *The Need for a National Land Use Law*

There are many tools and strategies that can be used to improve the success of local farmland protection efforts. However, we believe that even a better informed local use of these tools will not be sufficient to achieve healthy, productive landscapes and communities. Local communities are part of a spatial hierarchy (see Figure I.1), and decisions at higher levels have strong effects on land use decisions at the community level. A state or federal decision on the placement of a new highway can completely over-ride a town's decision on where growth should occur. Development in one community can spill into neighboring towns. Federal policies on immigration have a strong influence on the number of new residents that communities will have to accommodate, and federal trade agreements affect the viability of certain types of agriculture. "Think globally, act locally" is not a sufficient strategy; action is required at all levels.

Development pressures at the local level can overwhelm even a reasonably well prepared community. Although Monroe County, Pennsylvania has a comprehensive land use plan, half the development occurring since 1981 has been in areas not planned for growth by 2000, and total residential acreage in 1991 was three times that projected by the Plan (see Chapter 2, Box 2.4). Many communities are not as well prepared for growth as Monroe County. Master growth plans may be lacking, and local planning boards are often part-time, transient, and susceptible to peer pressure. For example, the zoning committees of four Wisconsin counties approved more than 90% of the 127 rezoning petitions submitted during a three-month period (Last 1995). The rezonings were variances to the adopted comprehensive plans of the counties, and resulted in scattered, unplanned development.

Planning boards are often captured by developers who have a huge financial interest in subverting farmland protection efforts (see Box 7.1). Zoning and other laws are often perceived as impermanent. Once farmland is paved, it is gone forever, but protected farmland can be assaulted year after year until development is approved. From Southeastern Pennsylvania (Case 3) comes the comment "*Zoning doesn t mean anything. If you have enough money, enough time, and hire the right lawyer, you can do anything you want as far as zoning is concerned.*" Agricultural zoning is not always stable through time (Coughlin 1993); one township in a southeast Pennsylvania county recently softened its agricultural zoning law after landowners sued for an increase in the amount of permitted development.

Without comprehensive land use planning, America's landscapes will be shaped by what Kahn (1966) referred to as the tyranny of small decisions. A five-acre homesite here, a small subdivision there, and elsewhere the paving of a gravel road— each action is of little significance by itself, but the cumulative effect is very significant.

In 1970, Senator Henry Jackson introduced a bill (S. 3354) that would require states to adopt federally approved statewide plans to retain agricultural land (Peterson 1983). Senator Jackson had the right idea. We believe that successful farmland protection at the national level cannot be achieved piecemeal through the uncoordinated actions of thousands of individual jurisdictions. What is required is a national land use policy mandated at the federal level, managed at the state level, and implemented at the local level. In the remainder of this chapter, we provide an outline of one possible program with clear goals and measurable endpoints. We also provide a list of some more modest changes in federal policy that would, in the interim, provide better support to local preservation efforts as well as reducing the restraints to local protection currently embodied in some federal laws.

Box 7.1   Hey, Lake Okeechobee: The suburbs are coming.

Something called the Policy Development Task Force has written the latest chapter in *How to Make Palm Beach County Look More Like Broward—While Costing the Taxpayers Millions*.

On Friday, a task force committee dominated by those who would profit from overdeveloping unplatted land near The Acreage voted—surprise!—12-4 to overdevelop roughly 13,000 acres north and west of Royal Palm Beach that are now mostly farmland. No one said the plan would overdevelop one of the county's last open areas, of course. But if the county commission adopts the policy this group recommended, there's nothing to keep sprawl from stretching to Lake Okeechobee.

The outcome actually has been clear since July, when commissioners decided to create new development rules. They asked the Land Use Advisory Board, which makes recommendations on planning and zoning, to appoint the Policy Development Task Force. The LUAB favors overdevelopment and sprawl because each county commissioner gets two appointments, and the commission favors overdevelopment and sprawl because those who benefit dominate campaign fund raising.

But for conflict of interest on display, it would be hard to top the Future Planning Area subgroup that cast Friday's vote. The chairwoman is Ellen Covert Smith, whose lobbying firm—Unruh, Smith & Associates—works for Seminole Groves, which owns 7,000 of the 13,000 acres. Another member is Kieran Kilday, who represents Callery Judge

*Continues*

Box 7.1  *Continued*

Groves, owner of 4,000 acres. Still another is attorney Gary Smigiel, who represents Mecca Farms, owner of another 2,000 acres. That's virtually the entire area in question.

Landowners hope the county commission will create "future planning areas." No one knows exactly what a "future planning area" is—that alone is enough to make anyone suspicious—but, clearly, it would be a way to maximize development in undeveloped, unplatted areas. Friday's vote asks the county staff to explore such a change to the comprehensive plan. The commission would have to approve any change, probably next year.

The county commission is well on the way to opening up 13,000 acres in the south county Ag Reserve. The county appears ready to do the same for about 10,000 acres near Jupiter Farms. All county plans for schools and roads assume little or no development in these areas.

Bills for those public services could run into the hundreds of millions of dollars for all taxpayers, since growth does not pay for itself. Add in the potential damage to Palm Beach County's public water storage areas. Then include the loss of runoff and the increased potential for flooding.

Then, if the county commission goes along, change "future planning areas" to "future bills for taxpayers."

— Editorial, The Palm Beach Post, November 11, 1997, p. 20A.

### A Proposal

Within the United States, Oregon's farmland protection program (Case 19) provides the best model for a proposed national program. In brief, the state mandates that each city and town delineate an urban growth boundary (UGB) within which urban development must occur. The UGB is positioned to enclose enough land to accommodate 20 years growth. Thus, conversion of farmland and rural land is not prohibited, but it is constrained in a way that reduces sprawl and promotes more efficient use of land. Land outside of UGBs is zoned for exclusive farmland or forest use, and construction of residential dwellings is restricted.

This type of hard edge separation of urban and rural land uses is also a key feature of Scandinavian land use programs (Case 22).

Oregon's experience with this model suggests one essential change. Within the state's law, UGBs can be expanded. Indeed, the premise of locating them to accommodate 20 years growth implies that expansion will have to occur with at least that frequency. The rate of farmland loss may be reduced, and urban growth may be more orderly, but as long as population increases, farmland will continue to be lost. In the long run, this is not sustainable. Even in the short run, population growth can tax the system. Since 1970, Oregon's population has increased by more than one million, and from 1987 through 1996, 144 UGB expansions totaling 12,541 acres occurred statewide. The population of the Portland primary metropolitan statistical area increased by 13.6% from 1980 to 1990, and an additional 10.6% from 1990 to 1994 (USDC 1996). In 1997 the Portland Metropolitan Service District added 4500 acres to its UGB.

Infinite growth is not possible on a finite planet. We would like to reiterate the message of Chapter 1 that continued population growth in the United States will overwhelm any efforts to preserve agriculture and rural landscapes. The exact number of people that can be supported indefinitely in the United States at current levels of affluence (the nation's carrying capacity) is unknown, but many studies suggest that we may have already exceeded that level (e.g., Grant 1992, Wackernagel and Rees 1996). It is certainly prudent to stabilize our population as soon as possible.

Census Bureau projections (USDC 1996) indicate that an immediate reduction in net immigration to between 200,000 to 300,000 per year would lead to a stabilization of U.S. population at around 300 million about the year 2030, an increase of 33 million from 1997. This population projection allows us to define an amount of land to be zoned for future urban expansion. Rural land conversion to accommodate this growth would be based on the 1982 development density of 0.34 acres per person (see Chapter 1; Appendix 1.2) or an increase of 11.22 million acres (0.34 acres per person times 33 million new residents) for the country as a whole.

The national increment of new urban zoning would be allocated among the states in proportion to each state's population. Thus, based on 1997 population estimates, California would receive permission to add 1,355,000 acres to its developed area, while Florida's share would be 609,000 acres. Each state then develops in conjunction with local authorities a state land use plan that describes how it will allocate its allotment by delineating UGBs for each town and city. In drawing their UGBs, states are encouraged to consider factors such as spatial patterns of prime or unique farmland and expected or desired patterns of population growth within the state.

Once drawn, a city's UGB can be expanded only if development rights are purchased from another urban area, shrinking the seller's UGB and keeping the national total of land within UGBs fixed. This is analogous to the transfer of development rights allowed now by some states (see Chapter 3). Thus, a free market mechanism is available for addressing unexpected shifts in population or the desire of some people to live less densely. Inside the UGBs, the market determines how the land is developed. Hopefully, the establishment of firm and known limits will encourage more creative use of land than is currently practiced, but the type of development is under local control without federal intervention. However, within a framework of permanent limits, the grab-bag of tools currently available to local communities (e.g., PDR, cluster zoning) is more likely to be effective. Locational advantages to agriculture are much more likely to be realized if urban boundaries are permanent and speculative increases in the price of agricultural land are avoided. As Robert Frost wrote, good fences make good neighbors, and this applies to the juxtaposition of agriculture and cities.

Non-federal lands outside of UGBs that are not set-aside for recreation or other non-production functions are zoned for exclusive agricultural or forestry use. New development in these areas is restricted to housing for farm labor or owners/operators and other structures directly supporting commercial agriculture. New vacation homes, hobby farms, and acreages are prohibited. Existing non-farm residences are grandfathered.

The federal land use program would include provisions for monitoring and enforcing state compliance. The Clean Water Act and The Clean Air Act provide models for a carrot-and-stick approach. States failing to develop a statewide land use plan that meets federal standards will be required to adopt a default federal plan. Lack of state enforcement would result in the withholding of a variety of federal monies. Citizen farmland protection groups would have the right to sue the state or particular towns for breaches of the plan.

On the other side of the ledger, the federal government would provide funding and technical assistance in developing state plans. Money would be available to assist in the redevelopment of decaying inner cities and inner suburbs, including mass transit. Tax breaks would be available to developers who construct compact, high quality communities within the urban boundaries. Some of the money for redevelopment would come from the savings resulting from the reduced cost of infrastructure for the compact new development.

Obviously, the details of a national land use policy are not as important at this point in the land use debate as is a focus on clearly stated goals and the basic approach to achieve them. We believe that the policy outlined above would preserve agriculture and other landscape functions in the United States, while providing the foundation for sustainable communities, and a sustainable quality of life for all Americans.

We doubt that many people would publicly define their vision for America as massive sprawl, degraded landscapes, gridlocked roads, energy- and eventually food-dependence on other nations, decaying inner cities, and a population largely isolated from nature. Yet that is what we are moving toward, a function of the tyranny of small decisions. Broader visions and plans offer a starting point for a debate on how to avoid the destiny that we are moving toward.

We challenge those who reject the idea of a national land use policy to articulate their vision of the future landscape of America, and propose how their vision might be achieved. Competing visions and plans of national scope are essential to the debate on what America should be and how we can get there.

### Removal of Constraints to Local Preservation Efforts

We are realistic, however, regarding the difficulty and lengthiness of such a debate. Given the current political climate, a national land use law as outlined above is unlikely to be adopted

anytime soon. Although we believe that anything less than a
national program will fail to adequately protect American agriculture and landscapes, there are changes in federal policies that
would at least be more supportive of and less restrictive to those
local communities that wished to preserve their farmland.
Current federal and state laws and policies often inhibit local
preservation efforts.

For example, federal and state funding of roads, sewers, and
other infrastructure is a major determinant of the location and
rate of new development. The 1.1 billion dollar Charlotte (NC)
outerbelt, supported by federal funds, is spawning sprawl at each
of its new interchanges, while threatening the viability of the
central city (see Chapter 2, Box 2.1). In Palm Beach County,
Florida, a $500,000 lobbying campaign by a small group of devel-
opers and land speculators resulted in the allocation of $102
million in state and federal funds to widen 23 miles of State Route
7 including 10 miles through the county Agricultural Reserve
(Engelhardt 1997). The road improvements greatly increased the
amount of development allowable under county rules in this
largely agricultural area.

Palm Beach County's efforts to control development are also
hindered by a state moratorium on concurrency, a policy under
which local governments can restrict or delay development if
adequate school space is not available to accommodate the additional students (see Box 7.2). Requirements for schools are one of
the main reasons that residential development does not generate
enough tax revenue to cover the cost of municipal services (see
Chapter 4, Box 4.3).

If the federal government will not take the lead in farmland
preservation, it should at least get out of the way of those communities that wish to protect their land, and act responsibly on
those issues related to farmland protection for which only the
federal government has authority. Those issues include:

*Population:* Only the federal government can establish a
national goal of stabilizing U.S. population. Immigration policy
is set at the federal level—states cannot control the movement
of people across their borders—and states such as California,
Texas, and Florida bear a disproportionate share of the burden.

Box 7.2   Control new crowding.

A statewide task force on school construction and
concurrency, which will meet today and Friday in Tallahas-
see, should strongly recommend to the Legislature and Gov.
Chiles that local school districts have the authority to set
their own rules to deal with growth that crowds schools.

The Public Schools Construction Commission doesn't quite
know what to do with the issue of concurrency, a policy that
would allow development only in areas with enough class-
rooms to handle the students. If school space was not
available, development could be restricted or delayed.

Some tentative recommendations before the commission,
such as giving more authority to charter counties—including
Palm Beach, where crowding is a serious problem—are good.
Others aren't, particularly the extension of the one-year
moratorium on concurrency the Legislature imposed in May.

The task force leans toward extending the one-year
concurrency ban, which developer-friendly legislators added
to House Bill 2121, until the rules are clarified. That's a
delaying tactic. The best way to get rules clarified is to let
local concurrency advocates—such as Students First! in
Palm Beach County—push ahead.

The panel also should make sure large counties aren't
crippled by its tentative recommendation that crowding be
measured districtwide rather than in smaller zones. A developer shouldn't be able to further crowd west Boca schools
simply because there's a school at capacity in Jupiter.

That policy might work in a small county. In Palm Beach
County, it would require absurd busing routes. Get
the point? Decisions should be made locally, not by the
legislature.

— Editorial, The Palm Beach Post, November 20, 1997, p. 22A

*Infrastructure*: Federal aid to state and local governments for highways approached $20 billion in 1996, and aid for construction of wastewater treatment facilities exceeded $2 billion in 1995 (USDC 1996). The Federal Farmland Protection Policy Act (see Chapter 3) should be strengthened to require not just an evaluation by federal agencies of the impact on farmland of their infrastructure expenditures, but the modification of spending plans to avoid significant farmland loss. A key to compliance should be compatibility with state, local, and private farmland protection programs. To assist in reaching compliance, rules restricting the expenditure of Highway Trust funds to highway construction should be broadened to include mass transit. States such as Oregon that have similar restrictions on the use of fuel tax proceeds should also allow more flexibility.

*Takings and givings*: Through legislation and court actions, the federal government should promote a restrictive definition of a regulatory taking. Zoning for exclusive farmland use should not be considered a takings because not all economic uses of the land have been prohibited (see Chapter 3). Alternatively, windfall profits accruing to landowners from the expenditure of tax dollars for roads or other infrastructure should be considered a givings, and at least a portion of any windfall profits should be captured by the state for funding farmland preservation or urban redevelopment programs. The landowners who successfully lobbied for the widening of Florida State Route 7 are gaining windfall profits of tens of millions of dollars from the expenditure of more than $100 million of tax money. Tax dollars should not subsidize speculators, particularly when farmland is lost as a result.

*Estate taxes*: The Taxpayer Relief Act (Public Law 105-34; Beretz 1997) has somewhat reduced the likelihood that inheritance taxes will force the sale of a farm to developers (see Chapter 3). However, more can be done. We recommend that 100% of the value of farmland encumbered with a permanent conservation easement be excluded from a decedent's taxable estate (see Chapter 3). In the meantime, county agents should do a better job of informing farmers of the existing estate planning options that can facilitate the intergenerational transfer of farmland.

The influence of the federal government on land use decisions is pervasive, so there are many other changes that could be made to indirectly reduce the development pressure on farmland. Examples include ending the tax deductibility of interest payments for mortgages on second homes, and avoiding trade agreements that reduce the economic viability of U.S. farmers. A thorough review of the direct and indirect effects of federal laws and policies on farmland loss is needed. State governments should follow suit.

### Support for Local Farmland Preservation

There are also many actions that the federal government can take to directly support community farmland programs. One of the most obvious is increased federal funding for purchase of development rights (PDR). State and local PDR programs provide permanent protection for farmland (see Chapter 3), but are very expensive. Funding is never adequate to protect more than a small amount of the farmland in any particular area (see Chapter 3, Table 3.3). The Farmland Protection Program (FPP), originally part of the 1996 Farm Bill, authorizes a total of $35 million over six years to assist state and local agencies in purchasing conservation easements on prime and unique farmland (Swords 1997). In 1996, the program helped to permanently protect 77,000 acres of farmland in 17 states; a large amount, but small compared to the more than 1 million acres of rural land converted to development during that year.

An increase in the FPP to $100 million annually might directly fund the permanent protection of 50,000 acres per year, more if it effectively leverages state and private efforts. This expenditure would still be less than .02% of the annual USDA budget. Considering USDA's interest in maintaining and increasing agricultural production, and considering that the agricultural productivity of paved land is zero, this level of increased funding for FPP seems modest. During the period 1990 through 1996, federal payments for farm income stabilization totaled more than $64 billion. Imagine how much farmland could have been permanently protected if taxpayers had demanded conservation easements in exchange for those subsidies.

Local communities wishing to develop comprehensive land use plans to protect farmland and enhance farming would benefit

from federal assistance, both financial and in the form of expertise. Minnesota's Community-Based Planning Act (see Case 12)
is an example of a voluntary, incentive-based planning framework
that could be implemented nationally to encourage and support
local land use planning. Case 4 describes a federally-funded
program to provide communities and citizens with access to
Geographic Information Systems and other internet-based tools
for evaluating trends in land use and development, and visualiz-
ing the effects of alternative development scenarios. NRCS and
other extension agencies should become more involved in training
community planners and facilitating land use planning efforts.

Current USDA research and policy agendas favor the input and
marketing sectors of the agricultural economy over the farming
sector, and multi-national corporations over the small farm.
Elimination of this bias would remove a major barrier to the
relocalization of agriculture and the accompanying incentive for
the preservation of local farmland. Some structural and policy
changes to support small-scale farmers are listed in Chapter 5,
Box 5.8. More recommendations are presented in *A Time to Act:
A Report of the USDA National Commission on Small Farms*
(USDA 1998).

## Conclusion

The United States is at a major crossroads, and the land use
policies that are implemented during the next decade will be decisive in determining the future quality of life in this country.
Americans have enormous power at this time to shape their landscapes. Energy is plentiful and cheap, the economy is booming,
and technological advances make it easier for many people to live
where and how they wish. No longer will distance or inaccessibil-
ity protect rural landscapes. The fate of the countryside rests
squarely in our hands.

Yet, as a group we seem to be using our wealth and power in a
mindless frenzy of consumerism, wanting more and bigger of everything, including roads, houses, building lots, and a place in
the country. An editor of the Charlotte (NC) Observer referred to
the "orgiastic devouring of countryside" occurring around his city,
the cumulative effect of thousands of individual decisions, unguided by consideration of the larger picture.

Figure 1.1 (p. 26) reminds us of a children's riddle: If a lily pad growing on a pond doubles in size every day and takes 50 days to completely cover the pond, when the pond is half covered, how many days are left before the pond is totally covered? The answer is simple—one day. It is after all a child's riddle. Yet, when it comes to understanding the implications of exponential growth, we are all children.

Our "pond" will never be literally covered by development (Figure 7.1). But there is ample evidence that the future we are creating will be unpleasant at best, and disastrous at worst. Dietrich Bonhoeffer, a Protestant theologian hanged by the Nazis in 1945, stated that "the ultimate test of a moral society is the kind of world it leaves to its children." Our society is in real danger of flunking the test.

Figure 7.1  A light-hearted view of our predicament. TOLES © 1997 The Buffalo News. Reprinted with permission of UNIVERSAL PRESS SYNDICATE. All rights reserved.

# References

1000 Friends. 1996. Agenda for Livability: Reforming State and Local Land Use Planning to Protect Oregon's Quality of Life in the 21st Century. 1000 Friends of Oregon, 534 SW Third Avenue, Portland, OR.

AFT. 1997. Saving American Farmland: What Works. American Farmland Trust, Washington, D.C.

Beretz, C. 1997. President Clinton signs farm estate tax relief into law. American Farmland 18(2):9.

Brecher, J., and T. Costello. 1994. Global Village or Global Pillage: Economic Reconstruction from the Bottom Up. South End Press, Boston.

Coughlin, R. 1993. The Adoption and Stability of Agriculture Zoning in Lancaster County, Pennsylvania. University of Pennsylvania, Philadelphia, PA.

Daniels, T., and D. Bowers. 1997. Holding Our Ground: Protecting America's Farmland. Island Press, Washington, D.C.

Engelhardt, J. 1997. How developers engineered the deal to expand SR7. The Palm Beach Post, 16 November, 1A, 25A-26A.

Grant, L. (ed.) 1992. Elephants in the Volkswagen. W.H. Freeman and Company, New York.

Kahn, A.E. 1966. The tyranny of small decisions: Market failures, imperfections, and the limits of economics. Kyklos 19:23-47.

Last, D.G. 1995. Incremental land-use decision making displayed by county zoning committees. Journal of Soil and Water Conservation (Jan-Feb):21-24.

Lehman, K., and A. Krebs. 1996. Control of the world's food supply. pp. 122-130. In: J. Mander and E. Goldsmith (eds.). The Case Against the Global Economy: and For a Turn Toward the Local. Sierra Club Books, San Francisco.

Liberty, R. 1997. Evaluating Oregon's land use program. Landmark 22:2-29.

Mander, J., and E. Goldsmith (eds.). 1996. The Case Against the Global Economy: and For a Turn Toward the Local. Sierra Club Books, San Francisco.

Olson, R.K., and C.A. Francis. 1995. A hierarchical framework for evaluating diversity in agroecosystems. pp. 5-34. In: R.K. Olson, C.A. Francis, and S. Kaffka (eds.) Exploring the Role of Diversity in Sustainable Agriculture. American Society of Agronomy, Madison, WI.

Peterson, G. 1983. Methods for retaining agricultural land in the urban fringe in the U.S.A. Landscape Planning 9:271-278.

Stokes, S.N., A.E. Watson, and S.S. Mastran. 1997. Saving
America's Countryside: A Guide to Rural Conservation, 2nd
edition. The Johns Hopkins University Press, Baltimore.

Swords, P. 1997. Full funding for farmland protection plan.
American Farmland 18(2):8-9.

USDA. 1998. A Time to Act: A Report of the USDA National
Commission on Small Farms. MP-1545. U.S. Department of
Agriculture, Washington, D.C.

USDC. 1996. Statistical Abstract of the United States, 1996. U.S.
Department of Commerce, Bureau of the Census, Washington,
D.C.

Van der Ryn, S., and S. Cowan. 1996. Ecological Design. Island
Press, Washington, D.C.

Wackernagel, M., and W. Rees. 1996. Our Ecological Footprint.
New Society Publishers, Philadelphia.

# Case Studies

1. Swanton, VT
2. Tompkins County, NY
3. Southeast Pennsylvania
4. Washington D.C. suburban counties
5. Fauquier County, VA
6. Albemarle County, VA
7. Tillery, NC
8. Lake County, FL
9. Ohio
10. DeKalb County, IL
11. Waukesha County, WI
12. Minnesota
13. Lincoln, NE
14. Lincoln, NE
15. Northwest Arkansas
16. Austin, TX
17. Rocky Mountain region
18. Western Washington
19. Oregon
20. Fresno County, CA
21. The Oxnard Plain, CA
22. Norway

# Case 1

## Swanton, Vermont: Farmland Conservation in the Green Mountain State

*Ethan Parke,*
*Vermont Housing & Conservation Board*

Vermont supports a vital and sustainable agriculture. According to the 1992 U.S. Census of Agriculture, Vermont's 5,436 farms keep 658,765 acres of cropland in active agricultural production. Agriculture represents the third largest sector of the state's economy, contributing more than $500 million in farm receipts annually. Dairy farming is the backbone of Vermont's agriculture with approximately 2,000 dairy farms contributing nearly 70% of the state's farm receipts. Vermont farmers also produce vegetables, apples, maple syrup, Christmas trees, and nursery crops. Most of Vermont's rural economy depends heavily on agriculture and therefore the availability of a plentiful agricultural land base is of prime concern to many communities.

The state's $1 billion tourist industry also relies on agriculture to maintain the scenic landscape that has made Vermont famous—green fields and hillsides dotted with cows, picturesque villages, and tidy farmsteads. But while tourism is a mainstay of Vermont's economy, it also poses a threat to the state's agricultural heritage. Sixteen million people live within a day's drive of

Vermont, and the state has become a second home haven to many city dwellers. The state also attracts those seeking a tranquil setting for their primary residence. As a result, many new homes are built on valuable farmlands. According to the U.S. Census, Vermont's population grew more than 10% from 1980 to 1990. The USDA publication, "The Changing Vermont Landscape II, 1991," documents that Vermont's urban and built-up land increased by approximately 9,700 acres between 1982 and 1987. About three-fourths of this acreage came from cropland and pasture. Agricultural statistics from Vermont also demonstrate this trend. From 1982 to 1992, the state lost 879 farms and saw 113,290 acres of cropland taken out of production, according to the U.S. Census of Agriculture.

## State Farmland Preservation Programs

The State of Vermont has a number of programs designed to help farmers stay in business. These include state-funded agricultural lending programs, a state-funded property tax stabilization program, and numerous extension education programs offered through the state university. The legislature has also passed several laws that regulate growth and development. Vermont's development review law (Act 250) was enacted in 1970, providing a framework for review of large scale or high impact development projects. Since then the legislature has also adopted subdivision regulations, and a statewide planning law (Act 200), which provides funding and planning guidance to municipalities. Vermont also has a program to fund the permanent protection of agricultural land through nonregulatory means. This is the purchase of development rights program administered by the Vermont Housing and Conservation Board (VHCB).

The Vermont Legislature formed VHCB in 1987 for the purpose of creating affordable housing for Vermonters, and for conserving and protecting Vermont's agricultural land, historic properties, important natural areas, and recreational lands. VHCB is funded by annual legislative appropriations. In recent years, proceeds from the sale of state general obligation bonds have formed the majority of VHCB's legislative funding. VHCB also receives a portion of the revenue from the state's property transfer tax. Total state appropriations have ranged from $7 million to $13 million annually. Supplementing these funds, VHCB also administers various federal programs, both in housing and conservation.

The VHCB, as a public instrumentality of the state, implements its mission through a cooperative process that involves nonprofit organizations, state agencies, and municipalities. The board awards grants to nonprofit developers of affordable housing throughout the state. These organizations build new housing or rehabilitate existing buildings in urban areas or in towns and villages. The board also funds a variety of conservation projects, including state acquisitions of forests, parks, or wildlife areas, and conservation acquisitions by nonprofits and local towns. The board uses a significant portion of its conservation funds to purchase development rights on farmland.

Since its inception, VHCB has spent $34,700,000 to conserve 192 farms totaling 65,935 acres, for an average cost of $534 per acre. Many projects leverage funds from private sources. While real estate prices have remained constant or have risen slightly, VHCB's average cost of conserving farms has decreased due to the extraordinary fund raising efforts of the program's nonprofit partners. During 1997, privately raised funds covered nearly one-third of the costs of purchasing conservation easements in Vermont.

## The Case of Swanton

The town of Swanton clearly illustrates VHCB's farmland conservation efforts. Swanton lies near the state's northwestern corner, where gently rolling fields of corn and alfalfa stretch down to the eastern shore of Lake Champlain. Many Vermonters consider Swanton to be the number one agricultural town in the state. USDA soil maps show that almost 60 percent of the soils in the town are of prime or statewide significance—a high percentage in a state largely covered by hills and mountains. Most Swanton farmers milk cows for a living; in fact, the town ranks third in Vermont for the number of operating dairy farms within its borders. Dairying is profitable in Swanton for a number of reasons, among them: Swanton farms typically have land that is easily tilled, and that grows forage in ample quantities for the long winters of confinement feeding; agricultural support services (e.g., feed and equipment dealers, veterinarians) are readily available; and the farms often abut one another, contributing to a lifestyle that is distinctly agricultural.

But Swanton farmland, like farmland throughout Vermont, faces threats from the encroachment of urban and suburban development. In 1990, 5,636 people lived in Swanton, compared to 5,141 in 1980. Linear projections of this growth rate indicate that 56 additional people a year will need housing, services, schools, and roads in Swanton. Already, an interstate highway interchange in town reduces the commuting time to major employment centers such as St. Albans and Burlington, making Swanton somewhat of a bedroom community. Summer residents of the area also spur development pressure. The nearness of Lake Champlain and Swanton's bucolic setting have encouraged the location of approximately 300 seasonal dwellings in the town.

Swanton's municipal plan calls for the concentration of new development in villages rather than strung out along country roads. The plan also recognizes the importance of agriculture to the local economy, and notes that the number of active farms in the town has been declining. The plan states that there were 65 active farms in the town in 1985, and only 54 in 1990. To counteract that trend, the town plan states: "...the town should continue its efforts to preserve and maintain agriculture as a viable economic activity and should also assist in the protection of significant open land resources by collaborating with land management and protection organizations such as the Vermont Land Trust and Vermont Housing and Conservation Board."

Responding to this call, VHCB and its nonprofit or state agency partners have invested, in a decade, more than $2 million to purchase development rights from Swanton farm owners. VHCB protects farmland by nonregulatory means, purchasing development rights from willing sellers based on appraised value. In choosing farmland for protection, the VHCB board examines the following criteria, in descending order of importance: soils, location, farm infrastructure, and management. Because of their good soil quality and their location in a strong farming community, Swanton farms have ranked high in this selection system.

The Vermont Land Trust (VLT) helped complete the first farmland protection project in Swanton in 1989. VLT, as a private nonprofit conservation organization, applied to VHCB, whose board agreed to fund the purchase of development rights on a 225-acre dairy farm in West Swanton. As in every subsequent project completed by this partnership, the conservation easement conveying the development rights was co-held by VLT, VHCB, and the Vermont Department of Agriculture. Having three co-holders provides assurance that at least one entity will always be available to monitor and enforce the easement provisions.

By 1992, VHCB was considering several farm applications from Swanton at each of its biannual funding rounds. The increase in landowner interest in the program resulted partly from outreach efforts to farmers conducted jointly by VHCB, VLT, and the Department of Agriculture. By the end of 1993, VHCB had made funding commitments to a total of seven farm projects in Swanton. Most of these farms were located in a fertile plain southwest of Swanton village, and since several of the farms were contiguous to each other, the completed projects began to form a block of protected land. The VHCB board came to believe strongly in the need for blocks of conserved farmland rather than isolated farm projects. Blocks provided a resource mass that was large enough to support the local agricultural supply and service industries, and to retain the feel of a farming community, as opposed to a rural residential or suburban neighborhood. From 1994 through the middle of 1997, VHCB committed funds to eleven more farm projects in Swanton, bringing the total of conserved farmland in the town to more than 4,400 acres, much of it in one contiguous block. These projects represented a public investment of approximately $3.25 million.

As the number of VHCB farm projects in Swanton grew, VHCB staff sought to maintain a dialogue with town officials. In the fall of 1994, the VHCB conservation director, along with staff of the VLT and the Department of Agriculture, met with the Swanton Selectboard and members of the Planning Commission. VHCB staff also responded to questions from Swanton tax assessors. Community leaders expressed mixed feelings toward the VHCB farm program. Earl Fournier, chair of the Swanton Selectboard, and a dairy farmer himself, supported the concept of conserving farmland in blocks, but questioned how much actual development potential there was in the areas where VHCB's money had gone. He also worried that conserved farms would contribute less to the town's property tax base, and would thereby increase the property tax burden on other farmers and home owners. Indeed, Swanton's tax assessors had taken the position that the sale of development rights lowered listed values, and therefore shifted some of the tax burden to other property owners.

"I can see why farmers are doing it," Fournier told VHCB staff. "It reduces debt so a farm can be sold to another farmer. It's the only way someone's going to get started nowadays." But, he added, "Overall, the majority of people in town wouldn't mind if no more [development rights] were bought up." Fournier did agree that in the long run, the VHCB program would benefit the public because conservation easements ensure that there will always be land available to farm, whereas without such protection, parcels become fragmented and ownership by nonfarmers increases.

Alan Bourbeau, chair of the Swanton Planning Commission, said the VHCB farm program had been good for the town because it had slowed residential growth in the outskirts of the town, where the provision of municipal services such as roads and school busing is more expensive. His observation supported the view that the net effect of conservation on property taxes could be advantageous because open land demands less in the way of municipal services and schools than developed land. He said the planning commission was trying to concentrate future growth in and around the village center and near the interstate highway interchange, and at the same time to slow down development in the rural areas. The VHCB program had become an important means of implementing that strategy.

The VHCB conservation dollars spent in Swanton have also helped to prime the local economy at a time when farm revenues have been low. By selling development rights, many farmers have been able to reduce and reorganize their debts, thereby improving their cash flows and allowing them to make new investments in land, machinery, farm buildings, or livestock. Tom Bellavance, vice president and loan officer for a nearby farm lending agency, said VHCB's farmland protection funds should be viewed as an investment by the state. Generally, because farming is a basic industry that turns raw materials into useful commodities, any money invested in agriculture multiplies throughout the economy. It has been said that every dollar spent in the farm sector turns over five to seven times, creating jobs and business gains throughout the community. A partial list of known Swanton businesses that depend on farmers includes one limestone quarry, four farm equipment dealers, two fertilizer companies, two grain dealers, one livestock dealer, three veterinarians, three meat packers, and four farm related manufacturers.

Another important outcome of the farm program in Swanton has been the conveyance of conserved farms to new owners. Five of the projects in Swanton involved transfers of the farms to new owners either at the time of the sale of development rights or soon thereafter. At least three more of the eleven projects will facilitate transfers in the near future as sons or daughters prepare to take over their parents' farm. The sale prices of these conserved farms are substantially lower than the unrestricted fair market values. For example, the sale of a newly restricted Swanton farm occurred in August 1995 when Stanley Jacobs sold development rights on his 226-acre farm and simultaneously sold the restricted farm to farmer Richard Longway. The restricted farm's sale price was $311,146, compared to the $430,000 appraised "before" value. This amounts to a discount of 28%. Other conserved farms in town sold for as much as 55% below the appraised unrestricted value, averaging a 39% discount as a result of removing the development rights.

The story of the Vosburg farm was particularly illustrative. Norm Vosburg had operated a dairy farm in Swanton on shares since 1958, but had been unable to purchase it at an affordable price from absentee owner Donald Wood. A VHCB grant to the Vermont Land Trust for the purchase of development rights brought the price within reach, and Norm and his son Mark now finally own the 336-acre farm. The total VHCB grant for this project was $198,418, with $184,000 for acquisition of development rights, and $14,418 for associated costs and stewardship. When the project closed, the farm was conveyed simultaneously to the Vosburgs for a price that was substantially less than the farm's unrestricted value. In this way, the seller, Donald Wood, realized a satisfactory return on his investment without having to sell the farm for building lots.

What might have happened in this instance, and what might the effect have been on the Swanton community if VHCB had not made this particular grant? Mr. Wood, an elderly gentleman in less than good health, might have placed the farm on the real estate market at its development value. Or, he might have sold portions of the farmland to other farmers, and retained a number of ten-acre lots as building sites. In either case, it is likely that an operating farm unit would have been lost, and the Vosburgs would have been displaced from their homes and out of work. This would have been a particularly tragic outcome because the

Vosburgs had put so much of their lives into the farm. Through the years they had built up a fine herd of Holstein cattle, had carefully maintained the buildings, had installed soil conservation measures, and had improved the fertility of the soils.

No discussion of Swanton would be complete without mention of the Abenaki people who have made their home there for at least 4,000 years. VHCB's conservation efforts in Swanton assisted the region's native Americans by protecting a 438-acre wooded tract near Lake Champlain that was a traditional hunting ground and cultural landmark. A developer planned to create house lots on the parcel, but regulatory agencies had delayed the project, giving the state Department of Fish and Wildlife time to negotiate a purchase and to apply for funds from VHCB. The local Abenaki tribal organization strongly supported the project. The state now owns the property subject to a conservation agreement that protects cultural resources and protects the right of the Abenaki people to use the land for traditional cultural and spiritual activities.

# Case 2

## Tompkins County, New York
## Local Agriculture and
## Farmland Protection

*Charles Schlough*
*Agriculture Planning Consultant, Ithaca, New York*

### Introduction

Location: Central Finger Lakes Region
County Seat: Ithaca
Population: 96,000
Land Area: 308,500 acres
Home of Cornell University

"Who in Tompkins County would want to save farmland?" This challenge from a retired upstate New York farmer, turned farmland broker, is a disheartening introduction to the many contradictions and conflicts around the topic of protecting agriculture and farmland. In another nearby county, a different challenge is just as enigmatic—how to help farmers out of cynicism and a downward economic dependence on dairy economics. Further entrenchment is expressed in the defensive refrain, "No one is going to tell me what I can do with my land. All they have to do is give us decent prices for our products and there won't be any farmland problem." And in one county, the farmer members of the Agriculture and Farmland Protection Board adamantly oppose even the discussion of land use planning or regulation.

Farmers are not the only ones entrenched in "positions." Preservationists, environmental groups, local and state governments, Cooperative Extension educators, traditional economic development practitioners, and consumers hold views and expectations that farmers often see as more self-serving than helpful.

The mind set of long time farmers often seems to be, "The problem was caused elsewhere, so the solution has to come from elsewhere." Many farmers keep waiting for the simple solution that will never come. To a great extent, the problem has been brought on externally, but the solution will have to be developed both locally and at larger scales.

Given the recent and long-term trends of farm and farmland losses, Tompkins County will probably experience losses between 10% to 24% per decade of both numbers of farms and acreage of productive farmland, and the associated losses of valuable direct and indirect benefits for the non-farm population.

With the advent of Agriculture and Farmland Protection Planning in 1995, Tompkins County is making progress, but not along a path focused solely on farmland preservation. The efforts being made illustrate an approach to farmland protection through dual strategies intended to strengthen local agriculture and build supportive land use policies—and thereby retain farmland.

## Views On Farmland Preservation

The popular preservation strategy of separating development rights from farmland has little support in most of the 44 rural towns of New York State. It is seen as impractical and ineffective where farmland is the dominant land use. If farmland were more scarce, it would be more precious to non-farmers. In counties where this is true, preservation strategies are being supported.

In this region there is a widely shared belief that the best way to preserve farmland is to keep it farmed. As one form of open space, farmland is not a natural resource; it is a man-made by-product of ongoing agricultural production. It is difficult to find a convincing argument that preserving farmland with conservation easements will maintain open space—unless scrub and woodland is the kind of open space for which people are willing to settle.

Pressure to convert farmland is much lower in most areas of Tompkins County than in more densely populated areas where farmland preservation measures such as purchase of development rights are applied. Because many Upstate New York counties have 30% or more of their total land area in farmland, any sense of its scarcity is difficult to detect except at the urban fringes. Suburban sprawl has been dampened over the past decade by a low rate of population and economic growth. Many villages still have active farms within their borders or have farm fields visible directly behind residential streets. In such rural areas, the pace of conversion is not fast enough to build a critical mass of citizens willing to "buy" farmland scenes. Beyond the urban fringe, breakup of the agricultural land base is less evident to the non-agricultural community.

Strong opposition to rural land use planning and regulation comes from farmers who wish to protect their option to sell building lots or large parcels as a source of cash when financial stresses occur, or more importantly, when retirement opportunities are considered. For many marginal farming operations, the hope for eventual sale of farmland offers the only exit from farming, or for many, an alternative to poverty. Windfalls for retirement have seldom been realized from such speculation. But the continuing fragmentation of farmland areas is increasingly evident as are problems with "city folk" who consequently move too close to farms and raise objections to normal and acceptable farming practices. Ironically, the attention given to preserving farmland from development is a distraction from the even greater loss (four times) of farmland through abandonment caused primarily by adverse economic pressures.

## Data, Trends, and Influencing Factors

### Conditions and Trends

Agriculture in Tompkins County is in transition. Structural changes in Tompkins County agriculture, as on the national level, continue to result in fewer and larger farms and more diverse smaller farms. According to the last Agriculture Census (1992), there are 215 part-time farms and 226 full-time farms with combined annual agricultural sales of $50 million.

Farmland acreage in Tompkins County has declined by 25% from 1978 to 1992 (1.8% per year); while the statewide decline has been 20% (1.4% per year). Even with this reduction in total farmland, average farm size in the county has varied only slightly in the 14 year interval, standing at an average of 208 acres per farm. Statewide, the average farm size has increased in the same interval by 5% to 231 acres. The number of farms in the county has also been steadily declining from 2988 in 1910 to 441 in 1992; falling by an average of 1.9% per year in the 14 year period from 1978 to 1992.

While dairy and field crop operations are fewer, their agricultural economic output has accounted for a steady increase in production and market value of dairy and commodity crops in Tompkins County. Meanwhile, farms and substantial amounts of farmland are disappearing in the mid-size range of 50 to 500 acres.

The number of small farms of less than 50 acres has increased slightly, primarily the 10–49 acre size that produce more than $10,000 annual gross sales. A number of these farms and those of 50–179 acres are the result of downsizing of former active, larger farms now run by semi-retired farmers who raise livestock and grow hay and other crops on a limited scale.

Small part-time farms raising livestock, fruits, vegetables, horses, and specialty agricultural and horticultural products are responding to opportunities from the proximity of an increasing urban population, appreciative of the rural character of the county and its farm products. Ornamental horticultural operations have also enjoyed growth due to the expanding urban/suburban population, and now represent the largest category of specialty agriculture enterprises in the county.

Farms of 500+ acres are generally profitable and expanding in Tompkins County. Consolidation of farm acreage into larger and more efficient units has resulted from decisions of the most competitive farmers who have responded to market forces, technological innovations, and economies of scale.

### Farmland Loss and Fragmentation

The "loss" of active farmland results largely from abandonment of formerly active farms and subsequent reversion to scrub and woodland. Only a small amount of "lost" farmland has been converted into land development, generally through random patterns of development that fragment and negatively impact viable agricultural areas.

Municipal land use planning, zoning and even the avoidance of planning have encouraged the conversion of prime agricultural lands to other uses without consideration for the negative impacts on farming profitability and farmland retention. This has partly resulted from the long-standing importance given to residential and commercial development as a means to build a larger tax base upon which to spread public service and infrastructure costs and ostensibly to reduce tax burdens among residents.

Affordability of farmland has been negatively impacted by assessment practices on farmland. The New York Farm Bureau reported in a 1996 study that New York has the highest average farmland taxes ($23/acre) of the top 20 agricultural states (20-state average of $14/acre). The New York State Office of Real Property Services (assessment) recently established the policy that undeveloped land should be valued on the basis of its "current use," not at its "highest and best use," as has been standard practice for many decades. Although the potential for reduction of taxes on active farmland is considerable in some areas, local and county assessors have been slow and sometimes resistant to adjust their valuation practices.

### Farmland Sales and Rental

In the 1994 Agriculture Survey, active farmers in Tompkins County reported selling a total of 1282 acres (of total farmland of 97,800 acres in 1992) in the past ten years. Of this small amount, 34% was developed for homes, 21% was idled, and 12% was sold to other farmers or to a buyer who rented it to a farmer. Another 30% reported multiple reasons, all of which included some portion of land sold for development. Farmland bought by farmers in the same ten year period totaled 4,826 acres, nearly four times as much land as active farmers sold.

Rented farmland, which accounts for as much as 30% of the county's harvested crop land, represents a considerable amount that is vulnerable to sale for non-farm use. Although it is often more cost effective for farmers to rent land than to buy it and pay the taxes, its continuing availability is at risk. There are reports that considerable development is occurring on farmland owned by non-farmers close to built-up areas.

## Lack of Continuity of the Family Farm

The lack of successors for aging farmers contributes to farm-land loss. Only half the full-time farmers surveyed in 1994 stated that after retirement the land would stay in farming either by selling to other farmers or transferring to family members who plan to farm. Another 10% said they would let the land idle or farm it modestly. The remaining 40% said they would sell land to non-farmers or to non-farming family members. A critical indication of the aggregate pressures on farming and farmland is that 55% of full-time farmers don't expect their family farm to continue past their own lifetimes.

## Outlook for Change

Tompkins County farmers, surveyed in 1994, reported that in the next ten years they expect to see a continuing reduction in the number of farms, increasing development in rural areas, increasing size of larger farms, increasing regulations, higher property taxes, and upon retirement, 40% expect to sell their land to non-farmers.

The non-farm community will suffer too. Continued losses of farming and farmland will adversely affect the economy and quality of life for all residents of the county through declines in exports, the property tax base of farms, farm jobs and farm support service businesses, fresh high-quality local food, non-food farm products used by consumers, cultivated open space, agricultural products, biodiversity, and attractiveness to tourists.

Changes that farmers seek most are improvements in product prices. How realistic are such expectations, given the present aggregate capacity for agricultural production, market control by major industrial-scale farming giants, continuing technological improvements, and the immeasurable impact of biotechnology on yields? How realistic is it for farmers to expect that higher product prices will assure their economic vitality? Few farmers are willing to acknowledge the counter-effect on prices that occurs when higher prices encourage higher production levels. Market forces of supply and demand will be unforgiving more than ever under the policies of the 1996 Farm Bill.

The decisions made by farmers, in response to many pressures and limited incentives, ultimately affect the loss or retention of farmland. Farmers in Tompkins County want to continue farming and to do it successfully. But they need incentives for investments and commitments, and support from local government to counteract the unfavorable trends underway.

## Public Policies

A low level of public policy support for agriculture throughout Tompkins County is a crucial impediment to keeping land in farming. Agriculture has a low profile among the non-farm population because the agriculture industry is highly decentralized, because it involves only about 2% to 3% of the population, and because accurate local information is not readily available. Overall, the contributions of agriculture to the non-farm population are not well articulated nor are they well understood and appreciated. In contrast, public policies are highly supportive of commercial business development, industrial job growth, housing development, and the infrastructure network of transportation, public water and sewer. These policies receive greater attention and are formed in an absence of knowledge about their impacts on agriculture.

Tompkins County has no Comprehensive Plan or any stated policy about agriculture. Land use plans and ordinances among its towns exhibit a wide, and ineffective, range of attention to the values, needs and future of agriculture. The existence of nine different town governments, in addition to the county and six municipalities, further complicates efforts for a meaningful and consistent approach to planning for a countywide population of less than 100,000 people.

Six of the county's nine towns have adopted land use plans. These Town Plans provide varying degrees of recognition of agricultural land use, but generally do not provide for the protection of the most viable farmland areas as unique agricultural resources for farming. In 1992, the Town of Ithaca recommended measures to protect agriculture within its boundaries, which have been incorporated in the Town of Ithaca Comprehensive Plan. It is the best attempt among the towns of Tompkins County to address the need for protecting farmland, and includes the approval to purchase conservation easements on 4000 acres of farmland and other open space.

# Strategies to Protect Farmland

## New York State's Approach to Agriculture and Farmland Protection

The New York State Department of Agriculture and Markets administers a grant program for counties to develop agriculture and farmland protection plans, which has spawned many local initiatives. While 24 counties pursue their own assessment of needs and solutions, the State has allocated $4,000,000 for the purchase of conservation easements on farmland. This allocation is consistent with the popular belief that sprawl and development are the primary cause of farmland loss. Unfortunately, no State funds have been directed toward efforts to strengthen agriculture at the local level.

An important missing piece at the State level is a food policy that addresses the importance of local food production and the food needs of local and State residents. The import of approximately 75% of the State's food consumption represents a huge loss of economic opportunity. In addition, there are the consequent economic costs of rural poverty, increased social and human services, lost local and state tax revenues, and decaying rural infrastructure.

## Tompkins County Planning

Funded by the N.Y. Department of Agriculture and Markets grant program, the Tompkins County Agriculture and Farmland Protection Board (AFPB) convened three Task Groups to develop a farmland protection plan. These Task Groups included AFPB members, representatives of organizations, and individuals in the community who are interested in supporting agriculture and farmland. The AFPB and Task Groups identified the following three Goals as the cornerstones of an approach to improve the county's agriculture industry and retention of farmland:

- *Education*: To have a high level of awareness and knowledge about economic and societal values of agriculture by community decision-makers, farmers, and the non-farm population.

- *Government Policies*: To have a supportive climate for continuation of farming through public policies and actions on land use, regulation and taxation that minimize disincentives for farming. Effective response and action is needed from various levels of government.

- *Agricultural Economic Development*: To strengthen the profitability of farm businesses through programs of education, business retention, and expansion, and the development of diverse agricultural enterprises.

Strategies and an implementation plan to meet these goals are currently under consideration by the county.

## Conclusion

Farmland without farmers is simply open space, no longer supportive of agriculture and at high risk of permanent conversion to non-agricultural uses. Effective policies to preserve farmland must include measures to increase the profitability and viability of the agricultural economy. Municipalities need to approach farmland protection from an integrated social, economic, cultural, and ecological perspective. The efforts underway in Tompkins County to protect agriculture and farmland are a beginning. The county's three goals are an attempt to address its current weaknesses in farmland protection policy in a unified manner in full recognition of the interdependence of the stakeholders, the issues, and the proposed solutions. It is hoped that this program will lead to new commitments and to a transition by farmers to join others to save our farmland.

# Case 3

## Southeastern Pennsylvania: Can Agriculture Be Sustained?

*Kate Smith, AUS Consultants, Moorestown, New Jersey*

If you drive through southeastern Pennsylvania,[1] beginning in center city Philadelphia and ending in Lancaster County, the trip is less than 60 miles. The city is part of a complex landscape that includes a thriving agriculture. Farming has been important to southeast Pennsylvania (SE Pa) for generations as evidenced by the more than 250 Century Farms[2] in the region. This agriculture is tremendously productive—the area's 10,358 farms and 1,182,282 acres of farmland produce 42% of the state's market value of agricultural products on just 23% of the state's farms and 16% of the state's farmland. County averages for the market value of agricultural products sold per farm in 1992 generally exceeded the state average of $79,567. For example, the average for Lancaster County was $206,705, while Berks County farms rang up average sales of $152,564 (Pennsylvania Department of Agriculture 1992). Lancaster County has the most productive non-irrigated agriculture in the United States.

Agricultural diversity is high. Farms include family-run dairies with 40 cows and 150 acres of cropland, 1,000-acre cash-grain operations spread over several townships, diversified Amish and Mennonite farms, greenhouse complexes producing tomatoes or peppers, and 10-acre farms raising specialty herbs and vegetables. While the most common farm types are dairy (27% of all farms), livestock (22%), and cash-grain (13%), the mix varies among counties. Dairies account for 1% of Delaware County farms and 38% of Lancaster County farms. Berks County is strong in both dairy and livestock (47% of farms), while Lehigh produces lots of grain (34% of farms). Fruits and vegetables (excluding horticultural specialties) range from 4% of farms in Chester, Lancaster, and Lebanon counties to 13% in Bucks and Delaware counties.

Despite the importance of agriculture to southeast Pennsylvania, the region lost 28% of its farms, with a total farm acreage decline of 21%, from 1969 to 1992. Farmland loss ranged from 9% (37,732 acres) in Lancaster County to 44% (35,008 acres) in Montgomery County (U.S. Department of Commerce, 1994). A recent study by the American Farmland Trust (Sorensen et al. 1997) listed the Northern Piedmont region, which includes SE Pa, as the second most-threatened agricultural area in the United States.

In addition to development pressures, farmers in SE Pa face challenges in resource management. In particular, the trend to put more animals on fewer acres has resulted in problems with manure and nutrient overloading. As part of the Chesapeake Bay watershed, SE Pa contributes to nonpoint source pollution in this important estuary, and changes in farming practices may be required as part of an integrated effort to alleviate this problem.

Agriculture helped shape the region and continues to provide vital economic, environmental and cultural benefits. However, concerns about the loss of farmland as well as the environmental and social impacts of the current system raise the question of whether agriculture in the region can be sustained.

## Assessing Barriers and Opportunities

As part of the Regional Infrastructure for Sustaining Agriculture project, an assessment involving more than 2000 participants was conducted of the barriers to and opportunities for sustaining the SE Pa food system (Hammer et al. 1996). Twelve hundred consumers were surveyed at 23 retail food markets, and 750 dairy and vegetable farmers responded to a mail survey. More than 300 individuals—including farmers, consumers, educators, marketers, planners, and policymakers—participated in 10 focus groups and three public forums. Key leaders responded to an additional written survey. From this process, the major issues affecting the viability of agriculture in SE Pa were identified.

### Barriers to Maintaining Agriculture

*Low profitability* was cited by more than a third of the farmers surveyed as the biggest problem facing their farm in the next 2 to 5 years. Many farmers are squeezed by low product prices and rising input costs. Production expenses continue to rise while prices received for farm products remain the same or decline.

The pressure to focus on short-term profits is strong. In the farmer survey, 68% of dairy and 62% of vegetable farmers "agreed" or "strongly agreed" with the statement, *"Farmers need to focus on maximizing yields today, because the future is unpredictable."* This short term focus has implications for making new investments in environmentally sound and "neighbor friendly" practices. Farmers are trapped between stewardship goals and low profitability.

*Development pressures* mean that in SE Pa land is often valued more for its development potential than for its agricultural productivity. In response to the statement, *"We could make more money by selling our farm than we can by farming the land,"* 64% of the dairy and 73% of the vegetable farmers "agreed" or "strongly agreed." A 1990 study of SE Pa found that 89% of the farmers surveyed believed they could make more money by selling their farm than by farming the land. Of those farmers, 66% reported they were approached by developers on a regular basis (Israel and Gillis 1990).

The farmers surveyed reported that the most common change in land use next to their farm was the introduction or expansion of housing developments. The number of dairy farms bordered by a housing development doubled between 1989 and 1994. Farmers whose operations neighbor a development are more likely to leave farming than farmers who are not near a development (Israel and Gillis 1990).

*Labor shortages*, particularly of skilled workers, often make the continuation or expansion of farming operations difficult. Both the high cost of labor and increasing federal regulation were cited as major barriers. Nearly 55% of both dairy and vegetable farmers reported a decrease in the availability of reliable farm labor. A related study found that labor scarcity was a "very important" reason why 23% of former farmers had left farming (Israel and Gillis 1990). Labor problems will likely worsen if production of fruits, vegetable, and other horticultural crops continues to grow because labor is the largest input, accounting for 37% to 44% of total production expenses.

*Declining support services* involve the closing or consolidation of farm-equipment sales and repair operations, feed and seed suppliers, lenders, and market outlets. Loss of these services increases farming costs. In a vicious cycle, more support businesses close as farm numbers decline. The number of farm-related equipment and supply dealers is declining throughout Pennsylvania. One equipment dealers association has seen its membership drop from nearly 600 in 1982 to 275 in 1993, with the eastern part of the state suffering the most loss (Siebert 1993). Nearly one-third of all the farmers surveyed in SE Pa reported a decreased availability of farm-machinery services.

*Burdensome tax policies* are directly related to development pressure. Farm profitability is reduced by valuing land for development potential rather than agricultural uses. In a 1990 study, 28% of the former farmers identified increased property taxes as a "very important" reason for leaving farming. Even those enrolled in the State's preferential tax program reported that property tax increases were a problem. Estate taxes are a related problem. Many farm families have little cash or other liquid assets with which to pay estate taxes when the principal property owner dies, and the family may be forced to sell the farm, often to a developer (Thompson 1992).

*Intergenerational transfer* of farms can be difficult due to low profitability, high estate taxes, lucrative off-farm job opportunities, and lack of financing for beginning farmers (U.S. General Accounting Office 1993). The farmer survey, consumer survey, focus groups, and literature review all indicate that SE Pa agriculture is threatened by a future lack of farmers. Some farmers said that they actively discouraged their children from farming because "*farming is such hard work for so little return.*"

*Nuisance complaints* from neighbors is another barrier. When residential development enters agricultural areas, new residents disturbed by farm odors or noise may file nuisance complaints against their farmer neighbors. Although Pennsylvania has right-to-farm laws that protect farmers from nuisance complaints, they still take a toll.

### Opportunities for Agriculture

Barriers to sustaining agriculture in SE Pa are significant and some may be too formidable to overcome. Some opportunities do exist, however, for farmers in the region, based in part on proximity to market. Forty percent of the U.S. and 60% of Canada's population is within 500 miles of Harrisburg, the state capital (Pennsylvania Department of Community and Economic Development 1997). Urban proximity provides opportunities for high-value direct marketing as well as off-farm employment. Forty-eight percent of the vegetable farmers reported an increase in market outlets during the past five years. Demographic shifts are also creating marketing opportunities. The growing Hispanic and Asian population in the region is stimulating new markets, and the average age of the population is increasing, a trend that tends to raise demand for fresh vegetables (Blair 1991). Some new dairy cooperatives are forming to take advantage of niche markets such as organic milk and cheese.

Other opportunities for agriculture exist in the form of state and non-governmental programs. PACE (Purchase of Agricultural Conservation Easements) is funded by the state along with counties and local municipalities to purchase development easements from farmers. Farm Link, incubated in the Center for Rural Pennsylvania, matches beginning farmers with farming opportunities. Clean and Green provides tax relief by assessing farmland for its agricultural value rather than its development potential. This state statute is administered through the county assessor's office. Collaborative initiatives supported by foundations such as the Pew Charitable Trusts and the W.K. Kellogg Foundation are bringing representatives from the farm, processing, education, and environmental communities together to support agriculture in the region. Some efforts are exploring the use of market driven incentives for dairy farmers to adopt sustainable agriculture practices. Others are involved in stream-bank protection and nutrient-management programs.

## What Can Be Done?

Barriers to maintaining the SE Pa food and farm system currently outweigh the opportunities. Changes in policies, programs, attitudes, and behavior are required for agriculture to survive. The participants in this assessment consistently identified the need to reduce development pressure on farmland. Growth must be targeted away from agricultural lands and directed toward more appropriate locations, and new development must use land more efficiently. In the 5 counties surrounding Philadelphia, a 3.5% population increase from 1970 to 1990 was accompanied by a 34% increase in developed land, resulting in a sprawling, low-density development pattern (Delaware Valley Regional Planning Commission 1994).

Some focus group participants expressed concern about the long-term effectiveness of zoning. One participant said, "*Zoning doesn't mean anything. If you have enough money, enough time, and hire the right lawyer, you can do anything you want as far as zoning is concerned.*" Agricultural zoning is not always stable over time (Coughlin 1993). For example, one township in a SE Pa county recently softened its agricultural zoning law after landowners sued for an increase in the amount of permitted development.

Some effort has already been directed to regional strategic planning. GreenSpace Alliance, a nonprofit organization dedicated to protecting and maintaining green space has recently completed a regional GreenPlan for five counties in SE Pa, including Philadelphia (Starr 1996). This elaborate, grass roots-driven plan contains innovative strategies for expanding and linking the region's green spaces, revitalizing existing towns and cities, managing suburban development to protect green space and minimize auto use, and protecting farmland.

The fastest growing metropolitan area in Pennsylvania since 1980 is Lancaster County. The resulting sprawl threatens the qualities that make Lancaster a uniquely beautiful place. Ronald Bailey, Lancaster's Planning Director, believes that by shaping new development in the form of traditional, compact communities, where homes, offices, and schools are close enough so people can walk to some of their activities, Lancaster can preserve all its prime farmland (Hylton 1995). To this end, after much soul-searching and debate, a coalition of businessmen, developers, farmers, and environmentalists endorsed a bold plan to protect farmland, revive the city of Lancaster and restore the town-center pattern of development. The plan designates 13 urban growth centers that contain sufficient land to accommodate commercial, industrial, and residential growth expected during the next 20 years. The growth boundaries include 45 of the county's 60 municipalities. The county has asked each to enact zoning compatible with these growth areas. So far more than 20 have complied. In conjunction with this, the county has prepared model ordinances for its municipalities that foster traditional, pedestrian-oriented communities.

Chester County officials are also showing promising leadership with a comprehensive plan to channel growth into already built-up areas, while reducing development in the still-ample rural expanses of what's known as Wyeth country. They plan to set growth boundaries and limit the reach of new utilities and roads into undeveloped areas.

Research and education to help farmers conserve resources and maintain profits continues to lag seriously behind need. By concentrating almost solely on product, agricultural research and education has led to increased yields, but at the expense of farmers, communities, and the environment. The extensive educational resources in the region must be mobilized to help consumers and community leaders recognize the importance and complexity of agriculture. For example, only 39% of the key leaders surveyed could identify three or more stakeholder groups in the food system. Developing a climate of communication and cooperation among farmers and consumers is essential for maintenance of the SE Pa food and farm system.

## Endnotes

1. Southeastern Pennsylvania includes 10 counties: Berks, Bucks, Chester, Delaware, Lancaster, Lebanon, Lehigh, Northampton, Montgomery, and Philadelphia.
2. Century Farms have been owned by the same family for at least 100 consecutive years, and a family member must still live on the land. The farm must also contain at least 10 acres of the original holdings and produce more than $1,000 per year from the sale of farm products.

# References

Blair, D. 1991. The Northeast Food System. The Northeast Network
Project, The Pennsylvania State University, University Park, PA.

Coughlin, R. 1993. The Adoption and Stability of Agriculture
Zoning in Lancaster County, Pennsylvania. University of
Pennsylvania, Philadelphia, PA.

Delaware Valley Regional Planning Commission. 1994. Land-Use
in the Delaware Valley: 1970 and 1990, Analytical Report #2.
Philadelphia, PA, 215-592-1800.

Hammer, J., J. Crosby, and K. Smith. 1996. Beyond The Last
Fencerow: The Future of the Food and Farm system in
Southeast Pennsylvania. A monograph obtained through the
Department of Agricultural Economics and Rural Sociology, The
Pennsylvania State University, 814-863-8649.

Hylton, T. 1995. Save Our Land, Save Our Towns. RB Books, Seitz
and Seitz , Inc., Harrisburg, PA.

Israel, D., and W. Gillis. 1990. Helping Farmers Survive the Pressures
of Development. Cooperative Extension, College of Agriculture, The
Pennsylvania State University, University Park, PA.

Pennsylvania Department of Agriculture. 1992. 1991-1992
Statistical Summary. National Agricultural Statistics Service,
Harrisburg, PA.

Pennsylvania Department of Community and Economic
Development. 1997. Pennsylvania the Food Processing
Advantage: The Competitive Advantages of Doing Business in
Pennsylvania. Governor's Action Team, 100 Pine Street, Suite
100, Harrisburg, PA 17101.

Siebert, S. E. 1993. Changing times claim landmark farm store.
The Philadelphia Inquirer, January 8, 1993, p. B2.

Sorensen, A.A., R.P. Greene, and K. Russ. 1997. Farming on the
Edge. American Farmland Trust, Center for Agriculture in the
Environment, Northern Illinois University, DeKalb, IL.

Starr, P.M. 1996. Green Plan for southeastern PA complete at last.
Green Plan Gazette, Pennsylvania Environmental Council,
Philadelphia, PA, Fall 1996.

Thompson, E. 1992. Estate tax squeeze. American Farmland
(Summer): 9-11.

U.S. Department of Commerce. 1994. 1992 Census of Agriculture,
Volume 1, Part 38, Pennsylvania State and County Data. Bureau
of the Census, Washington, D.C.

U.S. General Accounting Office. Farm Finance: Number of New
Farmers is Declining. GAO, Resources, Community, and
Economic Development. Report to the Chairman, Subcommittee
on Agricultural Credit, Committee on Agriculture, Nutrition, and
Forestry, U.S. Senate 93-95.

# Case 4

## County Planning and Suburban Expansion in the Washington, D.C. Region: Images for the Year 2020— What Have We Planned for Us?

*Margaret Stewart Maizel,*
*NCRI–Chesapeake Executive Director*
*George Muehlbach, NCRI–Chesapeake GIS Specialist*

### Introduction

The disappearance of green space from the Washington, D.C. metropolitan area is of increasing concern. Those sensitive to the environmental benefits afforded by open and agricultural green space cannot ignore the effects of the razing of trees, the stretch and spread of pavement, and the construction of strip malls and housing developments. By the time these effects are apparent, however, it is often much too late to change the course of development.

Geographic Information Systems are dynamic tools that allow us to approximate where, when, and how much development and expansion has and/or will take place and how much green space will disappear. The recent explosion of the world wide web and the rapid communication capabilities of the Internet, together with the effectiveness and efficiency of Geographic Information Systems and the tremendous educational power of computer

graphics offers local citizens unprecedented opportunities to analyze and interact with the local planning process. No longer are
Geographic Information Systems and massive data series and
layers confined to institutions of higher learning, government
agencies, and a small section of the private sector. Ecological,
sociological, economic, and agricultural production information
can now be widely distributed in a meaningful, tailored, and user-
friendly manner.

## Background

   Agriculture in the Washington, D.C. region is largely livestock-
based. Cropland is most often used for feed and grain production
to support poultry, dairy, beef and horse operations—the latter
two of which rely on significant pastureland acreage so characteristic of the storied Blue Ridge Piedmont.

   In March 1997, the National Center for Resource Innovations'
Chesapeake Office and *The Washington Post* collaborated on a
special three-part series entitled "Green, More or Less:
Washington's Vanishing Open Space." The study focused on urban expansion in the twelve-county, two-state region surrounding
the District of Columbia. By applying Geographic Information
System technologies to data from the U.S. Census, the Metropolitan Washington Council of Governments, aerial photography,
local land use plans, and planning statistics and projections from
county and state governments, NCRI compiled a series of maps
illustrating past and future patterns of open space and development in the Washington region.[1] One example of these images,
restricted to black-and-white for this publication, is presented as
Figure C4.1.

   Based on Figure C4.1 and other images of spatial patterns of
development, the NCRI study illustrated four major factors in the
loss of farmland and the rapid expansion of the Metropolitan area:

   1. Significant declines in the lowest density residential uses
      have already occurred and will continue. In fact, land with
      residential densities of 1 household per 50 or more acres (the
      lowest density analyzed) decreases from 500,000 acres in
      1980 to 300,000 acres in 2020.

2. As the lowest density lands disappear, all other higher density housing increases in an outwardly expanding halo surrounding the city.

3. Five-acre lot housing developments that had leapfrogged beyond urbanized areas by 1980 along major highways serve as outposts behind which "infilling" occurs in subsequent years.

4. Commercial development planned between now and the year 2020, primarily in Loudoun and Prince William counties, mimics the leapfrog pattern of the five-acre housing scenario of the 1980s;—and what's to follow ?—residential development attracted by jobs and commerce.

### 1973–1980

In 1973, the Washington, D.C. metropolitan area included the city proper, twelve surrounding counties, and five independent cities in Virginia, and encompassed 3,083,865 acres of land. Of this, agricultural land (cropland and pastureland) amounted to 37% of the land area, forest land comprised 29%, and water,

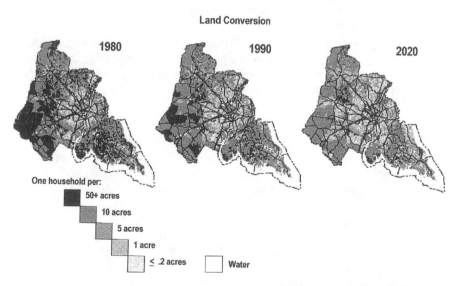

Figure C4.1 Housing densities in the Washington, DC region.

which includes significant portions of the Potomac River and the Chesapeake Bay, represented 16% (Table C4.1). Some 506,425 of those three million acres, or 16% of all available land in the D.C. metro area, was considered urban or built up.

From 1973 through 1980, seven years during which the real estate market was rapidly expanding, an additional 318,374 acres or 10.32% of all available land in the region was converted to suburban uses.[2] Roughly half of the land developed during this time period was converted from forest land. By 1980, more than one-quarter or 26.75% of the region had been urbanized.

## 1980–1990

From 1980 through 1990, land conversion continued throughout the Washington metro area, although at a slower rate than during the preceding decade (1973–1980). From 1980–1990, 210,642 acres or 6.83% of all land was converted to built land, as compared to 318,374 acres or 10.32% during the previous decade. More than half of the conversion (114,483 acres) occurred on agricultural land. By 1990, 33.6% of all land in the D.C. area was developed or built-up.

## 1990–2020

It is projected that more than 300,000 acres, almost all outside the D.C. city limits, will be developed between 1990 and 2020. Though somewhat pale in comparison to the urban wave that hit from 1973–1980, in this thirty year span almost an additional 11% of the metro land area will be converted from forest land, water, wetlands, barren land, and, in particular, agricultural land to urban land. In fact, as reported by *The Washington Post*, the D.C. area is slated to lose approximately 28 acres of green space per day between 1990 and 2020. In total, 43.7% of the land in the Washington metropolitan area will be converted to urban uses by the year 2020.

### Maryland Vs. Virginia: Polarized Viewpoints

Few Metropolitan areas are faced with the jurisdictional complexities afflicting the Washington, D.C. metropolitan area.

Table C4.1  Conversion of Washington, D.C. metropolitan area land to suburban/urban uses (1 house per 10 acres or less).

| Land Use/ Cover | 1973 Base acres | 1973–1980 Acres converted | 1973–1980 % region | 1980–1990 Acres converted | 1980–1990 % region | 1990–2020 Acres converted | 1990–2020 % region | Summary 1973–2020 Acres converted | Summary 1973–2020 % region |
|---|---|---|---|---|---|---|---|---|---|
| Agricultural land | 1,152,265 | 136,233 | 4.42 | 114,483 | 3.71 | 164,278 | 5.33 | 414,994 | 13.46 |
| Forest land | 889,473 | 162,072 | 5.26 | 88,275 | 2.86 | 139,841 | 4.53 | 390,187 | 12.65 |
| Water | 485,445 | 2,466 | 0.08 | 1,670 | 0.05 | 1,000 | 0.03 | 5,136 | 0.17 |
| Wetlands | 21,318 | 1,511 | 0.05 | 834 | 0.03 | 2,093 | 0.07 | 4,439 | 0.14 |
| Barren land | 28,939 | 16,091 | 0.52 | 5,381 | 0.17 | 3,824 | 0.12 | 25,296 | 0.82 |
| Total converted to suburban/ urban uses | | 318,374 | 10.32 | 210,643 | 6.83 | 311,036 | 10.09 | 840,053 | 27.24 |
| Total built-up land | 506,425 | 824,799 | 26.75 | 1,035,442 | 33.58 | 1,346,478 | 43.66 | 1,346,478 | 43.66 |
| Total land area | 3,083,865 | | | | | | | | |

Because D.C. is tightly tucked between Maryland and Virginia, the end result of identical development efforts spun from the city to the north (Maryland) may drastically vary from the results to the south (Virginia). Depending on which way growth flares, developers may be welcomed with open arms and weak growth management initiatives or carefully accommodated if not altogether shunned.

Though land restrictions and regulations are the usual prerogative of local governments, state leaders in Maryland and Virginia have set the land development tone. The different land development philosophies of Maryland Governor Parris Glendening and Virginia Governor George Allen are revealed via a glimpse of the respective governors' homepages. Governor Glendening's homepage may be accessed at www.mde.state.md.us/sg/sghome.html. Governor Allen's homepage can be accessed at www.state.va.us/governor/govhp.htm. While Governor Glendening's homepage encourages users to connect with topics such as "Smart Growth and Neighborhood Conservation," Virginia Governor George Allen's website asks the user to "[v]isit the Virginia Economic Development Partnership website and learn why "Virginia is Open for Business." Due to historical legal precedents within Virginia that have placed the onus on the town's elected officials while giving them little support as enjoyed by 'Home Rule' provisions in Maryland, Virginia has developed the reputation of being a servant to urban sprawl.

## A Closer Look: Montgomery County, Maryland

In Montgomery County in 1973, land outside of parks and other protected areas totaled 187,358 acres, while development covered 69,179 acres. By 1980, an additional 45,732 acres, mostly agricultural land, were consumed by urban expansion, leaving close to one half (44.79%) of the total land area of Montgomery County as urban or built-up land. By 2020, it is projected that 61.5% or 157,753 acres of the 256,537 acres available for development in the county will be developed. Most of the new development, however, is currently planned as in-fill, rather than more low density expansion.

# A Closer Look:
## Prince William and Loudoun Counties, Virginia

Prince William County, Virginia, dubbed by *The Washington Post* as "the county that can't say no," will experience a 13.40% increase in developed land from 1990–2020 as 20,592 acres of the 153,638 acres available in the county will be converted from mainly forest and agricultural land to urban or suburban status. Indeed, from 1973 through 2020, just over half of all available land within Prince William County will be urbanized.

Similarly, in Loudoun County, Virginia, another rapidly developing area west of Washington, D.C., development is expected to more than triple between 1990–2020 from development records for 1980 and 1990. By 2020, 105,967 acres or 32.94% of all agricultural and forest land, water, wetlands, and barren land will be developed or under development in Loudoun County. Though most of the development is occurring in the eastern portion of the county (closer to the District), there is also concern about the spread of development in the western half of the county, which is considered the heart of Loudoun County's already declining agricultural community.

Through special legislation, the Loudoun County government is exploring initiatives to purchase the development rights of farmers, thus offsetting the financial appeal of major land sales to developers. *The Washington Post* refers to this county land purchase practice as "Greenbacks for green space" (see below for virtual directions to *The Washington Post's* special series "Green, More or Less: Washington's Vanishing Open Space").

## Publicity for Public Planning: Letting the Sun Shine In

County planners and town councilors within the Washington metropolitan area struggle for acceptable solutions to allow for sensible, moderate, and appropriate development. While Loudoun County is proposing to pay its farmers to give up their right to sell land to developers, counties such as Montgomery County—already developed more extensively than Loudoun—challenge developers to pay for the public services that will be necessary once land is developed. Regardless of which "develabatement" method is examined by counties, a key part of the solution may be the application of GIS technologies to enable the public to evaluate the likely effects of development plans when the plans are proposed rather than after the plans are implemented.

What is so remarkable about NCRI's project with *The Washington Post* is that ecological, sociological, economic, and agricultural data is widely distributed in its raw or analyzed form to anyone around the world who is online. Not only can the location, timing, and extent of urban expansion be predicted, but the gigabits of information that have been traditionally used only by a select few can now be used by the general public to more effectively and efficiently plan America's urban future. NCRI and *The Washington Post* combined regional planning data in a geographic information system and world wide web technologies to reach out to local citizens to enable informed participation in the public planning process. Following publication of "Green, More or Less," citizens' groups began asking their local governments why and how such future plans came to be, and local officials began re-assessing their past decisions.

## How to Get There

Anyone with access to the Internet who is interested in projected plans or U.S. Census data for their county in the Washington metro area may access *The Washington Post* at www.washingtonpost.com. Once on *The Washington Post* home page, select "Metro," then click on "Special Reports," then scroll down to and click on "Growing Pains." Once within "Growing Pains," double click on any of the "Explore Further" subheadings. Related article titles will appear along with a map entitled "See how they grow." Click on an area of interest within the map and you will be connected to more detailed maps and U.S. Census data for the area you have selected.

## Endnotes

1. The statistics and graphics used in *The Washington Post* project do not take into consideration 1) conservation easements, 2) token green space on developed land, or 3) potential purchases of public land by federal or state governments in the Washington D.C. metro area.
2. Suburban uses include housing densities greater than one household per 10 acres.

# Case 5

## Fauquier County, Virginia: Agriculture in the Shadow of Suburbia

*G. Robert Lee, Fauquier County Administrator*

Fauquier County is located in northern Virginia approximately 40 miles west of Washington, D.C. The county is large by Virginia standards (660 square miles). The 1990 Census led to the official designation of Fauquier County as part of the Washington-Baltimore Metropolitan Area. The forces of land use change are coming from the east as the metropolitan area expands, seemingly inexorably, outward. In 1850, Fauquier County had a recorded population of 20,868. One hundred years later in 1950, the census showed growth to only 21,248. During the next 40 years, the population would more than double and today the estimated population exceeds 52,000. The growth in population has been attributable to net migration—defined as the number of persons who moved in minus the number of persons who moved out. Net migration has been influenced primarily by exogenous variables in the expanding metropolitan region. Fauquier County may be able to have more influence on where new residents locate than on the rate of migration.

Agriculture and the agricultural economy are central features of the heritage and cultural values of Fauquier County. The county ranks among the top five counties in the Commonwealth of Virginia in the following areas of production:

- Horses and ponies
- Grapes
- Hay
- Dairy cows
- Corn for silage

Increased losses of the open agricultural spaces that contribute to the scenic beauty for which the county is renowned have motivated the community to reexamine land use planning constructs for rural Fauquier. According to the U.S. Census of Agriculture (1992), Fauquier County witnessed a reduction in land devoted to agriculture of 27.5% from 1959 through 1992. In 1992 the county had 925 farms and the average farm size was 255 acres. Some of the reduction in land devoted to agriculture represents conversion for non-farm use and some of the loss is agricultural disinvestment associated with purchase of farms by land speculators.

Chapter 8 of the Fauquier County Comprehensive Plan is titled "Rural Land Use Plan" and represents the planning recommendations for more than 80% of the county's land. The accepted Comprehensive Plan prescription is that more than 80% of the population should occupy less than 20% of the county's land mass in areas of population concentrations known as Service Districts. Three of the ten stated goals in the Comprehensive Plan specifically address the rural areas including:

- To recognize the county's traditionally agricultural and rural character and the need for preservation of its open spaces and scenic beauty.

- To protect critical environmental resources and to maintain renewable natural resources so that they are not degraded but remain viable for future generations.

- To protect and promote the agricultural industry.

The rural area goals are widely acknowledged as public policy, but the means to promote the goals are the subject of debate and uncertainty. After many years of rural planning where Fauquier County was recognized as an innovator and leader in land use programs, the county's elected and appointed leaders recognized that the established planning mechanisms might not achieve the rural plan goals into the twenty-first century. This recognition led to the recruitment of an interdisciplinary team of nationally recognized experts to evaluate the existing rural planning framework and recommend enhancements and new directions for meeting planning goals.

The contract with the consultant team was signed in October of 1994 and the consultants delivered the Final Report titled <u>Rural Areas Land Use Plan</u> in December of 1995. The consultants worked with a team of local officials known as the Rural Plan Steering Committee made up of elected officials, appointed planning commissioners, and staff. The consultants' report made recommendations on county policies to strengthen the industry of agriculture in Fauquier County and to enhance the agricultural economy. Channeling future growth to Service Districts was identified as essential to accommodating anticipated population growth without sprawling across the rural landscape. This high-density/high-amenity growth district concept was already incorporated into other elements of the adopted Comprehensive Plan and was addressed by the consultants as a complementary policy that reinforced the proposed Rural Land Use Plan. One of the most interesting components of the consultant-prepared plan was the Visual Preferences Survey which was a community-based exercise to identify the visual landscape characteristics (both manmade and natural) valued by current residents.

Once the preferred types of settlement patterns and human edifices were identified, the consultants worked to develop planning programs that would lead to the preferred future based on the continuation of broadly accepted heritage components. More than one hundred separate recommendations were offered by the consultants and the Rural Plan Steering Committee. The broad categories were:

- Recommendations Regarding the Agricultural Economy and the Protection of Farmland

- Recommendations Concerning the Protection of Rural Environmental Resources

- Recommendations for Zoning and Subdivision Ordinance Amendments

- Recommendations for Other Techniques for Managing Land Development

Predictably, not all the recommendations were politically possible and some were not embraced by the required 'critical mass' of elected and appointed public officials. Some recommendations lacked adequate supporting justification. As this case study is submitted, the Fauquier County Rural Areas Land Use Plan is still an evolving document that has reached the final draft stage. The components reviewed here are those consultant and community proposals that seem likely to be incorporated into the county's planning program.

The residential development rights allocation under the Fauquier County Zoning Ordinance for the agricultural and natural resource conservation zoning districts will remain virtually unchanged. This sliding scale development rights allocation system[1] has been in place for almost two decades and has wide understanding, if not appeal. The planning effort did, however, elevate design over density. One of the more innovative plan prototypes, at least for Virginia, is a rural land division process which is referred to as the conservation subdivision design. This approach to rural land division for human habitation purposes is a continuing refinement of the Ian McHarg 'design with nature' concept that received much attention but little practical application in the 1970's. Randall Arendt and others have developed a stepwise pragmatic approach to accommodating limited human settlement while maintaining the sensitive natural features and ecosystem processes of a property subject to land division. This four step design process yields a rational and technically defensible rural residential subdivision. The process avoids fragmentation of conservation land and yields larger contiguous and integrated open space systems for production agriculture and natural resource integrity. One new component of the sliding scale development rights allocation that fits well with the conservation subdivision design process is the introduction of a small maximum lot size to replace the mandatory 85% open space of the existing zoning ordinance. The proposed two-acre maximum rural lot size will preclude future residential parcels that are too big to mow and too small to farm.

The requirement for conservation subdivision design includes a legal requirement to place a permanent easement on the open space with the first rural land division. This helps to ensure thoughtful build-out planning by landowners rather than the incremental and ad hoc approach of the conventional subdivision process that often results in open space that bears little relation to the productive capabilities of the original tract and ignores the defining natural and cultural resources of the property.

An optional set scale density allocation of one dwelling unit per fifty acres is being offered as another approach for public comment. This uniform density allocation could be combined with the small maximum lot size (two acres) or landowners could have the option of dividing parcels such that no single parcel is less than 50 acres. This format is easy to understand and is not unlike the quarter-quarter agricultural zoning in the western United States. One dwelling unit per fifty acres is a severe restriction on speculative land development in a metropolitan region in the eastern United States. Permitting tenant houses without requirements for land division, at one tenant dwelling per fifty acres, represents another option under consideration. This expeditious use of dwelling unit rights without subdivision keeps farms intact, while addressing housing needs for family members and farm labor.

Other measures under consideration to help retain the agricultural land base include purchase or lease of development rights and creation of a private Agricultural and Forestal Trust to hold land or land rights for continuation of agricultural use. Still other Rural Plan components that would complement and enhance the direct agricultural land preservation techniques include:

- Heritage Area designations

- Expanded Scenic River and Road designations

- Inducements to landowners for coordinated planning and resource conservation of adjacent properties in different ownership

- Permitting of off-site septic disposal to preclude use of prime agricultural soils for on-site waste disposal

Another important aspect of the community commitment to sustainable agriculture relates to the promotion of a strong farm economy. To save land for farming when farming is not economically viable is shortsighted. Fauquier County is one of only three communities in the State of Virginia that has established an Agricultural Development Office. The primary focus of this Office is to

work with the appointed Agriculture Advisory Committee to enhance and diversify the agricultural economy. Regulations that
limit the fragmentation of agricultural lands are necessary to
mitigate the speculative investment in farmland for non-farm
purposes, but farmers must be able to realize a fair return on
their investments if they are to support the policies that discourage premature conversion of land for non-farm uses.

Non-farmers also require education to support both land
use policies and economic investments to support production
agriculture. Many citizens can appreciate the bucolic attributes
of agriculture, but they need also to be convinced that public
investments for support of agriculture are justified. The most
provocative justification for preferential or differential real property assessment (also known as use value taxation) is documenta-
tion that farmland, even at a lowered rate of assessment, yields
a tax that exceeds the public service costs of that land use. The
county's Rural Plan consultant team included twenty-six separate
Cost of Community Service studies ( Revenue Generated by Major
Land Use Categories as a Percentage of Allocated Municipal
Expenditures) that demonstrate convincingly and conclusively
that retaining agricultural land, as opposed to conversion of land
for residential use, represents prudent and fiscally responsible
local policy. Use value taxation must be part of a local program
to protect production resources and restrain local tax burdens
in any community experiencing pressure for agricultural land
conversion.

The Fauquier County programs, both existing and proposed, to
retain the industry that has been the cornerstone of the county's
economy and heritage since the county was founded in 1759 are
critical to the retention of the enviable quality of life in a community that has been blessed with natural beauty and bounty. Failure to maintain viable agriculture of scale into the 21st century
will irrevocably degrade the quality of life for future residents and
betray the county's motto of "Progress with Reverence for Heritage." The farmers in Fauquier County are truly farming in the
shadow of suburbia and the policies and programs that are
adopted in the next few years will likely determine the fate of the
community's rural areas. Future observers will judge whether
Fauquier's elected officials exercised decisive leadership or suc-
cumbed to the vagaries of political vicissitudes. Agriculture is the
Fauquier heritage and the endowment for the future if current

elected and appointed officials evidence the political will to follow the advice of the experts who were engaged to recommend a definitive course of action. Indecisiveness and delay will set in place an impermanence syndrome that will be a self-fulfilling prophecy for the demise of the industry that defined the esteemed character of a vital and vibrant community for more than two centuries.

## Endnote

1. Sliding Scale Zoning is a residential development rights allocation system where the gross residential density declines as the size of the parcel increases. This zoning framework has been successful as an agricultural resources retention mechanism, and most Virginia applications were modeled on program examples from Pennsylvania.

# Case 6

## Albemarle County, Virginia: The Challenge of Turning Policy into Practice

*Tim Lindstrom, Piedmont Environmental Council*

For much of Albemarle County's existence it has been largely rural, dependent upon agriculture and the University of Virginia for its economic well-being. Thanks to air-conditioning and the growth of the University; Albemarle's proximity to Washington, D.C. and Richmond; its history; its beauty and a growing body of University alumni interested in living in the area, Albemarle in recent decades has more than doubled in population. Historically, population growth in the county (largely due to in-migration) has ranged between 2–2.5% per year. The county's current population is 75,500, which coupled with the 39,700 residents of the independent City of Charlottesville (which lies in the center of the county) results in an effective population for the area of 115,200.

The county has a rather typical comprehensive plan providing that future growth occur in designated "growth areas" where infrastructure and utilities are provided or planned, and the "rural areas," which cover nearly 450,000 acres or 96% of the county. Planning policy strongly discourages residential development in the rural areas. Consistently applied utility policy by the county has effectively insured that neither public sewer or water are available in the rural areas, limiting development to that which can be served by private well and septic field.

In 1981 the county undertook a substantial rezoning which dramatically reduced development potential in the county's rural areas (then designated the A-2 zone, with an allowed density of one dwelling for every two acres). The rezoning, which designated the A-2 zone the "RA" zone, meant that a tract of 220 acres which could have been divided into 110 residential lots in 1979 could only be divided into 15 lots in 1981. However, the number of lots allowed in the RA zone still provided more than a 50-year supply at current demand. Since 1990 the county has permitted the construction of nearly 2,000 new residences in the RA zone. In other words, the new ordinance does not appear to have significantly changed the prevailing pattern of suburban sprawl and farmland loss.

The 1981 rezoning may even have increased the rate at which farmland was converted to residential use by increasing the minimum size of many residential lots. In 1989, the county moved to correct this problem by allowing clusters of two-acre residential lots in exchange for the landowner's agreement to impose a permanent conservation easement on land outside the cluster. However, less than 10% of all RA residential lots created since 1989 have taken advantage of this voluntary clustering provision.

Current county RA zoning rules and the market demand for rural lots will ultimately lead to the conversion of most of the county's farmland and open space to low density residential use. However, although current agricultural economics are too weak to compete with the economics of a strong housing market for rural land, county planning policy still holds the potential to alter significantly the pattern of land use in the RA zone to achieve meaningful long-term conservation of farmland and open space.

## Geography and Agriculture

Albemarle County consists of 471,000 acres on the eastern slope of the Blue Ridge Mountains. Topography ranges from hardwood forested mountain ridges approaching 3,000 feet on the west to rolling pastures and woodlands bisected by numerous ravines at between 300 and 500 feet elevation. Average annual rainfall is 44 inches, and winter temperatures are mild. However, Albemarle is miserably hot and humid from late spring into early fall, a condition that kept the county (and much of the Southeast) insulated from significant population growth until the late 1950's and the advent of widespread air conditioning. Air conditioning, highway construction, and cheap labor have transformed the face of the South.

Poor soils limit crop production. Only about 40,000 of Albemarle's 188,567 acres of farmland were cropped in 1992. Most agricultural activity is devoted to hay production and raising livestock, often as part-time farming on 50 acres or less. Between 1982 and 1992, farm acreage declined by 12,432 acres, and farm numbers decreased from 830 to 757 farms. Average farm value increased during this period from $406,000 to $729,000 with per acre values increasing from $1,458 to $2,813. The market value of farm products sold in 1992 was $21 million, only a small part of a county economy that includes $218 million in retail sales and $95 million in tourist spending. The average value of farm products sold per farm in 1992 was $26,852, while average farm production expenses were $27,816.

Extensive acreage is devoted to fox-hunting, and many elegant horse farms grace the countryside. In 1995, Albemarle county had 12,200 horses, total annual horse related expenditures of $34,160,000, and 1,015 jobs associated with the horse industry. In addition, the horse industry is culturally and politically significant. Citizens involved in the horse industry have provided much of the political support for farmland protection.

## Patterns of Farmland Loss

In 1990 approximately 45,885 of the county's 68,040 citizens lived in the RA zone in 16,400 dwelling units, only 604 of which were farm dwellings. From 1988 to 1995 the county approved a total of 4,847 new residential lots, 1,783 of them in the RA zone. These lots averaged 11.38 acres each, representing the conversion of more than 20,000 acres of rural land to development. During the same period the county issued 6,606 residential building permits, 2,325 of them for construction in the RA zone.

The amount of land actually converted from farming or open space is small compared with the total of rural land in the county. However, a map of the patterns of residential development in the county since 1981 shows a network of residential sprawl reaching extensively into the countryside, fracturing farmland into ever more marginal bits and pieces. This pattern of development has had a multiplier effect on farmland loss as farmers have quietly become speculators in expectation of reaping development profits.

The principal causes of these destructive patterns are zoning rules which have failed to implement effectively the county's rural protection policies; steady population expansion; a strong preference by new residents for rural residential settings; and the weak economics of agriculture in the area.

## Organizations Influencing Land Use

Virginia has a highly centralized local government structure with only 120 independent agencies exercising governmental authority for land use decisions. In the case of Albemarle County, one government, headed by six elected supervisors, controls land use for 750 square miles. The supervisors are the ultimate arbiters of virtually all land use decisions and policies including zoning and planning, school locations, public utilities, and secondary roads. The centralized and extensive authority vested in the Supervisors by the state allows the possibility of truly effective rural protection policies and zoning.

The next most influential organization shaping land use in the county is the University of Virginia which has more than 25,000 full- and part-time students and 10,000 employees. The growth of the county is heavily influenced by the growth of the University. In recent years the University has become actively engaged in local real estate development and management through its investment arm, the University Real Estate Foundation (UREF). UREF is authorized to invest a portion of the University's substantial endowment in local real estate. As part of this effort UREF is currently developing a 500-acre research and office park, which could stimulate the formation of an additional 16,000 jobs in the county. It also owns another substantial office park, a major hotel, a retirement village and several other large office buildings.

Non-governmental organizations influencing land use in the county include such business and trade interests as the Chamber of Commerce, local realtors and homebuilders organizations, and the local chapter of the American Farm Bureau Federation. These

organizations carry significant political weight with respect to
land use decisions, often lobbying for more economic development
and greater safeguards for property rights. These positions tend
to place these organizations in opposition to additional restrictions on rural development.

Other non-governmental organizations having some influence
include several professionally staffed environmental organizations
that concentrate on land use in the county. There are also a number of smaller grass-roots volunteer organizations. Recently,
an organization representing a number of neighborhoods in the
county has become politically active, lobbying against new development projects. As the impacts of growth on the community
become more severe and obvious, these environmental and
grass-roots organizations will likely become increasingly active
and effective.

## Future Pressures and Influential Factors

Albemarle County and the City of Charlottesville are the economic heart of the region. They are surrounded by rural localities
that generally lack the infrastructure (and means of obtaining
infrastructure) necessary to sustain substantial economic growth.
Because the City of Charlottesville is essentially "built out," significant pressure on the county is unlikely to be generated there
either. Therefore, to a large extent, pressure on rural land in the
county will be stimulated from within.

Although Albemarle County is in a position to control its
own fate to an extent unusual for most localities, there is one exception—the potential expansion of the University, which is substantially influenced by the state legislature. If the University is
directed to expand enrollment (and there is growing pressure for
it to do so), it will trigger a chain reaction of growth in the county.
Other pressure will come from residential development resulting
from the successful marketing of the substantial amount of office
and retail zoning that the county has approved in past years.
Much of this land is owned by large development interests (including U.Va.'s UREF) capable of undertaking sophisticated and
effective marketing campaigns. The attractiveness of the area
coupled with consistently high rankings in national surveys of
"best places to live" suggests that the county will continue to

experience the relocation of corporate headquarters and other smaller businesses able to bring workers with them. The land use patterns that will be generated from this growth and development will be strongly influenced by several main factors.

### Excessive Zoning

Planning policies and ordinances, especially the zoning ordinance, establish the envelope within which the private market operates. In Virginia, the General Assembly has authorized localities to control both the rate and amount of growth and the location of that growth. The principal mechanism for this control is zoning. Although Virginia does not allow localities to manage growth by denying building permits, site plans or subdivision plats, it does allow considerable local latitude with respect to the amount of zoning allowed for residential and non-residential uses.

In theory, for example, a locality could determine through its planning process that during the next 20 years 7,000 new jobs will be needed and carefully limit its non-residential zoning to phase office, retail and industrial development to accommodate only 7,000 new jobs within a 20-year period. The same approach can be taken with residential zoning. Such carefully constructed zoning would create a very small envelope for the private market. This may be politically unpopular, but it is a very effective growth management technique.

The reality in Albemarle County is that county zoning has created such a large zoning envelope that planning policies and ordinances have relatively little influence on the rate or amount of growth, or the location of residential development. Because low density residential development (two-acre lots or larger) does not require public sewer or water, it can occur virtually anywhere in the county, in spite of the county's very careful control of the location of utilities.

A recent study by the Thomas Jefferson Planning District Commission (TJPDC), a regional planning agency that includes the county within its territory, showed that the county's RA zone regulations allow an additional 55,000 dwelling units to be built which could accommodate an increase in RA zone population of 144,000 people for a total of 190,000. The study adjusted for non-developable land and environmental restrictions.

This "build-out" analysis indicates that while 80% of land in the RA zone is currently in parcels of 21 acres or more (50-acre or larger parcels make up 70% of the RA zone), after build-out less than 4% of the RA zone would be in 21-acre or larger parcels. This potential for substantial new residential development allowed by RA zoning directly contravenes the comprehensive plan's strictures against any residential development in the county's rural areas. However, under Virginia law there is no requirement for consistency between the comprehensive plan and the zoning ordinance.

A similar build-out analysis of the county's light industrial zone undertaken by the Piedmont Environmental Council indicates that zone alone would accommodate as many as 65,000 new jobs. Yet the county projects a need for only 7,000 jobs during the next 20 years.

With zoning envelopes this big for residential and non-residential development it is clear that local planning policies and ordinances will have almost no influence on the rate, amount or location of growth. So far as public planning is concerned, influence on the timing and location of growth has been almost completely abdicated to the private sector. Exacerbating these dynamics for sprawl is the fact that local ordinances generally make it easier and cheaper for residential development to occur in the rural areas than in the areas the county has designated for growth.

### Voluntary Land Conservation

While the region has an active voluntary land conservation program managed through the Virginia Outdoors Foundation (a state sponsored foundation that holds conservation easements), only 14,000 acres are protected by easement in Albemarle. The county is considering initiating a purchase of development rights program, but the cost of even a modest "PDR" program makes significant farmland protection through this mechanism unlikely. Indeed, it may actually hinder rural protection by creating an impression that the county is aggressively protecting rural areas when in fact only a tiny fraction of land is effectively being protected.

### Real Estate Tax Relief for Rural Land

The county has adopted a "use value" assessment program for rural land which substantially reduces local real estate taxes on farmland and other rural land. Fair market value assessments on some Albemarle farmland are more than $5,000 per acre. The use value assessment can reduce such assessments to as little as $500 per acre. The program costs county taxpayers in excess of $5 million annually and yet remains a popular one, testimony to citizen support for farmland protection. However, the program poorly differentiates between farmers and developers and thus facilitates speculation in rural land by significantly reducing carrying costs for developers.

### Utility Policies

The county has been very diligent in limiting utilities to only those areas designated in the comprehensive plan for urban and suburban densities. In a significant victory, the county success-fully defended the denial of a site plan for a major residential de-velopment that was consistent with local zoning but inconsistent with the comprehensive plan's designation of the area for rural use only. The county denied the extension of utilities required by the development under a provision of state law that required the county to determine that proposed public facilities are consistent with the local comprehensive plan before approving them. Subse-quently the county rezoned the property to RA making it consis-tent with the comprehensive plan.

### Watershed Protection

A major goal of county planning policy is the protection of the public reservoir and its 200 square mile watershed. Concerns about the eutrophication of this reservoir due to pollution from development was a major factor behind the 1981 rezoning from A-2 to RA. As previously discussed, this rezoning substantially reduced development potential in the RA zone. In spite of consid-erable grumbling, this rezoning action was never challenged in court.

## Lessons (Which Should Be) Learned

The parenthetical suggests that not everyone has learned from the county's past mistakes. However, the lessons seem clear:

careful control of zoning, and regular evaluation of the cumulative effect of individual zoning decisions, are fundamental to controlling sprawl and managing growth. Another lesson learned years after the 1981 RA rezoning: reducing development potential without mandating (or at least allowing) clustering may actually accelerate the loss of farmland.

A bigger lesson is that the market, left to itself, will simply continue to trade farmland for suburban sprawl. The short-sighted and limited perspective of the economics implicit in the "willing buyer and the willing seller" scenario give development interests an upper hand in these transactions. As a growing body of knowledge about the fiscal impact of development confirms, it is the public subsidy of development (publicly funded roads, schools, police, etc.) that makes much development economically feasible. This is a lesson Albemarle's taxpayers are beginning to learn. It is one that is inspiring them to participate more aggressively in decisions about how, where and when they will subsidize the conversion of farmland.

## Suggestions for More Effective Farmland Protection

Any plans to improve the effectiveness of farmland protection in Albemarle must take into account the political reality that the Board of Supervisors is unlikely to reduce overall development potential in the RA zone. In view of this reality the key to more effective farmland protection lies in providing for more efficient and sensitive development of the potential 55,000 lots allowed in the RA zone under existing zoning rules.

For example, if all of these lots develop in the traditional manner, the TJPDC study indicates that an additional 250,000 acres of RA zoned land may be consumed, resulting in residential lots averaging a little less than five acres each. If each of these potential lots were limited to one acre and the remaining acres were protected by a permanent conservation easement, the total land area consumed could be reduced to less than 60,000 acres resulting in the permanent protection of nearly 190,000 acres of land.

Proper siting and clustering of residential lots in the RA zone could permit the use of all development potential and still accomplish one of the most effective farmland and open space protection programs in the Southeast. The effectiveness of clustering in this case is the result of the 1981 rezoning which, in spite of its flaws, significantly reduced overall density in the RA zone. An average density of approximately five acres per dwelling (roughly the density allowed on the developable land remaining in the RA zone) with dwellings clustered on two-acre lots can achieve approximately 60% open space protection. If densities had remained at two acres (as provided in the old A-2 zone), clustering would not work.

Specific goals for improving farmland protection in Albemarle include:

1. Limit the number of residential lots that can be developed by a landowner to no more than one per year unless lots are clustered. Clusters should be located using criteria that identify and permanently protect quality farm or forestland, or land that is otherwise environmentally sensitive. Protection would be achieved through permanent conservation easements. Limiting clustered lots to one acre in size would maximize the protection of farm land; would result in significant development cost savings as infrastructure (primarily roads) needs would be reduced; and would serve many people's desire for a rural homesite with limited maintenance responsibilities but guaranteed protection of rural surroundings. Septic easements on protected open land adjoining residential lots would facilitate the use of small lots. Limiting the numbers of unclustered lots allowed annually would eliminate the market for commercial residential development of such lots.

2. Strengthen the use value real estate assessment program by conditioning its availability on the landowner's agreement to keep the land in rural uses for a meaningful period of time. This would convert it from a subsidy for land speculators to an incentive for voluntary land conservation.

3. Create options for rural land owners to generate supplemental income on their land through means other than residential development (e.g., relaxed rules about rental of converted outbuildings) in exchange for the relinquishment of residential development potential.

4. Implement an already developed fiscal impact model to assist the public and county government in understanding the cost to taxpayers of residential development; the link between non-residential development and residential development; and the fiscal benefits of farmland and open-space, which local studies show generate substantial revenues in excess of service costs.

5. Establish a mechanism to automatically monitor the cumulative effect of rezonings and other planning actions.

All of these goals are within the legal authority of the county—and should be within the bounds of political acceptability as well. While a more aggressive approach could be more effective, political resistance would keep it from becoming reality. By building on popular sentiment for farmland protection and the county's already sound rural area policies (as opposed to RA zoning regulations), the county can stop the large lot sprawl now consuming Albemarle's rural areas. However, achieving protection of a viable agricultural economy would entail elimination of substantial development potential (probably beyond the political reach of the county at this time) and fundamental changes in either the market for the traditional agricultural products of the county or a fundamental restructuring of the way agriculture is practiced in the county, both beyond the authority of the county.

# Case 7

## "Here's My Mule: Where's My Forty Acres?" The Plight of Black Farmers and Farmland in Tillery, North Carolina

*Gary Grant, Concerned Citizens of Tillery*

Located in what is known by historians as the "Black Belt" of North Carolina, Tillery is a small community of people who come from largely farming backgrounds. Many here are now elderly settlers from Franklin D. Roosevelt's New Deal plan of the 1930s and 1940s, a plan that created more than 113 new farm communities throughout the country. The Tillery Resettlement Farm was one of the largest Resettlement Projects, and the largest of only eight African American Projects. The Resettlement Farm, whose name was changed to the Roanoke Farms in 1936, occupied more than 18,000 acres.

While these new settlers along with those who had been earlier sharecroppers in the Tillery community contributed significantly to the development of the community throughout the 1940s to the 1960s, a combination of troubles which escalated in the 1970s and climaxed in the 1980s caused a drastic decline in the life of the community. These troubles included the mechanization of the farming industry in the 1960s; the farm crisis of the late 1970s and early 1980s which affected small farmers throughout the country; the problem of heir property; and the increase in corporate agriculture. However, the crisis facing farmers in general has been exacerbated for Black farmers in Tillery by the pernicious reality of racism in the U.S. Department of Agriculture. Thus, in a protest rally held in Washington D.C. on April 23rd, 1997, Black farmers from Tillery and other rural Black farming communities throughout the country declared to Congress and the USDA with mule in hand, "Here's My Mule: Where's my Forty Acres?"

To answer the farmers' symbolic gesture and haunting question, we must take an historical journey through Tillery, identifying its many turning points: first, its historical geography; second, its history as a flourishing community; third, reasons for its decline; and finally, the challenges that this farming community has faced since the decline in Black owned and operated farms.

## Geographical Context

Tillery is located in Halifax County, N.C., one of the Black Belt counties that make up the rural Northeastern region of North Carolina. The county's population of about 57,000 is approximately 50% African American, 46% European American, 3% Haliwa Saponi Indian, and 1% Asian and others. The rural part of southeast Halifax, including the town of Tillery, has a population of about 15,000. According to the 1990 census, the median income for the county was $14,257 as compared to the state median of $17,831 and the national median of $20,137, while in Tillery proper the median income was less than $7,000. In the same period, Halifax County ranked 88 out of 100 counties in North Carolina in median family income. About one-quarter of the total population and about 40% of Blacks live in poverty. Yet in Tillery, 90% plus in the once thriving Resettlement Farm now live in poverty.

The main economic base has always been agriculture. Major crops in the area are cotton and peanuts; followed by soybeans, corn and tobacco. The climate of the area is well-suited to this type of farming. The average temperature is 59.9 degrees with a January average of 40.5 degrees and a July average of 75.8 degrees. Rainfall averages 43.4 inches per year with snowfall of 4 to 8 inches.

## Economic and Social History

Tillery was once one of many thriving communities. In the United States in 1920, one in every seven farmers was Black; however in 1982 only one in every sixty-seven farmers was Black. In 1950, Black farmers in North Carolina owned 1.2 million acres of land compared to 400,000 acres in 1982. At Tillery's height, there were more than 300 flourishing small farms, averaging 40 to 60 acres, which significantly contributed to the social, economic, political and spiritual wealth of the area. The settlers established seven different churches, several social clubs, an auto mechanic shop, and two grocery stores where farmers could market their own produce. At the center of much of the activity was the Tillery Chapel Elementary School, where not only academics, but also the arts, were encouraged. Plays, concerts and exhibits were held here. In the reflection of the elders of the community who still live here today, Tillery stood "in those days" as a self-sufficient, thriving community.

Graduates of the Tillery Chapel Elementary School remember the days when it was the "hub" of community life. Academics were stressed and what would be considered by today's standards as "troubled kids" were nurtured with a type of discipline that required them to rise above outside expectations of failure. While literacy programs today are held at the community center, the elementary school at that time was the site of early adult literacy efforts. Family reunions and community gatherings were also held at the school. After all, indoor facilities reached the school house long before they reached other sections of the community.

### Why the Decline?

A number of factors have contributed to the decline of the Tillery Community as it was once known by those who live to remember. One factor is the problem of "heir property." Many Black absentee heirs, who migrated away from the land and are able to make a living fail to recognize the significance of Black land ownership to their own political and economic well-being. They do not keep up on tax payments, or they give in to speculators' offers. Speculators know the value of the land and have perfected the art of double-talking working-class heirs into selling their property.

Another more compelling factor in the decline of Black-owned land in Tillery and other rural communities was the mechanization of the farming industry in the 1970s. During this time, numerous small farmers throughout the country overextended their loan potential in order to compete with larger, more advanced and incorporated agricultural systems. Furthermore, when devastating weather consumed crops in the early- to mid-1970s, many farmers were unable to recover and were forced into financial straits. The loss of crops for Black farmers in Tillery proved to be a major catalyst for their demise.

However, this devastation proved to be second only to discrimination in the USDA. When financial difficulties arose, many White farmers were able to refinance their loans or take out additional loans through USDA assistance programs to prevent foreclosure. Black farmers in the area were not extended these same privileges. In 1982, African Americans received only 1% of all USDA farm ownership loans; only 2.5% of all farm operating loans, and only 1% of all soil and water conservation loans. Thus, the decline in the number of Black farmers has been more rapid than that of White farmers.

Matthew Grant, a long time resettlement farmer and one who with his wife of fifty-seven years, Florenza Moore Grant, raised six children of their own and four extended family members on their farm, remembers well the tragedy. "When they foreclosed on us," Grant explained in a meeting with USDA officials, "they foreclosed on all of us at the same time...nineteen Black farmers." Pondering the legitimacy of this claim of racism, one official asked if they foreclosed on any White farmers at the same time. "Yes," came Mr. Grant's response, "Two. And they didn't own any land. This was in 1976."

Since 1976, all of the remaining Black farmers from the Tillery Resettlement Community have either lost their land to foreclosures or have simply been forced out of the farming business, unable to acquire operating capital and thus unable to turn a steady profit. Although one community resident estimates that 90% of the land still remains in the hands of Black landowners, only 5% of the land is being operated by Black farmers. Grant, however, has resisted the inclination to retreat. He and his family have been in a 22-year struggle with the USDA to prevent a foreclosure that many view as "inevitable."

## Present

The loss of land in the community has opened the area up to manufacturing, textile and livestock industries that employ persons with little or no technology skills. While taking Black land, agribusiness simultaneously creates for itself an exploitable Black working class for their non-union processing plants and textile mills. The industries brought into the northeast region of North Carolina seek to perpetuate the cycle of poverty. Such sweat shops as sewing factories, chicken processing plants and others who seek to avoid unionization locate in northeastern North Carolina. These low-paying, low-skill jobs are the ones that feel the nation's economic lurches or recessions immediately, while the state proudly proclaims itself a "right to work" state. The workers are constantly subject to layoffs and no increases in pay. In 1979, during an extensive period of this type of rapid growth, North Carolina became the nation's eighth most industrialized state, yet ranked 50th in the nation for average weekly wages for industry. As Black farmers faced imminent elimination in northeastern North Carolina, Perdue Farms Inc. (family farm) located a large portion of its billion-dollar poultry industry here, financed by a multi-million dollar USDA loan. The plant is infamous for its alleged low wages, unsafe working conditions, and intimidation of workers who apply for workers' compensation for job-related injuries.

In addition to this type of economic growth, Tillery and surrounding communities have felt the effects of industries that produce environmental hazards. Since the late 1980s Halifax County and other Black Belt counties have seen a rise in vertically integrated intensive hog production. Intensive hog operations are defined as factories with at least 740 sows; some have tens of thousands. These operations generate massive quantities of wastes that are stored in open cess pools prior to being spread on crop land. The growing houses and cess pools threaten ground and surface water and expose surrounding populations and workers to potential bacterial hazards, respiratory hazards, and an extremely noxious odor that has been linked with psychological problems. There are now seven intensive hog operations in the county.

## Strategies to Combat the Trend

The issues facing Halifax County and Tillery in particular are not unique among poor African American communities. What is unique is southeast Halifax's history of successful organizing in the African American community especially around the small town of Tillery. Concerned Citizens of Tillery (CCT), an organization of approximately 350 people has used its extensive grassroots support, in conjunction with a cooperative County Health Department, to introduce an Intensive Livestock Ordinance giving the County Health Department regulatory authority over intensive livestock operations, authority to instigate ground water education and monitoring programs, and to help motivate citizen demands for other local regulation, state monitoring, and representation on a State commission charged with studying the impacts of corporate hog operations.

CCT was established in 1978 to save the Tillery Chapel Elementary School and has grown in its goals and outreach. Following in the footsteps of previous community organizations that have led struggles for human rights, CCT's goal is to empower African American citizens in southeast Halifax. CCT aims to break the isolation experienced by both Tillery residents and the residents of other rural communities in eastern North Carolina by enabling citizens to rely on themselves while also ensuring connection and support from all sectors of society including government, academia, social service, business and finance. CCT organizes its efforts by addressing the needs and concerns of all stages of the community: the Nubian Youth, the Grown Folks Group and the Open Minded Seniors. Each of these groups meets regularly to discuss issues relevant to them and to organize activities that will benefit the community.

CCT has also organized a twice monthly Health Clinic that brings in doctors and medical students from state medical schools to address the health issues of local residents. In addition, the Southeast Halifax Environmental Reawakening Project which began in September 1996 works to support rural and semi-rural communities in efforts to recover environmental values that have become subject to certain types of corporate development. CCT is also the founding organizer of an environmental justice coalition, the Hog Roundtable, which brings together grassroots, legal and traditional environmental organizations.

A fundamental objective of this group is to organize across race and class barriers in order to make an impact on local, state and national policy that determines the future of the environment and agri-business in the state.

## Conclusion

While significant strides have been made in addressing the many issues raised by the loss of Black-owned land in the Tillery community and the subsequent loss of political and economic leverage, a considerable amount of work is yet undone. Education is a key component of this work. Children of farmers who were a part of the great out-migration of Blacks from rural areas to urban centers in the 1950s and 1960s, and who are now returning to homesteads need to understand both the tactics used by unscrupulous business people to acquire land, and the tax laws often administered by corrupt and racist local officials. Environmentalists who work for the preservation of surface water to the exclusion of groundwater need to understand the history of environmental racism. Politicians who court agri-business as a means of bolstering economic growth without considering the necessity of economic development need to understand the long-term consequences of having one without the other. And community people, long excluded from the political and economic processes that determine their future, need to come to understand the power that comes from consolidating resources to work together for the common good.

In Tillery we have learned that agri-business and its twin, corporate development, are not only affecting our own local spaces, but also national and international spaces. Thus, the magnitude of challenges is great; education is key; and perseverance is a necessity.

# Case 8

## Lake County, Florida: Citrus, Suburbs, and a Changing Way of Life

*William H. Good, Board of County Commissioners*

With more than 1600 named lakes and 1,163 square miles of land mass, Lake County, Florida is rich in sun and water, abundant wetlands and abundant biodiversity. The county has a rich agricultural history and until recently was a prosperous and thriving agricultural community—a community with a people knowledgeable and proud of their relationship with the land.

Lake County had traditionally grown a variety of crops for its own consumption as well as for market and export. As early as 1887, when the county was founded, Lake County produced citrus, grapes, fruits, vegetables, forage crops, livestock and poultry. More recently, the county made the tragic mistake of investing too much of the community agricultural infrastructure in one monocrop. That monocrop—King Citrus! Whether this policy of specialization of agricultural production was made by intent or born only in the marketplace is not of consequence. What matters is that a recent series of freezes in 1981–83, 1985, and 1989 forever changed the physical environment of Lake County. The resulting devastation of agricultural productivity, even after some replanting—90,000 acres of land that once produced a food crop now does not!

Despite these setbacks, agriculture is still an important factor in Lake County. By 1995 (as reported by the Cooperative

Extension Service), the economic impact from agriculture was $988.62 million. Other contributions to Lake County from agriculture included:

1. 1.5 million gallons water per acre per year captured or recharged into the Floridian Aquifer (the county's, and much of Florida's main source of potable water),

2. agricultural parcels listed on the tax rolls in 1994 assessed at $438 million, and

3. approximately 9,870 people employed either full-time or seasonally by agriculture.

The county struggles to rebuild its base of agricultural productivity, but many economic, social and cultural factors have made this task more difficult. The close proximity to major theme parks (e.g., Disney World, Sea World, MGM Studios) in Orlando has created "off the farm" jobs and "spin off" economic development. This new economy has provided for the community by creating wealth of a different sort. As the economic base has shifted to the development of retirement housing and tourism with some distribution and light manufacturing, major political and social changes have followed. The new rallying cry is "More fire protection, more deputies, more schools, more sidewalks, more roads," and all these cost money. At this point, it becomes a very good question as to whether the county commission can continue to lower the millage rate assessed on ad valorem property. For the past three years, the Board of County Commissioners has set the ad valorem tax rate at the "rollback" rate.

The suburbanization of the rural landscape is apparent and the focus on construction and suburban sprawl has caused a shift in the economy. It has also caused a change in many of the values of rural youth who can "make more money" at the mall and working in the emerging construction and service industries that are demanded by the proliferation of retirement communities that have evolved as farmers have sold their family lands to quickly "create wealth" by planting rooftops in this land of sunshine, beautiful lakes and rolling hills. The result has been devastating to the agricultural productivity of Lake County and has splintered the agricultural community as children of farmers sell their land and become suburbanites. The agricultural community that remains is fragmented into enclaves around the county with a few agribusiness producers and processors scrambling to compete for labor with higher wage industries.

As a science instructor in the public schools, I have watched as the agriculture curriculum, which once focused on food production, has been replaced by programs that focus on horticulture and the managing of suburban infrastructure. This is readily seen by the institutionalization of the Tech Prep Programs such as "turf grass management" and horticulture and landscape maintenance programs, often at the expense of curriculum focused on the production of food and fiber. In one local high school, the focus of the Exceptional Student Education Program has shifted from agriculture to gardening and auto detailing. 4-H programs teach some of the traditional production project programs, but tend to focus on educational programs training youth in traditional skills for "fair competitions." A loss of production knowledge, forage production skills, and the infrastructure for agricultural production have left Lake County's agricultural production capabilities diminished and our rural way of life in jeopardy.

Although in recent years the number of youth participating in the Lake County Fair has increased to the point of severely straining the fairground's capacity, plans to increase the facility have been placed on hold due to local politics. The recent retirement of the Fair director has left a void in the leadership of the County Fair, which has traditionally served as the showcase for the Lake County agricultural community.

Many economic and social impacts are being seen throughout our changing communities. Being lumped into the Orlando Metropolitan Area for the purposes of gathering statistics has grossly skewed the data used by Lake County to develop policy. This can be seen in the inflation of the average wage and income data, and also in the inflation of the average cost of affordable housing in Lake County. Low unemployment is inflating wages and the costs of goods and services. Many of Lake County's youth grapple with the problems of newly evolving suburban lifestyles and the morals of a society in rapid transition. This is seen in the skyrocketing of our Lake County juvenile crime statistics, and the recent reports of violence in our schools.

The immigration of new persons from outside Lake County accelerates the rate of social and economic change. While the basis of rural Lake County and its values still remains, much has changed. We have some very successful rural and suburban youth, but as the meeting places of our society change, the common sense of the feed store is rapidly being replaced by the convenience store mentality.

## The Process—How Did We Get Into This Position?

The basis for our arriving at this position is clear—greed and the quick buck account for how we arrived at our present predicament. A few people have benefitted greatly from the changes, but as usually occurs in times of rapid transition, others have been exploited. Few profit while a great many follow along.

The politics of this change are fascinating and worthy of comment. In the late eighties and early nineties, the local Board of County Commissioners, Planning and Zoning Board, and Board of Adjustments were "taken over" by realtors and developers (to the exclusion of others). When an agricultural person spoke out, she or he was criticized as grandstanding, or out of touch with the times. The few production agriculturalists who are involved in the politics of change have been accused of working for their own political purposes by those who promote a new direction at the expense of rural ways.

## The Result—More Suburbs, Less Agricultural Production

The result was that few agrarians, not always the most likely to involve themselves in politics anyway, were involved in making the decisions about land use and the future development of the Lake County environment and economy. On the Board of County Commissioners, the land boom mentality still remains, even though in recent years some changes have been made. The Board of County Commissioners' policies proclaim lofty goals for the agricultural sector of our economy, but the programs still focus on suburban economies and lifestyles. This is in spite of a recent report, The Economic Impact of Agriculture on Lake County, by the Lake County Soil and Water Conservation District, which concluded that 1) suburban development was accompanied by expensive demands for services that exceeded the taxes government receives from the development, and 2) that agricultural

lands more than paid in taxes for the costs of the services that
they demanded.

In spite of the fact that the County Commission recently increased the impact fees paid by developers before building permits are issued, the cost of suburban service delivery is still
greater than the fees and taxes derived from suburban development. Yet, building permits continue to be pulled at an expanding
rate. The Lake County of past years has given way to King Growth
of residential development often supported by the suburban
Chambers of Commerce.

The school board, responsible for educating the next generation
of Lake Countians has no representative from the agricultural
community. Instruction in horticulture and the processing of citrus grown elsewhere has replaced the production of food and fiber
for local consumption. The regional economy and agricultural
imports have become the basic sources of food for Lake County's
growing population of 190,000. Few people seem concerned about
this turn of events for the economy is booming, unemployment
figures are low, businesses are "coming to town," and the pension
and social security checks from retirees from the last five years
total $2.25 billion. Property taxes are still relatively low
(countywide millage rate 4.733), and a boom town mentality exists for those who are profiting.

But, what are the costs? The future of, and the ability for, agricultural production in Lake County have been forever changed.
The necessary infrastructure for agricultural production is disappearing as labor converts to the construction industry and a
slightly higher average wage than those employed in agriculture.
The opportunity for local agriculture still exists, but many of the
larger agriculture parcels have been sold off, and fragmentation is
reducing many of the parcels to a size that challenges the
economy of scale for many of the agricultural operations attempting to use them, leaving only the most intensive operations as
being recognized by the property appraiser as "bona fide agricultural operations."

As Chairman of the Value Adjustment Board, I see the applications for the agricultural classification of property that entitles
property owners to a "Greenbelt exemption." As reported by the
Lake County Property Appraiser's Office, the number of parcels

classified as being in agricultural use in 1995 was 7792. In 1997, the number of agriculturally classified parcels in Lake County was 8082, but their size and yield had decreased. The zoning and classification of land uses have produced a deceptive system that identifies many vacant parcels as agriculture, which are really marginally productive silvaculture operations at best, and at worst are only schemes by developers to gain tax exemptions from agricultural classification of land. A change is needed if we are to encourage local agricultural productivity.

## The Solution?

A lack of information about agricultural production and practice prompted the Lake County Board of County Commissioners to establish the Agricultural Advisory Committee to the Board. This committee is charged with the following tasks (Lake County Ordinance No. 1996-79):

1. Identification of opportunities for diversifying Lake County's agricultural production.

2. Working with Federal and State Departments of Agriculture, and the University of Florida, to develop a Lake County Agricultural Plan.

3. To identify and recommend means to overcome challenges and constraints to implementing sustainable agricultural practices.

4. To provide an annual report to the Board of County Commissioners on the condition of agriculture in Lake County. This report is to include a section on the quality and quantity of Lake County's food supply, and may include local and regional sources and the identification of distribution systems involved in the delivery of food products to the consumer.

Although this seems like a very complicated charge, it is the hope of this commissioner that the results will serve to improve community awareness and understanding of what is involved in improving the security of community food supplies. It is also hoped that the networking among various government agencies and the private sector agricultural community will help to bring about a safer and more secure food supply for the citizens of Lake County.

Another proposal being discussed is a cooperative venture for the establishment of The Palatlakaha Environmental and Agricultural Reserve (PEAR). A proposal is being drafted by members of the community for the development of a joint park and community farm/gardens on the historical site of the University Research Farm. This site, on the environmentally sensitive Palatlakaha Creek south of Leesburg, Florida has been the home of the development of seedless watermelons and many varieties of Florida grapes by the Institute of Food and Agricultural Sciences (IFAS) researchers. Only time will tell if PEAR and the other efforts described will be successful in making Lake County a more food safe and food secure community.

# Case 9

## The State of Ohio Farmland*

### The American Farmland Trust

The Great Seal of Ohio depicts a sheaf of wheat beside a bundle of 17 arrows (showing that Ohio is the nation's 17th state) on a cultivated field. Behind the field, a stylized blue river flows by a mountain range beneath a many-rayed, rising sun.

If that seal were redesigned today, it might look a little differ-ent. The wheat and field advertise that agriculture is still Ohio's number one industry. But beyond the river—meant to represent the Scioto, which divides the state into east and west—the artist might dot the horizon with houses and commercial buildings. Development is sprawling over the state's best farmland—espe-cially that east of the Scioto in a broad northern swath along Lake Erie —at an alarming rate.

This pattern is clear on American Farmland Trust's "Farming on the Edge" map (see Spring-Summer 1997 *American Farmland*, pp. 12-13), which shows where especially rapid development is consuming each state's highest quality agricultural land. AFT ranks the Eastern Ohio Till Plain, in the northeastern part of the state, as the seventh most threatened farming region in the nation.

*Reprinted with permission, *American Farmland*, Fall 1997, pp. 15-17.

In August 1996, Ohio Governor George V. Voinovich signed an executive order establishing the Ohio Farmland Preservation Task Force to "serve our urban and rural citizens as they search for incentives, not mandates, to preserve Ohio's precious farmland resources in a manner that will benefit us all." Staffed by AFT, the task force of 21 representatives from agriculture, business, government, academic and environmental concerns studied the issue of farmland loss in the state. In June, the task force submitted its report to the Governor, with recommendations for future action to protect the integrity of Ohio's agricultural economy.

The group's principal findings: Ohio should declare farmland protection to be a top priority and establish an Office of Farmland Preservation within the state's department of agriculture. Just days after receiving the task force report, Voinovich added $400,000 to the state budget to fund the new OFP for the next two years. The proposed scope of the OFP, says AFT's Director of Field Programs Bob Wagner, makes it the most comprehensive agency of its kind in the nation. "Ohio's office will coordinate statewide policies and regulations to ensure that they promote agriculture and discourage sprawling development," Wagner explains. "That's a much broader mission than other states have given their farmland protection programs."

Ohio Lieutenant Governor Nancy P. Hollister says the state faces a unique challenge with respect to farmland conservation: "Ohio is both very urban and very rural. We've got seven major metropolitan areas, yet the landmass of the state is two-thirds rural. Lately, the loss of farmland and the urban population's moving 'out to the country' have signaled the need for comprehensive land use planning for the counties, townships and cities." Hollister was a co-chair of the Task Force, along with Ohio Department of Agriculture Director Fred L. Dailey and Dr. C. William Swank, former executive vice president of the Ohio Farm Bureau Federation.

With sprawling suburban development come rising land prices and property taxes, and the loss of an area's agricultural infrastructure—from farm-related businesses to farm-tolerant neighbors. And as farmland increases in value, fewer young people can afford to buy farms of their own, and landowners' estate tax burden grows, making it more difficult for farmers to pass their land on to the next generation. Hollister says that in addition to the far-reaching activities of the new OFP, the state is now designing a program to make grants or loans available to new farmers in Ohio. "Although the state has provided grants and incentives to agribusinesses for some time," she notes, "we've never really addressed the problems of small farmers," especially young people who are having a hard time buying their first farm.

"Our report got a great deal of newspaper and TV coverage throughout Ohio," says task force co-chair Fred Dailey. "I think that shows people are starting to recognize that our agricultural lands are a finite resource and that saving them is an important issue. What really surprised me is that there's every bit as much support for farmland protection from the urban and suburban communities as from the farm communities."

There are plenty of reasons for Ohioans to value their state's farmland. In addition to the $56.2 billion in annual income generated by the Ohio agriculture industry, which also provides one-sixth of the state's jobs, farmland provides fresh food and other farm products, open space, wildlife habitat and a host of other environmental and "quality of life" benefits. Preventing further sprawling development in the state will mean revitalization of areas already developed—more good news for residents of Ohio's cities, towns, and older suburbs.

"I think we've made great progress," Lt. Gov. Hollister declares. "It turns out that by protecting farmland, you're also addressing a multitude of important issues, both urban and rural. When the task force issued its recommendations, my feeling was that this is not the end—it's just the beginning."

## Recommendations of the
## Ohio Farmland Preservation Task Force

The June 1997 report by the Ohio Farmland Preservation Task Force to Ohio Governor George V. Voinovich outlined the many political, social and environmental issues related to farmland loss in the state, and called on the governor to "endorse a policy statement establishing that it is a priority of the State of Ohio to preserve the state's productive agricultural land and protect against its unnecessary and irretrievable conversion to nonagricultural uses." Following are the key recommendations of the task force:

*Create an Office of Farmland Preservation (OFP) within the Ohio Department of Agriculture to administer a Farmland Preservation Program for Ohio.* The OFP will work cooperatively with existing institutions, organizations and governmental entities to compile and distribute information on the importance of agriculture to Ohio and the importance of protecting agricultural resources. This may include:

- developing youth and adult educational programs on agriculture;

- organizing and conducting informational and technical programs on farmland preservation;

- collecting, analyzing and mapping land use trends;

- promoting public and private options and the activities of land trusts, including the donation of conservation easements, to preserve farmland; and

- identifying and disseminating model community plans, planning methodology and zoning codes, and programs for farmland preservation.

*Develop a set of state guidelines and suggested criteria for local comprehensive land use plans* to encourage farmland protection, efficient public infrastructure investment, agriculturally supportive zoning and the managed expansion of urban and suburban areas.

*Create a Farmland Preservation Program at the state level* to be coordinated and matched with local initiatives, including an Agricultural Security Area Program.

*Administer a pilot Ohio Farmland Preservation Fund* to leverage matching federal, local and private funds to protect farmland.

*Develop and administer an Ohio Farmland Preservation Strategy* to coordinate the planning and review of all state programs and actions with respect to their impact on farmland conservation.

*Prepare, with the Ohio Department of Development, a biannual report to the governor* on the progress of programs and activities to coordinate the preservation of farmland with economic growth and development for agriculture in the state.

*Establish an advisory board for the OFP,* representing the rural and urban constituents with a stake in agriculture, to examine farmland conservation and related issues.

# Case 10

## DeKalb County, Illinois:
## Land Use in the Urban Shadow

*Patrick A. Stewart, Arkansas State University*
*Lawrence W. Libby, The Ohio State University*

DeKalb County, Illinois is a prime example of competition between urban and rural uses of land in the face of the growing urban five o'clock shadow of commuters desiring inexpensive land and rural lifestyles. Located less than sixty-five miles from downtown Chicago and within twenty-five miles of rapidly growing suburbs, DeKalb County has all the assets of country living, such as limited congestion, crime and noise as well as clean air and water, while being within easy reach of Chicago's cultural amenities and business opportunities. As a result, the city of DeKalb grew by 2,000 people from 1990 to 1995, to a population of 37,000 residents (Comprehensive Plan 1995:24-30). A survey of new city residents in 1992 showed that 35% moved from outside the county.

At the same time, DeKalb County historically has emphasized agricultural production, focusing primarily on soybeans and corn. Ninety percent of the county is farmland, and 98% of that land is classified as prime farmland. In addition to possessing some of the finest agricultural land in the world, DeKalb County was the first county in the nation to create a county Farm Bureau and appoint an Agricultural Extension Advisor. It is also home to DeKalb Ag Research Corporation, a major producer of hybrid seed corn. While farming is a major part of the local economy, farmers make up only 3.5% of the work force. Additionally, trends in the county reflect those nationwide with a decrease in the number of farmers while farm size increases (Paulson and Gehl 1997). This does not bode well for preservation of agricultural land. As fewer people are intimately involved with agricultural production, fewer people are likely to appreciate high quality farmland.

As a result of DeKalb County's prime farmland and prime location near Chicago and its suburbs, there is an imminent land use conflict, a conflict first forecast in 1972 when the county developed its initial comprehensive land use plan. Therefore, we consider DeKalb County's current comprehensive land use plan and assess its effectiveness before looking at a recent legal challenge and the resultant legislative actions.

## Comprehensive Land Use Plan

While DeKalb County is not considered to be directly pressured by metropolitan growth, the current comprehensive land use plan addresses growth pressures from the Chicago area. Because the 1972 comprehensive plan, which implemented inclusive agricultural zoning based on a five-acre minimum rural residence lot size, was unsuccessful in discouraging farmland conversion, the plan was changed in 1974 to better ameliorate the conflict between agricultural and residential land use (NALS 1980). The major points of the plan assert the need to preserve prime agricultural land and other natural resources and their uses while accommodating controlled growth.

As a result, DeKalb County zoning protects agricultural and other natural resource lands by only allowing development coterminous with existing municipalities, and only when full utilities are provided (Comprehensive Plan: Executive Summary 1995). The land use plan establishes two types of agricultural zoning (A-1 and A-2) and two types of residential zoning (R-1 and R-2). A-1 zoning has a minimum lot size of 40 contiguous acres, of which at least 25 acres have been used for agricultural pursuits in the last three years. A-2 zoning has a 15-acre minimum lot size as this land is not necessarily seen as permanently retained in agriculture, typically because of proximity to municipalities and villages. R-1 zoning allows residential construction, usually as subdivisions, near municipalities and villages, and prevents

premature disinvestment in agriculture by accommodating necessary growth. R-2 zoning refers to the construction of primarily
residences on land to be served by public sewer and water distribution services, that is, within city limits (DeKalb County 1991).

The effectiveness of DeKalb County's comprehensive land use
plan was tested in a study of farmland value (Stewart and Libby
1997). The study used multiple regression techniques to assess
the effects of various factors on the price of DeKalb County farmland non-contiguous with municipalities and villages. Land zoned
as small lots (less than the 40 acre minimum) before the comprehensive land use plan was implemented had an average added
sales value of $11,065 per acre. This is presumably due to the
market value of hobby farms. In other words, the price of production farmland is constrained through the large lot A-1 zoning
established by the comprehensive plan.

However, farmland in the study was not immune to the effects
of speculation. Proximity to highway interchanges, which benefits
commuters, was a strong and significant variable, with every mile
from the highway interchange decreasing the sales price of the
property by $390 per acre. This implies that while DeKalb
County's agricultural zoning may effectively limit the price of
farmland, there is still the expectation of growth.

The study suggests that government plays a role in both giving
and taking value from land. Through increased sales prices of
agricultural land close to highway interchanges, government
gives value by redistributing taxpayers' money that pays for
transportation infrastructure in proximity to the land. Through
large lot zoning, government takes value from agricultural land
by restricting its development. The owners of agricultural parcels
that avoided large lot zoning restrictions, due to being zoned
less than forty acres before the comprehensive plan took effect,
benefitted financially from restrictions placed on their neighbors
and thus were the recipients of government givings.

## Wolfenberger Vs. County of Dekalb

In spite of its comprehensive land use plan, it is expected that
DeKalb County will experience intense growth pressure in the
near future. As a result, conflict regarding development patterns

and zoning ordinances is expected. An example of potential zoning conflicts is the <u>Dennis Wolfenberger et al. vs. County of
DeKalb</u> lawsuit decided in DeKalb County's 16 Judicial Circuit
Court September 16, 1997. In this case, Wolfenberger, the owner
of 146 acres approximately 2½ miles north of Sycamore, one of
two major cities in DeKalb County, brought suit to rezone his
agricultural land from A-1 to R-1 residential to develop a subdivision. One hundred thirty-nine of the 146 acres were tillable, and
were leased for $135 per acre per year cash rent. The land was
bordered to the south by Plank Road, a high traffic county road
moving commuters from the northwestern Chicago suburbs to
Sycamore and the city of DeKalb. While this added to the development value of the land, the subdivisions already in place to the
south, east and north were not fully developed.

### Precedent

Legal precedent used to decide this case was <u>La Salle National
Bank of Chicago vs. County of Cook</u>, 12 Ill.2d.40 (1957). The decision from this case is seen as establishing many of the principles
of law for judicial review of municipal zoning matters in Illinois.
Key statements from that case are: "It is well established that it is
primarily the province of the municipal body to determine the use
and purpose to which property may be devoted, and it is neither
the province nor the duty of the courts to interfere with the discretion which such bodies are vested unless the legislative action
of the municipality is shown to be arbitrary, capricious and unrelated to the public health, safety and morals. By the same token,
however, if the restrictions imposed bear no real or substantial
relation to the public health, safety, morals, comfort and general
welfare, the ordinance is void." The Court goes on to state, "each
zoning ordinance must be determined on its own facts and circumstances." Of these facts and circumstances, which are six in
total (see below), no one factor is controlling.

The second case considered "truly important" to this case was
<u>Racich vs. The County of Boone</u>, 254 Ill.App.3d 311 (1993). This
case is pertinent because it exhibits the legal application of the
LESA (Land Evaluation Site Assessment) system, in turn establishing agricultural land value through the evaluation of soils.
The first part of this system is consistent throughout the nation
and rates soils on a scale of 0–100; a rating of 76 or more points
indicates prime agricultural land. The second part of the system

varies from county to county and is developed by persons involved
with agriculture and zoning in that county. This part entails a
site assessment rated on a scale of 0–200 based on 14 factors. If a
parcel receives a combined rating for the two parts of the system
that sums to more than 200 points, the land is considered prime
agricultural land and may be kept in that use because it promotes the "health, safety, morals or general welfare of the public."

### Decision

While it was recognized that "The plaintiff has gone to great
efforts to design and propose an excellent subdivision plan," the
Court used six standards (italicized below) established by La Salle
Bank and made the following findings:

1. *The existing uses and zoning of nearby property.* The uses
   and zoning of nearby property are consistent with both an
   agricultural and a residential use, and are thus compatible.

2. *The extent to which property values are diminished by the
   particular zoning restrictions.* The plaintiff contended that
   property values were diminished by about $2,000 per acre
   due to zoning restrictions. While the Court agreed there was
   some diminution in value, it did not believe the extent of loss
   was almost 50% of the property value, and felt "the property
   supports a good value as farm land without further expenditure of costs to develop."

3. *The extent to which the destruction of property values of the
   plaintiff promotes the health, safety, morals or general welfare
   of the public.* Here, the Court utilized the LESA system,
   although it was considered less than perfect because of its
   use at the county level by people potentially biased or preju-
   diced in favor of the system and the use of prime agricultural
   land for farming. However, the Court stated that "there is no
   question that the subject land is prime agricultural land."
   Further, because the county stated in their comprehensive
   plan that public health, safety, morals and general welfare
   are maintained by a public policy where prime farmland
   should not be developed into residential areas, the public
   interest as stated, and as supported by Racich vs. County of
   Boone should prevail.

4. *The relative gain to the public as compared to the hardship imposed upon the individual property owner.* The Court believed that $135 per acre cash rent was a fair and equitable return, and through favorable use-value tax assessment, the net revenue available from farmland did not impose a severe hardship on the property owner.

5. *The suitability of subject property for zoned purposes.* In the words of the Court "There seems to be no question that this property is suitable for use as agricultural land and consistent with property which immediately adjoins it as well as property which surrounds it for several miles."

6. *The length of time that the property has been vacant as zoned considered in the context of the land development of the area in the vicinity of the subject.* With this final factor, the Court recognized that nearby land that had been re-zoned for development was generally located in areas with brush and trees and had less productive soil, hilly or rocky conditions, or other factors that kept it from being economically productive farming acreage.

Based upon the La Salle Bank case and supported by the weight and authority of Racich, the Court decided that given "the appropriateness of the comprehensive plan and legislative decision which favors agricultural use of prime farmland, the current zoning is not arbitrary and capricious." As a result, the decision favored the County of DeKalb on the basis of the underlying power of a legislative body to adopt public policy that favors agricultural land use in place of residential land use in rural areas.

As noted by the Court in Wolfenberger vs. County of DeKalb, the challenge was not to the constitutionality of the entire DeKalb County Ordinance, but to the specific property. The potential for further legal challenges led to an amendment to the Illinois Counties Code to grant counties the authority to establish a minimum lot size for residences on agricultural land. This amendment, introduced as House Bill 1188, passed the General Assembly and was signed by the Governor on July 30, 1997, effective January 1, 1998 (Paulson and Gehl 1997).

## Conclusions

DeKalb County provides an important case study of conflict between speculation on potential residential land use and current agricultural production use by showing the effect of zoning on farmland values and the potential lawsuits that might come about. While the 1972 comprehensive land use plan was quickly discovered to be faulty, the current land use plan, in place since 1974, has been successful to date. Not only has the comprehensive land use plan had the desired impact on farmland prices, it has also withstood recent legal challenges. However, as the Chicago urban area expands, and with it greater demand for rural and small town lifestyles, so too will legal challenges. While the amendment to the Counties Code will do much to forestall the revocation of comprehensive plans throughout Illinois, the relinquishment by the state of land use authority to *both* counties and municipalities can lead to suburban sprawl when counties and municipalities disagree about the benefits and negative aspects of growth and work at cross-purposes.

## References

Comprehensive Plan (DeKalb County). 1995. Kuhlman Design Group, St. Louis, MO.

DeKalb County Zoning Ordinance. 1991. DeKalb County Planning Department, Sycamore, IL.

NALS (National Agricultural Lands Study). 1981. The Protection of Farmland: A Reference Guidebook for State and Local Governments. U.S. Department of Agriculture, Washington, D.C.

Paulson, J., and S.J. Gehl. 1997. DeKalb County: First in Agriculture. Working Paper #97-12. Center for Agriculture in the Environment, DeKalb, IL.

Stewart, P.A., and L.W. Libby. 1997. Determinants of Farmland Value. Working Paper #97-10. Center for Agriculture in the Environment, DeKalb, IL.

Wolfenberger, D., et al. vs. County of DeKalb, 96 MR 16. 16th Judicial Circuit, DeKalb County, September 16.

# Case 11

## Understanding the Rules, Practices and Attitudes Regarding Land-Use in Waukesha County, Wisconsin, 1996

*Susan Jo Gehl, Farmland Policy Consultant*
*Lawrence W. Libby, The Ohio State University*

Waukesha County, located immediately west of Milwaukee County in east-central Wisconsin, encompasses 580 square miles. With its proximity to Milwaukee and its unique landscape of hills, kettles, lakes and streams, Waukesha County is a pleasant place to live. As subdivisions and strip malls rapidly replace farmland throughout the entire county, many current residents believe that suburbanization and the disappearance of farmland is inevitable. However, the type of growth that is occurring is not inevitable. Development occurs as a result of a collection of rules, practices and attitudes that determine how, where and when growth occurs.

### The Current Situation

Seventy-two percent of the total area of Waukesha County was non-urban land in 1990, with about half the open land in wetlands, woodlands, surface water, quarries, and landfill sites, and the other half in agriculture. The number of farms and land in farms in Waukesha County declined from 1982 to 1992

(Table C11.1), as is the case in most counties in Wisconsin. Average farm size increased only slightly, reflecting a relatively modest amount of consolidation. This is primarily a dairy county, though the number of milk cows declined by 30% in ten years. Other livestock sales and inventories declined more dramatically, with the broiler industry dropping from 26 to eight farms from 1982 to 1992. Waukesha farmers are getting older, up to an average of 54 years in 1992.

Although agriculture is still the predominant land use in Waukesha County, farmland is rapidly being converted to urban uses. Much of this conversion is low-density residential development, characterized by on-site septic systems and private wells, and located outside of planned urban service areas. By its very nature, sprawl significantly increases the rate and amount of farmland developed for urban uses.

Table C11.1  Agriculture in Waukesha County.

|                               | 1992    | 1982    |
| ----------------------------- | ------- | ------- |
| Farms (number)                | 691     | 974     |
| Land in farms (acres)         | 114,184 | 149,259 |
| Harvested cropland (acres)    | 82,953  | 111,436 |
| Average age of operators      | 54      | 51      |

### Cities and Villages

Waukesha County has seven cities and 18 villages which encompass 36% (206 square miles) of the total area of the county. Each city and village is governed by an elected board that possesses both administrative and legislative powers. Under Wisconsin Statutes, municipalities have home-rule power, allowing cities and villages to make development decisions that cannot be challenged by county or town governments. Although the State can intervene in specific situations, it rarely chooses to involve itself in zoning, subdivisions and annexations.

### Transportation

Waukesha County is served by four freeways running primarily east and west. In addition, north-south and east-west arterial routes occur at one to three mile intervals throughout the entire county. These freeways and arterial routes provide transportation from the western, southern and northern parts of the county to the eastern edges and the Milwaukee area. With 83% of the roads operating at less than capacity, travel from one area to another is relatively fast and efficient. This ease of movement has opened much of the county for residential, commercial and industrial development and contributed to scattered development patterns.

### Public and Private Utilities

On-site septic systems have been a major contributor to urban sprawl and the conversion of farmland because they allow development in rural areas. Today there are two types of septic systems: the traditional and the mound system. The traditional system must be placed in specific soils to work effectively, while the mound system can function in many soil types. With the use of the mound system, rural lands with soils not suited for traditional systems can now be developed and soil type is basically removed from the factors that limit urban development.

Public water is currently supplied by 16 municipal and 61 private or cooperatively owned water supply systems. In 1993, 12% of the area of the county and 58% of the population was served by such systems. The remaining residents are served by private wells. Additional development will easily be accommodated by new and existing water systems or private wells. Hook-up to electric power, natural gas and communication services is readily available throughout the county.

### Real Estate

Milwaukee ranks seventh among the top 10 U.S. cities in regard to home equity growth. Property values have risen steadily in the Milwaukee metropolitan area (of which Waukesha County is a part) during the past decade, resulting in a strong real estate market that shows few signs of slowing down. Unlike the East and West Coasts, the Milwaukee market has not fallen victim to huge upswings or downswings in home values. This stability has made homes one of the most secure and lucrative investments for Milwaukee area residents during the past ten years with residential values rising on average 7.1% per year since 1986.

In addition to the financial advantages of settling in Waukesha County, people are buying houses in the area simply for the desirable urban/rural lifestyle. It is the scenic beauty of the glaciated terrain with its hills, lakes, rivers and farmland that attracts people to the area, and it is the availability of land that allows them to stay. Waukesha County developers are finding that residents want open space and lot sizes of one, three and five acres; the suburban lifestyle with half-acre lots is no longer in high demand. Unfortunately, the widespread desire for large lot sizes has accelerated the pace of farmland conversion, and Waukesha County residents are destroying the very lifestyle they moved to the area to attain.

### New Development

Tax Incremental Financing (TIF) is a local financing mechanism used by cities, villages and towns to attract private development in a designated area through the use of public investment. The funds to finance the improvements within a TIF district are generated by the taxes collected on the increases in taxable property values within a 23 year period. In 1993, 26 TIF districts existed in 14 Waukesha County villages and cities. To qualify for designation as a TIF district, at least 50% of the property must be blighted, in need of rehabilitation or conservation, or suitable for industrial use according to Wisconsin Statute 66.52 (66.46). Therefore, TIF is primarily used for the redevelopment of downtown areas or to build new industrial parks. Although farmland cannot be considered a blighted area according to the statutes governing TIF, it can be considered an area suitable for industrial use. Under 66.52, the state declares that it will promote industrial development in order to provide residents with greater employment opportunities and relief from tax burdens through an expanded tax base. Therefore, cities, villages and towns are authorized to pay for industrial development through the use of tax increment financing. For example, the city of Muskego is proposing to develop an industrial park on 260 acres of farmland with the use of tax increment financing.

## Why Did Waukesha County Agriculture Decline?

Aware of their proximity to Milwaukee (not more than thirty-five miles), Waukesha County farmers decided 30 years ago that eventually they would sell their land for development. They knew that urbanization would reach their farmyards, and that in the absence of use-value assessment and other tax credits, property taxes would be higher than in other rural areas of the State. Therefore, according to these farmers, farming would no longer be viable. Despite the fact that very little in life is inevitable, the mere fact that farmers believed development was inevitable has conditioned all aspects of their business and personal planning and has fulfilled the prophecy of development.

Today, most farmers publicly say:

- Property taxes are too high; therefore they cannot make a living.

- None of their kids want to farm; therefore, there is no one left to inherit the farm.

- The land is their retirement; therefore, they need to sell it for development.

- There are not enough contiguous acres of farmland; there-fore, they cannot expand and/or continue to farm long-term.

- The nearest implement dealer is in a neighboring county; therefore, it is difficult to get needed equipment and services.

But these reasons are only symptoms of the real barrier to farmland preservation—urban sprawl and widespread uncertainty about the future pattern of development. Urban sprawl has given the farmer the potential to sell his or her land for more money than can be gained through farming, and the overwhelming majority of farmers cannot find any substantial reasons to sacrifice the possibility of receiving such an offer.

## Government Programs: Tax Relief

### Farmland Preservation Program

In 1977, the state legislature acknowledged the existence of financial difficulties for farmers statewide by establishing the Wisconsin Farmland Preservation Program. Under this program, Waukesha County farmers are entitled to income tax credits if their land is part of an exclusive agricultural zoning district.

Seven years later, in 1984, Waukesha County adopted the Waukesha County Agricultural Land Preservation Plan to promote the Wisconsin Farmland Preservation Program. In accordance with the plan, exclusive agricultural zoning districts were incorporated into the Waukesha County Code thereby enabling farmers under the jurisdiction of this code to participate in the farmland preservation program and take advantage of income tax credits. However, each municipality and the majority of towns are not under the jurisdiction of the Waukesha County Code, and, despite the recommendation of the plan, many of these local governments did not adopt agricultural zoning districts.

It is probable that many local governments did not implement the Farmland Preservation Program because the rules are inadequate to attract wide participation:

- Tax credits are insufficient. Credits are based on gross household income from both non-farm and farm sources. If income is greater than $37,000 and taxes are more than $6,000, the maximum tax credit a farm family can receive is $600.

- Most farmers want the option to sell for development, which is not possible with their land zoned as exclusive agricultural.

- Farmers in the program are penalized for selling to developers through a fee equal to the total income tax credit for the previous ten years.

### Use Value Assessment

With the realization that the Farmland Preservation Act has done little to help preserve agriculture in Wisconsin, the Wisconsin State Legislature passed a law in 1995 to assess farmland on the basis of its use-value rather than its market value. The legislation froze the assessed value at 1995 levels for 1995 and 1996. After 1996, assessed values will be reduced to use values over a ten year period. Farmland affected by this law is defined as land used for raising livestock or for the production of crops. Non-pasture wetlands and forest lands are not eligible. Currently, the law is under attack by some city governments and tax payer groups concerned about the loss of revenue and shift of tax burden to non-farm property owners. The Wisconsin Supreme Court is expected to rule on use-value assessment in mid-1997.

Unlike the Farmland Preservation Program, all agricultural lands regardless of zoning are assessed according to use-value, and only those landowners who sell their land after owning the land for less than five years are required to pay a penalty. This penalty is equivalent to 5% of the difference between the sale price and the use-value during the last year of ownership. Thus, while the new program may be expected to provide substantial property tax relief to all owners of farmland, it will do so without attaching any significant restrictions on the land.

## Government Policy: Past and Present

### The Regional Land-Use Plan

Waukesha County is one of seven counties in the Southeastern Wisconsin Region. Although none of these counties has county-specific land use plans as of fall 1996, there is a Southeastern Wisconsin Regional Plan that can be referred to by county officials when making land-use decisions. The first regional plan was adopted in 1966 and has since been revised twice. The current plan has a design horizon of 2010. Like the first two plans, the current plan recommends that growth occur in a centralized rather than decentralized pattern with predominantly medium density rather than low density development. These recommendations were designed to encourage development near areas served by municipal facilities, such as sewer, water and mass transit, and to preserve environmentally sensitive areas and the remaining prime agricultural land.

Simply designating land as prime agricultural land and recommending the end of leap-frog development, however, cannot

guarantee that prime agricultural land will remain undeveloped
and urban sprawl will not occur. The Southeastern Regional
Land-use Plan is just that—a plan. Since the plan's adoption in
1967, the plan has not been followed by county, municipal or
town officials in Waukesha County, and the current zoning is
markedly different from what the plan recommends.

### Current Zoning

According to 1993 data, 52% of the county (302 square miles)
is zoned for urban residential use. Almost 90% of this land is
zoned equally for low-density and suburban-density development.
Of the 302 square miles zoned for urban residential use, 165
square miles is currently undeveloped, much of it still in agriculture. Upon full development of such lands, an additional 230,000
persons will be accommodated.

It is apparent that current zoning throughout the county does
not reflect the recommendations of the Southeastern Wisconsin
Regional Planning Commission (SEWRPC). The reasons for this
lack of *congruency* can be summarized by understanding the
history of zoning, the legal relationship between the county
and the towns, and farmer preferences. Prior to the creation
of SEWRPC in the early 1960s, the entire county was zoned
primarily as one-acre lots. At that time, urban pressure was
minimal and one-acre lots adequately discouraged growth. In
1967, SEWRPC completed the first Southeastern Regional Land-
Use Plan. The plan, as noted above, called for more restrictive
zoning in order to preserve agricultural land and environmental
corridors. Under Wisconsin Statutes, proposed zoning changes
needed the approval of both county and town governments, otherwise one-acre zoning would remain in effect. Therefore, the
county could not impose SEWRPC recommendations on the
towns and was limited to approving any town proposals that
were more restrictive than one-acre zoning. The zoning in 1996
is basically a reflection of the changes proposed by the towns in
the 1970s. Although some towns desired protection of environmental corridors and prime agricultural lands, most towns
resisted placing severe development restrictions on their land.
For example, the Town of Merton zoned the entire town for one-
and three-acre lots.

# Government Policy: The Vision for the Future

## *County Land-Use Plan*

With concerns regarding the current patterns of development and the need to better coordinate decision-making between the county and towns regarding the development of unincorporated areas, Waukesha County began in 1993 to prepare its first county-wide land-use plan. The Development Plan Advisory Committee designed the plan to meet three objectives:

- Promote relatively compact, centralized development by encouraging new development within or near existing urban centers and prevent the development of areas where sewer, water and mass transit are not provided.

- Preserve, in open and natural uses, the remaining environmental corridors.

- Preserve the remaining prime farmlands.

These objectives are identical to the objectives of the regional land-use plan. However, there are two significant differences between the sets of rules guiding the creation of the two plans:

- The definition of prime agricultural lands.

- The method for determining the amount of land allocated to the various land-use categories.

The Waukesha County Development Plan Advisory committee identified prime agricultural areas as land in farm units of at least 35 acres, with at least 50% of the area covered by USDA designated prime farmland soils and in a contiguous block of similar farmland of at least five square miles in size. The omission of soils of statewide importance and the increase in the farming block size criterion from 100 acres to five square miles or approximately 3,200 acres substantially reduced the amount of land that qualified as prime agricultural land. In formulating these standards, the Advisory Committee stated that it was attempting to balance the need to preserve agricultural resources with the difficulties faced by farmers in maintaining farms in an urbanizing county.

## Submission of the Preliminary County Land-Use Plan for Local Review

After the Advisory Committee completed the Preliminary County Land-Use Plan, it was submitted to local governments for review. Many town governments were outraged by the plan. Their collective vision for the community and their land-use plans as previously noted were significantly different from the county's vision and the county's plan. The general consensus was to "take the word farming out of the plan" (Stevens 1996). Although the Advisory Committee was reluctant to remove prime agricultural areas from the plan, they were forced to do so as a result of their own definition of prime agricultural land. Land in nearly all of the five square mile blocks designated as prime agricultural land had been recently subdivided unbeknownst to the Advisory Committee. Therefore, only a few five square mile blocks of farmland remain.

## The Revised County Land-Use Plan

With the new information regarding the recent subdivision of farmland, the land-use plan was revised. Although the Revised County Land-Use Plan is similar in many ways to the preliminary plan, the revised plan identifies significantly less prime agricultural land than did the preliminary plan. In the preliminary plan, 52 square miles of land were identified as prime agricultural land; in the revised plan, only 17 square miles or 2.9% of the total area of the County is identified as prime agricultural land. Large areas of land formerly classified as prime farmland were reclassified as urban land, rural residential, other agricultural lands or other open lands to be preserved. This allows for a 4.2% increase in developable land.

Town governments are generally pleased with the revised plan because prime agricultural zoning districts were removed almost entirely. The only area that is designated for preservation in farming is a small area in the northeastern corner. If the Revised Plan is adopted by the County Board, virtually every farmer will have the county's official support in developing his or her land and rezonings of prime agricultural land will be easily obtained. According to Kurt Bauer of SEWRPC, "clustered development will be about the only way that the county will save what privately owned open space is left" (Gould 1996). Virtually every person interviewed for this project agreed with Kurt Bauer's assessment.

# Conclusion

Planning, zoning and special tax laws have failed to protect prime agricultural land in Waukesha County. With the lure of profits from selling to developers, operators of both profitable and non-profitable farms have pushed for zoning ordinances and land-use plans that allow the development of agricultural lands. In late 1996, virtually the entire county is zoned for development, and it appears as if the majority of agricultural lands remaining will soon be lost.

Despite the grim forecast, agriculture can still be saved in Waukesha County with innovative tools requiring public and private partnerships between farmers and the non-farming community.

**Public Partnerships:** The county or individual townships and municipalities can raise money to purchase the development rights from interested farmers. Those farmers interested in continuing to farm would keep their land and gain income equal to the value of the development rights. Farmers interested in retiring could receive the full value of their land by selling the development rights to the community and the land at its agricultural price to another farmer. This would allow the retiring farmer to receive substantial compensation for his land and enable another farmer to begin farming.

**Private Partnerships:** Individuals with an interest in having a home with a rural setting could buy a farm at its development price, build a house on one or two acres and establish a conservation easement restricting the remaining land to agricultural use and allowing the owner to take a tax deduction. Subsequently, the land would be rented or sold to a farmer according to its agricultural value. In many cases, several individuals would have to buy contiguous tracts to provide a farmer with enough land to sustain a viable operation.

The fact that these preservation tools exist, however, will do nothing to save farming in Waukesha County without public will, leadership, public education and support from the agricultural community. Today, very few people, if any, want to see the demise of agriculture and the development of open spaces. Farmers say they are sad to see houses instead of corn or pasture. A developer said it made him sick to look at all the land being developed non-contiguous to the municipalities, and nearly everyone agrees that a future of widescale development for Waukesha County is unpleasant at best. Therefore, there is strong public desire to preserve agriculture, but most residents feel powerless to do so.

Waukesha County desperately needs a leader who can convert the widespread desire to save agricultural lands into public action. The county and township governments are not willing to assume this leadership. Therefore, a group of private citizens will have to take the initiative. This group of citizens will need to educate themselves and the general public about the social, environmental and economic costs of sprawl, the community benefits of active farming and the public and private partnerships needed to secure the future of their county that they truly prefer.

### References

Gould, W. 1996. Suburban sprawl: A creature of the car.
    Milwaukee Journal Sentinel, August 19, p. 5A.
Stevens, J. 1996. Town: Nix ag land from Plan. Lake County
    Reporter, January 4, p. 17.

# Case 12

## Protecting Minnesota's Farmland: Lessons from the Fields

*Michael Pressman, The Land Stewardship Project's 1000 Friends of Minnesota Program*

The non-profit Land Stewardship Project (LSP) began in 1982 as an organization dedicated to fostering an ethic of stewardship toward farmland in the Midwest. It grew out of a rural humanities education program, known as the American Farm Project. Having just celebrated its 15th year, LSP is actively working on a variety of projects focusing on farmland protection and sustainable agriculture.

From LSP's first days, it has been a leader in the sustainable farming movement in the Midwest. Through a variety of cultural, educational, organizing, and policy programs, LSP has worked closely with farmers, community organizers, legislators, agency staff, and the media to widely promote and apply the concepts of sustainable agriculture. LSP staff members have gained a reputation for being effective facilitators and respected policy advocates.

Currently, LSP's farmland protection work includes strengthening the recently passed Community-Based Planning Act, which provides a statewide framework of 11 sustainable development goals to guide local planning. Simultaneously, LSP is leading a coalition of seven private and public organizations to develop a Green Corridor through two counties in the Twin Cities

Metropolitan area. During the next several years, LSP's farmland protection work will include making the Community-Based Planning Act a successful and effective framework for local planning. We will also work to implement proactive land conservation projects that help communities to identify lands that need to be protected and give land owners new incentive-based options besides subdivisions and strip malls.

## Making Land Use Planning Part of the Public Dialogue

Building on its work in sustainable farming, LSP saw the need for dedicated efforts to protect our rapidly diminishing farmland. This work began in the 1980s with its Farmland Preservation program, motivated by *"Turn Here Sweet Corn,* a video essay about food, farming, and the land...just before the shopping mall arrives." This was the first time LSP took the issue of farmland loss on the road—an approach that was so successful that it has guided its work ever since.

As the Farmland Preservation program continued, LSP began developing effective models for growth management, including strengthening the Metropolitan Agricultural Preserves Act to protect farmers from all urban services assessments. LSP also launched the Minnesota Land Trust (a statewide land trust with local chapters working to protect open space through the use of conservation easements), successfully urged passage of a local cropland preservation ordinance in a rapidly urbanizing St. Paul suburb, and built momentum for statewide growth management legislation. Throughout its work, LSP used a highly effective combination of community organizing, education, policy work, and advocacy. LSP's unique blend and style of work was well displayed when hundreds of local residents attended a rally, press conference, and prayer of care and stewardship for the land to protest the proposed annexation of a fourth generation farm to the City of Stillwater on the fringes of the Twin Cities metropolitan area.

With momentum growing behind its work, LSP broadened its metro farm focus to incorporate a variety of land use issues throughout the state. As part of this work, LSP created a national Telly award winning video, *"Houses in the Fields,"* which featured singer-songwriter, John Gorka, and told the story of the urban-

ization of Minnesota's farmland. LSP continued to develop policy
initiatives to protect farmland including strengthening the Metropolitan Agriculture Preserves Program and helping to establish
the Governor's Sustainable Development Task Force. LSP's learning curve on land-use issues increased dramatically after joining
the National Growth Management Leadership Project (NGMLP).
LSP also started the Minnesota Environmental Fund, a workplace
giving program designed to help broaden funding for Minnesota's
environmental community.

Through this and other work, LSP achieved its goal of moving
farmland conversion, suburban sprawl, and land use issues into
the public eye. To enhance its growth management efforts, LSP
began its 1000 Friends of Minnesota program to implement new
visions and tools to help achieve a sustainable future for Minnesota. One of 1000 Friends' first projects was a Cost of Community
Services Study for three metro suburbs that showed how residential land uses require more in government services than they contribute in tax revenues, while farmland and other open space
uses contribute roughly twice the amount of tax dollars that they
receive in services. This analysis has been instrumental in getting
communities to rethink their costly and ineffective strategy of
"increasing the tax base" through residential development.

## Turning Public Concern Into Effective Policy

Much of the work of LSP's 1000 Friends of Minnesota program
(and the various programs that preceded it) culminated with the
1997 passage of the Community-Based Planning Act (CBPA). For
1000 Friends, the CBPA is the policy implementation arm of all of
its work on community education, local organizing, and advocacy
around land use planning issues. It builds on the notion that protecting our farmland, natural areas, and other open spaces requires solid land use planning and the creation and maintenance
of livable communities that discourage sprawl. By passing the
CBPA, Minnesota joined an elite group of states, including Oregon, Florida, New Jersey, and Vermont that have enacted laws to
bring consistency and predictability to local comprehensive planning efforts.

The CBPA sets forth a new incentive-based planning framework
that integrates statewide sustainable development principles into

local comprehensive plans and provides financial and technical assistance for planning. The law lays out 11 goals that define the basic framework for community-based plans. These goals address the long-term interest of the state in responding to growth and change. The law requires that communities participating in the program actively involve citizens in the planning process and cooperate with neighboring communities and all units of government. It also created an 18-member Advisory Council to recommend policy changes to flesh out the act.

There are five key components to the bill:

- **Voluntary:**  Local planning under the CBPA is entirely voluntary. One responsibility of the CBPA Advisory Council is to develop a set of incentives to encourage communities to plan under the Act. In the long run, LSP's 1000 Friends of Minnesota believes that if the CBPA is to succeed, all counties in the state should plan under the Act. This belief is borne out by other states that have implemented similar legislation.

- **Funding:**  If a community chooses to complete a plan under the CBPA, the state will provide funding and technical assistance to the community. The state benefits when communities create sound, citizen-supported comprehensive plans, so the state is willing to provide resources to make that happen.

- **State Goals:**  The heart of the CBPA is the 11 goals for comprehensive planning, which provide guidelines for planning throughout Minnesota. The goals are intentionally broad, to allow for flexibility within the diverse situations found in counties throughout the state.

- **Citizen Participation:**  The CBPA Advisory Council created criteria for citizen participation in local planning that involves community members throughout the process, not just at the required public hearings. A critical objective of the CBPA is to get citizens active in planning for the future of their community.

- **Enforcement:**  Once a community has completed its plan and shared it with adjoining communities, the plan is sent to the State's Office of Strategic and Long Range Planning (Minnesota Planning) for review and comment on its consistency with the 11 goals. If the plan is found to be inconsistent, the community may make the suggested changes or enter into binding dispute resolution with the state. If the community chooses to ignore Minnesota Planning's comments, it may still implement the plan, but must return funding to the state.

The 11 goals of the CBPA include:

1. Citizen Participation
2. Cooperation
3. Economic Development
4. Conservation
5. Livable community design
6. Housing
7. Transportation
8. Land-Use Planning
9. Public Investments
10. Public Education
11. Sustainable Development

The Act also designated funds for four pilot projects that will help flesh out the details of the Act while addressing critical planning needs for targeted communities. Interest in the CBPA is evidently quite high as competition for the planning grants among counties was strong.

Within four months of their appointment, the CBPA Advisory Council held 24 meetings around the state to solicit public input. Throughout that time, 1000 Friends was actively organizing in local communities, getting the word out, and promoting participation in the Advisory Council meetings. More than 1,000 citizens attended the meetings. In spite of the vast differences among the many regions of Minnesota, several common themes emerged from the meetings:

- *Communities realize that planning is a powerful and effective tool to manage growth.* Even in places where planning has been likened to socialism, there are signs that more and more people understand the value of strong comprehensive

planning. More than that, they understand the importance
of and difficulty in implementing a plan.

- *Citizen involvement and cooperation are by far the most
  important goals and they are also the most difficult to achieve.*
  There was common agreement that if citizens are not involved in a meaningful way, the Community-Based Planning
  Act is doomed to failure. Equally critical is achieving true
  cooperation among the counties, cities, and townships that
  implement planning.

- *Minnesota's changing demographics are generating widespread concern for affordable housing, transportation, and
  livable wages.* While greater Minnesota's elderly population
  is growing, its youth are leaving to seek higher paying jobs in
  the metro area.

- *People are concerned with the destruction of Minnesota's
  natural resources and the future of agriculture.* How can we
  balance economic development with natural resource protection? Local units of government, seeking that elusive tax
  dollar, find that they are degrading the natural resources
  that are the very reason for their economic growth, be it the
  agricultural land of southern and western Minnesota, or the
  lakes and forests of the north and east.

## Proactive Conservation Planning

LSP's 1000 Friends of Minnesota recognizes that for policy initiatives such as the Community Based Planning Act to be successful, they must result in and be complemented by
on-the-ground local efforts to protect natural resources and promote responsible growth. In recognition of this, the Land Stewardship Project spearheaded an effort to create a Green Corridor
of permanently protected natural areas, farmland, and other open
spaces in two rapidly suburbanizing counties on the eastern
fringe of the Twin Cities Metropolitan region.

A coalition of seven public and private organizations led by LSP,
The Green Corridor Project is dedicated to helping Washington
and Chisago County residents keep the beautiful countryside,
farmland, and special natural areas that make them a great place

to live. Green corridors are areas of open spaces that are linked together throughout the community. In addition to retaining important open spaces, green corridors protect water quality, maintain scenic and rural character, provide wildlife habitat, and help ensure that we have productive farms for future generations. Around the Midwest and throughout the country, green corridors have worked to help communities keep their valuable farmland and other open spaces while accommodating growth. Communities from Massachusetts and Michigan to Colorado and Oregon have used green corridors to protect important open spaces while improving the appeal of neighborhoods and supporting their long term tax base.

LSP began working on this initiative in 1996. The State of Minnesota recognized the value of this innovative approach to protecting open space and awarded the coalition a $500,000 grant to develop the project. LSP also received important funding from the McKnight Foundation and the Carolyn Foundation. Other members of the coalition are: Chisago County, Minnesota Farmers Union, Minnesota Land Trust, Rural Community Initiative, The Trust for Public Land, and Washington County.

The Green Corridor Project will link already protected lands with other important open spaces in Washington and Chisago Counties. Extensive input from local residents, public officials, and government agency staff is being sought to help shape the corridor's location and composition.

Currently, the coalition is undertaking a land base inventory to identify areas that should be protected, developing educational resources, conducting a public survey on financing options for land protection, researching similar programs around the country, and developing a handbook for local officials and staff. During the next year and a half, the coalition will work closely with local communities to help implement new programs and tools to make the Green Corridor a success.

As part of the project's outreach efforts, more than forty public meetings will be held within the project area and around the state. The Washington and Chisago County meetings will provide the coalition with an excellent opportunity to engage local residents in designing the project. The statewide meetings will be used to introduce new, incentive-based tools for land protection that can be applied in other communities as well.

## Tools to Keep Open Spaces

Four voluntary, innovative tools will be the primary mechanisms used to create the Green Corridor. The first three tools—*Donated Conservation Easements, PDR,* and *TDR*—are **voluntary** programs in which participants retain ownership and control of their land. They can sell or transfer their property at any time, but a conservation easement permanently protects the land from development. The land remains affordable for open space uses such as agriculture because it is appraised at its open space value. The fourth tool, *Land Acquisition,* gives landowners a way to **voluntarily** sell or donate their land to city, township, county, or state government.

**Donated Conservation Easements** are voluntary, legal agreements between a landowner and a land trust or government agency that allow property owners to permanently limit or prohibit development on their property. Conservation easements run with the title so that all future owners of the land are bound by the original agreement.

**Purchased Development Rights (PDR)** are voluntary, legal agreements that allow owners of land meeting certain criteria to sell the right to develop their property to township, city, county, or state government, or to a nonprofit organization. A conservation easement is then placed on the land. This agreement is recorded on the title to limit the future use of the land to agriculture or other open space uses.

**Transferred Development Rights (TDR)** are enabled by local or regional ordinance. TDR ordinances create a *sending area*, or preservation area and a *receiving*, or high density *area*. Landowners in the sending area receive *development right credits*, which they can sell in exchange for not developing their land. Real estate developers can then purchase *development right credits* and use them to increase existing or planned densities in receiving areas.

**Land Acquisition** is used in select cases when willing landowners want to conserve their land by selling or donating it outright to a public agency. This mechanism allows a government entity to have full control of a property's future.

The project has been a natural fit for the communities in the Green Corridor Project area. During the last several years, as public debate rose about land use, sprawl, and the loss of farmland and natural areas, several community concerns emerged. Residents have consistently demonstrated their desire to protect the landscape that is key to their quality of life while encouraging responsible growth. The Green Corridor Project has demonstrated that it is possible to simultaneously achieve these goals. In so doing, it has begun to bring together seemingly disparate members of the community to focus on shared objectives and to create new, incentive-based tools to help protect their landscape. Throughout this work, the coalition is focusing on facilitating the community's vision. We are working hard to give the community ownership of this project. We have received widespread support for our open, community-based approach.

The Legislative Commission on Minnesota Resources made it clear in their appropriation that they view the Green Corridor Project as an important pilot project for the entire state. LSP sees it as another important way to demonstrate that there are win-win strategies that can help communities keep their important farmland and other open spaces while accommodating growth.

## Learning All Along the Way

Throughout the course of its work on public education and building momentum behind land use issues, LSP learned some vital lessons:

- **Make it local:** With limited free time and dollars, people are most concerned with issues that affect them locally. By focusing on how statewide issues affect local communities, LSP has helped to develop an impassioned, educated, and energized constituency.

- **Be persistent:** Keep your eyes on the prize. Five years ago, LSP members were being called 'communists' and 'tree huggers.' And in that short span of time, many rural community leaders have embraced the need for community-based land use planning.

- **Good ideas have a way of moving fast:** When LSP began a
  series of public forums in January 1997 to begin to develop a
  statewide framework for local land use planning, it had no
  idea that the legislature would pass a bill within four
  months. To accomplish this, LSP had to give up 'ownership'
  of the framework much sooner than anticipated and be able
  to consistently adapt to changing situations. The speed of
  legislative decision-making can often seem frantic to those
  who value careful, deliberate, grassroots policy development.

- **Good organizing, public accountability, and public humil-
  ity can lead to pressure to make change:** With so much
  important work occurring, it's impossible to be everywhere at
  once. Local activists are key components to successful
  campaigns and programs. Many would-be activists are
  craving information on how to run meetings, set an agenda,
  and get media attention. By training activists and effectively
  using the media, public exposure and scrutiny can be
  wielded as a powerful tool for change.

- **Make your work open, professional, and broad based:**
  Part of the appeal of LSP's programs is that we approach
  them in the role of community facilitator. LSP wants to
  create dialogue and help people of divergent viewpoints
  create common solutions. It constantly seeks to appeal to
  diverse audiences and reach out to a broad array of community players. All of LSP's programs have a very professional
  approach and it strives to have everyone feel that they are a
  valued participant whose ideas are respected and incorporated into the work.

- **Draw on the links among issues:** One of the successes of
  the Community-Based Planning Act was its ability to address
  diverse local issues in a context of statewide goals. In organizing around the issue, LSP highlighted the links among
  urban blight, concentrated inner-city poverty, 'white flight,'
  suburban sprawl, farmland loss, destruction of natural
  areas, traffic congestion, air quality, and quality of life. LSP
  tried to show people how their local issues were intimately
  tied to issues of statewide concern and worked with them to
  develop solutions that promoted statewide values in a way
  that encouraged and respected local flexibility.

## The Larger Picture—Putting It All Together

The goal of LSP's 1000 Friends of Minnesota program is to encourage sustainable development patterns that conserve farmland, forests, and natural resources and promote healthy, livable communities. This goal envisions a sustainable landscape where finite natural resources are protected, cities are vital and livable, and all citizens have access to clean air, water, and soil, as well as food, jobs, and housing. In this goal, the cities do not sprawl into the countryside but are concentrated around existing infrastructure and offer transportation alternatives to the automobile. Planning and zoning would be done locally under the umbrella of a statewide policy framework with common goals that had been developed by the people of Minnesota.

Achieving this goal requires work at a variety of levels. An integrated approach to natural resource conservation and land use planning incorporates the five elements of policy, planning, implementation, monitoring, and enforcement. Work in these areas should address environmental, social, and economic issues in an integrated program that includes land protection, growth management, community development, and transportation. It must also be applied across the rural to urban spectrum and address issues and initiatives from the local to the statewide level, and occasionally include national policy and international issues as well.

Such a broad-based program can seem intimidating. It certainly would have seemed so to the few, dedicated individuals that decided to put together a video entitled *Turn Here Sweet Corn* back in 1990. At that time, no one would have thought that in seven years LSP would have initiated a statewide framework for local land use planning. None could have predicted that within several short years LSP would be uniting seemingly disparate interests to develop a Green Corridor. Back then, a few good folks decided to do something about their concerns about the loss of farmland. They got together, picked a few achievable tasks, developed some creative programs that brought the message to the hearts and minds of local citizens, and got to work. During the past decade it has become clear to many people throughout Minnesota from the urban city council member to the suburban homeowner to the farmer in the Red River Valley that sprawl is not good. Through projects like the CBPA and the Green Corridor, LSP is proving that it is also not inevitable.

# Case 13

## Lincoln, Nebraska, Public School Systems: The Advance Scouts for Urban Sprawl

*W. Cecil Steward, Dean, College of Architecture, University of Nebraska*

There is a Chinese fable that cautions, "Be careful what you wish for, it may come true." The "garden city" planners and Frank Lloyd Wright's sub-urban planning concept, "broad acres," gave Americans of the industrial revolution era images of the detached, single family frame house, with a private car in every driveway, sitting in the midst of lush green gardens, connected neighbor-to-neighbor by tree-lined paved streets—and all in sight of (or at least within short walking distance of) their childrens' pastoral haven for recreation, knowledge, and social values (where they would be taught by others). Since then, and continuing now, the image of the public school, as the center of America's image of a utopian, better future, has given almost reverent power to public school planners to control the form and future of our cities. This case study, from planning/development activities in Lincoln, Nebraska, supports the premise that the public school system in environments of moderate-to-intense population growth is the most influential planning entity, either public or private, promoting the proto-typical sprawl pattern of American cities.

Lincoln is a middle-sized, capitol city in the agricultural heartland of the United States. Since about 1965 it has experienced moderate, to recently accelerating growth, of approximately 1.5% per year, to reach its current population of more than 200,000 residents. During this period the city's jurisdictional limits have grown from 41.36 square miles to today's area of 69.45 square miles. In the same period the facilities owned and operated by the Lincoln Public Schools (LPS) have increased from three high schools, seven middle schools, one center, and 28 elementary schools, to the present inventory of four high schools, ten middle schools, three centers, and 37 elementary schools. The facilities manager for the LPS reports that the system also currently owns "about one dozen" vacant sites to accommodate planning for "potential" future facilities. The majority of these sites have been selected with elementary school requirements in mind, at an average size of approximately 25 acres each.

The city is currently debating the need and feasibility of a specific route for an outer-ring highway "beltway," which would force (and accommodate) growth on the south and eastern quadrants of the city. According to the city's comprehensive plan, these new developments would be primarily of the single-family, detached frame housing type, marketed by the developers for middle-to-upper income sales. Thus, the majority of the LPS land purchases have, not by coincidence, been consummated in these two quadrants, and in the area between the current city limits and the proposed locations of the belt-way right-of-way. Where prime farmland would be priced at around $1,500 to $2,000 per acre in the surrounding county, the school system is paying $15,000 to $25,000 per acre for these edge sites.

It has become standard practice for the school system planners to attempt "to anticipate future growth directions of the city." And, to be the first to acquire developable property in key locations, in advance of other development interests. Their criteria for selection and purchase are not dissimilar from the private developer's interests. The school system wants the best location at the cheapest price; they want good topographic features, such as adequate drainage, buildable terrain, stable soil, and flexible orientation of building and playground sites on the "campus;" they also want good vehicular access, and assurance from the city of inexpensive access to city utilities and publicly maintained infrastructure.

The director of planning for the City of Lincoln acknowledges early and frequent sessions with the school system to discuss the above parameters during the school's bond planning and site selection process. On more than one occasion, the site selected by the school system has led to changes, and/or acceleration of the city's capital improvements planning and expenditures for infrastructure, such as sanitary sewers, water mains, and/or street and thoroughfare extensions.

Immediately behind (or in some cases, parallel to) the school system's planning will be one, or more, private developers with the same "lowest cost, highest value" objectives on the as-yet undeveloped edges of the city. It is not uncommon for these common interests to become overlapping and interactive, and for negotiations to be conducted between the developer and the school system for "win-win" trading of property parcels, development costs, and the formation of "informal" coalitions to influence the plans of the city. Two recent new school sites, for instance, were acknowledged to have been moved three times each, before the "trading and negotiations" were finalized with the final developer-of-record for the surrounding suburban neighborhoods.

While the city's planning and administration staffs are making significant efforts to carry out joint (or "trilateral") planning in the best interests of the public, such as coordination of schools; trails, parks and recreation facilities; and public access accommodations, the policy and practices of school system planning is a "growth at the edges" strategy. This strategy, however, (in the absence of a "central city reinvestment" strategy for revitalization of older schools and neighborhoods) places the local school system in the enviable position of always being able to predict the outcome of its own self-fulfilling prophecy—"we had to build here, because the new families will demand it."

We now have what we have wished for—wonderful new schools and neighborhoods (some of which we can no longer afford; some of which we cannot protect and make safe from ourselves; some of which have no convenient access to the services of the city; and within some, neither "neighborliness," nor "spirit of community" can be found)—while the vitality of our city's center is bled dry by the relentless blade at the edges.

# Case 14

## Antelope Commons: Building on the Border between Urban and Rural

*Alexander Maller, University of Nebraska, Lincoln, Nebraska*

One March evening in my sophomore year I was sitting alone in my room after supper. There had been a warm thaw all day, with mushy yards and little streams of dark water gurgling cheerfully into the streets out of old snow-banks. My window was open, and the earthy wind blowing through made me indolent. On the edge of the prairie, where the sun had gone down, the sky was turquoise blue, like a lake, with gold light throbbing in it. Higher up, in the utter clarity of the western slope, the evening star hung like a lamp suspended by silver chains—like the lamp engraved upon the title-page of old Latin texts, which is always appearing in new heavens, and waking new desires in men.

— Willa Cather, *My Antonia*

People moving to the Great Plains of the American Midwest may find the place a last frontier: a place you reach coming back from the vibrant ocean fronts, a place to be rediscovered and settled, a place to relax and stay, the Heartland of America. One of these places is Lincoln, the capital of the State of Nebraska. The city embodies most of the urges and dreams of the new residents: a comfortable community with a well-balanced economy, an above average public school system, a large state university and several smaller private colleges, reasonably compact in its territorial distribution and surrounded by a pastoral rural context.

This attractive setting and its livable conditions are the city's strengths, but ironically, the city's attractiveness to potential residents presents a major threat to its ability to sustain these very livable conditions. The city population is currently growing at an accelerating pace and has recently exceeded 200,000. Future growth can take one of two forms:

1. an explosive suburban development sprawling into the surrounding county, with its dreams and paradoxical illusions of "urban villages;" or

2. an energetic intensification of the urban development inside the existing city limits.

Lincoln is at a crossroads. Its future will be determined by decisions made in the coming years. These decisions, political as they always are, will be inspired and influenced by ideas the professional community can provide and should advocate. This case study describes a set of ideas for a mixed residential development on the urban/rural border: Antelope Commons.

One of the key positions adopted by Antelope Commons' design and development team[1] was a respect for the vulnerability of the adjacent farmland and rural living conditions. The main objective of the project, the need to provide community-oriented living conditions integrated with local ecological features and circumstances, was developed to respond to the special location of the site. The project proposes to address this concern by establishing a clear boundary between metropolitan development and its rural context. The design team believed that the border should be clear, coherent and poignantly expressed in terms of its urban content and form, yet friendly, in its performance and appearance, to its rural vicinity.

## Reading the Site

For three generations, the Antelope Commons site has been used as a nursery by Nebraska Nurseries. One legacy of this use is a broad inventory of existing trees. The site is nearly 70 acres and is part of a 2,000-acre subarea drainage basin whose prominent feature is Holmes Lake, located in the center of a major recreation park of Lincoln. To the north, the site is bordered by Pioneers Boulevard, an east-west artery that serves as a three mile long local connector between neighborhoods in the southern part of Lincoln. The northern side of Pioneers Boulevard is lined by conventional suburban neighborhoods. To the west, the site shares Antelope Creek with another suburban residential scheme sprawling out into the southern neighboring area. The eastern border coincides with the city limit. Across this border lies an unannexed acreage area with lots varying between one and two acres.

Antelope Commons is located in the core of a metropolitan subarea that is undergoing rapid suburban residential development. The undeveloped sites within this subarea are crossed by small creeks surrounded by trees and other indigenous vegetation. The existing urban development and the emerging conventional suburban developments have not considered natural features as qualitative assets. Those developments have followed the requirements of the zoning ordinances and the legally rigid interpretations provided by the Planning and Public Works Departments and familiar to the typical developer. As a consequence, many of the natural features of sites in the subarea have been bulldozed.

Antelope Commons' design and development team recognized from the beginning the need to preserve and respond to natural features and consider them valuable assets. We recognized that the preservation and enhancement of these features can provide an improved urban ecology, improved living conditions, greater residential appeal, and ultimately a greater economic value.

## Design Principles

The unique edge location of the site in the metropolitan area dictated our consideration of solutions specific to the location. The alternatives considered were:

- to merge into the general suburban profile of the surrounding areas; or

- to accentuate the particular part of the metropolitan fabric
  in which the site was located and mark the "corner edge" of
  the city.

We selected the second option with the intention to emphasize
the clear separation between urban and rural, to let the urban be
urban and the rural be rural, without compromising the qualities
specific to each type of settlement. We also based the design on
our belief that enhancing the urban character of the scheme does
not have to come at the expense of:

- existing natural assets (to the contrary, natural assets have
  a significant role to play in the urban context); and

- the well being of the adjacent developments (to the contrary,
  the intent was to preserve their rural character and reduce
  the tendency to expand the suburban sprawl).

Livable urban development depends on the preservation of
natural resources and, at the same time, needs to be integrated
with private and community needs. The design was intended to
address existing ecological patterns of the region in a responsive
way and to make Antelope Commons an integral part of these
regional patterns.

The rural areas adjacent to Antelope Commons, located outside
the city limits, provide valuable living qualities to current residents. One important attribute of the rural areas is their low density and open spaces. The presence of these attributes in the
immediate vicinity of Antelope Commons will also benefit the new
residents of the development. At the same time, the new qualities
introduced by Antelope Commons are likely to serve the existing
neighborhoods as well. These mutual benefits will be better preserved and enhanced by the Commons' role as an inhabited landmark meant to establish an edge. It was assumed that a
deliberate differentiation between urban and rural, rather than a
blurred transition, would be more suitable for city dwellers. Such
a differentiation better expresses the richness of urban living and
is more effective in preserving rural assets and rural character.

We rejected the conventional suburban sprawl model, agreeing
with those that find living conditions in sprawling suburbia
unsatisfactory, dominated by confinement and conformism.
Conventional sprawl usually relies on maximum land subdivision,

making this type of development uniform and inconspicuous. The extreme dependency of suburbia on the automobile makes its development aggressive toward the natural environment and wasteful in terms of natural resources.[2]

We identified and incorporated a set of territorial design principles into the project that help shape the relationship between the overall scheme and its surrounding areas:

- priority to pedestrians without excluding motored transportation, motored transportation that is brought to a great degree of "calm";[3]

- a congested layout of private lots that encourages accidental encounters between residents;

- an overall density that is below the maximum density required by the zoning ordinance (though residential clusters may be more dense than the maximum, the overall density is reduced by the existence of open common spaces);

- a hierarchy of common spaces that provides a range of common activities and spatial scales from intimate and local to wide communal spaces;

- a certain degree of space obsolescence (Nelson 1957) in the common areas, generates a sense of surprise, change and convenient local character for each common and cluster;

- an overall landscape design that adopts land development practices sensitive to existing ecological features, a consistent integration of mature trees in the layout of private lots and commons, surface drainage and a preference for indigenous vegetation; and

- a set of design guidelines that do not indicate any architectural style, but encourage diversity of individual expression (unexpected and ever changing close and distant views and a unity through diversity limited only by the need to preserve the quantitative limitations of the site's zoning and its ecological attributes).

The scheme is expected to provide a variety of living conditions that balance the comforts of privacy with opportunities to connect

in informal ways. Common open places set the stage for accidental encounters and recreational activities. This diversity will make
the living conditions of this scheme significantly richer than the
suburban "cookie-cutter" lifestyle—no one style, architectural or
social, is promoted. As such we expect that the design approach
adopted in Antelope Commons will make it possible for people of
diverse backgrounds and interests to live harmoniously together.

As part of an organized association, the residents will enjoy the
benefits of the preserved natural resources, commons and community gardens. They will contribute to the maintenance of these
facilities through financial commitments and, for those interested, physical involvement in landscape and management works.
People living in rural areas rarely enjoy these benefits, while suburban dwellers hardly ever have access to them. It might seem
paradoxical, but this scheme, in spite of its urban expression, will
perform more as a pedestrian and socially interconnected community than the pseudo-rural regional developments, sprawling
suburbs, and rural acreages, which are all highly dependent on
automobiles and distance services.

## Proposition

The overall scheme is designed to create a medium density, low
to medium height, mixed residential development that includes
recreational and local commercial services. The Lincoln planning
authorities approved 365 dwelling units and 35,000 square feet of
commercial area. The common areas make up 40% of the total site
area. Approximately 50% of the dwellings are single residences,
with the rest distributed between rowhouses and apartment houses.

The design of the development is divided into three components
(Figure C14.1):

1. The eastern component, which includes a sequence of one
   and two floor single and duplex residential clusters placed
   along both sides of the continuation of 80th Street, called the
   Boulevard;

2. the western part, which includes three clusters of two-floor
   residential row houses; and

3. the northern part consisting of multiple midrise dwellings placed along the border with Pioneers Boulevard.

The three parts will enclose a main commons. The massing of the residential clusters of the scheme around the commons, in a rather condensed manner, enables the neighborhood to develop a visible but not obtrusive urban form. The perforated urban mass is filled with clusters and screens of trees. Nebraska Nurseries, the owner and developer of the site, has initiated the reconstruction of the portion of Antelope Creek that forms the southern and southwestern boundaries of the development into wetlands. The wetlands provide a rich recreation area for the development including two interpretative centers, a segment of the city-wide bike trail, and a boardwalk along a portion of the waterfront. The wetlands are also a major filtering device for the drainage basin.

This infill of the urban fabric with natural material is meant to create a comfortable balance between buildings and landscape, without losing the visual cohesiveness of the development. The enhanced physical cohesiveness of the scheme is expected to enable it to perform as a cohesive community and as an urban anchor which establishes, in visual and tangible terms, the southeastern corner of the city.

The eastern border between Antelope Commons and the acreages appears to be a rigid line in the plan. However, we sought a more elaborate definition of this border. Using a diversified pattern of lot positioning along the border, different setbacks, the preservation and enhancement of the existing tree resources, and a variety of building designs and orientations, the border will become an articulated built front. This mix is intended to generate a jointed screen, providing depth and diversity in its physical expression, visually permeable and conducive to friendly "across the fence" contacts.

Pioneers Boulevard, which runs parallel to the northern border, has been designated in Lincoln's comprehensive plan to become an artery connecting neighborhoods between the southwestern and southeastern corners of Lincoln, with a permissible maximum speed of 45 miles per hour. We believe that this artery should not become a traffic commuter corridor, but instead develop as a real Boulevard; a place for people to be and enjoy the public and commercial activities that will take place along its sidewalks and the

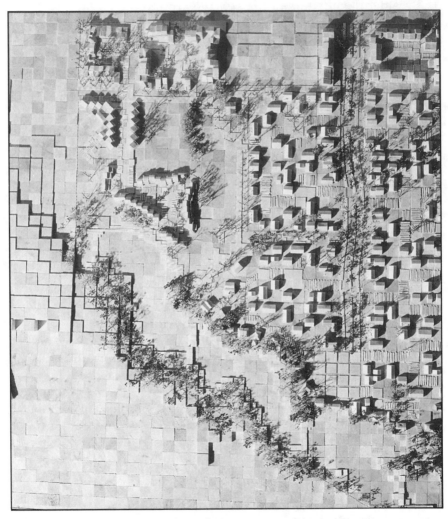

N

Figure C14.1  Overall view of the Antelope Commons model. The reconstructed wetlands and creek lie southeast to northwest along the southern boundary of the development. On the western side of the development, the Main Common is bounded by row houses, single and duplex residences, and commercial space. The eastern portion of the model shows a treed boulevard flanked by clusters of residences each centered on their own commons.

existing and future street vegetation. The area of Antelope Commons bordering Pioneers Boulevard is designed to respond to this intent. Other parts of the Boulevard, to the west of Antelope Commons, already include several new commercial centers. The question remains whether the city, as part of its road improvement plan, will recognize the merit of the living qualities an inhabited Boulevard can offer or will persist in implementing its current preference for speeding cars and concrete surfaces. A commuters' corridor will create a divisive and hostile no-man's-land that separates and alienates the adjacent parts of the community. Such conditions are already evident along similar corridors in other parts of Lincoln.

The commercial center located on the northwestern corner of Antelope Commons will be integrated with the residential uses by including residences on the second floor of its southern wing and by extending its commercial activities to the east, into the ground floor of the adjacent multiple dwelling. In spatial terms, the center will participate in the shaping of a common open space, a town square enclosed on its other edges by mixed residential and commercial buildings and a parallel sequence of row housing.

## Conclusion

This case study describes the design developed for the Antelope Commons residential scheme in Lincoln, Nebraska. The design emphasizes the relationship between the new development and the adjacent suburban neighborhoods and rural vicinity. It also incorporates and in some cases enhances existing natural features such as streams and trees. Clustering of dwellings around common areas, the inclusion of commercial space as part of the development, and a design that favors pedestrians rather than automobiles will all serve to foster a sense of community among the residents. We believe that the successful implementation of this design will enable Antelope Commons to generate and sustain outstanding urban living conditions for its residents and help preserve the mutually rewarding relationship between urban and rural settings.

382    Under the Blade

## Endnotes

1. The design and development team included: (1) developer
and project manager Richard Speidell, President of Nebraska
Nurseries; (2) urban planning and design team leaders and
coordinators, Arch. K. Dubas and Arch. A. Maller; (3) traffic engineers Kirkham Michael & Assoc.; (4) road and utilities engineer,
Ehrhart, Griffin & Assoc.; (5) landscape designer, Nebraska Nurseries; and (6) initial land surveyors, H.W.S. Lincoln.

2. We also considered and rejected the regional urbanization
model proposed by Benton MacKaye (1962) and promoted by
R. Yaro, R. Arendt, H.L. Dodson and E.A. Brabec (1988). This
idea, attractive as it might appear initially, encourages the evolution of suburban sprawl, penetrates the natural reserves and
later takes over in its full brutality. The resulting developments,
adapted to accommodate an increasing demand, will begin to cut
into the natural reservation and farmland. As such, this process,
by camouflaging its subversive intentions, is bound to destroy
natural resources more effectively from within. In the long term,
this process of urbanization will fail to sustain the initial qualities
of the original scheme, lose its community cohesiveness and deteriorate into a highly uncontrollable sprawling mass that will consume any available land. Therefore, we actually consider the
MacKaye model a suburban sprawl in disguise and therefore
more dangerous than conspicuous conventional sprawl.

3. "Traffic calming" is a current, commonly held notion that
describes means to increase traffic safety by reducing automobile
speed. The model we adopted and developed in Antelope Commons is based on the principle that residential areas with mixed
motor and pedestrian traffic and a deliberate preference for the
pedestrian are achievable if (a) the need is clearly indicated by
traffic signage and regulations, and (b) the physical urban setting, its landscape and urban architecture are designed to promote this goal. In Antelope Commons, all cluster commons
operate as mixed traffic environments. Limited traffic also crosses
the main common. Through the highly articulated spatial design
and road pattern of the commons, including the Boulevard (88th
Street), drivers are prevented from elevating their speed and are
made aware of the presence of pedestrians. In time we hope and
expect that the diverse and elaborated architecture of buildings
and landscape will encourage residents to walk in the neighborhood rather than drive.

# References

MacKaye, B. 1962. The New Exploration: A Philosophy of Regional Planning. University of Illinois Press, Urbana.

Nelson, C. 1957. Problems of Design, Whitney Publishers, New York.

Yaro, R.D., R. Arendt, H.L. Dobson, and E.A. Brabec. 1988. Dealing with Change in the Connecticut River Valley: A Design Manual for Conservation and Development. University of Massachusetts, Amherst, MA.

# Case 15

## Land Use Conflicts Between Poultry Production and Residential Development in Northwest Arkansas

*Allen H. Olson, National Center for Agricultural Law Research and Information*

### Land Use Conflicts

Northwest Arkansas leads the nation in poultry production. Washington and Benton Counties are in turn the two largest poultry producing counties in the region. In 1995, Washington County farmers raised 111,836,000 broilers and 3,133,000 turkeys, while Benton County farmers produced 130,145,000 broilers and 2,915,000 turkeys. Several million additional birds were maintained in table egg production and hatchery supply flocks.[1]

Northwest Arkansas has also produced a bumper crop of houses. It is the fastest growing region in the state, and eighth fastest in the country.[2] Between 1980 and 1996, the combined population of Washington and Benton Counties rose from 178,609 to 260,849, a 68% increase. Approximately 50,000 people have been added to the region since 1990.

People and poultry are now competing for the same land. Poultry houses can be found within a few yards of new subdivisions, and conflicts occur between the two land uses. Homeowners complain of odor and noise from poultry facilities, and worry that poultry waste will contaminate their water supplies and that air-borne particles will cause or aggravate respiratory conditions.

Farmers must deal with their neighbors' complaints and also with increased theft and vandalism. Traffic from the new subdivisions makes it more difficult to move farm vehicles on the public roads. Trespass is an increasing problem as subdivision dwellers on small lots use the farmers' land for outdoor recreation. Farmers worry that complaints by neighbors will result in increased regulation of their agricultural activities by state and local agencies.

Other poultry facilities are bulldozed as farmers sell to developers, furthering the expansion of the region's cities into the countryside. In some cases, these farmers are simply tired of dealing with the land use conflicts. In others, the farmers are cashing in on escalating land prices. The developer's offer is simply too good to turn down. The result is the same in either case; the land is permanently taken out of agricultural production.

Poultry production is a $421.8 million per year industry in Northwest Arkansas.[3] The region is home to several of the country's largest processors such as Tysons, Hudson Foods and Cargill. The industry employs tens of thousands of people at its many levels. As the region's population continues to grow, land use conflicts between poultry production and residential development will increase.

The poultry industry is vertically integrated. In broiler production, the processors own the birds and contract with farmers to raise the birds to slaughter size. The processors deliver chicks to the farmer's broiler houses and deliver feed for the birds throughout the production cycle. When the birds reach the proper weight, the processors send trucks and laborers to the farm to retrieve the birds and deliver them to processing plants. The farmers clean out the broiler houses at least once a year, disposing of the litter by land application, often on the farms where the birds are raised. The litter fertilizes crop and pasture land, but may contaminate streams and groundwater if applied in too great a quantity or too close to stream banks.

The majority of processing plants and processor-owned feed mills in Northwest Arkansas are located along the Highway 71 corridor running north from Fayetteville to the Missouri line. Rail service is available in this corridor. Residential development is also concentrated along this corridor, and as development continues, poultry production will be pushed eastward and westward. This will increase the processors' transportation costs for birds and feed. With the exception of Highway 412 going west toward Oklahoma, east-west roads in Northwest Arkansas are generally limited to two lanes, and drivers must negotiate tight curves on the hilly terrain.

There are limits to how far processors can travel to service farmers before they are forced to relocate processing plants and feed mills. Ultimately, less land will be available for poultry production, and processors will either have to reduce production in the region or increase the amount of production on the remaining farms. Higher levels of production will exacerbate waste disposal problems. More waste will have to be applied per acre with the potential for environmental damage and increased complaints by neighbors, or the wastes disposed of off-farm with the attendant higher costs. Both approaches could subject the industry to greater government regulation.

The land use conflicts between poultry production and residential development are largely unregulated in Northwest Arkansas at the present time. Land application of dry poultry waste does not currently require a permit from either the United States Environmental Protection Agency or the Arkansas Department of Pollution Control and Ecology. The Arkansas Right-to-Farm Act, as yet untested in the Arkansas appellate courts, may provide poultry producers with a limited defense against suits by neighboring property owners based on common law nuisance theories. However, no laws have been adopted to reduce land use conflicts by separating poultry production and residential land uses. Neither Washington nor Benton Counties have adopted any form of zoning in their unincorporated areas. Outside of the city limits, no statutes or ordinances prohibit one type of land use from being located next to any other type of land use. Indeed, rural zoning of any type is relatively uncommon in Arkansas.

## Possible Solutions

There is presently little public discussion of solutions to the farmland conversion problem in Northwest Arkansas. Should citizens, local governments and the poultry industry eventually decide to address the issue, they should consider at least two different approaches.

### Agricultural Zoning

Agricultural zoning is a remedy available to local governments in Northwest Arkansas to reduce land use conflicts between poultry production and residential development. By limiting or prohibiting residential development in agricultural zones, these conflicts can be minimized. Fewer households will be affected by odors, noise and waste disposal practices, and farmland will be less likely to be sold for non-agricultural uses. It will be easier to maintain a critical mass of farmland necessary to support the poultry processing infrastructure of the region, and more land will remain available for land application of poultry wastes. This in turn may avoid the need for more stringent regulation of waste disposal.

Section 14-17-206 of the Arkansas Code authorizes counties to adopt a county plan. The plan may address, among other matters, "[t]he conservation of natural resources" and "[a]reas of critical environmental concern" to include "prime agricultural and forestlands." The plan shall "give consideration to protective mechanisms which seek to regulate activities or development therein." Such mechanisms may include "special zoning districts."

Section 14-17-209(a) of the Code then grants counties the authority to enact zoning ordinances to implement the plan. A zoning ordinance may include provisions regulating "open space," "density and distribution of population," and the "uses of land, buildings and structures." The ordinance may provide for "districts of compatible uses" and for "the control and elimination of uses not in conformance with provisions of the ordinance..."

A county that adopts agricultural zoning will most likely also create non-agricultural zones where residential uses are preferred. Commercial and industrial zones may also be designated. New residential development and non-agricultural commercial development will then be directed into the appropriate zones and away from the agricultural zones. The amount of land to be included in each zone will be determined by the County Planning Board and the Quorum Court. The Arkansas statutes require, however, that zoning ordinances be consistent with the adopted county plan (see Chapter 3 for a description of different types of agricultural zoning).

It is unlikely that courts would hold that well-drafted agricultural zoning ordinances, based on sound planning to protect the poultry industry, would cause a taking under the Fifth Amendment to the United States Constitution or under the takings provision of the Arkansas Constitution. Most poultry producers acquired their land for farming purposes. Few will be able to show that their "distinct investment-backed expectations" in acquiring their land were to develop it for residential purposes. Even when this was the case, agricultural zoning proponents could argue that the county's dual interests in protecting an important segment of the region's economy from the adverse effects of residential development and protecting people from excessive exposure to poultry wastes outweigh those expectations.

### Purchase of Development Rights

While agricultural zoning is an option legally in Northwest Arkansas, it may not be an option politically. The public in Arkansas, like in much of the South, tends to show an aversion to land use regulation. If local governments fail to adopt agricultural zoning, the poultry industry should consider funding a purchase of development rights (PDR) program to protect its substantial investment in the area's agriculture.

Each poultry company could pay its contract growers for the development rights on their farmland. In return, the growers would place permanent conservation easements on their properties severely restricting residential and non-agricultural commercial development of the land. The conservation easements would be held and enforced either by a non-profit organization dedicated to that purpose or perhaps by local government agencies (see Chapter 3 for details of PDR programs).

The poultry companies should not hold the easements. This avoids anticompetitive effects that might keep a grower from switching companies. It also prevents companies from trying to sell or terminate easements in an unfavorable economy.

The program would be voluntary, and legal safeguards should be enacted to prevent a poultry company from terminating a contract or refusing to enter into a contract with a grower solely because the grower refused to sell his development rights. However, a company could provide additional contract incentives to farmers whose land is already protected by conservation easements.

Local governments could participate in such a PDR program by providing supplementary funding for purchasing development rights on farms that they have planned for long term agricultural production. This could in turn save local governments millions of dollars in infrastructure costs for these areas. Farmers could use the development rights payments for a variety of purposes including retiring farm debt, buying new equipment, retirement, and funding the inheritance of those of their children who will not continue farming.

PDR programs are expensive, but conservation easements afford permanent protection. Zoning is a much less costly approach, but zoning can be changed at the whim of elected officials.

## Conclusion

Poultry production and processing are major economic engines for Northwest Arkansas. Farmland loss threatens the viability of the industry, and either government or the poultry industries, or preferably both, must act soon if adequate farmland is to be preserved.

## Endnotes

1. Cooperative Extension Service & Arkansas Agricultural Statistics Service, *Arkansas Poultry Production Publication* (June 1996).
2. This ranking is based on growth rates of Washington and Benton Counties from 1990 to 1994. U.S. Census Bureau, Department of Commerce, *Population Estimates of Metropolitan Areas and Large Cities*, Vol. 30, No. 11/12 (Nov./Dec. 1995).
3. This figure is the value added dollar amount for poultry and egg production and poultry processing in Washington and Benton Counties in 1994. Telephone facsimile received from Wayne Miller, Extension Economist-Economic and Community Development, University of Arkansas *citing* data provided by Minnesota IMPLAN Group, Inc. (May 28, 1997).

# Case 16

## Water Fights: Citizens Struggle to Shape a City in Central Texas

*Lauren Ross and Jeanine Sih*
*Glenrose Engineering, Austin, Texas*

This is a story of Barton Springs, the cool, clear, constant flow of water just three miles from the Capitol Building in Austin, in the heart of Texas. It is a story of the Springs and its relationship to the aquifer that feeds it; a story of the dependence of the aquifer upon the natural character of the contributing zone. It is also the story of the Austin community and politics as we fight, compromise, legislate and litigate the rights of land owners, land developers, and the rest of us to preserve that which we love most.

### Barton Springs

Barton Springs is created where part of the Edwards Aquifer discharges its accumulated flow into a natural, 944-foot long swimming pool. The water temperature is 68° F year round. In the summer, the water and its banks are an oasis of natural coolness under the hot Texas sun. In the winter, brave souls, self-described as the "polar bears," show up each day for their rejuvenating dip.

The use and enjoyment of Barton Springs predate the use of air conditioners. Artifacts collected from its banks indicate that the

Springs has been a refuge from summer heat as long as human habitation in Central Texas. Within the memory of some of Austin's oldest citizens, evening summer dances were held on the bank above. A 50-foot wide, 10-foot deep pit, lined with concrete, rigged with steps for seats, and emblazoned with their mascot remains where the Elks created a comfortable summer meeting place. Probably the most famous Barton Springs conversations were those of J. Frank Dobie, Walter Prescott Webb, and Roy Bedichek.

For all of the period of human habitation and about 170,000 years predating our first footsteps here, the Edwards Aquifer and its flow at Barton Springs have been sustained by rainfall runoff on a very particular area of land known as the contributing zone. The contributing zone is the watersheds of 6 creeks: Barton, Williamson, Slaughter, Bear, Little Bear, and Onion, above the outcrop of the Edwards Limestone.

These watersheds that comprise the contributing zone lie across the land west of Austin, part of an area called the Texas Hill Country, which sits between the piney forests of east Texas, the coastal plains, the northern prairies and the western desert, with its own distinctive landscape. The vegetation is dominated by juniper and shrub oak. Grasses are thin. In the era of Lyndon B. Johnson's grandfather Samuel Ealy Johnson, this land supported immense herds of cattle. For a few glorious years (1867–1871), Texas ranchers would drive their herds north to the Abilene, Kansas railhead and return with saddlebags full of gold coins. During this short time span, centuries of accumulated soil were eroded through overgrazing. In the 1870s cotton farmers further over-taxed this soil, until it took 4 acres to yield one bale of cotton.

What remains today through most of the Texas Hill Country is scattered ranching of cattle, goats, and a small number of sheep. Part of the value of the livestock on some properties is the state property tax relief afforded by agricultural exemptions. The native landscape is dotted by small rural communities. Even though the soils are thin, rainfall on this natural landscape is filtered, stored, and slowly released through small springs and tributaries. Within the Barton Springs contributing watersheds, this creek flow accumulates until it crosses the outcrop of the Edwards Limestone.

The Edwards Limestone is what remains of several thousand feet of mostly calcium carbonate materials deposited when shallow, warm seas covered Texas. Sixty-six million years ago, the seas receded and the Edwards Plateau uplifted. Along a line across Texas known as the Balcones Fault Zone, the weight of sediment deposition created large faults and fractures in the Edwards Limestone. Naturally acidic rainwater moved through the fault and fracture openings and began to dissolve the calcium carbonate.

Through millions of years, this dissolution process has created an intricate pattern of sinks, caves, solution openings and honeycombs within the rock. Creek flow moves through openings in the limestone to recharge the karst limestone aquifer known as the Edwards Aquifer. The 354 square mile contributing watershed area recharges an average of 36,000 acre-feet per year into the aquifer.

## Early Efforts to Protect the Springs

Austin's expanding urban sprawl seriously threatens the natural soil, vegetation, and geologic systems that sustain flow at Barton Springs. Where there was nothing but open space 20 years ago, now sits a shopping mall. Where 10 years ago there were only dirt roads, there are now six-lane roadways and residential housing.

More than 20 years ago, Austin citizens began to be concerned about the effects of changes in the landscape on Barton Springs. City staff started monitoring the quality of creek water and urban runoff. Research in the Austin area supported results of similar studies across the country. The change from a landscape of natural soils and vegetation to lawns, buildings, parking lots and roadways profoundly changes the quality of creek water. The single best measure of urbanization to predict creek water quality and flow changes is the amount of impervious cover.

Responding to both the local and national research, Austin began to pass ordinances to protect water quality. The first water quality ordinance, passed in 1979, applied to the watershed of Barton Creek. Barton Creek contributes to the Edwards Aquifer and is closest to the Springs. Between 1979 and 1986, four more water quality ordinances were passed, culminating in the Comprehensive Watersheds Ordinance, which restricted development in all areas within the city limits and extraterritorial jurisdiction. Each of the water quality ordinances was constructed upon the same elements: limits to impervious cover, requirements to leave natural buffers along stream channels, treatment of stormwater runoff, and construction-phase erosion controls.

Despite the passage of these water quality ordinances, Austin citizens continued to worry about the consequences of rapid development near creeks. One source of concern was whether the ordinances would actually preserve the creeks as natural features and habitat. Nowhere in Austin was the concern higher than for the lovely and fragile creeks feeding the Aquifer and Barton Springs. A second worry was the large number of developments that proceeded under "grandfathering" provisions: special exemptions, waivers, exceptions, and variances. Five years after passage of the Comprehensive Watersheds Ordinance, for example, 86% of the development in the interim period had proceeded without complying with its provisions.

The match that ignited this concern into a political firestorm was a proposed 3,363-acre Planned Unit Development by a subsidiary of Freeport MacMoRan. This development was to be built within the Barton Springs contributing zone, on the very edge of the Edwards Limestone outcrop. A City of Austin public hearing to approve development agreements began at 4p.m. on 7 June 1990. The hearing lasted through the night to 6a.m. the next morning. Hundreds of Austin citizens spoke, sang, cried, and read poetry expressing their opposition to this large development and its potential impact on Barton Springs. When the hearing was over, the City Council denied the requested development permits and the next round of debates on the protection of Barton Springs began.

## The Debate Continues

In October 1990, the Council declared a moratorium on the approval of development permits in the Barton Springs contributing and recharge zones. In February 1991, the Council passed an interim ordinance that strictly limited impervious cover and eliminated the exemptions that allowed development to proceed without complying with the earlier ordinances. Three months later, in the last hours of their terms, lame duck City Council members chose not to make the interim ordinance permanent law. The responsibility to pass a permanent ordinance was deferred to the incoming Council.

The incoming mayor created a task force. The Planning Commission held long hearings. Citizens and the engineering and legal communities debated water quality issues in front of civic organizations and in the local news media. Virtually all of Austin's environmental organizations came together to form the Save Our Springs (SOS) Coalition. With sound technical information and astute political advice, SOS kept the fire burning for a strong water quality ordinance. As weeks passed, however, it seemed likely that the protections of the interim ordinance would be compromised in the final ordinance.

The proposed final ordinance would allow the exemptions, exceptions, and variances under which development could proceed without complying with the technical components of Austin's water quality ordinances of the last 12 years. This proposed ordinance also reinstated higher impervious cover limits.

SOS fears were realized when the City Council ratified the final "composite" water quality ordinance for the Barton Springs Zone on 17 October 1991. In the days following passage of the Council's ordinance, SOS drafted its own water quality ordinance, and proposed to pass it by citizen's referendum. If passed by referendum, it would require a vote by 6 out of 7 Council members to amend. Major provisions of the SOS ordinance were simple. This ordinance limited impervious cover to 15% to 25% of the flat areas away from the creeks. It required water quality controls so that the average annual pollutant loads after development would not be more than the estimated loads prior to development. It gave development with existing plan approvals a limited period of time to complete construction. Most significantly, the SOS ordinance eliminated any variances or exemptions to its conditions.

As soon as the ordinance was drafted, petitions were circulated to get it on the ballot. When the required number of signatures was obtained, the city council defied a judicial order to place the ordinance on the 2 May 1992 ballot, and the elections were delayed until 8 August. Between 2 May and 8 August 1992, 248 development applications, compared with 26 in the preceding five months, were filed and exempted from SOS requirements. On 8 August, however, when the votes were counted, Austin citizens overwhelmingly supported the SOS ordinance by a 2-to-1 margin in one of the largest election turnouts in Austin history.

Although SOS was the law, applications filed before its passage allowed development to continue without having to comply with its provisions. Within a few months of its passage, the validity of the ordinance was challenged in a hearing before the Texas Natural Resource Conservation Commission. After months of legal discovery and depositions, opponents of the ordinance withdrew their challenge in the opening moments of the hearing process.

A more serious legal challenge to the SOS ordinance was tried in the Hays County District Court. Most of Austin lies within Travis County, and Hays is the next county south. Hays County is primarily rural and often perceives its interests and perspectives as at odds with its urban neighbor. Although elderly owners of small tracts of land were the featured plaintiffs in the case, their legal fees were paid by representatives of two of the largest developers in Austin: Freeport MacMoRan and the Circle C Corporation. One of Austin's most prominent lawyers, Mr. Roy F. Minton, ably represented the plaintiffs. In December 1993, the court ruled that the SOS ordinance was not valid on every count.

Within days of the ruling, a new, environment-friendly Austin City Council appealed that judicial ruling, and passed another ordinance, attempting to achieve as much water quality protection as possible within the constraints of the ruling. Acting on questionable legal advice from the city's attorney, the City of Austin suspended enforcement of the SOS ordinance, pending the appellate court decision.

## Enter the State

In the next chapter of this saga of Austin's water quality ordinances and their application, enter the Texas Legislature. In 1993 the Legislature, led by representatives of other communities with sizable campaign contributions from Austin's developers, had passed a bill further limiting Austin's authority to regulate development. The bill required the City of Austin to approve development if it complied with ordinances in place at the time of original submittals. Unlike almost every other city in Texas, Austin had simple procedures that allowed original submittals to remain viable projects indefinitely. Because most of the land within its jurisdiction had approved preliminary plats from the boom years in the early 1980s, this bill would have virtually eliminated the application of current ordinances.

The bill limiting Austin's ability to implement its water quality ordinances was vetoed in 1993 by the Democratic Governor Ann Richards. When a similar bill was passed in 1995, however, Republican Governor George Bush signed it into law. A year later, on 30 July 1996, when the appellate court overturned the lower court decision, very little property would have to comply with the once-again-legal SOS ordinance. The 1995 legislature also passed a law allowing owners of tracts of land larger than 1,000 acres to create "water quality protection zones" exempt from Austin zoning, ordinances, or annexation for at least 20 years.

## An Unfinished Story

There are more chapters in the story of the application of the SOS ordinance to protect Barton Springs. In 1997, in a legislative action that has been characterized as an accident, the 1995 bill limiting Austin's powers was repealed. On the effective date of the repealing ordinance, 1 September 1997, one legal interpretation is that all development in Austin requiring any city approvals became subject to the city's current ordinances—including the SOS ordinance. Four days later, on 5 September, the City Council passed an ordinance that allowed developments with existing approvals a window of 18 months to 3 years to be completed under the old standards.

The SOS ordinance is not a perfect tool. Limiting impervious cover on each development site will only slow the sprawl that threatens to engulf the entire rural Hill Country, stretching even beyond Barton Spring's contributing zone. To be effective, Austin must form alliances with neighboring communities. In the absence of authority from the State of Texas to control land use, the City of Austin's only hope is to develop creative ways to voluntarily achieve the goals of its citizens: healthy growth and long-term preservation of cherished natural features.

Certainly the final chapter in this long story between those with interests in land development, and those most interested in preserving Barton Springs and the natural landscape, has yet to be written. The story will continue to involve the city, the state legislature, the Texas Natural Resource Conservation Commission, the judiciary, and the public. In the meantime, we will continue to swim in those chilly waters on misty mornings, sit on the banks discussing diapers and Texas politics, speak up in public hearings, and work to elect politicians who speak for the citizens of Austin and for what we love most.

# Case 17

## Subdividing the Rockies: Ranchland Conversion in the New West

*William E. Riebsame, University of Colorado*

Ranching is both a business and a lifestyle in the Rockies. Besides producing livestock, it accounts for a majority of the region's private open space. Ranching is also an industry struggling for economic survival and social respect, like much of the American farm sector, and facing the pressure of economic change with little help from a citizenry out-of-touch with agricultural issues. Westerners take their open spaces for granted, but rapid population growth and development is changing the look of the landscape—and some of them are noticing it. In addition to the never-ending debates about public lands, the next big land concern in the Rocky Mountain West will center on protecting private ranchlands from development, not so much for food security or local economics, but as a cultural, ecological, and growth management issue.

Throughout the Rocky Mountains, growing demand for residential and commercial land offers ranchers a "golden parachute" out of the squeeze between low returns on investment and the hassle of grazing on the federal lands. They can get some nice cash out of their ranch—something rarely derived from the cattle or sheep business itself. And more ranchers are deciding this is the way either out of ranching or into a big, deeded spread on the Great Plains.

These times are a critical watershed in Western ranching. Federal lands grazing, essential to Rocky Mountain ranches, is under a major policy re-evaluation as Americans demand more recreation and ecological values from the public lands. The private ranchlands are under pressure for development in a landscape more than half of which (the federal lands) is not developable. Westerners face a decision about the future of the rural West: Do we want to support, maybe even "protect" ranching as a way of life, a culture, and as an industry, even in the face of rapid population growth and land value escalation?

This may seem an arrogant question to a rancher, who might prefer if the rest of us had less say in her future, but, for better or worse, "we are all in this together" and Western landscapes, Western towns, and Western ranches will change because of the attitudes and actions of all Americans—their support for environmental protection, their sense of fairness in agricultural policy, their willingness to practice "givings" and "takings" of social values, and their consumption of agricultural products.

## A Land Use Watershed

Sometime in the last two decades, ranchlands in the region, after consolidating into larger and larger units since first agricultural settlement, began to sub-divide (Riebsame et al. 1996). The ski resort boom in the Rockies is certainly the most obvious covariate with the epidemic of ranchland development, but other, more deeply rural, places see the same changing land use pattern. Jackson County, Colorado, and neighboring Carbon County, Wyoming, are unusual among Rocky Mountain counties because neither grew in population during the 1990s. Yet, even here county officials report that land is sub-dividing, and the number of property owners, if not permanent residents, is growing.

Non-resident land ownership is proliferating throughout the Rockies. Either non-ranchers buy and operate ranches (Ted Turner and Jane Fonda's ranch near Bozeman, MT, perhaps the most famous case), or ranches subdivide into "ranchettes" and more typical, high density subdivisions. These modern homes on the range are often owned by a new landed and mobile gentry with permanent residence elsewhere, a class attracted to the imagery of the Old West, the Rocky Mountain landscapes, and the cachet of owning a piece of it.

Though no region-wide assessment is available, anecdotal and case study evidence suggest that Rocky Mountain ranchland subdivision is widespread (Gersh 1996). It is occurring in Montana's Madison Valley (Wyckoff and Hansen 1991), all around Yellowstone National Park (Rasker 1993), and throughout the Colorado mountains (Riebsame et al. 1996).

## Driving Forces: What's Going On Here?

The current boom in Rocky Mountain ranchland is not a classic suburbanization process, nor the result of a dynamic agricultural-land market. Ranchland, which might be valued at $1,500 to $2,000 per animal unit in the Rockies, now sells for twice to ten times that amount, sometimes for ranching and sometimes for residential development. Some of the new residential land owners maintain agricultural land taxation by "hobby ranching." Other "ranches" may be owned for a variety of different reasons. Many of the larger cities in the Rockies, Denver in particular, own what might be called "water ranches"—ranches purchased for their water rights. They may still be ranched now, but eventually the growing cities will sever the water and send it to town, the ranch becoming much less agriculturally useful (if it can be used at all) without the water rights.

As part of a national population shift to the South and West, the interior West states grew faster than the United States as a whole in the 1970s and 1980s, and the pace quickened in the 1990s. Colorado boasted ten of the fifty fastest growing counties in the United States during 1990–95. The fastest growing county was a Denver suburb, and second place went to Summit County, UT, preparing to host the 2002 Winter Olympics. Idaho, Colorado, Montana, Arizona and Utah grew faster than all other states during 1995.

The Rockies' current boom, not tied to a particular commodity like silver or beef, seems different than past migrations and is difficult to characterize. *Time* magazine's cover story hyping the 1990s "Boom Time in the Rockies" (Bonfante 1993) offered anecdotes about high-tech telecommuters, retirees, and trust-funders seeking a Western lifestyle. The newcomers have been called lifestyle refugees, modem cowboys, lone eagle entrepreneurs, and amenity migrants. New Western homesteaders have also been vilified for their precious lifestyles, inconsistent preservationist attitudes, and for carving up the West's open spaces. In short, a significant migration to the Rocky Mountains is underway and expected to continue in the near future.

### Economic Change on the Range

Ranchland conversion in the Rockies plays out in a complex ecological and political landscape. Ranching settlement began in earnest after the 1872 Homestead Act, often based on the transportation infrastructure and markets developed for mining. Agricultural settlement was difficult, though, due to terrain and climate, and extensive lands remained in government ownership (more than 80% of some mountain counties), complicating the geographical patterns of later development. Public lands were closed to residential and most commercial development at the turn of the century, but have now become an important attraction to amenity migrants (e.g., Rudzitis 1993). Anecdotal evidence suggests that public lands attract new residential development to the more deeply rural areas.

The first century and a half of Rocky Mountain settlement was driven by extractive industries, chiefly timber, mining, and grazing, often in boom and bust cycles. Energy development (oil, gas, and coal) caused the last of the great commodity boom-and-bust cycles during the 1970s and early 1980s; the service, retail, and real estate sectors then grew to dominate most mountain areas in the 1980s and 1990s. Tourism and recreation are increasingly important in the regional economy, but the recent residential boom also reflects growth in high-wage, highly mobile professional employment such as engineering, law, financial services, health, and higher education (Rasker 1993, Culbertson et al. 1993, Cromartie 1994).

### Emerging Land Use Patterns

This amenity migration has created two new rural land use patterns in the Rockies. Small towns, with and without ski resorts, are booming (Ringholz 1992) as is affluent, low density residential development of former ranchlands. The pastures and rangelands are platted into both dense subdivisions and large-lot ranchette developments of homes scattered across valley bottoms and far up the mountain slopes (Theobald et al. 1996).

Widespread residential development outside of traditional town sites began in the 1970s and mushroomed into an important landscape feature in the 1990s. Two socio-economic trends fuel this rural subdivision and building pattern. First, second home construction is burgeoning as affluent urbanites acquire a house in the country. Many of the mountain counties exhibit roughly half absentee home ownership according to U.S. Census Bureau statistics, including counties without ski resorts. Second, rural residential development is encouraged by the decentralization of many businesses, along with improved transportation and tele-communications, that allows greater mobility and more flexible work patterns including working at home (i.e., telecommuting). Although statistics are rare, numerous news and business maga- zines have described the recent boom in small, footloose indus- tries and entrepreneurs moving into the Rocky Mountains (e.g., Bonfante 1993). A mixture of employment at nearby (or even dis- tant) recreational facilities, retail sales and service, retirement, and telecommuting to jobs in distant urban areas, offer mountain immigrants a great deal of locational flexibility—enabling them to live in remote, charismatic rural settings.

### *The Ranchette*

The ranchette, large lots each with an isolated, large house, are built for people who want some of the qualities of ranch life (open space, natural surroundings, and space to board and ride horses), but who do not wish to purchase an operating ranch. In a revealing instance of political impacts on landscape, state laws in the Rockies tend to set the size of ranchette lots through stat- utes giving county governments authority over subdivision plan- ning (including requirements for water, sewer, access, etc.) only for subdivisions comprised of parcels below a certain size (e.g., 35 acres in Colorado and Wyoming, 160 acres in Montana). Colorado developers thus tend to design rural subdivisions with parcels just over 35 acres to minimize regulatory constraints, creating a landscape carved into extensive lots dotted with dispersed houses. Ranchettes introduce roads, pets, and human presence into large areas previously disturbed only by livestock grazing. They also frustrate local planning officials because not only do ranchettes lessen their ability to guide land use, they consume large amounts of land and require more infrastructure (e.g., roads) per home.

In some respects, the ranchette phenomenon fills the spatial niche between traditional, small-lot subdivisions near towns, and extensive ranches (Wyckoff and Hansen 1991). In another way it has begun to link ranchers and urbanites, especially environmentalists and "slow-growthers." Some environmentalists worry that the remorseless workings of the market could eventually accomplish what the most strident anti-grazing activists could not—the disappearance of widespread Western ranching. The dissolution of ranching means the loss of important open spaces—the so-called cows vs. condos problem. Alternatively, George Wuerthner, an ardent anti-grazing activist, feels that even the subdivision of all home ranches in the West would be ecologically acceptable if it got all cows off the public range (see Wuerthner 1994, Knight et al. 1995). I disagree. But, even this simple perspective—"the ranch as open space"—is complex. First, many ranchers don't want their land considered open space! Many, maybe most, ranchers, just don't respect the part of the economy that we've come to call "amenity resources." All those "tertiary activities"— recreation, wildlife watching, fly fishing—are for people who have too much money and too much time on their hands, and do not reflect a truly sound economy, one that produces meat, metal, lumber, and other commodities from the earth.

Regardless of our perspective, we must pay attention to what's happening to Rocky Mountain ranchlands because they comprise a critical part of the Western landscape. And, the land use dynamics on that land are changing rapidly.

## The East River Valley

The East River Valley in southern Colorado's Gunnison County illustrates the region's land use transition. Homesteaders established cattle operations in this high mountain valley during the 1880s, and some 30 ranches existed by the turn of the century. Ranch numbers then declined throughout much of the 20th century, though ranch size increased—a pattern common to much of American agriculture as less efficient operations were acquired by expansive ones. Only half as many ranches could be identified in the valley by 1978, and only six were in business in 1994 (Theobald et al. 1996). Yet there is a world of difference between the ranch number decline before the 1970s, caused by ranches growing in size, and the decline in the 1990s, caused by ranches selling land for residential and commercial development. The total acreage of ranchland in the valley remained stable prior to the 1970s. The recent pattern, in which ranch land is sold to residential developers, rather than to neighboring ranchers, marks the first time since initial homesteading that the average size of land ownership parcels in the valley has declined.

Roughly 20% of the private land in the valley has been divided into parcels smaller than about 45 acres, parcels that cannot economically support agriculture. Most development has been single family housing, except in 1980–85 when mostly apartments and condominiums were built to accommodate skiers, and workers in nearby mines. Recent development emphasizes ranchettes. Though the simple number of lots created was greatest in 1970– 75, the total land area subdivided increased dramatically in the 1990s (Figure C17.1), reflecting the switch to a more dispersed residential pattern. One 700-acre base property subdivided into 19 dispersed homesites each on 35 acres! I won't go into all the effects of such land use changes, except to note that they're generally negative for wildlife and other ecological values. This is inevitable when you take, for example, several hundred grazed acres that had two houses, a few outbuildings and some dirt roads and replace it with a dozen big trophy homes, miles of two-lane graded roads, and the other infrastructure that comes with subdivision.

Lifestyle conflicts among residents and visitors in the valley have intensified. Ranchers report increasing conflict with recreationists such as mountain bikers, fishers, and hikers on their National Forest grazing allotments, especially that bane of every ranchers' existence, gate and fence problems. At a more fundamental level, land use conversion has also eroded a long-standing relationship between cattle ranching and the landscape. Cattle were traditionally moved from the lower valley in the spring, with a pause in the mid-valley, up to the high range in mid- and late-summer. This stair-step migration put cattle on different ranges just as the grass was ready, it protected resources by reducing grazing on any given pasture, and it eased cattle transport logistics. Residential development of the key, mid-valley stop-over pastures disrupted this pastoral arrangement, and seasonal cattle drives on highway right-of-way between pastures became difficult and stressful to the animals, forcing ranchers to more expensive trucking.

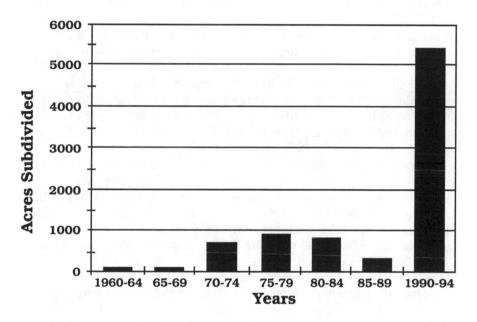

Figure C17.1   Recent trends in the subdivision of ranchland in the East River Valley, Gunnison County, Colorado.

Irrigated hay fields have dominated the valley-bottom since the late 1800s, but as subdivisions replace meadows, less local hay is available and winter feeding costs escalate. Irrigated fields were also an important element in the visual quality of the valley. In both Gunnison and Routt County, Colorado, local groups have recently won significant grants of state lottery money to buy ease-ments on key ranch properties, particularly irrigated hay fields. Tourist-related business owners and local officials are especially sensitive to the effect of development on landscape aesthetics.

Like elsewhere in the Rockies, the cows vs. condos debate created an unlikely coalition of ranchers and environmentalists in the east River Valley, fueled by their perception that loss of agricultural land is the chief threat to the valley's cultural and ecological well-being. This coalition is fragile because it divides environmentalists themselves: some feel that the negative effects of grazing are worse than the residential development that replaces ranches and others argue that ranching better maintains natural biodiversity than development. This difference of opinion has reduced environmentalists' willingness to cooperate with agricultural organizations in the Rockies, but, at least in the East River, the local environmental group broke with national organi-zations and argued that ranching, done properly, has less impact on local ecosystems than residential development (Sprung 1994).

One local developer attempted to meld ranching and residential land uses by clustering homes on a ranchette subdivision so that the remaining open space can still function as a cattle ranch and wildlife habitat—no mean feat given the poor cattle market and the stellar real estate market. Clustering reduces the number of lots carved out of the former ranch (only 11% of the original 4,900 acres is divided into 15 building sites), while the remainder is protected from development by conservation agreements requiring that home owners allow a rancher to graze cattle on the property. Such "green" subdivisions are most feasible where prospective residents appreciate, and will pay highly for, the common open space provided by either fewer homes, clustered homes, or both. In most cases, the developer must also be willing to forgo some potential profit, though this is mitigated in the Rockies by rapid real estate inflation. The apparent inevitability of widespread residential subdivision of private land in the Rocky Mountains clearly calls for more land use innovations like this. Some conservation groups, notably The Nature Conservancy, have purchased and preserved small amounts of Colorado ranch-land (Wright 1993), but the potential landscape protection provided by ranches that shift from agriculture to private conservation use remains to be evaluated.

## The Future Rocky Mountain Landscape

Population growth and agricultural land conversion in the Rockies creates a landscape irony. Immigrants are drawn by the natural spaces, views, recreational opportunities, and vestiges of the "Old West." But their arrival changes these very landscape attributes by reducing agricultural operations; drying up irrigated meadows; blemishing valley slopes with roads and houses; decreasing access to public lands; and increasing recreational use and conflicts. Yet, in many ways, this "neo-homesteading" of the Rocky Mountains is similar to past migrations—a rush is on to own and settle a charismatic landscape. Economic and social mobility in the United States would seem to assure continued population growth in the Rocky Mountains and the landscape transformations described here are likely to intensify.

The East River, Jackson County, and other Rocky Mountain situations also speak to another side of the story. A rancher in Jackson County recently sold off 150 acres for development, a move to raise cash that will help keep that ranch in business. So, the strategic sales of land can be an important aid to ranching. Of course, I hardly need mention the ambivalence that ranchers themselves feel about land use change in the West. They hate to see agricultural units go out of business, they know it weakens the whole social fabric that supports agriculture in the rural West, but they also support—quite profoundly—the right of land owners to do with their land as they please, and they may need to sell the ranch in the future to retire without big debt (something most suburbanites take for granted)! Given this facet of the issue, we must be very careful when considering, as many Western states and counties are right now, policy to restrict the rate of ranch subdivision.

Yet, despite ambivalent attitudes about government or even private land trusts meddling in land use, several Rocky Mountain places under threat of development have efforts, mostly with the ranchers' support I think, to protect private ranchlands. They are creating mechanisms, like the purchase of development rights (PDR), that meet community open space goals and help ranchers achieve their family and production goals. Routt County, Colorado, voters recently approved a one-mill property tax levy for PDR aimed mostly at agricultural lands. The largest proportion of YES votes came from the town of Steamboat Springs, and some rural parts of the county voted NO, but it is my understanding that the ranching community generally supports the county's open lands protection program because it is voluntary and, they believe, is one way to get a handle on what is otherwise a purely market, mostly outsider-driven phenomenon.

Are efforts like this, in places like Jackson, Wyoming or Montana's Gallatin Valley just delaying tactics, or might they be the roots of a new approach to sustainable pastoral land uses in at least some areas of the Rockies? This is not an easy question to answer.

## References

Bonfante, J. 1993. Boom time in the Rockies. Time 142 (September 6):20-27.

Cromartie, J. 1994. Recent demographic and economic changes in the West. Statement before the U.S. House of Representatives, Committee on Natural Resources, hearing on "The Changing Needs of the West." April 7, Salt Lake City, UT.

Culbertson, K., D. Turner, and J. Kolberg. 1993. Toward a definition of sustainable development in the Yampa Valley of Colorado. Mountain Research and Development 13:359-369.

Gersh, J. 1996. Subdivide and conquer: Concrete, condos, and the second conquest of the American West. The Amicus Journal 18 (Fall):14-20.

Knight, R.L., G.N. Wallace, and W.E. Riebsame. 1995. Ranching the view: Subdivisions versus agriculture. Conservation Biology 9:459-461.

Rasker, R. 1993. Rural development, conservation, and public policy in the Greater Yellowstone Ecosystem. Society and Natural Resources 6:109-126.

Riebsame, W.E., H. Gosnell, and D. M. Theobald. 1996. Land use and landscape change in the U.S. Rocky Mountains I: Theory, scale and pattern. Mountain Research and Development 16:395-405.

Ringholz, R. 1992. Small Town Blues: Voices from the Changing West. Peregrine Smith Books, Salt Lake City.

Rudzitis, G. 1993. Non-metropolitan geography: Migration, sense of place, and the American West. Urban Geography 14:574-585.

Sprung, G. 1994. Open space and the future of western ranching. High Country Citizens' Alliance Newsletter. Crested Butte, Colorado.

Theobald, D.M., H. Gosnell, and W.E. Riebsame. 1996. Land use and landscape change in the U.S. Rocky Mountains. II: A case study of the East River Valley, Colorado. Mountain Research and Development 16:407-418.

Wright, J.B. 1993. Rocky Mountain Divide: Selling and Saving the West. University of Texas Press, Austin.

Wuerthner, G. 1994. Subdivisions versus agriculture. Conservation Biology 8:905-908.

Wyckoff, W., and K. Hansen. 1991. Settlement, livestock grazing, and environmental change in Southwest Montana, 1860–1990. Environmental History Review 15 (Winter):45-71.

# Case 18

## Western Washington State Urbanization, Agricultural Changes, and Farmland Protection

*Linda R. Klein, LRK Communications*
*John P. Reganold, Washington State University*

The portion of Washington State to the west of the Cascade Mountains represents less than one-third of the state's total land area. The region's climate, scenic beauty, proximity to recreation areas, and economic opportunities, however, made it home in 1992 to nearly 75% of the state's 5.1 million people, resulting in a population density three times greater than the state's. The temperate climate and the rich, alluvial soils of the region's river valleys create a unique environment conducive to many agricultural enterprises. Although only 5% of the state's farmland occurs in western Washington, more than 33% of the state's farms are located here, accounting for nearly 23% of the total agricultural sector earnings. Western Washington farms produce a majority of the state's berries, Christmas trees, green peas, lettuce, silage corn, milk, eggs, broiler chickens, and nursery and greenhouse products.

Western Washington residents have supported some form of local farmland protection legislation since the early 1970s, evidence of their belief that the land market is not adequately protecting farmland. Due in part to the limited success of these county-level farmland protection measures, the Washington State legislature enacted the 1990 Washington State Growth Management Act (GMA). The GMA requires the most populated and fast-est-growing counties to adopt comprehensive land-use plans in-cluding provisions for the protection of agricultural lands of long-term commercial significance for the production of food or other agricultural products (RCW 36.70A.060).

We used county-level data from the Washington State Office of Financial Management, the U.S. Census of Agriculture, and the U.S. Bureau of Economic Analysis to describe trends in popula-tion and agriculture in 14 of the 19 counties in western Washing-ton between 1974 and 1992. We chose these 14 counties (referred to as "western Washington") because they are the most populous or the fastest-growing as defined in the GMA (RCW 36.70A.040.) and, therefore, most likely to contain farmland under develop-ment pressure. These counties were further divided into eight metropolitan and six nonmetropolitan counties, which allowed us to study relationships between the degree of urbanization and the amount and structure of agriculture. A survey of western Wash-ington planning departments also provides insight into local con-cerns and issues surrounding farmland resources and an assessment of the effectiveness of farmland protection strategies since 1985.

## Regional Trends

### *Population Pressures*

Between 1974 and 1992, more than 80% of the State's total population increase occurred in western Washington, with 90% of the western increase occurring in the eight metropolitan counties. A similar partitioning is expected for population growth between 1992 and 2012, resulting in a projected increase in population density from 549 persons/mi$^2$ in 1992 to 739 persons/mi$^2$ in 2012 for the metropolitan counties and from 55 persons/mi$^2$ to 70 persons/mi$^2$ for the nonmetropolitan counties. This population growth and associated development ensures that agricultural resources in western Washington will continue to be under ex-treme pressure for conversion to nonagricultural uses.

### *Farm and Farm Operator Characteristics*

The number of farms in western Washington declined about 20% between 1982 and 1992 after having increased from 1974 to

1982. Seventy percent of the farms are located in the metropolitan counties. The average farm is small and getting smaller. Between 1974 and 1992, the average size of a metropolitan-county farm decreased from 77 acres to 59 acres, and the average size of a nonmetropolitan-county farm decreased from 141 acres to 99 acres. The percentage of farms in western Washington less than 10 acres in size nearly doubled during this same time period (Table C18.1).

Table C18.1   Selected farm and farm operator characteristics (Source: Bureau of the Census 1977, 1994).

|  | Farms < 10 acres (% of total) | | Farms < $5,000 sales[1] (%[2] of total) | | Operators[3] < 34 years old (%) | |
|---|---|---|---|---|---|---|
| REGION | 1974 | 1992 | 1974 | 1992 | 1978 | 1992 |
| Western WA | 12.4 | 23.1 | 57.5 | 58.9 | 12.5 | 6.6 |
| Metropolitan | 14.9 | 26.3 | 57.2 | 59.8 | 12.5 | 5.7 |
| Nonmetropolitan | 5.8 | 13.7 | 58.4 | 56.1 | 12.5 | 6.8 |

[1]Values for "sales" are defined as the gross market value (not adjusted for inflation) before taxes and production expenses of all agricultural products sold or removed from a farm for any one census year, but not necessarily crops harvested in that year, regardless of who received the payment.

[2]These percentages are based on current dollar values and are not directly comparable without considering the efect of inflation. If adjusted for inflation, the 1992 dollar figures would be worth less in terms of the buying power compared to 1974 dollar figures.

[3]Operator age data only applied to sole proprietorships and family partnerships in the 1974 census year, whereas this characteristic was collected from the senior partner or person in charge on all farms for 1978-1992. Therefore, 1974 data were excluded due to lack of comparability with subsequent census years.

Most farm operators in western Washington are hobby farmers who earn an additional income by producing agricultural products as a secondary, part-time business. By establishing their land in an agricultural use, hobby farmers reap the benefit of lower property taxes under Washington State's Open Space Taxation Act (RCW 84.34). In 1974 and in 1992, almost 60% of western Washington farms grossed less than $5,000 in annual sales of agricultural products (Table C18.1). The average age of western Washington farm operators increased from 51 years in 1978 to 54 years in 1992, whereas the proportion of operators under the age of 34 declined by nearly one-half (Table C18.1).

### Farmland Area and Tenure

In 1992, about 10% of western Washington's nonfederal land area was farmland and more than 60% of this farmland was located in the metropolitan counties. After a net gain of land in farming between 1974 and 1982, western Washington's farmland area declined 16% from 1982 to 1992 (Table C18.2), a rate of decrease 3.5 times greater than that for the state as a whole.

Table C18.2   Changes in farmland area and tenure (Source: Bureau of the Census 1977, 1984, 1994).

| | Farmland changes: 1974-82 | | Farmland changes: 1982-92 | | Rented farmland (% total) | |
|---|---|---|---|---|---|---|
| REGION | Acres | %[1] | Acres | %[2] | 1982 | 1992 |
| Western WA | 31,091 | 3.69 | -138,688 | -15.86 | 28.5 | 33.1 |
| Metropolitan | 33,231 | 6.42 | -85,045 | -15.43 | 26.8 | 31.8 |
| Nonmetropolitan | -2,142 | -0.66 | -53,643 | -16.59 | 31.2 | 35.2 |

[1]The absolute change in total farmland from 1974 to 1982 as a fraction of 1974.

[2]The absolute change in total farmland from 1982 to 1992 as a fraction of 1982.

In 1992, 72% of all farm operators in western Washington owned all the land they farmed. The percentage of farm operators who relied on rented land for part or all of their farming operation remained steady between 1982 and 1992. However, about 96% of the total decrease in farmland area during this same 10-year time period was land *owned* by farm operators, which may explain the increase in the percentage of rented land from 29% in 1982 to 33% in 1992 (Table C18.2). An increase in the proportion of land rented for agricultural uses may signal instability in the agricultural resource base. Economic conditions may be making it difficult for farmers to buy land, and landowners may be renting to farm operators while waiting for land prices to increase before selling for development.

### Agricultural Sector Earnings

Western Washington's agricultural sector earnings (adjusted for inflation) declined 18% between 1974 and 1992, and contributed less than 1% of the region's total economic output. However, the region's agricultural sector earnings grew by approximately 50% between 1982 and 1992, despite the concurrent 16% decrease in farmland area. The region also increased its share of the total state agricultural sector earnings from 17% in 1974 to 23% in 1992. Metropolitan counties accounted for about 70% of the region's total agricultural sector earnings.

## Analysis of Relationships

### Urbanization and the Structure of Agriculture

The majority of farms, farmland, and agricultural sector earnings in western Washington are associated with the metropolitan counties. This suggests that farming in these metropolitan areas may offer locational advantages including a larger consumer base, more efficient transportation systems, shorter distances to local markets and shipping facilities for foreign markets, and direct marketing opportunities. Part-time, small-scale farming operations are common. Environmental conditions and plentiful local markets are conducive to the production of high-value crops such as fruits, vegetables, and nursery and greenhouse products, that can be grown profitably on small acreages. In addition, the greater opportunities for off-farm employment in urbanized areas may increase the prevalence and stability of small, part-time farms.

### Population Pressures and Farmland Changes

We found that population increases were not always associated with concurrent losses of farmland. For example, during the 1978–1982 period, both farmland and population increased. In addition, the highest population growth rate of any agricultural census period (15% between 1987 and 1992) did not correspond with the highest rate of farmland decline (10% between 1982 and 1987). Furthermore, the metropolitan counties experienced farmland increases with concurrent population increases during two consecutive agricultural census periods, 1974–1978 and 1978–1982. Agricultural growth or decline is a complicated process and is influenced by factors in addition to population growth and degree of urbanization, such as general economic conditions, political climate, environmental regulations, or availability of other land for nonfarm uses.

## Survey Results

The 14 western Washington county planning departments indicated in our 1995 survey that the protection of agricultural land at the county level was important for maintaining the agribusiness sector, maintaining local food supplies, preserving rural lifestyles, and preserving open space.

### Causes of Farmland Conversion

All but one of the county planning departments (Kitsap) indicated that increases in land values and property tax assessments are placing moderate or high pressure on farmers to sell their land for nonfarm uses. The planners generally agreed that future population increases will increase the demand for, and therefore the value of, land for nonagricultural uses. All counties reported that there will be moderate or high development pressure to convert agricultural land to urban or built-up uses between 1995 and 2012. A 1985 survey of county planning departments (Christensen 1986) found that residential development was primarily responsible for farmland conversion in western Washington. In our 1995 survey, 13 out of the 14 counties also rated some form of residential infrastructure (e.g., residential growth at urban fringes, rural subdivisions, and large-lot zoning) as the primary cause of agricultural land conversion since 1985.

Urban expansion, however, can sometimes be an indirect response to another cause of farmland decline. In some western Washington counties, stringent environmental regulations have resulted in the reduction of land in dairy farms as well as the consolidation of smaller dairies into larger, more efficient operations. These regulations, aimed at protecting ground- and surface waters, require expensive and complex measures for livestock waste management which many smaller dairy operators have been financially unable to implement. Nine of the 14 county planning departments rated the influence of government regulations on farmland conversion as high or moderate.

### Effectiveness of Farmland Protection Strategies

County planning departments were asked to rate the overall effectiveness of their farmland protection strategies (Table C18.3) for slowing the conversion of agricultural land to urban uses since 1985. We compared the 1995 responses to the corresponding responses in the 1985 survey. Only one county (Skagit) increased its rating from moderate in 1985 to high in 1995, five reported the same rating as in 1985, one county (King) dropped from high to moderate, and one county (Clark) dropped from moderate to low. One county (Mason) had no farmland protection strategies implemented in 1985 but rated their current strategies as having "no effectiveness." Comparisons for five counties were inconclusive because they either did not respond to the question in 1985 (Clallam), had no farmland protection strategies in place in 1985 or 1995 (Jefferson, Lewis), had no farmland protection strategies in place in 1985 and their new strategies had not been implemented yet (Pierce), or had no farmland strategies in place in 1985 and their new strategies had been implemented so recently that an evaluation was not justified (Thurston). Overall, these responses suggest that farmland protection strategies in western Washington such as large-lot zoning, agricultural zoning, promotion of open space taxation, and right-to farm ordinances are no more effective and perhaps even less so than they were 10 years ago.

Ten of the 14 counties identified and designated for protection agricultural land of long-term commercial significance as required by the GMA [RCW 36.70A.030.(10)] (Table C18.3). Many of the current and proposed farmland protection methods, however, are no different than previous strategies and, based on past performance, are unlikely to slow the conversion of agricultural lands or to provide much permanent protection in the future. Most county planning departments believed that the influence of the State's GMA would result in only slightly greater effectiveness, if any, compared to that of the previous strategies enforced by local jurisdictions alone.

Farmland preservation programs that are voluntary and provide compensation to the landowner for decreases in land value, such as Purchase of Development Rights (PDR) or Transfer of Development Rights (TDR), tend to be politically more favorable and to provide permanent protection. We found, however, that counties having proposed TDR and PDR programs (Table C18.3) are uncertain that they will receive the necessary financial or political support from county residents to enact these measures. And, despite the "permanence" of these types of programs, they are not always able to protect the "best" agricultural soils nor do they guarantee that a current farming operation will continue to be economically viable or that someone will be willing to farm the land in the future.

Most planning departments felt that farm operation profitability, farm operator age, farm operator plans for his/her land at retirement, and farmland tenure were either of high or moderate importance to the future of farming in their counties, yet these four characteristics were rarely used as criteria for designating agricultural land of long-term commercial significance. The primary criterion used by the counties for designating farmland for protection was if the farmland soils were mapped as prime, unique, or locally-important under the Important Farmland Classification System used by the Natural Resources Conservation Service.

## Conclusions

Significant negative changes have occurred in western Washington's agricultural resource base, despite the many farmland protection strategies in place in the 14 counties. In just 10 years (1982–1992), the number of farms decreased by approximately 20% and farmland declined by nearly 16%, a rate 3.5 times faster than the state's. Population projections suggest that western Washington, particularly the metropolitan counties, will

continue to be under extreme pressure for the conversion of farmland to nonfarm uses.

Western Washington's farmland protection programs have been
ineffective and we question the criteria used for designating farmland to be protected. In addition to population pressures, there
are economic, political, and social forces that influence a farm
operation's profitability or a farm operator's decision to discon-
tinue farming. These factors have been given little, if any, consideration when designating and designing strategies to protect
important agricultural lands in western Washington. It makes
little sense to protect agricultural land resources based on the
presence of high quality soils unless there is someone willing to
farm, the farm operation is profitable, and the local community is
able and willing to lend financial and political support.

Table C18.3  Amounts of farmland and methods for protection as
required by the GMA (Klein 1995).

| County | Agricultural land of long-term commercial significance[1] (acres) | Total farm-land (acres) | Methods for protection (current and proposed) used with comprehensive planning[2] |
|---|---|---|---|
| Clallam | 7300 | 24254 | promotion of open space taxation, residential clustering in agricultural zones, TDR and PDR |
| Clark[3] | 85204 | 82972 | large-lot zoning, promotion of open-space taxation, TDR |
| Island | 19302 | 19527 | large-lot zoning, agricultural exclusive zoning, TDR, promotion of open space taxation, right-to-farm ordinances |
| Jefferson | 0 | 9603 | "resource production zones" (1 homesite/5 acre min. lot size, but not strictly enforced)[4] |
| King[3] | 43002 | 42293 | large-lot zoning, agricultural non-exclusive zoning, PDR, purchase and resale or lease with restrictions, promotion of open space taxation, development of permit system[5] |

*Continues*

Table C18.3   *Continued*

| County | Agricultural land of long-term commercial significance[1] (acres) | Total farm-land (acres) | Methods for protection (current and proposed) used with comprehensive planning[2] |
|---|---|---|---|
| Kitsap | 0 | 10302 | promotion of open space taxation, right-to-farm ordinances[4] |
| Lewis[6] | n/a | 112269 | n/a |
| Mason | 0 | 10967 | promotion of open space taxation, exemption from some county environmental regulations[4] |
| Pierce | 17537 | 58753 | agricultural non-exclusive zoning, promotion of open space taxation |
| San Juan | 10826 | 20530 | large-lot zoning, agricultural non-exclusive zoning, promotion of open space taxation, development permit system |
| Skagit[3] | 95805 | 92078 | large-lot zoning, agricultural non-exclusive zoning, promotion of open space taxation, development permit system, right-to-farm ordinances |
| Snohomish | 69705 | 74158 | large-lot zoning, agricultural non-exclusive zoning, promotion of open space taxation |
| Thurston | 12000 | 59892 | agricultural exclusive-use zoning, residential clustering in agricultural zones, promotion of open space taxation, TDR and PDR |
| Whatcom | 93966 | 118143 | large-lot zoning, agricultural non-exclusive zoning, promotion of open space taxation, hold harmless agreements on plats/subdivisions near farming activities, right-to-farm ordinances, TDR |
| Western WA[7] | 454645 | 623471 | |

[1]"Includes the growing capacity, productivity, and soil composition of the land for long-term commercial production, in consideration with the land's proximity to population areas, and the possibility of more intense uses of the land." [RCW 36.70A.030 (10)].

[2]All counties use comprehensive planning.

[3]Total farmland is less than commercially significant land due to land being protected that does not fall into definition of farmland per U.S. census of agriculture.

[4]Policies exist to encourage farming in rural zones even though no strict agriculture zone designations.

[5]All funds exhausted for PDR or purchase and resale programs.

[6]Lewis County's comprehensive plan is in infancy stages because not included in GMA until 1993.

[7]Lewis County total farmland excluded from state total farmland.

## References

Bureau of the Census. 1977. 1974 Census of agriculture. Geographic area series: Washington State and county data. U.S. Department of Commerce. Washington, D.C.

Bureau of the Census. 1984. 1982 Census of agriculture. Geographic area series: Washington State and county data. U.S. Department of Commerce. Washington, D.C.

Bureau of the Census. 1994. 1992 Census of agriculture. Geographic area series: Washington State and county data. U.S. Department of Commerce. Washington, D.C.

Christensen, G. R. 1986. Protecting agricultural lands in Washington State: Concerns, issues, and effectiveness. M. S. thesis. Department of Environmental Science and Regional Planning, Washington State University, Pullman, WA.

Klein, L. R. 1995. Population influences on agriculture in western Washington from 1974 through 1992. M.S. thesis. Department of Crop and Soil Sciences, Washington State University, Pullman, WA.

# Case 19

## Saving Oregon's Farmland

*Remarks by Richard P. Benner, Director
Department of Land Conservation and Development to
the Oregon Board of Agriculture, December 11, 1997*

For more than three decades, the State of Oregon has sought to protect agricultural land from urban sprawl and leapfrog subdivisions. Our state often is hailed as a leader and an innovator in the nationwide effort to save farmland from uncontrolled development. But that acclaim raises some questions. What is Oregon doing to protect farmland, and how well is it working? My comments today will center on those two issues.

### How Oregon Protects Farmland

In 1961, the Oregon legislature created a program to keep farmers from being forced out of business by the higher property taxes caused by land speculation and development. The law required that farmland "zoned exclusively for farm use" be assessed at its lower farm value rather than at a higher "true cash value" based on its potential for development.

In 1963, the legislature expanded on that idea. It established a dual tax program, calling for preferential farm tax assessment on lands zoned for farm use and allowing property tax deferrals for farms outside of such zones. The 1963 legislature also adopted provisions for the "exclusive farm use" or EFU Zone. As the name implied, the EFU Zone was to be a district within which only agriculture and other uses compatible with agriculture would be allowed.

Through its first decade of use, the state's EFU Zone provisions were optional. Counties could apply the zone as they saw fit, and many did apply it to at least some farmland. In 1973, the legislature elevated the state's role. With Senate Bill 101, the legislature passed into law a strong policy to preserve "the maximum amount of the limited supply of agricultural land"—not just prime farmland but the *maximum amount of agricultural land.* Also in 1973, the legislature adopted the now-famous Senate Bill 100, thus creating a strong statewide program for land use planning. The bill directed the newly created Land Conservation and Development Commission (LCDC) to "give priority consideration to" several resources, including "agricultural land."

That state policy to protect farmland and the law calling for statewide planning and zoning have been in effect ever since. The combination of those two laws has led to a system of farmland protection that is arguably the strongest in the country. Some 16 million acres of agricultural land have been protected by the combination of strong state standards, local planning, and exclusive farm use zoning. Those 16 million acres amount to half of all the privately owned land in the state.

EFU zones vary somewhat from one county to another. For example, Hood River County calls its main farm district the Exclusive Farm Use Zone, while nearby Jefferson County protects its farmland with an A-1 Zone. The two zones differ not only in name but also in some of their provisions. However, both zones have the same basic purpose and satisfy state requirements for exclusive farm use zoning set forth in ORS Chapter 215.

The EFU Zone protects farmland in two main ways. First, it limits development by prohibiting land uses that conflict with commercial agriculture. Subdivisions, shopping malls, fast-food shops, and most other urban uses are prohibited in the EFU Zone. Second, the zone specifies a minimum lot size to keep farmland from being divided into pieces too small for commercial agriculture. As a result of legislation passed in the 1993 Legislature, the minimum parcel size for cropland is 80 acres, for rangeland, 160 acres.

EFU zoning is reinforced by another key element of the state-wide planning program: the "urban growth boundary" or "UGB." Statewide Planning Goal 14 requires each of Oregon's 240 cities to establish such a boundary, and all of them have done so. The boundary marks the outermost limit of the growth and development planned by a city for the next 20 years. It is the line between urban lands, which are expected to be served and developed at urban levels sometime in the future, and rural lands, most of which are protected for commercial agriculture and forestry.

The result of the system I have just described is a "planscape" consisting of urban lands inside urban growth boundaries, farmlands, exception areas (rural areas zoned for development), and lands zoned for forest conservation.

## How Does Oregon "Lose Farmland?"

Within the system that has been created to protect farmland, conversion of farmland can still happen in three ways:

- by cities expanding onto farmland;

- by land in EFU zones being rezoned for development;

- by a proliferation of the uses allowed by state law in the EFU Zone.

### Cities Expanding Onto Farmland

Many people visualize an amoeba-like expansion of cities as the biggest consumer of farmland. That may be true in other places, but not in Oregon. This is one of the big success stories of our statewide planning program: UGB's work to protect farmland.

During the ten years from 1987 through 1996, a total of 144 UGB expansions occurred statewide in Oregon (an average of 14 per year). They took in 12,541 acres, but only 4,963 of those acres were farmland. Using those numbers to calculate an average, we find that we are losing farmland to UGB's at a rate of only 500 acres per year.

This low figure may surprise people who drive down I-5 and other highways in the Willamette Valley and see "all that development going onto prime farmland." For the most part, what they are seeing is development occurring inside UGB's that were established long ago. Yes, the development is occurring on farmland, but it is occurring as the result of a conscious policy choice, not because UGB's are marching across the landscape. The policy choice in the early 1980's was between not letting cities grow, or providing at least some new land for growth, even when some of that land was good for farming. In most cases, vacant land for growth was included in the UGB's, and some of it had to be farmland. That was inevitable, because most of our cities were established on farmland more than a century ago.

Expansion of UGB's may prove to be a larger consumer of farmland in the future, for several reasons. First, UGB's were adopted in the late 1970's and early 1980's. Most were comfortably large, but some are becoming a bit snug. The number of expansions proposed in the future therefore is likely to become larger than the number we've seen in the recent past. The Portland Metropolitan Service District, responsible for the UGB around Portland and 23 other cities in the region, recently decided to add 4,500 acres to its UGB (a 2% increase). But nearly all the new land to be taken into the UGB is currently designated Rural Residential, not EFU, in order to comply with LCDC's Goal 14 (Urbanization).

Second, some small cities are seeing huge proposals for development unlike anything in their history. Lincoln City, for example, recently approved a new subdivision with almost 2,000 lots. At build-out, the development will double the population of the city. Proposals like that will almost certainly result in some UGB expansions.

### Rezoning of Farmland

The second way that we lose farmland is through rezoning. To rezone land from EFU to, say, Rural Residential takes an exception to Oregon's statewide planning goals. The standards for exceptions are high, so here, too, we see success. Rezonings are not taking much farmland.

During the ten years from 1987 through 1996, 18,366 acres were rezoned from EFU to some type of rural development zone (through the exceptions process). A single rezoning of some 14,000 acres in Morrow County from EFU to Industrial accounted for most of that. If we include that one big rezoning in our calculation, we find that our average loss of farmland to rezoning during the past ten years has been 1,840 acres per year. If we do not include it, the average loss is only 430 acres per year.

### "Internal Conversion" of Farmland

The third way in which we lose farmland is through what I will call "internal conversion." By that, I mean the taking of farmland out of production for uses *allowed* in the EFU Zone—uses such as golf courses, schools, RV parks, and especially dwellings. I believe that this is the greatest threat to farmland because it is insidious and because there's so much pressure to provide opportunities for "a place in the country."

I call this threat insidious because we can't see new dwellings on farmland as readily as we can see a new subdivision in a city. New dwellings on farmland are built one at a time on sites far from most roads. They are largely invisible. But they are being built: for the past four years, the average number of new dwellings being approved in EFU zones has been just under one thousand per year. About one out of every 20 new houses or manufactured homes in the state is placed in an EFU zone. When you drive by a new subdivision of 200 houses in Gresham or Tigard or Eugene, remember: another 10 new houses that you can't see are being built somewhere out on the farmland.

In 1994, a total of 1,137 new dwellings were approved on land zoned EFU. That was up 30% from the previous year. One third of those were "farm dwellings," that is, homes to be occupied by the owner/operator/employee of a commercial farm. Most were approved under the much lower standards in effect before LCDC adopted new rules for farm dwellings in February 1994.

At that time, LCDC adopted a two-tier system of higher standards for new farm dwellings. LCDC had considerable evidence to indicate that new standards were needed. A study done in the late 1980's had shown that most new "farm dwellings" were in fact not associated with commercial farming at all. The study looked at a sample of 330 new farm dwellings a few years after they were approved. It found that three-fourths of them were on farms—or perhaps I should say "nonfarms"—that grossed less than $10,000 per year from the sale of agricultural products. More than a third of the so-called farms had gross agricultural sales of zero.

## LCDC's New Rules for Farm Dwellings

You probably have heard and read about the new farm dwelling standards that LCDC adopted in 1994. They have generated considerable controversy, so I'll take a moment to explain them.

The lower tier of standards applies to the great majority of land under EFU zoning. This tier offers three different ways to get a permit for a new farm dwelling. A permit applicant can choose the way that works best for his or her situation. Each of the three ways involves a set of standards designed to ensure that the parcel proposed as the site of the new farm dwelling is indeed a bona fide farm.

The criteria from those three approaches involve, respectively, parcel size, median annual gross sales from nearby farms, and a gross farm income test. A permit applicant can qualify for a new farm dwelling if his or her farm has at least 160 acres of cropland or 320 acres rangeland. Or, the applicant can qualify if the farm can produce gross annual sales equal to or greater than the median produced by nearby commercial farms. Or, a permit can be granted if the farm has produced gross annual sales of at least $40,000 or the median of commercial farms in the county.

The other tier is simpler. It applies to "high-value farmland"— soils that are prime, unique, Class I, Class II, or that support certain crops, such as orchards. The test for a new farm dwelling on this high-value land is that the farm must have produced at least $80,000 in annual gross sales of farm products in recent years.

The $80,000 test drew a lot of criticism from people who argued that the number was too high. I believe, however, that such criticism overlooks five important points.

First, the test is a measure of *gross* sales. Farms and ranches have high overhead, typically 80% or more. The net profit from gross sales of $80,000 therefore is likely to be $16,000 or less. That's a pretty small income to support a household.

A second point overlooked by many critics is that bona fide commercial farms in areas with good soils typically have gross sales far higher than $80,000. The 1992 Census of Agriculture shows that the average gross income of commercial farms in many counties—Marion, Yamhill, and Washington, for example— exceeded $200,000 per year.

Third, the $80,000 test applies only to the very best land, land that often can gross $3,000 or $4,000 per acre. For example, an applicant for a new farm dwelling on high-value farmland in Marion County could meet the test with 30 acres of hops, 28 acres of blackberries, or 19 acres of strawberries.

Fourth, the standard is by no means an arbitrary number. The $80,000 test grew out of several years of research, including a major study commissioned by the Oregon legislature. LCDC conducted public hearings and received a great deal of testimony from farmers and agricultural experts. The commission also established a technical committee made up of experts in agriculture to advise LCDC about appropriate standards. The $80,000 test originated in that committee.

Finally, the $80,000 test is only for farm dwellings. There are other types of dwellings permitted by Oregon's statutes and rules for EFU zones—lot-of-record dwellings, nonfarm dwellings, dwellings for farm help, and so on.

If our standards for farm dwellings are too low, our laws and rules for the other types of dwellings are rendered meaningless. If almost anyone can meet the standards for a farm dwelling, then they need not bother about meeting the standards for lot-of-record dwellings, nonfarm dwellings, or any other type of dwelling. The standards for different types of dwellings are like the dikes and levees along our rivers: the flood pours through where the barriers are lowest.

A second problem is that if standards for farm dwellings are too low, we lose farmland without even knowing it. Suppose, for example, that we approve 1,000 new "farm dwellings." Let's further suppose that our standards are so low that half of those dwellings wind up being owned by people who really aren't farmers and only wanted a place in the country. We lose at least 500 acres to their home sites, and we may lose a great deal of production, since the new residents are not committed to commercial agriculture. But our records will show no loss of farmland at all, even though the land itself will be changing. Large farms will become small farms, which will become ranchettes and hobby farms. Admittedly, a thousand new dwellings may not sound like much when you spread them across 16 million acres in 36 counties. But the steady development of new dwellings in EFU zones threatens to convert at least some of the areas that we describe today as "farmland" into rural subdivisions.

Here are some statistics on that point that I believe will surprise and even alarm you.

- Hood River County has 31,360 acres of land in EFU zoning, with 2,700 dwellings on that land—one dwelling for every twelve acres.

- Washington County has one dwelling for every 33 acres of land in its EFU zone.

- Samples from many sections of Clackamas County suggest that it has about one dwelling for every 23 acres of land in its main EFU zone.

My chief concern is about dwellings, but I also would call your attention to the growing list of other uses authorized in the EFU Zone. The Exclusive Farm Use Zone is becoming much less exclusive. In almost every legislative session, another use or two gets added to the growing statutory list of uses permitted in the zone. In 1995, for example, bills were passed to allow veterans homes, armories, and log-truck parking in EFU zones. When you examine any one of those uses, the reasons for allowing it in an EFU zone may seem quite valid. However valid those reasons may be, such uses do consume farmland—a great deal of farmland.

For example, in 1994, about 180 nonfarm uses other than dwellings were approved on EFU-zoned land. The parcels involved in those approvals total more than 10,000 acres. Not all of that land will be taken out of agricultural production. For example, mineral and aggregate operations were approved on 20 parcels involving 5,900 acres, but the mining itself will affect only a portion of that acreage. Farming can occur on one part of a parcel while aggregate is extracted from another. But other uses do remove the entire parcel from production. For example, the four golf courses approved on EFU-zoned land in 1994 will remove a total of 768 acres from production.

The data for these other uses are too imprecise to let us conclude exactly how much farmland they take out of production. But the data do enable us to conclude that the nonfarm uses allowed by statute in EFU zones take several thousand acres of farmland out of production every year.

I fear that all these numbers may become tiresome, so I will summarize here and get to the bottom line. There are three main ways that Oregon can lose farmland: from the spread of cities, rezoning of farmland, and internal decay of our EFU zones from approval of too many dwellings and other nonfarm uses. I believe that the third process—the proliferation of dwellings and nonfarm uses on farmland—is the biggest threat of the three. Like a slow-growing cancer, it is difficult to see, but its long-term effects are profoundly destructive.

However, I will not end my remarks on such a gloomy note. With the passage of House Bill 3661 in 1993, the Oregon legislature took some measures to curb the proliferation of dwellings on farmland. The bill established the two-tier system that provides stronger protection for high-value farmland and for the Willamette Valley. LCDC reinforced those measures in 1994 by adopting the higher farm-dwelling standards that I described earlier. These new laws are having their intended effects. The number of new farm dwellings plummeted 75%—from 372 to 88— from 1994 to 1996. The number of nonfarm dwellings rose 44%—from 293 to 422. But virtually all nonfarm dwellings will be sited on less productive land (they are severely limited on high-value farmland). No new golf courses, schools or churches were built on high-value farmland, now prohibited by law.

Opponents of LCDC's rules for high-value farmland challenged them in court. In a key ruling this summer, <u>Lane County vs. LCDC</u>, the Oregon Supreme Court upheld the rules.

Oregon will not abandon its longstanding commitment to protect farmland. We face formidable challenges, but we have overcome similar challenges during the 23 years of our statewide planning.

# Case 20

## Fresno County, California

*Greg Kirkpatrick, American Farmland Trust*

If the Midwest is the breadbasket of the world, then California's San Joaquin Valley is its salad bowl. More than 250 crops are produced in the Valley generating more than $13 billion annually in agricultural sales. The Valley's productivity can be attributed to a unique combination of factors that create an ideal setting for agriculture: a mediterranean climate, deep alluvial soils, an adequate supply of irrigation water, an intricate marketing and transportation infrastructure for moving crops to market, and some of the best-trained and technically advanced farmers in the world. This setting cannot be duplicated anywhere in the nation or, probably, the world. San Joaquin Valley agriculture is truly a national treasure.

Fresno County lies at the heart of the San Joaquin Valley and exceeds all of its neighboring counties in agricultural production. Irrigated agriculture began in Fresno in the 1870's and grew steadily as water was diverted from local rivers and streams flowing from the Sierra Nevada. Agriculture in Fresno County boomed in the 1950's and 1960's as technology for extracting groundwater from wells advanced and federal and state water projects began making deliveries. In 1950, Fresno County overtook Los Angeles County as the top-producing county in the nation in terms of gross agricultural sales.

Today, Fresno County generates $3.1 billion in gross agricultural revenues on approximately 1.2 million acres of irrigated farmland. As a basic industry, agriculture builds wealth in the community because much of the operating expenses, as well as profits, remain in the local economy. Agriculture and related businesses contribute more than $8 billion annually to Fresno County's gross domestic product.

## Population Growth and Agriculture

The San Joaquin Valley is also one of the most rapidly urbanizing regions in California and the nation. While the state's population is expected to double during the next 45 years, the Valley's population is expected to triple. According to the California Department of Finance, Fresno County is expected to grow from its present population of 674,000 to 2,498,000 by the year 2040. This growing population must be provided with food, jobs and housing to maintain the economic health of the community, which in turn creates enormous pressure for the conversion of farmland to subdivisions, shopping centers and industrial parks.

The recent pattern and density of growth has contributed significantly to the loss of farmland in Fresno County. Since World War II, most new residential development in Fresno County and the San Joaquin Valley as a whole has occurred in subdivisions that provide only about three houses per acre. A 1995 study by American Farmland Trust (AFT) found that if we accommodate Fresno County's expected population increase of 1.8 million new residents at historic land use densities, approximately 234,000 acres of land will be converted from agriculture to urban uses during the next 45 years. By the year 2040, Fresno County would lose approximately 18.9% of its irrigated farmland and experience annual losses of $698 million (22.6%) of the $3.1 billion of farm revenue earned in 1994.

Rapid population growth has been occurring in Fresno County for many years, and therefore a number of land use policy tools have been developed, with varying degrees of success, to slow the loss of productive farmland. Land use in all of the cities and unincorporated areas is governed by General Plans and zoning. Exclusive agricultural zoning with minimum parcel sizes of 20 to 80 acres has been established on most of the irrigated agricultural land in the county and minimum parcel sizes of 40 to 640 acres have been established on foothill rangeland. The Williamson Act provides farmers with property tax relief in exchange for a commitment not to develop farmland for 10 years, and more than 90% of the prime farmland in Fresno County is enrolled in this program. Annexations are governed by the Local Agency Formation Commission (LAFCo), a board including city and county representatives that has the authority to establish specific criteria for approval that may include farmland protection policies.

Even with these growth management policies and ordinances in place, the magnitude of population growth continues to overwhelm these modest protection efforts. Lack of consistency by local decision-makers in supporting farmland protection policies has also eroded the effectiveness of these tools. General Plans and zoning designations are frequently amended at the request of a landowner or developer and Williamson Act contracts can be canceled without penalty if a city filed a protest when the contracts were originally issued.

## Building Consensus for a Better Future

It has become apparent to AFT that growth patterns might play a more important role in the loss of farmland to urbanization than population growth itself. Replacing urban sprawl with more compact and efficient patterns of growth on the urban edge and directing growth inward through infill development and neighborhood revitalization can accommodate the same number of people on much less land. We also realized that controlling or changing population growth trends would be nearly impossible, but that it might be possible to change patterns of growth, especially if a grass roots consensus for better land use planning could be developed among local stakeholders. This has been the focus of our Central Valley Alternative Growth Futures initiative during the last two years.

The first step in this consensus building process was to build recognition of the problems associated with urban sprawl and the need for better land use planning. Fortunately, many of the private business, building and farming organizations in Fresno County recognized the problem and were prepared to take action. Business organizations recognized the need to build more livable communities in order to attract new economic investment as well as the need to protect agribusiness as the driving force of the local economy. Builders had been frustrated by their inability to build more affordable housing by making more efficient use of land and infrastructure investments. The agricultural community recognized the threat that urban sprawl posed to maintaining a critical mass of farmland that would ensure the future viability of their industry.

A few initial discussions among organizations representing the business, farming and building communities led to initial steps toward action. In July, 1996, The Building Industry Association of the San Joaquin Valley, the Fresno County Farm Bureau, the Fresno Chamber of Commerce, and the American Farmland Trust jointly issued a letter to the City of Fresno encouraging our local leaders to adopt policies that would encourage and facilitate compact growth and urban infill to accommodate anticipated population increases. These organizations agreed that moderate increases in urban density were likely to have positive benefits for the local citizenry and economy including:

- reduced conversion of agricultural and natural land to urban uses

- lower housing costs as a result of greater efficiency in the use of infrastructure

- greater feasibility of regional transit systems such as light rail

- stronger sense of community and neighborhood

- revitalization of urban centers and retention of infrastructure investments in the urban core

- improved delivery of public services and emergency response

- greater ability to attract new businesses due to improved quality of life

Even with this initial agreement, bringing together groups with widely divergent interests to discuss specific policies for achieving compact growth was a difficult challenge. Initial attempts to convene a publicly appointed task force to study land use issues were met with hesitancy and skepticism by some key stakeholders. It became apparent that an intermediate step was needed to build trust and to provide an opportunity to discuss issues more freely than would be possible in a public forum.

In January 1997, the groups that signed the letter to the City of Fresno along with the Fresno Business Council formed the Growth Alternatives Discussion Group. The group met throughout 1997 to reach consensus on specific policies and implementation strategies for achieving compact growth and infill development. The primary objective of the Growth Alternatives Discussion Group was to develop a common vision for the future of Fresno County and its cities that would guide urban development and protect our most important agricultural resources during the next 25 to 30 years. The consensus building process was also intended to increase the understanding of the importance and needs of agriculture, building trades, and business among the participants and the community-at-large. To our knowledge, this is the first time anywhere in the country that leaders of the agricultural, development, and business communities have collaborated to set a course of action to accommodate new growth in a manner that provides a wide range of affordable housing, protects vital natural resources, and improves the quality of life.

Two representatives from each organization plus their executive director or manager participated in the discussions, which were facilitated by American Farmland Trust. The group identified the barriers to achieving compact growth and urban infill in Fresno County and then sought solutions to overcome these barriers. The group reviewed a variety of land use policies and guidelines that had been applied in other places around the country and discussed their practicality and feasibility. At the end of the process, the discussions were summarized into more than 40 policy statements and implementation strategies. Each organization ranked the statements by priority and had the opportunity to veto any principle that they could not support. The policy statements and implementation strategies were then compiled in a white paper along with more detailed descriptions of what the group was suggesting.

## Elements of Consensus

As the discussion proceeded, three main themes emerged for which their was broad agreement. These became the guiding principles around which specific policies and implementation measures were developed. All of the policy recommendations agreed upon by the discussion group fall under one or more of these guiding principles:

- Use urban land as efficiently as possible.

- Encourage the development of livable communities that emphasize pedestrian or transit-oriented design.

- Recognize the importance of agriculture and the need to protect agriculture by directing growth away from productive agricultural land.

The implementation strategies developed by the Growth Alternative Discussion Group focus on actions that should be undertaken by broader coalitions if not the entire community to enact the guiding principles. The strategies emphasize further collaborative efforts and public participation to define the specific standards within each community rather than dictating one-size-fits-all solutions.

Changing land use patterns to create compact and efficient growth, while building stronger pedestrian-based neighborhoods and directing growth away from productive agricultural resources may seem like a daunting task. One of the strongest barriers to compact growth has been the natural resistance to change from neighboring residents and a lack of political will by local elected officials. Citizens often react to projects that propose higher density with fear that is driven by the myth that density creates crime, congestion, and will reduce their property values. When these projects come up for approval, local leaders are often faced with an angry mob who may not understand the key role that these projects play in building livable and economically viable communities. A common vision for community growth must be agreed upon *before* these projects come up for approval and local leaders must review and approve projects based upon that vision.

The Fresno Growth Alternatives Discussion Group and its member organizations strongly believe that the community, as a whole, will benefit greatly from the adoption and implementation of these planning principles. The Fresno Chamber of Commerce, the Fresno County Farm Bureau, the Building Association of the San Joaquin Valley, the American Farmland Trust and the Fresno Business Council are firmly committed to continue working together to create a constituency for change that recognizes the benefits of building better communities and is committed to take appropriate action.

As a next step, representatives of the discussion group will present our vision to all of the local governments in Fresno County and in public workshops. It is our hope that local elected officials, planning commissioners, city and county personnel, and the public at large will review these planning principles and adopt them as their own. The Group has also formed a technical advisory committee that will participate in the development of the specific standards and guidelines necessary to build a healthy, diverse, and vibrant community *and* economy.

> A community is an economy: the two are one and the same...a web of practical interrelationships between neighbors who understand their mutual dependency and honor it by competently caring for their work, their town, their offspring, and each other.
>
> — James Howard Kunstler, The Geography of Nowhere.

Note: Updates on the progress of the Fresno Growth Alternatives Discussion Group can be obtained through the American Farmland Trust homepage at http://www.farmland.org.

# Case 21

## The Oxnard Plain, Southern California: The Economics of Agriculture in the Urban Fringe

*Michal C. Moore, California Energy Commission*
*Rasa Dale, University of California, Davis*

Urban influences can be blatant or subtle depending on the community and the distance from the urban boundary. Throughout Southern California, many different planning regulations and political tools have been employed to mitigate urban impacts on agriculture. The success of each has been limited, and their effectiveness is often short lived as regulations or rule-making bodies change with time, and as economic forces interact with land use planning.

In this case study, we review the economic issues involved with farming in the proximity of urban areas in the Oxnard Plain, southern Ventura County, California. We identify and quantify some external costs associated with farming in these areas and review mechanisms used by landowners to cope with these costs. Finally, we explore the phenomenon of urban conversion of agricultural lands and review the public planning tools designed to limit or restrict conversion.[1]

The issue is a critical one for many communities, especially those surrounded by unique production lands that contribute to the economy through direct sales and employment as well as the pastoral proximity value that can be added to local residential properties. Preserving land or stabilizing rates of conversion is a high priority even when so-called food security is eliminated from the calculus.

## Nature of Costs

The costs of agricultural operations in the proximity of urban areas can be broadly classified as either direct or indirect. Direct costs are borne by agricultural producers, either landowners or renters, in the process of developing, harvesting and transporting crops to market. They include land acquisition cost (or lease), land taxes (secured and unsecured property), and production costs (labor and factor inputs).

Indirect costs arise from factors not controlled by the land-owner. These can be either regional (affecting all owners more or less equally) or local (property specific in nature). Air pollution and road congestion are examples of indirect *regional* impacts. On a *local* scale, indirect impacts include vandalism, theft of products or machinery, and shifts in land prices from urban bids.

### *Locational Cost Impacts on Agriculture*

Field interviews revealed topical rather than specific complaints on the part of farmers in the Oxnard Plain regarding the influence of urban activities. The interviews revealed costs in the following areas:

- *Theft of product and vandalism* were the two most cited problems of agricultural operators close to an urban area. Not surprisingly, the rows of crops closest to a subdivision tend to be the most affected, with crop production in the first two rows reduced by as much as 20%. Theft can also occur due to mechanized gangs stealing from remote areas. The greatest damage reported for vandalism was from the inadvertent effects of horse riders, walkers and joggers. There is also deliberate vandalism of vehicles and farm equipment, which must be stored in more secure areas, increasing costs.

- *Air pollution* costs have already been internalized industry-wide for farms on the Oxnard Plain, in terms of price reductions and an approximately 10% decrease in yields. *Noise* from normal farm operations is a frequently cited complaint of urban dwellers near agricultural operators. As a result, local governments have imposed noise-abatement regulations, which have contributed to increased costs of farming.

- *Traffic congestion* on narrow agricultural roads inconveniences both urban and rural drivers. More time is required to move machinery between parcels, and field operations must sometimes be delayed in order to avoid peak traffic periods.

- *Water availability and cost* remain major concerns to agricultural production. The Oxnard Plain maintains its competitive advantage from rich soils, moderate climate, and access to adequate water supplies. Agriculture constitutes a large portion of the overall water use and competes directly with current and perceived future residential needs for water.

Urbanization of agricultural lands may increase the demand for water. For example, water demand of a citrus crop is 1.6 acre feet/acre/year, and row crops are 3.2 acre feet/acre/year. In contrast, residential demand for 5 homes on one acre with 2.7 people per home is 3.1 acre feet/acre/year. If one acre of row crop agriculture is displaced by 5 new homes, the water usage will remain about the same. If five houses replace one acre of citrus, the water usage will double, increasing competition for the available water and increasing costs.

Although the majority of locational costs are due to the factors discussed above, additional costs accrue from the need to create buffer zones, the spread of crop disease, increased liability insurance, and the disruption of the timing of operations. In general, our field interviews suggest that, other than those costs borne through increased property values (discussed below), the costs of operations near or adjacent to urban areas are largely internalized by landowners. On average, increases of costs due to proximity to urban sites appears to be about 5% of total variable costs. This can be attributed largely to the increased management required of agricultural operators, and their tendency to discount the value of their own labor (essentially to zero).

## Land Prices

The impact of changes in land price and shifts in land use can be significant, especially when viewed in the context of market entry. If the cost of the mortgage is significantly higher than the net return from a single harvest or lower value added crops, few new agricultural operators will enter and some may even have to leave the market.

Field evidence indicates that actual land acquisition prices are in the range of $25,000 to $35,000 per acre, especially in the proximity of urban expansion areas. Using a citrus example where land acquisition costs must be below $10,000 in order to produce a profit, land sales at $25,000 to $35,000 per acre encourage conversion, either to a much higher value crop or ultimately to urban land use, because agricultural operators would be unable to stay in business. One of the reasons for the high prices is the increased demand from urban sectors that bids up the land value around the cities.

Ventura County's current agricultural operations remain in agriculture either because owner operators bought land at much lower prices or owners who lease their land out for farming as a holding action receive immediate returns. However, the owners who are leasing will eventually develop or sell the land to recoup their investment.

## Agricultural Land Owner Response

As agricultural land owners face urban conversion pressure, they tend to alter practices and behavior. In the field area, the following general trends have appeared:

- A trend to more specialized agricultural operations, including changes to higher value-added and more exotic crops.

- Greater reliance on technology to maximize returns, minimize water use, and provide more efficient pesticide application.

- Greater acreage aggregation of agricultural units by corporate owners and disaggregation and higher diversity for smaller individual land owners.

- Continued escalation of agricultural land entry prices with corresponding shifts in intra-agricultural diversity and location.

## Local Government Response

### California Planning Tools

Land use planning in California relies on three principal tools to attain and exercise local control of development: the general plan, zoning ordinance, and subdivision ordinance. Other planning guidance is provided by state government, the regional governments and the Local Agency Formation Commission (LAFCo).

The zoning ordinance is the primary implementation document for the general or community plan. Functionally, it is a set of specific ordinances regarding individual land use types and a coordinating map dictating the location and extent of the applicable ordinances. The broad functions of the zoning ordinance include: (1) the separation of incompatible activities, (2) integration of compatible activities through mixed use zones, and (3) encouragement of positive externalities and restriction of negative externalities through development control standards.

Zones may be changed or modified when the general plan is updated or they may be interpreted by the decision-making body through "variances." Other tools beyond strict zoning are available and include differential tax assessment, circuit breaker taxation, centralized land use policies, exclusive agricultural zoning, creation of agricultural districts and right-to-farm ordinances. These tools act to encourage particular uses for the land.

Traditionally, zoning districts have been divided by use classification into four basic types: residential, commercial, industrial and agricultural. Agriculture in turn can be classified as agricultural or open space, both of interest and concern to the community.

### Agricultural Zones

Except for totally urbanized communities, zoning ordinances provide for agricultural use zones. California legislative policy strongly favors the preservation of open spaces and agricultural zoning and establishes zones to accomplish this goal.

### Agricultural Land Conservation Contracts

Pursuant to the California Land Conservation Act of 1965 (known as the Williamson Act), cities and counties are authorized to establish agricultural preserves of at least 100 acres, or smaller preserves if necessary due to the unique characteristics of the agricultural enterprises in the area. The purpose of an agricultural preserve is to prevent premature conversion of agricultural land to urban use. If an owner of agricultural property agrees to temporarily relinquish his right to develop, for a minimum duration of 10 years, such is considered an enforceable use restriction and the property is taxed as agricultural property rather than based on the market value of the land as established in accordance with normal assessment practices.

Participants in the program must signal during a window period each year that they wish to withdraw, otherwise they are automatically renewed for the next ten-year period. A notice of withdrawal typically signals a wish to either sell, subdivide or otherwise reconfigure the use of the property. Changes in the tax structure have led to decreased enrollment in the Williamson Contract statewide as the tax advantage of participating has diminished. The program was successful historically in enrolling large quantities of agricultural land, but the majority of acres enrolled were not close to urban boundaries.

### Open Space Zones

Both the California legislature and the courts have recognized that open space land is a limited and valuable resource that must be preserved. Accordingly, every city and county is required to prepare, adopt and submit to the secretary of the resources agency a local open space plan for the comprehensive and long-range preservation and conservation of open space land within its jurisdiction.[2]

### Annexations and Incorporations

Each of California's counties has a regulatory body (LAFCo) that has the authority to review and approve (or deny) annexations, boundary changes, city incorporation and disincorporation, and the formation of special districts. They have a tremendous impact on urban development patterns throughout the state. The LAFCo must plan for the development of vacant and non-prime agricultural land within urban spheres, while preserving existing open space, agricultural farmland resources, and important environmental features outside of the spheres.

Special provision is made to plan for and design future expansion changes, accomplished by the delineation of three critical boundaries:

**Urban limits or city boundaries:** This adopted line defines the current incorporated extension of the city for the provision of services. Beyond this line, services are provided by the county or state.

**Sphere of influence:** Defines the area that is assumed to be developable by the city in a reasonable time frame, usually 20 years. Although unincorporated, this zone is thought of as future city territory and is often "pre-zoned" to indicate likely land uses prior to annexation proposals.

The State law established four factors that must be considered by local LAFCO's in determining spheres of influence: (1) the present and planned land use in the area, including agricultural and open space, (2) the present and probable need for public facilities and services in the area, (3) the present capacity of public facilities and adequacy of public services that the agency provides or is authorized to provide, and (4) the existence of any social or economic communities of interest in the area if the commission determines that they are relevant to the agency.

**Urban reserve:** This zone, beyond the Sphere of Influence, is meant to define the ultimate expansion area of a city. Typically this zone will be moved until it becomes coterminous with that of a neighboring community, defining the outer limits of urban influence. Generally, no land in this area can be considered for development without first being included in the Sphere of Influence and finally being annexed.

### Designated Greenbelts

Cities and counties employ the designation of so-called greenbelts to define urban boundaries, create buffer zones between urban and rural uses, and to encapsulate existing areas of agriculture deemed to need protection.

Greenbelts are typically presented as "permanent," although they are functionally non-binding zones of guidance. Greenbelts are reviewed periodically if in an interagency agreement or as part of the general plan. Depending on the agreement reached between agencies, a greenbelt may include the designation of the land as a bank for expansion or a prohibitive zone designed to prevent leap-frogging development. Greenbelts are most often associated with Agricultural Protection Zones in the zoning element.

## Assessing the Effectiveness of Three Planning Tools

To test the effectiveness of the public planning process, we used a field sample of approximately 3,000 agricultural properties encompassing five incorporated cities and their spheres of influence on the Oxnard Plain. The objective was to determine whether the principle planning tools (General Plan Designation, Zoning, and Sphere of Influence relationship) were effective in maintaining agricultural ownership in the face of urban pressure for expansion.

The test involved using a surrogate (per acre land price) to measure:

1. The effectiveness and extent of enrollment in the Williamson Land Conservation Act.

2. The restrictive power of the Sphere of Influence designation.

3. The efficiency of greenbelts in stabilizing agricultural land prices.

A Geographic Information System (GIS) was used to spatially array data on farmland holdings within the case study area on a parcel by parcel basis. The GIS allowed the parameter of linear distance from the urban boundary to be assigned to each parcel in addition to acreage and value characteristics.

In addition, a dummy variable was assigned to each parcel to proxy for its proximity to and assumed influence by the planning policies of the cities in the case study area. A city's general plan can greatly influence the price of land close to the city. If a city has a more permissive development policy, the price of agricultural land outside of the sphere of influence increases in expectation that development will soon be allowed. Table C21.1

shows the relative permissiveness of the planning policies of the five cities in the Oxnard Plain case study. Also included is the county, which because of its limits to residential development, tends to act as a market datum. In our analysis, there was a significant positive correlation between land value and permissiveness of city policies.

Table C21.1   Relative restrictiveness of planning policies.

| Municipality | Relative Restrictiveness of  Planning Policies |
|---|---|
| County | Most restrictive |
| Fillmore | Moderately restrictive |
| Santa Paula | Neutral |
| Ventura | Neutral |
| Camarillo | Moderately permissive |
| Oxnard | Least restrictive |

### Williamson Act Enrollment

The Williamson Act is designed to encourage long term commitment of land to agricultural use. The designers of the system anticipated that the tax incentive would work equally well in areas adjacent to urban boundaries as in those further removed. This has not proved to be the case in the Oxnard Plain, with the probability of a parcel being enrolled in the program decreasing with proximity to those urban areas where the most permissive planning environments can be found. For example, the probability of enrollment is very low for land near Oxnard, known for expansion, compared to high probabilities for land near Ventura, which has stricter development guidelines.

In general, enrollment in the Williamson Act seems to reduce land prices, thus reducing conversion pressures. However, when combined with the locational effect described above of lower rates of enrollment near the more permissive cities, we still find a significant bid up in land price, suggesting future pressure to withdraw from the contracts and allow conversion to take place.

### Sphere of Influence

Local government use of Spheres of Influence dictates not only the direction but ultimately the nature of growth and residual agricultural holdings. Because Spheres of Influence are derived from the local general plans and zoning, their ability to direct and assign time parameters to development proposals should cause land markets to follow.

Field evidence suggests, however, that owners value market information more than the actual statements of policy from the plans. The upshot of this is increased pressure from land market speculators and land owners to change the underlying nature and control of the general plan, often far in advance of the expected plan life or review period.

This is illustrated by the land values shown in Chart C21.1, which records average land values for a range of areas near the Sphere of Influence boundary, but outside existing city boundaries. The urban conversion potential is clearest in higher values for existing agricultural land for the two cities with relatively permissive growth controls (Oxnard and Camarillo) and less for cities where growth is more tightly regulated.

### Greenbelts

Greenbelts have been used by local governments for many years to protect both agricultural lands and open space areas. This planning tool, while optional and usually non-binding, is meant to signal to market players that areas so designated are not typically candidates for near-term development.

Field research suggests that the market may overlook the designation and bid up land values beyond their rate of agricultural return. Under totally protected circumstances we would expect (*ceteris paribus*) that land values would vary relatively little across greenbelt areas, and that proximity to more or less permissive planning authorities would not influence land prices. This was not true in Ventura County, where higher land prices and greater price differentials between boundary and interior greenbelt parcels were recorded for those greenbelt areas adjacent to urban areas with more permissive growth controls, which are more likely to review and possibly redraw greenbelt boundaries.

Chart C21.1 Per acre land prices by city and greater county area with sphere of influence relationships.

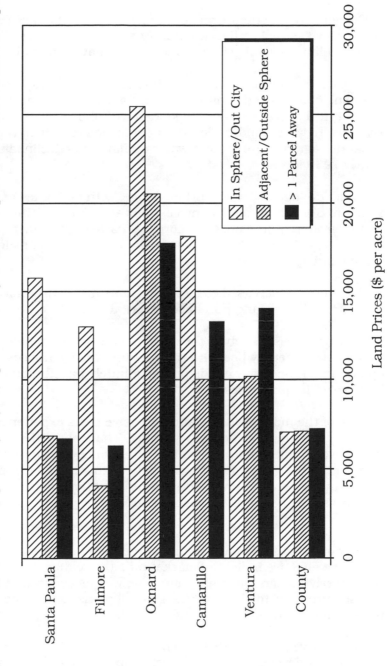

Land Prices ($ per acre)

## Conclusions

Conversion of agricultural land imposes costs that are felt by landowners as well as the community at large. In the case of the Oxnard Plain, several general conclusions may be drawn:

The cost of access to water has increased, reflecting increased pumping charges and conservation mitigation requirements. Agricultural operators have responded with more efficient delivery systems, however, and while urban usage has remained relatively constant, agricultural ground water demand has declined to nearly 1980 levels.

Costs do increase at the urban fringe, with estimates as high as 5% to 6% of total operations cost per acre. Most of this cost results from requirements for more intensive management and direct oversight of activities such as the regulation of pesticide timing and application.

The highest increased cost of operations at the urban fringe is the entry price for land purchase or rental.

Intangible costs such as the effects of air pollution on crop yields have generally been internalized into the overall costs of operation on the Plain, not disproportionately distributed to urban proximity properties.

One of the most insidious and pervasive costs experienced by growers is the most difficult to quantify. That cost is the value of the grower's time, whether spent in compliance with new regulations or in changing agricultural practices to forestall complaints by urban residents, even when current operations are perfectly legal (this may be most visible in the area of pesticide application).

Planning tools such as zoning or greenbelt designations may not prove effective in light of market bids that cause the nature of the underlying agriculture to change as well as generating increased pressure to alter existing general plans to allow development opportunities.

Alternative planning tools such as dedicated buffers that are acquired by developers on their own properties between new development and agriculture, and the use of dedicated easements to freeze property conversion will ultimately prove to be more effective in protecting agricultural areas than traditional tools, which respond to rather than lead the land market.

## Endnotes

1. This case study is developed from field research and interviews conducted in 1993 through 1995.
2. California Government Code 65563.

# Case 22

## Forests Belong To Everyone: Public Use of Private Lands in Norway

*Charles Francis, University of Nebraska,*
*Lincoln, Nebraska*
*Helle Margrete Meltzer, University of Oslo, Norway*

"Every Norwegian is born with skis on" is a popular and humorous anecdote that delights visitors to this green Nordic land. If we ignore the physical impossibility or obvious discomfort to the mother, this metaphor clearly describes an entire culture's affinity to the outdoors and an underlying attitude that shapes behavior, custom, and even law regarding land use. It relates to land preservation, and a society's willingness to accept strict zoning on the forest resource. In a practical sense, forests belong to everyone in Norway.

This is clear to visitors and citizens alike, who are impressed with the 360 degree view available from the television tower high atop Volksenkollen, about 600 meters above the Oslo harbor and 10 kilometers north of the city center. Emerging after a 10-story elevator trip, we are greeted with a spectacular panorama of the vibrant city that fills the low area at the head of Oslo Fjord. The harbor is alive with local ferry boats, small sailboats, and a large cruise ship bound for Copenhagen. But in spite of development of the greater capital city area with a current population of 1,000,000 and some building up the surrounding slopes, there is forest everywhere. Most of the forests are privately owned, but there is access for everyone.

What does this mean? According to Norwegian law, these private forest lands are strictly controlled by the Oslo Commune (county government) and any person is allowed to enter and roam freely on foot or skis, picnic, camp, ride, or cycle on paths and tracks, and pick berries, mushrooms and flowers. The *Allemansretten* ('all man's right' or law of access) law of 1957 is based in ancient, time-honored custom, and guarantees general access to woods, fields, mountains, rivers and lakes irrespective of who owns them. Visitors must not leave litter behind or cause any damage, and there is no hunting or cutting of trees allowed, but there is access to enjoy these natural resources.

The results of strict zoning and adherence to the law are obvious from the Volksenkollen tower. To the east, there is a beautiful lake, with apartments and single dwellings right up to the dam, and beyond is only forest. To the west there is city, some light industry, and development up to a point—beyond are only farms and forest. To the north are seemingly unending forests, with an occasional town visible from the tower, and each of these towns is well contained within its development limits. Apparently zoning can work, when there are laws in place and a people and outdoor culture that work in harmony to support them.

The actual use of the forest lands is also obvious. Just below the tower is a huge parking lot that holds more than 300 cars, parking for those hiking the forest or skiing during winter. At 42 degrees North, the days are short in winter. Thus there are ski lifts and cross-country trails with street lights for evening illumination. Most times of year the hiker can see moose in the forest— the latter are willing to share their space without conflict except when with their young in May and June. Nothing can keep Norwegians out of the woods.

It is impressive to see how people, wildlife, and forest habitat can coexist in such close proximity. Although there is an obvious need for land to accommodate this economically successful capital city, the Norwegians have focused development on existing built-up lands, preserving the centers of cities, and pursuing a relatively high density strategy. Similar land use patterns exist for all of the major cities and most towns.

Another type of forest is the common land owned by each municipality. This is available for grazing to those who have dairy or beef cattle, but the numbers are strictly controlled and you must seek a permit each year for an allocation for grazing. There is a date after which you are allowed to put your cattle in the forest, and this is determined each year depending on weather conditions and growth of forages. There is also a date before which all the cattle must be removed. As the owner, you are responsible for keeping track of your animals, although the forests are so large that a multi-family round-up is needed each fall to find all the livestock. In an interesting twist on responsibility, there is a long tradition that is now in law that neighboring landowners have responsibility to fence out your cattle from moving onto their production fields, rather than the responsibility falling on those who use the forest to graze their cattle. Thus there may be a phone call one day in July that your cattle are out in my grain field—it is a call to let you know they should be taken back into the forest and common land, but there is no cost to you for damages to my fields or crops.

A similar law, passed in 1972, protects access to beaches and coastline in Norway. Since that time, people have been prohibited from building within 100 m of the shore line and must allow public access to the beach. Existing houses near the beach were allowed to remain and, not surprisingly, their prices have shot up during the last 25 years. Nonetheless, the law now in place protects the beach for everyone's use.

This multiple use of land and combination of private ownership with public use represents a rational zoning and strict compliance by the population. This combination has allowed the continued use of an invaluable natural resource for private gain, for public use, and for posterity. We would do well to study such models for the future. In some parts of the world, they have figured out how to use resources wisely, kept them protected for the long term, and kept them from falling "under the blade."

# Index